FERRARI
ALL THE CARS

FERRARI
ALL THE CARS

**Every Ferrari ever made
described and illustrated**

First published as *Tutto Ferrari* in Italy in 2004 by
Arnoldo Mondadori Editore/Giorgio Nada Editore
This English-language edition published in 2005 by Haynes Publishing

A catalogue record for this book is available from the British Library

ISBN 1 84425 312 0

Text and technical data by Leonardo Acerbi

Published by Haynes Publishing, Sparkford, Yeovil, Somerset BA22 7JJ, UK
Tel: 01963 442030 Fax: 01963 440001
Int.tel: +44 1963 442030 Int.fax: +44 1963 440001
E-mail: sales@haynes.co.uk
Website: www.haynes.co.uk

Printed and bound in Italy

Index

Ferrari 166 MM Zagato 1949	*Sport*	20-21
Ferrari 166 Inter 1949	*GT*	22-23
Ferrari 275 F1 1950	*F1*	24-25
Ferrari 340 F1 1950	*F1*	26-27
Ferrari 375 F1 1950	*F1*	28-29
Ferrari 195 S 1950	*Sport*	30-31
Ferrari 195 Inter 1950	*GT*	32-33
Ferrari 340 America 1951	*Sport*	34-35
Ferrari 212 Export 1951	*Sport*	36-37
Ferrari 212 Inter 1951	*GT*	38-39
Ferrari 342 America 1951	*GT*	40-41
Ferrari 500 F2 1951	*F2*	42-43
Ferrari 375 Indy 1952	*Indy*	44-45
Ferrari 225 S 1952	*Sport*	46-47
Ferrari 250 S 1952	*Sport*	48-49
Ferrari 340 Mexico 1952	*Sport*	50-51
Ferrari 250 MM 1953	*Sport*	52-53
Ferrari-Abarth 166 MM/53 1953	*Sport*	54-55

Index

Index

Index

Index

Index

Introduction

The myriad of Grand Prix victories and world championships won by Scuderia Ferrari in Formula One over the last six years is certainly attributable to Michael Schumacher and his colleagues, but also to men, women and equipment of the first order, all contributing to consolidating the legend of the Prancing Horse and taking Maranello back to the very summit of motor racing.

Those results come from the long process of reconstructing of the Ferrari Racing Department, much changed in the Nineties by the then new president, Luca Cordero di Montezemolo. The organisation was further strengthened by the arrival of Jean Todt as motor sport director in 1993 and culminated at the end of 1995 with the engagement of Schumacher, who had just won the world drivers' championship with Benetton. After a first year of bedding in, during which 1996 still produced three victories for the Rosse in Spain, Belgium and at Monza, the Scuderia's success in Formula One from 1997 until today has matured and multiplied due to a driver of exceptional quality and the perfect interaction of the Department's men, strategies and material.

The last 10 years have also seen the Prancing Horse return to being a leading contender in sports car races, which were the unquestioned preserve of Maranello during the Fifties and Sixties. This time, the winning cars were the Ferrari 333 SP and those of the Grand Touring category, with the various 348s, F 355s and the 360 Challenges in a series of single marque championships open to Ferrari's sporting customers, once called gentlemen drivers.

The old red brick Maranello factory, with its big yellow Ferrari logo and a stone's throw from the Cavallino restaurant where Enzo Ferrari liked to hold his most delicate negotiations, has made way for a major industrial installation. One that will become even larger over the next few years, transforming the whole complex into a mighty technological nerve centre.

That is the Ferrari of 2005, the solid concrete reality that the youngest tifosi see today; but they were still in their cradles in the days of Niki Lauda and Clay Regazzoni, for instance.

Today's Ferrari, recounted and documented by the media down to the smallest detail, is born of another Ferrari, one that put down its roots as it created more than 50 years of motor racing history. A Ferrari that was, certainly, less technological and more artisan-like, whose life spanned the entire second half of the 20th century. A different Ferrari, but nevertheless the winner of many championships, which have now either disappeared or changed radically. They are the reason why Formula One has been just one piece in the motor sport jigsaw, a number of moments in the Scuderia's history. Maranello's is an extremely complex and intricate story, which also meant a constant commitment to Formula Two, long distance racing on track and road, hillclimbs and Grand Touring events.

Covering the history of the Prancing Horse, a subject about which so much has been said and written, permits us to recreate that enormous jigsaw puzzle in this book. The individual pieces are represented by races of undying fascination, such as the 24 Hours of Le Mans, Targa Florio and the Grand Prix of Monaco, and by cars synonymous with the Ferrari legend like the Testa Rossa, the 250 GTO and the 250 Le Mans. But, more than anything else, Ferrari's is a story of men and women, the ingenious designers, able technicians, mechanics, champions and other drivers, some of whom even gave their lives while helping to create the myth.

Many avenues present themselves when considering how to tell the glorious Ferrari glorious story: a long and unique narration; a text embellished with fascinating period pictures and more recent shots in colour; a chronological succession of all the Ferraris model-by-model, from the 1940 Auto Avio Costruzioni 815, to the pre-Ferrari Ferraris and the F 2005 Formula One car, told, analysed and, more than anything else, illustrated. And that is the route we have chosen here.

The Ferraris illustrated by the prestigious hand of Giorgio Alisi, who has been able to catch even the smallest difference between one model and another with precision and accuracy, and has brought together in one single gallery, a virtual museum made up of Formula One, sports racers and Grand Touring cars.

The illustrator, with his unique and innate evocative ability, was given the task of resurrecting the shapes and colours of an everlasting epoch, of an extraordinary slice of Italian history, and not on the sporting front alone.

Leonardo Acerbi

Foreword

Each thumbnail sketch of Maranello's many cars is published here in chronological order and begins in 1940, the year in which the Auto Avio Costruzioni 815 first appeared as a kind of Ferrari 'preview'. They extend through to the F 2005, the car with which Michael Schumacher won the 2005 Formula One World Drivers' Championship, his fifth consecutive title in Ferrari and a record seventh in all.

Each sketch is an individual treatise in its own right, in some cases devoted to a single model of which there were two versions. The Ferrari 308 GTB and the corresponding GTS – the first appeared in 1975, the second in 1977 – or the 365 GTC and GTS of 1969 can, for example, be found in the one description, as they are nothing other than different versions of the same model. The two different items on the 365 GTB/4 Daytona and the corresponding 365 GTS/4 roadster are no contradiction of this system. While two versions of the same car, we believe it is right to devote an individual profile to each model, given the historical importance of the sports saloon body and the open road car version. In some cases, such as the 1953 375 MM, it has been decided to separate the closed and roadster derivatives, the two being so different from each other, both from the aesthetic and sporting history standpoints.

Using this means of cataloguing the Ferraris, one sometimes also comes across the opposite situation: models that are different but are accounted for in one specification. The 1955 118 and 121 LM barchettas are a case in point: they were largely indistinguishable from each other as far as their bodies were concerned, but had very different engines – a 3.7-litre for the 118 LM and a 4.4-litre for the 121 LM. In addition, their sporting lives, which did not last long, would not have justified individual treatment.

Each specification includes the technical data of the model, giving the main characteristics of the engine, transmission, body, chassis, dimensions, weight and performance.

Where a single-seater, sports racing model or prototype competed for more than one season or, in the case of Grand Tourers, remained in production for a number of years, each treatise contains the principal modifications to which the car was subjected in brackets: these include an increase in power, the adoption of different fuel feed systems, ignition and a different location for the gearbox.

The main problem encountered while compiling these technical specifications was discrepancies in the data, figures and values provided by the various sources we consulted. Where such situations arise, we have chosen to use data taken directly from the official Ferrari web site, which uses a system of specifying the cars model-by-model. Where it was not possible to obtain accurate data from any of our sources, no information has been included under the respective sub-headings.

Cars with special bodies and prototypes built over the years by the carrozzieri on Ferrari rolling chassis have not been included in this publication, among them the 365 P Speciale, 250 P5, 512 S and Modulo. These were all Pininfarina concept cars and have been left out because they were experimental models, which were used purely for shape study: they were never produced and had no sporting history. However, documented participation in even a single race induced us to include cars like the 1950 Zagato-bodied 166 MM and the 166 MM/53, built by Abarth in 1953.

Ferrari all the cars

Carrozzeria Touring of Milan asked the great Alberto Ascari to pose with the Auto Avio Costruzioni 815, the lines of which were clearly inspired by the soft, flowing Touring body for the 1939 Alfa Romeo 6C 2500 SS. It was Ascari who gave this Ferrari forerunner its motor sport debut in the 1940 Mille Miglia, in which he led his class for much of the race before retiring.

TECHNICAL SPECIFICATION

ENGINE
Front, longitudinal, eight cylinders in line

Bore and stroke	63x60 mm
Unitary cubic capacity	187
Total cubic capacity	1496
Valve gear	single overhead camshaft
Number of valves	two per cylinder
Compression ratio	7.5:1
Fuel feed	four Weber 30DR2 carburettors
Ignition	single, one distributor
Coolant	water
Lubrication	damp sump
Maximum power	72 hp at 5500 rpm
Specific power	48 hp/litre

TRANSMISSION
Rear-wheel drive

Clutch	single dry disc
Gearbox	en bloc with engine, four gears + reverse

CAR BODY
Two-seater barchetta

CHASSIS

Chassis	longitudinal and cross members
Front suspension	independent, transverse leaf spring, dampers with helicoidal springs
Rear suspension	live axle, longitudinal semi-elliptic springs, anti-roll bar, dampers
Brakes	drum
Steering	worm and sector
Fuel tank	108 litres
Tyres front/rear	5.50-15 all round

DIMENSIONS AND WEIGHT

Wheelbase	2420 mm
Track front/rear	1240/1240 mm
Length	-
Width	-
Height	-
Kerb weight	625 kg

PERFORMANCE

Top speed	160-170 km/h
Power to weight ratio	8.7 kg/hp

Auto Avio Costruzioni 815   1940

After having worked at Alfa Romeo for 10 years, during which he ran the company's racing department under the Scuderia Ferrari banner, Enzo Ferrari left Portello in 1939 due to continual disagreements with the directorship, in particular the new technical boss, Spaniard Wilfredo Ricart.

In that difficult situation, Ferrari signed an agreement that would stop him becoming involved in any form of motor racing with the Scuderia brand for at least four years. But that obstacle was soon overcome. With the money he received in double settlement for his departure from Alfa Romeo and the cessation of the Scuderia, the future constructor formed a new company called Auto Avio Costruzioni in Modena in 1940. From the workshops of the new organisation came two roadsters built almost exclusively from Fiat materials and components. The chassis of longitudinal and cross members and the 1496 cc eight-cylinder in-line engine came from the Fiat 508 C Balilla 1100. A modest number of people worked with Ferrari on that adventurous undertaking, including Alberto Massimino and Vittorio Bellentani.

Carrozzeria Touring of Milan penned the gentle, flowing lines of those two two-seater cars built by Ferrari and called the 815, which competed in the Grand Prix of Brescia – in actual fact the 13th Mille Miglia – on 28 April 1940. Crewed by Lotario Rangoni Machiavelli-Enrico Nardi and Alberto Ascari-Giuseppe Minozzi, the cars dominated the up to 1500 cc Sport category until a broken rocker arm on Ascari's car and a transmission failure on the Rangoni 815 brought a promising debut to an end. Ascari sold his car to Enrico Beltrachini, who raced it in at least eight post-war events. Lotario Rangoni was killed during the Second World War and the second car was passed on to his brother Rolando, only to be scrapped in 1958.

Tuning the Ferrari 125 S, Gioachino Colombo's first designs for which go back to the summer of 1945, was long, complex and required numerous test sessions in which various drivers alternated, including Nando Righetti pictured at the wheel of the car. Those early tests always took place under the watchful eye of Enzo Ferrari, who is on the right, next to his first "true" creation.

TECHNICAL SPECIFICATION

ENGINE
Front, longitudinal, V12 (60°)

Bore and stroke	55x52.5 mm
Unitary cubic capacity	124.73
Total cubic capacity	1496.77
Valve gear	single overhead cam
Number of valves	two per cylinder
Compression ratio	7.5:1
Fuel feed	three Weber 30DCF carburettors
Ignition	single, one distributor or two magnetos
Coolant	water
Lubrication	damp sump
Maximum power	118 hp at 6800 rpm
Specific power	78.8 hp/litre

TRANSMISSION
Rear-wheel drive

Clutch	single dry disc
Gearbox	en bloc with engine five gears + reverse

BODY
One/two-seater barchetta

CHASSIS

Chassis	longitudinal and cross members
Front suspension	independent, double wishbones, transverse semi-elliptic springs, hydraulic dampers
Rear suspension	live axle, longitudinal semi-elliptic springs. anti-roll bar, hydraulic dampers
Brakes	drum
Steering	worm and sector
Fuel tank	75 litres
Tyres front/rear	5.50-15 all round

DIMENSIONS AND WEIGHT

Wheelbase	2420 mm
Track front/rear	1255/1200 mm
Length	4500 mm
Width	1550 mm
Height	1500 mm
Kerb weight	750 kg

PERFORMANCE

Top speed	170 km/h
Power to weight ratio	6.3 kg/hp

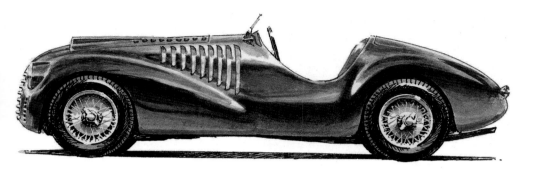

Ferrari 125 S   1947

Now free of all ties with Alfa Romeo, in 1945 Enzo Ferrari began to warm to the idea of building a car that would finally carry his own name. A good "agitator of men", as he liked to define himself, Ferrari resumed contact with some his Alfa colleagues, including technician Giuseppe Busso, test driver Luigi Bazzi and designer Gioachino Colombo. He gave Colombo the task of laying out the first "real" Ferrari, which made its debut in the spring of 1947 after a long gestation period. Setting the eight-cylinder to one side, Ferrari and his designer were agreed on taking the ambitious and difficult road that led to the 12-cylinder. It was a power unit that had always attracted the Modena constructor's interest: he had been fascinated first by the American V12 built by Packard and then the glorious Thirties power units of Auto Union, as well as his personal experience at Alfa Romeo, exposed to projects like the unit for the 1936 12 C single-seater. That format also seemed a good choice for possible use in Grand Prix category cars, needing only the simple addition of a supercharger.

So the Ferrari 125 S began to take shape on that basis. The two-seater roadster, with its wraparound wings integrated into the bodywork, made its debut on 11 May 1947 at the Circuito di Piacenza, driven by Franco Cortese. But the car's race came to an end three laps from the finish while in the lead, after a long tussle with the Maserati 6CS 1500s. Victory was only postponed for 14 days, though, for Cortese won the Grand Prix of Rome on the Caracalla circuit a fortnight later. After just five months in business, Ferrari had chalked up six wins from 14 races, five of which went to the 125 S and one to the type 125 S Corsa.

Raymond Sommer's Ferrari 159 S just before the start of the Grand Prix of Turin at the Circuito del Valentino on 12 October 1947. After having covered only 30 laps, the French driver was way ahead of all the other competitors, confirming the total superiority of the car and taking a significant and encouraging victory, ahead of Delage driver Eugène Chaboud and a gaggle of Talbots and Gordinis.

TECHNICAL SPECIFICATION

ENGINE
Front, longitudinal, V12 (60°)

Bore and stroke	59x58 mm
Unitary cubic capacity	158.57
Total cubic capacity	1902.84
Valve gear	single overhead camshaft
Number of valves	two per cylinder
Compression ratio	8.5:1
Fuel feed	three Weber 30DCF carburettors
Ignition	single, two magnetos
Coolant	water
Lubrication	damp sump
Maximum power	125 hp at 7000 rpm
Specific power	62 hp / litre

TRANSMISSION
Rear-wheel drive

Clutch	single dry disc
Gearbox	en bloc with engine five gears + reverse

BODY
Single or two-seater sports saloon

CHASSIS

Chassis	longitudinal and cross members
Front suspension	independent, double wishbones, transverse semi-elliptical spring hydraulic dampers
Rear suspension	live axle, longitudinal semi-elliptic springs. anti-roll bar, hydraulic dampers
Brakes	drum
Steering	worm and sector
Fuel tank	75 litres
Tyres front/rear	5.50-15 all round

DIMENSIONS AND WEIGHT

Wheelbase	2420 mm
Track front/rear	1255 / 1200 mm
Length	3550 mm
Width	1470 mm
Height	1120 mm
Kerb weight	750 kg

PERFORMANCE

Top speed	180 km/h
Power to weight ratio	6.0 kg/hp

Ferrari 159 S   1947

The history of this car was so short that it was made in just a few races, all of them in 1947. With the early victories of the 125 in Sport and Racing forms to his credit, Ferrari went to the Circuito di Pescara with only one car on 15 August. From the outside, the 159 S looked the same as the integrally bodied 125 S, but it was powered by a 1902.84 cc, 12-cylinder engine for the first time, following increases in its bore and stroke to 59x58 mm; to generate 120-125 hp at 7000 rpm. The car was driven by Franco Cortese, who had led the race, but he eventually came second behind Vincenzo Auricchio's Stanguellini: the 159 S won its class. A Racing version with motorcycle-type wings was also built and that competed during the second half of the season with lukewarm results. The 159 S was thwarted by the competitiveness of the fast and agile single headlight Maserati A6G.CSs of Giovanni Bracco, Gigi Villoresi and Alberto Ascari and the Cisitalia D46s. In that climate of uncertainty, the car was entered for the Grand Prix of Turin on the Circuito di Valentino on 12 October. As Ferrari was concentrating mainly on planning for the 1948 season, only one 159 S single-seater was entered for the talented French driver Raymond Sommer who, after starting from the second row, scored a providential victory, confirming that the almost two litre engine had achieved reliability and performance. The car was retired at the end of 1947, as it was a transition model between the 125 S and the new 166 ranges, which would soon nourish the young and ambitious Maranello company's production.

The 1950 version of the Ferrari 125 F1, driven by Alberto Ascari in that year's Grand Prix of Monaco. He recorded a lap time of 1'53"8 in practice, started from the third row of the grid and clocked 3'00"6 to come second to Fangio's winning Alfa Romeo 158. By the end of 1950, Portello had clinched the first F1 world championship with Nino Farina, having dominated the season.

TECHNICAL SPECIFICATION

ENGINE
Front, longitudinal, V12 (60°)

Bore and stroke	55x52.5 mm
Unitary cubic capacity	124.73
Total cubic capacity	1496.77
Valve gear	single overhead camshaft (twin-cam in 1949)
Number of valves	two per cylinder
Compression ratio	6.5:1
Fuel feed	one Weber 40DOC3 or 50 WCF carburettor and one single stage supercharger (two stage in 1949)
Ignition	single, two magnetos
Coolant	water
Lubrication	dry sump
Maximum power	230 hp at 7000 rpm (280 hp at 8000 rpm in 1949)
Specific power	153,6 hp/litre (187 in 1949)

TRANSMISSION
Rear-wheel drive

Clutch	single dry disc (multi-disc in 1949/50)
Gearbox	en bloc with engine five gears + reverse

BODY
Single-seater

CHASSIS

Chassis	longitudinal and cross members
Front suspension	independent, double wishbones, transverse semi-elliptical spring, Houdaille dampers
Rear suspension	oscillating drive shafts, torsion bars, Houdaille dampers (De Dion axle in 1950)
Brakes	drum
Steering	worm and sector
Fuel tank	120 litres (140 in 1949)
Tyres front/ rear	5.50-15/7.00-15 5.50-16/6.50-16 in 1949)

DIMENSIONS AND WEIGHT

Wheelbase	2160 mm (2320 1949)
Track front/rear	1278/1250 mm
Length	3685 mm
Width	1400 mm
Height	1025 mm
Weight (running order)	710 kg

PERFORMANCE

Top speed	260 km/h
Power to weight ratio	3.08 kg/hp (2.5 1949)

Ferrari 125 F1 1948

When Enzo Ferrari and Gioachino Colombo decided to take the 12-cylinder 1500 cc route for the 125 S, they had already thought of using the same power unit in a Grand Prix single-seater, the forerunner of the modern F1 car.

Regulations in force at the time required the use of a 1.5 litre engine with supercharger. The 1500 cc booster project was developed by Colombo in parallel with a normally aspirated version, and was the origin of the first Grand Prix Ferrari, the 125 F1, initially called the GPC or Grand Prix Compressore. Testing started during the second half of 1948 and immediately confirmed it would be a long and complex business. Still boosted by a Roots single stage supercharger, the engine was afflicted by a chronic loss of power, especially at high revs, which stopped the car matching the performance of the eight-cylinder Alfa Romeo 158 and the four-cylinder Maserati 4CLT. By way of compensation, the light Gilco chassis with a wheelbase of only 2160 mm meant the 125 F1 was compact, handled well and was suited to any circuit.

The single-seater's debut took place on 5 September 1948 at the Grand Prix of Valentino. Three cars were assigned to Prince Bira of Siam, Nino Farina and Raymond Sommer, who took an encouraging third place behind an Alfa Romeo and a Maserati. That result was of historic importance, because it convinced Enzo Ferrari that he should continue Grand Prix motor racing, when he was on the point of giving up due to its already high cost. In 1949-50, the Ferrari 125 F1 was modified in both its mechanics with a new two-stage supercharger, and its body, with changes to the radiator grill and tail.

The Grand Prix of the Autodromo di Monza, 26 June 1949: Juan Manuel Fangio (photo) in the pits for a fast refuelling and tyre change stop for his single-seater 166 F2, entered by the Automobile Club of Argentina. The future five-times F1 world champion won, scoring his first top level victory on the European continent in a season that saw him driving for both Ferrari and Maserati. He won his five F1 world titles between 1951 and 1957.

TECHNICAL SPECIFICATION

ENGINE		CHASSIS	
Front, longitudinal, V12 (60°)		Chassis	longitudinal and cross members
Bore and stroke	60x58.8 mm	Front suspension	independent,
Unitary cubic capacity	166.25		double wishbones, transverse
Total cubic capacity	1995.02		semi-elliptic spring,
Valve gear	single overhead camshaft		hydraulic dampers
Number of valves	two per cylinder	Rear suspension	oscillating drive shafts,
Compression ratio	11:1		torsion bars, hydraulic
Fuel feed	three Weber 32DCF carburettors		dampers (transverse
Ignition	single, two magnetos		semi-elliptic spring 1949,
Coolant	water		De Dion axle 1950)
Lubrication	damp sump (dry sump in 1949)	Brakes	drum
		Steering	worm and sector
Maximum power	155 hp at 7000 rpm	Fuel tank	130 litres
Specific power	77 hp/litre		150 litres 1950
		Tyres front/rear	5.50-15/6.25-16
TRANSMISSION			(5.25-16/6.50-16 1950)
Rear-wheel drive			
Clutch	multi-disc	DIMENSIONS AND WEIGHT	
Gearbox	en bloc with engine, five gears + reverse (en bloc with differential, four + reverse from 1950)	Wheelbase	2160 mm (2320 1949)
		Track front/rear	1200/1200 mm
		Length	-
		Width	-
		Height	-
BODY		Kerb weight	550 kg
Single-seater			
		PERFORMANCE	
		Top speed	235 km/h
		Power to weight ratio	3.5 kg/hp

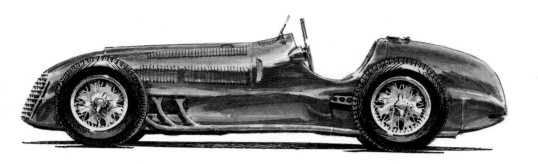

Ferrari 166 F2 $\qquad$ 1948

The Formula Two Drivers' Trophy, which only became a championship in 1967, was instituted in 1948. The first set of regulations, which covered a series of rounds on circuits throughout Europe, permitted the entry of normally aspirated two-litre or supercharged 500 cc single-seaters. The publicity implications of a category structured in this way were too substantial, so Ferrari decided not to take part from the start, but built a single-seater that completely exploited the opportunities provided by the regulations. Conceived around the two-litre (1995.02 cc) engine, which already powered the closed wheel 166, the F2 car had its output increased to about 150 hp by the installation of three Weber 32DCF carburettors instead of the single unit of the sports racing car. The gearbox, which was en bloc with the engine, had five speeds plus a reverse on the 1948-49 166 and became a single unit with the differential with four speeds in 1950. The motor racing career of the 166 F2 began in the best possible way with Raymond Sommer's win at the 1948 Grand Prix of Florence, an event he led from the start and lapped all other competitors. But 1949 was the consecration of the 166 F2, which had been given a new engine and a completely re-designed chassis that was lighter and more agile. After an uncertain start to the season, the 166 F2 won in Rome, Naples, Bari, Monza and Reims. Its successful drivers included a man who competed in a number of races at the wheel of a 166 F2 entered by the Automobile Club of Argentina, in its unusual yellow and blue livery. The 'young' hopeful did not take long to confirm his extraordinary driving talent and won at Monza - his name was Juan Manuel Fangio.

Bruno Sterzi and Fernando Righetti started the 1948 Mille Miglia in the same car: a Ferrari 166 S Allemano barchetta (MI 111176) in which Clemente Biondetti and Igor Troubetzkoy had won the Giro di Sicilia a month earlier. But the result of the Mille Miglia was not so favourable: after passing through the Padua time control in 20th place overall, they were forced to retire before Forlì.

TECHNICAL SPECIFICATION

ENGINE		CHASSIS	
Front, longitudinal, V12 (60°)		*Chassis*	longitudinal and cross members
		Front suspension	independent,
Bore and Stroke	60x58.8 mm		double wishbones, transverse
Unitary cubic capacity	166.25		semi-elliptic spring hydraulic
Total cubic capacity	1995.02		dampers
Valve gear	single overhead camshaft		
Number of valves	two per cylinder	*Rear suspension*	live axle, longitudinal
Compression ratio	6.8:1		semi-elliptic springs, anti-roll
Fuel feed	one Weber 32DCF carburettor		bar, hydraulic dampers
Ignition	single, two distributors	*Brakes*	drum
Coolant	water	*Steering*	worm and sector
Lubrication	damp sump	*Fuel tank*	72 litres
Maximum power	110 hp at 6000 rpm	*Tyres front/rear*	5.90-15 all round
Specific power	55 hp/litre		
		DIMENSIONS AND WEIGHT	
TRANSMISSION		*Wheelbase*	2620 mm
Rear-wheel drive		*Track front/rear*	1270/1250 mm
Clutch	single dry disc	*Length*	-
Gearbox	en bloc with engine	*Width*	-
	five gears + reverse	*Height*	-
		Kerb weight	900 kg
BODY			
Two-seater barchetta		PERFORMANCE	
		Top speed	170 km/h
		Power to weight ratio	8.2 kg/hp

Ferrari 166 S Allemano   1948

Ferrari's first real racing season was in 1948 and it marked the debut of the 12-cylinder engine in two-litre (1995.02 cc) form, with bore and stroke values increased to 60 x 58.8 mm respectively. The unit, called the 166, was installed in new models for both the Sport and Formula Two categories. At the time, Ferrari car denominations were derived from their unitary cubic capacity, obtained by dividing the total by the number of cylinders into their total cc: in this case, 1995.02 divided by 12 = 166.25, rounded down to 166.

A single-seater version of the 166 S almost always competed as a works entry, while the Sport often raced under the private Scuderia Inter banner, which entered Allemano-bodied 166 S barchetta number 36 for the Giro di Sicilia on 4 April 1948. Not meant exclusively for racing, the chances of this rather clumsy and ungainly looking car doing well were rather poor, given the presence of the works Maserati A6G.CSs of Alberto Ascari and Gigi Villoresi. But in the talented hands of great road racer Clemente Biondetti, who had already won the 1938 and 1947 Mille Miglias and was accompanied at the last minute by the less expert Igor Troubetzkoy, it beat its powerful opposition and won the Sicilian race, giving Ferrari another important victory. But the same car was not so lucky in the year's Mille Miglia driven by Bruno Sterzi and Fernando Righetti, who retired it with a broken engine.

The introduction of the new two-litre power unit was the start of a long and successful line of Rosse: the Tipo 166 earned Ferrari further prestige with its first international victories.

Tazio Nuvolari's Ferrari 166 SC being pushed to scrutineering In Brescia's Piazza della Vittoria by a mechanic, before the 1948 Mille Miglia. The car had small motorcycle-type mudguards, a headlight either side of the radiator grill and a cramped second seat for mechanic Sergio Scapinelli: a seat that broke away from its anchorage points during the race – as did many other parts of the car.

TECHNICAL SPECIFICATION

ENGINE
Front, longitudinal, V12 (60°)

Bore and stroke	60x58.8 mm
Unitary cubic capacity	166.25
Total cubic capacity	1995.02
Valve gear	single overhead camshaft
Number of valves	two per cylinder
Compression ratio	11:1
Fuel feed	three Weber 32DCF carburettors
Ignition	single, two magnetos
Coolant	water
Lubrication	damp sump
Maximum power	130 hp at 6500 rpm
Specific power	65 hp / litre

TRANSMISSION
Rear-wheel drive

Clutch	single dry disc
Gearbox	en bloc with engine five gears + reverse

BODY
Two-seater roadster

CHASSIS

Chassis	longitudinal and cross members
Front suspension	independent, double wishbones, transverse semi-elliptic spring, hydraulic dampers
Rear suspension	live axle, longitudinal semi-elliptic springs, anti-roll bar, hydraulic dampers
Brakes	drum
Steering	worm and sector
Fuel tank	75 litres
Tyres front/rear	5.90-15 all round

DIMENSIONS AND WEIGHT

Wheelbase	2420 mm
Track front/rear	1240 / 1240 mm
Length	-
Width	-
Height	-
Kerb weight	680 kg

PERFORMANCE

Top speed	170 km/h
Power to weight ratio	5.2 kg/hp

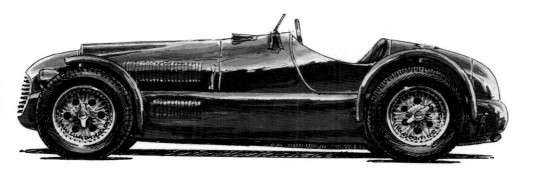

Ferrari 166 SC   1948

The Corsa version of the 166, also called the Inter after the Besana brothers' Scuderia of the same name as they often raced the car, had motorcycle-type mudguards detached from sides of its body and was equipped with the classic two-litre (1995.02 cc) engine. The car will forever be associated with Tazio Nuvolari's legendary drive in the 1948 Mille Miglia. Suffering from an illness that would claim his life in 1953, the Flying Mantuan should not have even entered the race. However, both Alfa Romeo and Ferrari were desperately in need of a driver on the eve of the Brescia marathon and the two had approached him. Gentleman driver Igor Troubetzkoy had suddenly withdrawn, after which Enzo Ferrari secured Nuvolari's services at the wheel of a 166 SC: supported by mechanic Sergio Scapinelli, the great racer did not disappoint. Having started from Brescia at 4.30 am with number 1049, Nuvolari was sixth at Padua, third at Forlì and first in Rome. At Bologna, the last hourly control before the finish, the Mantuan was leading by 29 minutes from second placed Clemente Biondetti, in a Ferrari 166 S. Only a broken spring after an earlier collision in which the 166 SC had, among other things, lost its bonnet, deprived Nuvolari of a memorable victory, one of many in his long and extraordinary career.

The competitive life of the 166 SC was fairly long: it raced throughout the 1948 season and most of the '49 in both long and short wheelbase versions, with different kinds of radiator grills and without mudguards, with cigar-shaped or wraparound bodies, depending on the circuits involved.

Clemente Biondetti and Giuseppe Navone aboard their Allemano-bodied 166 S, awaiting the start of the XV Mille Miglia. Having begun meekly, Biondetti soon drove a hard race and moved steadily up the field, in part due to the retirement of leading adversaries, to win in Brescia for a third time, clocking 15 h 05'44" at an average 121.277 km/h.

TECHNICAL SPECIFICATION

ENGINE
Front, longitudinal, V12 (60°)

Bore and stroke	60x58.8 mm
Unitary cubic capacity	166.25
Total cubic capacity	1995.02
Valve gear	single overhead camshaft
Number of valves	two per cylinder
Compression ratio	7.5:1
Fuel feed	one Weber 32DCF carburettor
Ignition	single, two distributors
Coolant	water
Lubrication	damp sump
Maximum power	110 hp at 6000 rpm
Specific power	55 hp/litre

TRANSMISSION
Rear-wheel drive

Clutch	single dry disc
Gearbox	en bloc with engine
	five gears + reverse

BODY
Two-seater sports saloon

CHASSIS

Chassis	longitudinal and cross members
Front suspension	independent, double wishbones, transverse semi-elliptic spring, hydraulic dampers
Rear suspension	live axle, longitudinal semi-elliptic springs, anti-roll bar, hydraulic dampers
Brakes	drum
Steering	worm and sector
Fuel tank	80 litres
Tyres front/rear	5.50-15 all round

DIMENSIONS AND WEIGHT

Wheelbase	2620 mm
Track front/rear	1270/1250 mm
Length	-
Width	-
Height	-
Kerb weight	800 kg

PERFORMANCE

Top speed	170 km/h
Power to weight ratio	7.2 kg/hp

Ferrari 166 S Allemano   1948

As always, the most important race of the 1948 season was the Mille Miglia on 2 May. Ferrari had only entered one 125 S the previous year for Franco Cortese and the car went more or less unnoticed. But in '48, he fielded five cars; in practice his entire model range of the period, showing that the interest and publicity impact of the Brescian classic was extremely important, especially for a young marque. Cortese, paired with Adelmo Marchetti, started in an old 125 S with an integral body, but brothers Gabriele and Soave Besana were in a 166 SC powered by a 2000 cc engine, entered by Scuderia Inter; Tazio Nuvolari also drove a 166 SC, as did Bruno Sterzi with Fernando Righetti. The line-up was completed by an Allemano closed bodied 166 S coupé that also had the new two-litre engine, driven by Clemente Biondetti and Giuseppe Navone – and theirs' was the only Ferrari to finish, winning the 15th Mille Miglia by almost 90 minutes from the Fiat 1100 S of husband and wife crew Alberto Comirato and Lia Dumas. It was Biondetti's third victory in the Brescia-Rome-Brescia dash.

The same Allemano sports coupé (chassis number 003 S) competed in the following year's Mille Miglia in an elegant new pearl grey livery. This time, the car was driven by Giampiero Bianchetti, one of the Prancing Horse's first regular customers, with Giulio Sala. Unlike the previous year, the 166 S had wind-up glass windows instead of sliding Perspex units, but its crew did not repeat the 1948 result and retired soon after Pescara.

A stand that was spartan to say the least hosted the Touring-bodied 166 MM (Mille Miglia) for a preview of the new Maranello model at the 1948 Turin Motor Show from 15 September. The car's body was elegant but at the same time essential, underlined by a slight ribbing along its flanks, and was much admired by both critics and public. The example shown on this occasion was sprayed red and had a real leather interior.

TECHNICAL SPECIFICATION

ENGINE
Front, longitudinal, V12 (60°)

Bore and stroke	60x58.8 mm
Unitary cylinder	166.02
Total cubic capacity	1995.2 5
Valve gear	single overhead camshaft
Number of valves	two per cylinder
Compression ratio	8.5:1
Fuel feed	three Weber 32DCF carburettors
Ignition	single, two distributors
Coolant	water
Lubrication	damp sump
Maximum power	140 hp at 6600 rpm
Specific power	70 hp/litre

TRANSMISSION
Rear-wheel drive

Clutch	single dry disc
Gearbox	en bloc with engine five gears + reverse

BODY
Two-seater barchetta/sports coupé

CHASSIS

Chassis	longitudinal and cross members
Front suspension	independent, double wishbones, transverse semi-elliptic spring, hydraulic dampers
Rear suspension	live axle, longitudinal semi-elliptic springs, anti-roll bar, hydraulic dampers
Brakes	drum
Steering	worm and sector
Fuel tank	100 litres
Tyres front and rear	5.50-15 all round

DIMENSIONS AND WEIGHT

Wheelbase	2250 mm
Track front/rear	1270/1250 mm
Length	4120 mm
Width	1490 mm
Height	1150 mm
Kerb weight	680 kg

PERFORMANCE

Top speed	220 km/h
Power to weight ratio	4.8 kg/hp

Ferrari 166 MM Touring   1948

Enzo Ferrari entrusted Carrozzeria Touring of Milan with the creation of the Auto Avio Costruzioni 815's body in 1940 and they produced a car of sober yet elegant lines, giving that first-born an unmistakable personality.

Eight years later, when Ferrari wanted to go into production with a car that qualified unequivocally as a racer conceived for the sports category, it seemed inevitable that he would assign the task once again to the Milan atelier, noted for its "Superleggera" or super-light bodies. Maranello created a great deal of interest when it unveiled the first much admired example of the 166 MM Touring barchetta at the Turin Motor Show on 15 September 1948. The lines of the car were, once again, sleek and coherent at the same time, but without that angular appearance that had characterised earlier Ferraris, especially those bodied by Allemano. The long strengthening ribs that ran down both flanks, linking the front and rear wings, earned this 166 the name barchetta. Ferrari also turned to the two-litre version of his 60° V12 engine for that model, which could generate up to 140 hp at 6600 rpm. All that power in a relatively light body with a 680 kg kerb weight turned the 166 MM into an excellent racing car, which also won at an international level. Driving the fast and agile Touring barchettas Luigi Chinetti, future North American importer of Ferrari cars, won the 1948 12 Hours of Paris. The following year, he won the 24 Hours of Le Mans, in which he drove for 23 consecutive hours – Ferrari's first major victory on French soil - as well as the 24 Hours of Spa-Francorchamps. That same year, Clemente Biondetti also won the Mille Miglia in a 166 MM, ahead of Felice Bonetto and Pasquale Cassani in a similar car.

The Zagato-bodied Ferrari 166 Panoramica of Antonio Stagnoli and Aldo Bianchi at the start of the 1950 Mille Miglia. After a positive first half and arriving at Rome eighth overall, the car's performance fell off gradually and Stagnoli finished 36th at Brescia. The same car reappeared at the 1950 Grand Prix of Senigallia as a profoundly modified barchetta.

TECHNICAL SPECIFICATION

ENGINE
Front, longitudinal, V12 (60°)

Bore and stroke	60x58.8 mm
Unitary cubic capacity	166.25
Total cubic capacity	1995.02
Valve gear	single overhead camshaft
Number of valves	two per cylinder
Compression ratio	8.5:1
Fuel feed	three Weber 32DCF carburettors
Ignition	single, two distributors
Coolant	water
Lubrication	damp sump
Maximum power	140 hp at 6600 rpm
Specific power	70 hp/litre

TRANSMISSION
Rear-wheel drive

Clutch	single dry disc
Gearbox	en bloc with engine five gears + reverse

BODY
Two-seater sports coupé/barchetta

CHASSIS

Chassis	longitudinal/cross members
Front suspension	independent, double wishbones, transverse semi-elliptic spring, hydraulic dampers
Rear suspension	live axle, longitudinal semi-elliptic springs, anti-roll bar, hydraulic dampers
Brakes	drum
Steering	worm and sector
Fuel tank	100 litres
Tyres front/rear	5.50-15 all round

DIMENSIONS AND WEIGHT

Wheelbase	2200 mm
Track front/rear	1270/1250 mm
Length	-
Width	-
Height	-
Kerb weight	-

PERFORMANCE

Top speed	210 km/h
Power to weight ratio	-

Ferrari 166 MM Zagato   1949

After a long working relationship in the Thirties that saw Zagato body numerous Alfa Romeos for Scuderia Ferrari, ranging from the 1750 to the 8C 2300, the paths of the Maranello constructor and the Milan stylist crossed again in 1949. Antonio Stagnoli, a Piaggio scooter concessionaire in Milan and an amateur racing driver of reasonable ability, acquired 166 MM chassis number 0018 M, which had a wheelbase of only 2200 mm; he turned to Ugo Zagato to create a Ferrari that was, possibly, lighter and more aerodynamic, suitable for racing. From the first design produced in mid-1949 emerged a rounded two-seater sports saloon of soft, flowing lines. It had ample lateral windows in Plexiglass, in line with other cars Zagato was building on Fiat and Lancia rolling chassis at the time, which they called Panoramica. The car was dubbed the Ferrari 2000 Panoramica speciale in a 1949 page of advertising, which included a picture of the new model with a plain aluminium body. The short wheelbase, the use of Plexiglas even for the rear window and the car's highly aerodynamic line, with its stubby rear end in which the fuel tank and spare wheel lay, made the 166 MM Zagato look like a real racing car.

But the speciale's racing career was short lived: Stagnoli took third place in the 1949 Circuito di Senigallia, won the 1950 Coppa Intereuropa at Monza, came a modest 36th in the Mille Miglia and scored class wins in the Aosta-Gran San Bernardo and Parma-Poggio di Berceto. The car appeared again at the Circuito di Senigallia on 20 August, but this time with a barchetta body and separate motorcycle-type mudguards, the form in which Stagnoli raced the 166 MM Zagato again in 1951.

The two-seat 166 Inter coupé built by Carrozzeria Touring of Milan. This car (chassis number 007 S) with its 1949 body and slightly shorter wheelbase of 2420 mm instead of subsequent models' 2500 mm, is shown in an official Touring photograph, taken in Piazza Santorre di Santarosa in Milan. Compared to the barchetta, recourse to chromed components and of moulding is more marked in this case, especially along the flanks.

TECHNICAL SPECIFICATION

ENGINE		CHASSIS	
Front, longitudinal, V12 (60°)		*Chassis*	longitudinal and cross members
Bore and stroke	60x58.8 mm	*Front suspension*	independent,
Unitary cubic capacity	166.25		double wishbones, transverse
Total cubic capacity	1995.02		semi-elliptic spring,
Valve gear	single overhead camshaft		hydraulic dampers
Number of valves	two per cylinder	*Rear suspension*	live axle, longitudinal
Compression ratio	7.5:1 (7:1 in 1951)		semi-elliptic springs, anti-roll
Fuel feed	one or three Weber 32DCF or		bar, hydraulic dampers
	36DCF carburettors	*Brakes*	drum
Ignition	single, two distributors	*Steering*	worm and sector
Coolant	water	*Fuel tank*	80 litres (85 in 1951)
Lubrication	damp sump	*Tyres front/rear*	5.50-15 all round
Maximum power	110 hp at 6000 rpm		(5.90-15 all round in 1951)
	(105 hp at 6000 rpm in 1951)		
Specific power	55 hp/litre	**DIMENSIONS AND WEIGHT**	
	(52 in 1951)	*Wheelbase*	2420 mm (2500 in 1951)
		Track front/rear	1250/1200 mm
TRANSMISSION			1270/1250 in 1951)
Rear-wheel drive		*Length*	-
Clutch	single dry disc	*Width*	-
Gearbox	en bloc with engine	*Height*	-
	five gears + reverse	*Kerb weight*	800 kg (900 in 1951)
BODY		PERFORMANCE	
Two-seater coupé/cabriolet		*Top speed*	170 km/ (180 km/h in 1951)
		Power to weight ratio	7.6 kg/hp (8.2 kg/hp in 1951)

Ferrari 166 Inter 1949

The Ferrari 166 family of cars was blessed with a new coupé at the 1949 Paris Motor Show on 6 October: it was called the 166 Inter, like the Sport category single-seater and Formula Two racers. Construction of the body for this two-seater was once again assigned to Touring of Milan, who maintained their consolidated tradition by designing a clean and elegant body. Seen in sharply defined profile, this Ferrari had something of the Alfa Romeo 6C 2500 Villa d'Este about it - a car built by Touring in the mid-Forties - especially its tail. As with the 166 MM barchetta, of which the Inter can be considered the grand touring version, the flanks were furrowed by two ribs, which began respectively from the front wing and the rear, extending first along the edge of the door and then right to the end of the tail, in proximity with which it curved downwards slightly. The engine, once again, was the 1995.02 cc 60° V12.

The many victories Ferrari had achieved by racing in both Italy and Europe generated great notoriety for the company and attracted all the leading carrozzieri of the period to working on Maranello's rolling chassis. After Touring, the first to propose an unusual body for the 166 Inter was Ghia, who came up with a coupé designed by Mario Boano, of which only one was built in white; that same year, Stabilimenti Farina conceived the sober yet elegant coupé shown above, which was extraordinarily similar to the Cisitalia 202, first shown in Paris 1947. In 1950-51, Vignale designed an interesting series of coupés, which embodied some styling features that would became regulars on future Ferraris, while Farina and Bertone extended the Inter range with two cabriolets.

They did not look it, but the two 275 Ss entered for the 1950 Mille Miglia were powered by a 3322.34 cc V12 engine designed for Formula One. The first was assigned to Alberto Ascari and Senesio Nicolini and the second to Gigi Villoresi and Pasquale Cassani (photograph). Both cars retired with broken transmissions, much stressed by the exuberant power of their V12s.

TECHNICAL SPECIFICATION

ENGINE
front, longitudinal, V12 (60°)

Bore and stroke	72x68 mm
Unitary cubic capacity	276.86
Total cubic capacity	3322.34
Valve gear	single overhead camshaft
Number of valves	two per cylinder
Compression ratio	10:1
Fuel feed	three Weber 42DCF carburettors
Ignition	single, two magnetos
Coolant	water
Lubrication	dry sump
Maximum power	300 hp at 7300 rpm
Specific power	90.3 hp/litre

TRANSMISSION
Rear-wheel drive

Clutch	multi-disc
Gearbox	en bloc with engine five gears + reverse

BODY
Two/single seater barchetta

CHASSIS

Chassis	longitudinal and cross members
Front suspension	independent, double wishbones, transverse semi-elliptic spring, Houdaille dampers
Rear suspension	oscillating drive shafts, transverse semi-elliptic spring, Houdaille dampers
Brakes	drum
Steering	worm and sector
Fuel tank	195 litres
Tyres front/rear	5.50-16/7.00-16

DIMENSIONS AND WEIGHT

Wheelbase	2320 mm
Track front/rear	1278/1250 mm
Length	3937 mm
Width	1428 mm
Height	960 mm
Weight (in running order)	850 kg

PERFORMANCE

Top speed	280 km/h
Power to weight ratio	2.8 kg/hp

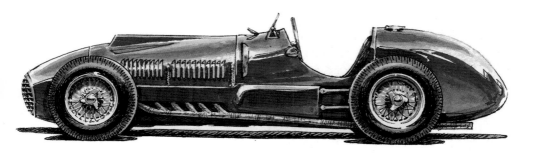

Ferrari 275 F1   1950

The first round in the Formula One World Championship was flagged away on 13 May 1950 at Silverstone and was called the Grand Prix of Europe. With new changes to the motor racing regulations for 4,500 cc normally aspirated and 1500 cc super-charged engines, the debate inside Ferrari as to which car and power unit to use in the new category raged on. But while remaining faithful to 12 cylinders it was decided to drop the supercharger, which had caused a number of problems in the 125 F1, and to design a new aspirated unit, which could later also be transferred to the Scuderia's sports racing and Grand Touring cars. The task of designing the engine was given to Aurelio Lampredi, who took over technical management of the Prancing Horse from Gioachino Colombo. The new man decided to achieve his target of 4.5 litres in successive stages.

The first step was a 12-cylinder engine of over 3.3 litres, which initially appeared as a test case in two sports racers. Ascari and Villoresi were entered for the 1950 Mille Miglia of 23 April in the two Touring barchettas, which were much like the 166 MM, but boasted the new engine for which the model was named the 275 S. Villoresi went through the Pescara control in the lead, but he was forced to retire when his transmission broke, as was Ascari soon after the same town. That engine, the power of which was increased to 300 hp, was immediately installed in the 275 F1 single-seater, which Alberto Ascari raced for the first time at the Grand Prix of Belgium at Spa-Francorchamps on 18 June. Despite his modest fifth place, the move to 4.5 litres had begun and, after another sporadic appearance in practice for the Grand Prix of France, the 275 F1 was soon joined by the 4101.66 cc 340 F1.

Alberto Ascari was given the job of debuting the 340 F1, a stopgap car en route to the 4.5-litre, at the 1952 Grand Prix of Nations for F1 single-seaters in Geneva. The car's power enabled Ascari to start from the front row, but the outcome of the race was not so favourable, as the Milanese driver retired with engine trouble. Alfa Romeos took the first three places.

TECHNICAL SPECIFICATION

ENGINE
front, longitudinal, V12 (60°)

Bore and stroke	80x68 mm
Unitary cubic capacity	341.80
Total cubic capacity	4101.66
Valve gear	single overhead camshaft
Number of valves	two per cylinder
Compression ratio	12:1
Fuel feed	three Weber 42DCF carburettors
Ignition	single, two magnetos
Coolant	water
Lubrication	dry sump
Maximum power	335 hp at 7000 rpm
Specific power	81.7 hp/litre

TRANSMISSION
Rear-wheel drive

Clutch	multi-disc
Gearbox	en bloc with differential four speeds + reverse

BODY
Single-seater

CHASSIS

Chassis	longitudinal and cross members
Front suspension	independent, double wishbones, transverse semi-elliptic spring, Houdaille dampers
Rear suspension	De Dion axle, oscillating drive shafts, transverse semi-elliptic spring, Houdaille dampers
Brakes	drum
Steering	worm and sector
Fuel tank	195 litres
Tyres front/rear	5.50-16, 7.00-16

DIMENSIONS AND WEIGHT

Wheelbase	2420 mm
Track front/rear	1278/1250 mm
Length	3937 mm
Width	1428 mm
Height	960 mm
Kerb weight	850 kg

PERFORMANCE

Top speed	300 km/h
Power to weight ratio	2.5 kg/hp

Ferrari 340 F1 1950

Ferrari brought out a new single-seater to join the 275 F1. It was called the 340 F1 and competed for the first time in the Grand Prix of Nations at Geneva on 30 July 1950. The new car was an intermediate step on the way to a car powered by a 4.5-litre unit, the limit imposed by regulations for normally aspirated engines. A logical evolution of its predecessor, the 340 F1 was also designed by Aurelio Lampredi, who concentrated his attention on increasing the engine's cubic capacity to 4101.66 cc by expanding its bore and stroke to 80 x 68 mm to generate 335 hp. The rear suspension was also new and included a De Dion axle, which had been much tested on the Formula Two car, as had the four-speed gearbox that was en bloc with the differential. Ascari started from the front row in the car's maiden race, next to Juan Manuel Fangio's Alfa Romeo 158 and in front of Gigi Villoresi in a 275 F1, and led for most of the race. Only engine trouble forced him to give way to eventual winner Fangio and his Alfa, the car that dominated that first world championship. In spite of that negative result, the 340 F1 showed its competitiveness for as long as it raced and competed again at that year's Grand Prix of Spain in Barcelona, where it came third in the hands of Piero Taruffi, behind winner Alberto Ascari and second-placed Dorino Serafini in Ferrari 375s.

The 375 F1 had made its debut at Monza on 3 September and it was with that car that Aurelio Lampredi achieved his 4.5-litre engine objective, which meant Ferrari was finally able to go up against the Alfa Romeo 158/159 of Nino Farina and Juan Manuel Fangio and fight it out for its first race victory in the Formula One World Drivers' Championship.

Silverstone, England, 14 July 1951: the great day finally arrived. Jose Froilan Gonzalez, aka El Cabezon, drove the Ferrari 375 F1 to victory in the Grand Prix of Great Britain, beating Juan Manuel Fangio's Alfa Romeo 158 to add Ferrari's name to the Formula One World Championship roll of honour for the first time. It was the first of a long series of wins that continue to the present day.

TECHNICAL SPECIFICATION

ENGINE
front, longitudinal, V12 (60°)

Bore and stroke	80x74.5 mm
Unitary cubic capacity	374,47
Total cubic capacity	4493.73
Valve gear	single overhead camshaft
Number of valves	two per cylinder
Compression ratio	11:1
	(12:1 in 1951)
Fuel feed	three Weber 42DCF
	carburettors (three Weber
	46DCF3 in 1951)
Ignition	single, two magnetos
	(double, one magneto in 1951)
Coolant	water
Lubrication	dry sump
Maximum power	330 hp at 7000 rpm
	(380 hp at 7500 rpm in 1951)
Specific power	77.9 hp/litre (84.5 in 1951)

TRANSMISSION
Rear-wheel drive

Clutch	multi-disc
Gearbox	en bloc with differential
	four gears + reverse

BODY
Single-seater

CHASSIS

Chassis	longitudinal and cross
	members
Front suspension	independent,
	double wishbones, transverse
	semi-elliptic spring,
	Houdaille dampers
Rear suspension	De Dion axle, transverse
	semi-elliptic spring,
	Houdaille dampers
Brakes	drum
Steering	worm and sector
Fuel tank	195 litres
Tyres front/rear	5.50-16/7.00-16

DIMENSIONS AND WEIGHT

Wheelbase	2320 mm (2420 mm in 1951)
Track front/rear	1270/1278 mm
	(1250/1250 in 1951)
Length	3937 mm
Width	1428 mm
Height	960 mm
Power to weight ratio	850 kg

PERFORMANCE

Top speed	320 km/h
Power to weight ratio	2.5 kg/hp (2.2 in 1951)

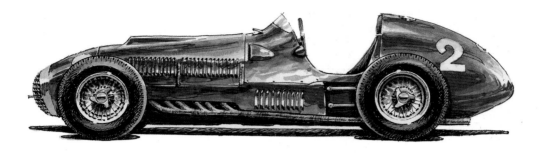

Ferrari 375 F1   1950

The 4.5 litre objective had already been achieved in 1950 with the 375 F1, which may well have looked like the 340, but under the skin was hidden all the principal new developments of the 12-cylinder engine, with a cubic capacity increased to 4493.73 cc after enlarging the bore and stroke to 80x74.5 mm respectively. The first two examples of the car made their debut at Monza on 3 September, driven by Dorino Serafini and Alberto Ascari. Ferrari's future world champion came second behind the Alfa Romeo of Nino Farina, who won the first F1 world drivers' title with that victory. The potent 375 dominated the subsequent Grand Prix of Barcelona, a non-championship race, with the win going to Ascari and second place to Serafini. At the start of the 1951 season, the new Ferraris became the biggest threat to the new Alfa Romeo 159 in the fight for the world championship.

During that season, the 375 F1 was modified numerous times: it was given a new kind of double ignition with only one magneto, and new Weber 46DCF3 carburettors. After three consecutive second places during the first three races, all won by Alfa Romeo, the Argentine driver Jose Froilan Gonzalez was able to beat the Portello cars to win the 1951 Grand Prix of Great Britain at Silverstone on 14 July and inscribe the Ferrari name on the Formula One World Championship role of honour for the first time. It was a moment of extraordinary significance to Enzo Ferrari, who had run Alfa Romeo's motor sport department from 1929-1939. When he received a telegram of congratulations from engineer Quaroni, managing director of Alfa, the only message with which he could reply was: "Rest assured that I still have the adolescent tenderness of a first love and deep affection for a mother for our Alfa".

Renzo Castagneto, an organiser of the great Mille Miglia, lowers the chequered flag on the Touring-bodied 195 S sports saloon number 724 of Giannino Marzotto and Marco Crosara as they win the 1950 Brescia-based marathon. The two were first across the finish line in the city and clocked an average 123.209 km/h, over seven minutes ahead of the Serafini-Salami 195 S Touring barchetta.

TECHNICAL SPECIFICATION

ENGINE
front, longitudinal, V12 (60°)

Bore and stroke	65x58.8 mm
Unitary cubic capacity	195.08
Total cubic capacity	2241.02
Valve gear	single overhead camshaft
Number of valves	two per cylinder
Compression ratio	8.5:1
Fuel feed	three Weber 36DCF carburettors
Ignition	single, one coil and two distributors
Coolant	water
Lubrication	damp sump
Maximum power	170 hp at 7000 rpm
Specific power	72.6 hp/litre

TRANSMISSION
Rear-wheel drive	
Clutch	multi-disc
Gearbox	en bloc with engine five speeds + reverse

BODY
Two-seater barchetta/sports saloon

CHASSIS
Chassis	longitudinal and cross members
Front suspension	independent, double wishbones, transverse semi-elliptic spring, hydraulic dampers
Rear suspension	live axle, longitudinal semi-elliptic springs, anti-roll bar, hydraulic dampers
Brakes	drum
Steering	worm and sector
Fuel tank	-
Tyres front/rear	5.50-15/6.00-15

DIMENSIONS AND WEIGHT
Wheelbase	2250 mm
Track front/rear	1278/1250 mm
Length	-
Width	-
Height	-
Kerb weight	720-780 kg

PERFORMANCE
Top speed	200 km/h
Power to weight ratio	4.2-4.6 kg/hp

Ferrari 195 S   1950

As tradition would have it, the Giro di Sicilia inaugurated the series of 1950 events for sports racing cars on 2 April. Ferrari entered the usual 166 MM Touring models, as well as two cars for Alberto Ascari and Giannino Marzotto that did not seem so different from the 166. Ascari's was an open top and Marzotto's a sports saloon. But the main advance was under the bonnet, where a 60° V12 engine lurked: its power output had been upped to 170 hp by increasing the diameter of the pistons to 65 mm, while the total cubic capacity was raised to 2341.02 cc. The two 195 Ss – that was the official denomination attributed to the new model – were both forced to retire, but three cars were entered for the year's Mille Miglia: one for Dorino Serafini and one each for brothers Vittorio and Giannino Marzotto. The latter turned up in the Piazza della Vittoria in Brescia for scrutineering at the wheel of his 195 S Touring sports saloon rendered even more elegant by its unusual light blue livery. That year's Mille Miglia was run in fairly adverse weather conditions, with rain along almost the whole route. Giannino Marzotto exploited the undoubted advantages of the closed 195 S: he had taken the lead by the Ravenna control and, with a consistent performance, was first across the finish line in Brescia after 13h 39'20" of racing. He climbed out of his winning Ferrari wearing an elegant double-breasted suit that was slightly dampened by the odd raindrop, which, at least as he tells the story today, he wore throughout the event, convinced that his race would only last a few hours on 10 June. Marzotto also won the 3 Ore Notturna di Roma in the same elegant sports saloon, which had taken second place in the Coppa della Toscana driven by Franco Cornacchia.

Carrozzeria Vignale in Turin designed a number of different versions of the 195 Inter. The photograph shows the body on rolling chassis 099, built in 1951. It has an elegant dual-tone livery, which distinguished Vignale-bodied Ferraris. In the early Fifties, the Turin atelier built bodies almost all the Ferraris of the period, from the 212 to the 340 and on to the 250.

TECHNICAL SPECIFICATION

ENGINE		CHASSIS	
front, longitudinal, V12 (60°)		Chassis	longitudinal and cross members
Bore and stroke	65x58.8 mm	Front suspension	independent, double wishbones, transverse semi-elliptic spring, hydraulic dampers
Unitary cubic capacity	195.095		
Total cubic capacity	2341.02		
Valve gear	single overhead camshaft		
Number of valves	two per cylinder	Rear suspension	live axle, longitudinal semi-elliptic springs, anti-roll bar, hydraulic dampers
Compression ratio	7.5:1		
Fuel feed	one Weber 36DCF carburettor		
Ignition	single, one distributor		
Coolant	water	Brakes	drum
Lubrication	damp sump	Steering	worm and sector
Maximum power	130 hp at 6000 rpm	Fuel tank	82 litres
Specific power	55.5 hp/litre	Tyres front/rear	5.90-15 all round
TRANSMISSION		DIMENSIONS AND WEIGHT	
Rear-wheel drive		Wheelbase	2500 mm
Clutch	multi-disc	Track front/rear	1270/1250 mm
Gearbox	en bloc with engine five speeds + reverse	Length	-
		Width	-
		Height	-
BODY		Kerb weight	950 kg
Two-seater coupé			
		PERFORMANCE	
		Top speed	180 km/h
		Power to weight ratio	7.03 kg/hp

Ferrari 195 Inter   1950

The notoriety that came from the Giannino Marzotto/Marco Crosara victory in the 1950 Mille Miglia driving a 195 S led Ferrari to promote a less powerful version of the sports saloon in the classy grand touring market. So on 5 October at the Paris Motor Show, the Prancing Horse unveiled the 195 Inter. Built on a 2500 mm wheelbase rolling chassis by Carrozzeria Vignale, who had already created the 166 Inter, Michelotti gave the new coupé clean and essential lines. Shown in an elegant black livery, the 195 Inter went on to diversify into a series of individual examples, some with dual-tone paintwork, built on request. In line with its use predominately as

a tourer, the fuel feed to the car's 2341.02 cc V12 power unit was modified by the adoption of a single Weber 36DCF carburettor in place of the three fitted to the S version: that made power generation smoother and more progressive. Performance was also diminished to return a top speed of 180 km/h.

Carrozzeria Ghia unveiled its interpretation of a car on a 195 rolling chassis at the 1951 Geneva Motor Show. Their effort was shown in white at the Turin show and had with a generous radiator grill, underscored by a large chrome bumper bar. At the same show Touring, a long-time Maranello partner, displayed a dual-tone 195 Inter; but the Milan body stylist was showing signs of a creative crisis. It was unable to come up with anything really new and limited itself to going over the old stylistic ground already covered by the 166 sports saloons.

In 1951, Salvatore Ammendola had Motto build a 195 S coupé, in which he came 15th overall in that year's Mille Miglia.

The 220 hp, 4100 cc 340 America Vignale was quite a handful for Gigi Villoresi and Pasquale Cassani, so problems along the 1951 Mille Miglia route were inevitable. The car was in the lead at Bologna, though, the last time control before the finish, after 11h 22' 28" of racing at an average 117.016 km/h. The Bracco-Maglioli Lancia Aurelia B20 came second.

TECHNICAL SPECIFICATION

ENGINE
front, longitudinal, V12 (60°)

Bore and stroke	80x68 mm
Unitary cubic capacity	341.80
Total cubic capacity	4101.66
Valve gear	single overhead camshaft
Number of valves	2 per cylinder
Compression ratio	8:1
Fuel feed	three Weber 40DCF carburettors
Ignition	single, one coil, two distributors
Coolant	water
Lubrication	dry sump
Maximum power	220 hp at 6000 rpm
Specific power	53.6 hp/litre

TRANSMISSION
Rear-wheel drive

Clutch	single dry disc
Gearbox	en bloc with engine five speeds + reverse

BODY
Two-seater barchetta/sports saloon

CHASSIS

Chassis	longitudinal and cross members
Front suspension	independent, double wishbones, transverse semi-elliptic spring, hydraulic dampers
Rear suspension	live axle, longitudinal semi-elliptic springs, hydraulic dampers
Brakes	drum
Steering	worm and sector
Fuel tank	135 litres
Tyres front/rear	6.40-15 all round

DIMENSIONS AND WEIGHT

Wheelbase	2420 mm
Track front/rear	1278/1250 mm
Length	-
Width	-
Height	-
Kerb weight	900 kg

PERFORMANCE

Top speed	240 km/h
Power to weight ratio	3.9 kg/hp

Ferrari 340 America   1951

The 340 F1 entered for the Grand Prix of Nations at Geneva in July 1950 and powered by a 4101.66 cc, 12-cylinder engine was a stepping stone towards the 4.5-litre limit imposed by F1 regulations. Less than three months later, that same unit was installed in a Touring sports racing car very similar to the 166 MM and was unveiled at the Paris Motor Show on 5 October. The Paris car's bodywork was sprayed black and its interior was in dark green leather. The newborn was christened the 340 America and Ferrari's intention was to consolidate its presence in the U.S. market with a car that could be entered for Sport events and, later, be offered as a grand tourer to an elite clientele. After the Paris preview, the real launch of the 340 America took place at the following year's Turin Motor Show, also attended by the designer of the car's potent four-litre power unit, Aurelio Lampredi.

As always the Mille Miglia, scheduled for 29 April that year, was considered the best event in which to test the qualities of the new 340, which was entered in Touring barchetta form for Vittorio Marzotto, Alberto Ascari and Dorino Serafini and as a coupé by Vignale for Gigi Villoresi-Pasquale Cassani. It was the coupé that fought a tooth and nail battle with the Giovanni Bracco-Umberto Maglioli Lancia Aurelia B20, which, even though way down on power at just 1991 cc, used its tremendous stability and handling qualities that the 340 America could not match to great effect on the wet, tortuous parts of the route. But on the straights, the Ferrari was way ahead and scored big time on the Adriatic coast and the plains to win.

The Giannino Marzotto-Marco Crosara Ferrari 212 Export at the start of the 1951 Mille Miglia. With this Carrozzeria Fontana-bodied car, the two became exciting protagonists of the first half of the race, moving into the lead at the Ravenna control with 5'17" over Gigi Villoresi's Ferrari 340 America. But Marzotto's race ended before he got to the Pescara time control.

TECHNICAL SPECIFICATION

ENGINE
front, longitudinal, V12 (60°)

Bore and stroke	68x58.8 mm
Unitary cubic capacity	213.54
Total cubic capacity	2562.51
Valve gear	single overhead camshaft
Number of valves	two per cylinder
Compression ratio	8:1
Fuel feed	one Weber 32 DCF carburettor
Ignition	single, two distributors
Coolant	water
Lubrication	dry sump
Maximum power	150 hp at 6500 rpm
Specific power	58.8 hp/litre

TRANSMISSION
Rear-wheel drive

Clutch	single dry disc
Gearbox	en bloc with engine five speeds + reverse

BODY
Two-seater coupé/sports Saloon/barchetta

CHASSIS

Chassis	longitudinal and cross members
Front suspension	independent, double wishbones, transverse semi-elliptic spring, hydraulic dampers
Rear suspension	live axle, longitudinal semi-elliptic springs, hydraulic dampers
Brakes	drum
Steering	worm and sector
Fuel tank	-
Tyres front/rear	5.90-15 all round

DIMENSIONS AND WEIGHT

Wheelbase	2250 mm
Track front/rear	1270/1250 mm
Length	-
Width	-
Height	-
Kerb weight	800 kg

PERFORMANCE

Top speed	220 km/h
Power to weight ratio	5.3 kg/hp

Ferrari 212 Export   1951

Despite Gioachino Colombo leaving Ferrari in January 1951 due to tension that had been building built up between him and Aurelio Lampredi for some time, Maranello continued to develop engineering projects conceived by the departed engineer. In particular the 12-cylinder, two-litre originally installed in the 166, which was advanced to 2,562.51 cc. That unit was lowered into a new model, the name of which confirmed Ferrari's growing interest in overseas markets: the Vignale-bodied 212 Export made its debut as a cabriolet at the 1951 Geneva Motor Show. Numerous carrozzerie built bodies for the high performance grand tourer, including the usual Vignale and Touring sports saloons and cabriolets, and extended to extravagant interpretations by Motto and Fontana. Carrozzeria Fontana of Padua built bodies for two of the cars at the request of the Marzotto brothers: one was an odd-looking barchetta, not surprising dubbed the 'Sicilian cart', with which Vittorio won the 1951 Giro di Sicilia. The other was a rounded sports saloon, known to the fans as 'Marzotto's Egg', in which Giannino competed in the Mille Miglia without success.

He remembers, "Those cars may have been ugly, but they were much lighter and faster than the other Ferraris. When the Commendatore saw the Egg for the first time, he blanched; he was speechless, as if an evil curse had violated his creation." But Marzotto's Egg was competitive, light and fast, enabling him to lead the race before retirement. The Egg reappeared at the 1952 Mille Miglia, crewed by Guido Mancini-Adriano Ercolani, but came nowhere.

Pinin Farina's first Ferrari was this Inter 212 cabriolet, commissioned by Georges Filipinetti in 1952. Right from that first creation, the Turin carrozziere was able to confer great sobriety and elegance on Ferrari grand tourers, further enhanced here by a black body and a light coloured leather interior. The 212 Inter marked the beginning of a long and fruitful relationship between Maranello and the talented stylist.

TECHNICAL SPECIFICATION

ENGINE
front, longitudinal, V12 (60°)

Bore and stroke	68x58.8 mm
Unitary cubic capacity	213.54
Total cubic capacity	2562.51
Valve gear	single overhead camshaft
Number of valves	two per cylinder
Compression ratio	7.5:1, 8:1
Fuel feed	one Weber 36 DCF or three Weber 32DCF carburettors
Ignition	single, two distributors
Coolant	water
Lubrication	damp sump
Maximum power	155/170 hp at 6500 rpm
Specific power	60.5-66.3 hp/litre

TRANSMISSION
Rear-wheel drive

Clutch	single dry disc
Gearbox	en bloc with engine five speeds + reverse

BODY
Two-seater coupé/cabriolet

CHASSIS

Chassis	longitudinal and cross members
Front suspension	independent, double wishbones, transverse semi-elliptic spring, Houdaille dampers
Rear suspension	live axle, double longitudinal semi-elliptic springs, Houdaille dampers
Brakes	drum
Steering	worm and sector
Fuel tank	105 litres
Tyres front/rear	5.90-15 or 6.40-15 all round

DIMENSIONS AND WEIGHT

Wheelbase	2600 mm
Track front and rear	1278/1250 mm
Length	4100 mm
Width	1500 mm
Height	1380 mm
Kerb weight	1000 kg

PERFORMANCE

Top speed	185-200 km/h
Power to weight ratio	6.4-5.9 kg/hp

Ferrari 212 Inter   1951

As was the case with 195 - the Sport derivative of the 195 S came out first and the 196 Inter grand tourer later - the less "sporty" version of the Ferrari 212 was the first to appear: the 212 Inter made its debut at the 1951 Paris Motor Show. Carrozzeria Vignale devised the initial sober and elegant-looking Inter with a wheelbase increased to 2600 mm. The car had almost the same mechanics as the previous model: a 60°, 2.5-litre V12, still with a single Weber 36DCF carburettor, which would later be replaced by three 32DCFs. Many stylists built 212 Inter bodies between 1951-53. After Vignale, who also produced some cabriolets and consolidated its relationship with Maranello with this car, Ghia came up with a 2+2 coupé and a four-seater saloon, inaugurating new territory for the Prancing Horse. Meanwhile Touring, now going through the worst of its creative slump, came up with yet another sports saloon similar to its 166 and 212 Export. The 212 Inter played a particularly important role in Ferrari's genealogy, as it marked the start of a long and successful relationship with Pinin Farina, who built two elegant cabriolets in 1952, one in black commissioned by Swiss customer Georges Filipinetti, and the other in metallic silver, presented at that year's Paris Motor Show.

The sales success of the 212 Inter, especially in the U.S. market, was assured by the prestigious victory of Piero Taruffi and Luigi Chinetti in the 1951 Carrera Panamericana driving a Vignale 212 coupé, ahead of Alberto Ascari and Gigi Villoresi in a similar car. The effect of that win was of great importance, helped along by Maranello's substantial advertising campaign.

Pinin Farina showed this cabriolet built on the Ferrari 342 America rolling chassis at the 1953 New York Auto Show. The car was impressive for its rather generously proportioned, prominent radiator grill and the sobriety of its line, for which every single detail had been carefully designed to make the most of its cleanliness of surface. For instance, note the recessed door handle with a chrome profile in the lower area.

TECHNICAL SPECIFICATION

ENGINE
front, longitudinal, V12 (60°)

Bore and stroke	80x68 mm
Unitary cubic capacity	341.80
Total cubic capacity	4101.66
Valve gear	single overhead camshaft
Number of valves	two per cylinder
Compression ratio	8:1
Fuel feed	three Weber 40 DCF carburettors
Ignition	single, two carburettors
Coolant	water
Lubrication	dry sump
Maximum power	200 hp at 5000 rpm
Specific power	48.8 hp/litre

TRANSMISSION
Rear-wheel drive

Clutch	single dry disc
Gearbox	en bloc with engine
	Four speeds + reverse

BODY
Two-seater coupé/cabriolet

CHASSIS

Chassis	longitudinal and cross members
Front suspension	independent, double wishbones, transverse semi-elliptic spring, Houdaille dampers
Rear suspension	live axle, double longitudinal semi-elliptic springs, Houdaille dampers
Brakes	drum
Steering	worm and sector
Fuel tank	105 litres
Tyres front/rear	6.40-15 all round

DIMENSIONS AND WEIGHT

Wheelbase	2650 mm
Track front/rear	1325/1320 mm
Length	4550 mm
Width	1600 mm
Height	1430 mm
Kerb weight	1200 kg

PERFORMANCE

Top speed	186 km/h
Power to weight ratio	6 hp/kg

Ferrari 342 America   1951

Riding the wave of the Villoresi-Cassani win in the 1951 Mille Miglia in the 340 America, Ferrari decided to begin production of a grand touring version of the car. So an imposing Ghia coupé called the 342 America was given its first outing in October at the 1951 Paris Motor Show. But it was Pinin Farina who created the most original and elegant body for the new car soon after having begun its long working relationship with Ferrari. Aimed at an elite clientele anything but sporting, the 342 was powered by a de-tuned 4,101.66 engine with its revs reduced to 5,000 rpm against the 6,000 of the racer. A longer, 2,650 mm wheelbase and a four-speed synchromesh gearbox helped increase the comfort and driveability of the car, suiting it to road use. One of its first customers was ex-King Leopold of Belgium, who had Pinin Farina grace his rolling chassis with a black cabriolet body with beige interior - in which the 4,493.73 cc engine of the 375 was installed. Soon afterwards, Pinin Farina displayed another silver 342 cabriolet at the 1953 New York Auto Show, the car's clean and elegant lines already seen on the 212 Inter. The Turin atelier also blessed the 342 range with two coupés, one silver and the other black, both with prominent radiator grills, panoramic rear windows and each with its own unmistakable styling personality. The art of Pinin Farina lived up to the expectations of Ferrari who, still searching for a stylist able to give his grand tourers originality, began to turn increasingly to the Turin body stylist.

Alberto Ascari (photo) winning the Grand Prix of Switzerland at Bern on 23 August 1953 to take his second consecutive Formula One World Championship with a race in hand. That season, the driver conceded almost nothing to his opponents and took five of the nine GPs, an indication of his Ferrari 500 F2's undoubted supremacy.

TECHNICAL SPECIFICATION

ENGINE
front, longitudinal, four cylinders in line

Bore and stroke	90x78 mm
Unitary cubic capacity	496.21
Total cubic capacity	1984.86
Valve gear	twin overhead camshafts
Number of valves	two per cylinder
Compression ratio	11.5:1 (13:1 in 1953)
Fuel feed	four Weber 45 DOE carburettors (two Weber 50 DCOA in 1953)
Ignition	double, two magnetos
Coolant	water
Lubrication	drum sump
Maximum power	165 hp at 7000 rpm (185 hp at 7500 rpm in 1953)
Specific power	83.1 hp/litre 93.2 in 1953

TRANSMISSION
Rear-wheel drive

Clutch	multi-disc
Gearbox	en bloc with differential four speeds + reverse

BODY
Single-seater

CHASSIS

Chassis	longitudinal and cross members
Front suspension	independent, double wishbones, transverse semi-elliptic spring, Houdaille dampers
Rear suspension	De Dion axle, transverse semi-elliptic spring, Houdaille dampers
Brakes	drum
Steering	worm and sector
Fuel tank	150 litres
Tyres front/rear	5.25-16/6.00-16

DIMENSIONS AND WEIGHT

Wheelbase	2160 mm
Track front/rear	1278/1250 mm
Length	3988 mm
Width	1402 mm
Height	1050 mm
Kerb weight	560 kg

PERFORMANCE

Top speed	240 km/h
Power to weight ratio	3.4 kg/hp (3.0 in 1953)

Ferrari 500 F2 1951

The 500 F2 was a car of special importance to the Prancing Horse, as it was the first not conceived around a 12-cylinder engine, yet it enabled Alberto Ascari to add the Ferrari name to the Formula One World Championship roll of honour. The new category, instituted in 1950, was already of little interest by the end of 1951, because few teams competed and especially because of Alfa Romeo's retirement from racing. So the International Federation decided to let Formula Two single-seaters compete in the top championship for two years. Enzo Ferrari was the only constructor not to be caught on the hop, as he had earlier told Aurelio Lampredi to design four-cylinder 2.5 litre (2,490 cc) and two-litre (1,985 cc) engines, the latter installed in a new concept car called the 500 F2. In 1952-3, there was no serious opposition for that light and agile car, during the design of which Lampredi paid great attention to weight distribution to further enhance the small four-cylinder's performance. The 500 F2 won 14 out of a possible 15 races, 11 of them going to Alberto Ascari, who had won the world title by the end of both years.Mike Hawthorn and Piero Taruffi also won with the car. The 500 F2 needed no particular modification during those two seasons, although a "lengthened" version was introduced with a more prominent nose for use on high speed circuits. The unopposed domination of the 500 F2 was broken in 1953 by a new regulation that fixed cubic capacity at 2,500 cc, inexorably overtaking the small Ferrari cars.

The official picture of the 1952 NART-Ferrari Indianapolis car, with Alberto Ascari at the wheel of the 375 Indy. Others in the photograph include Giovanni Canestrini (right, with pipe), the Auto Italiana track correspondent. As it was not known whether or not the car would compete as a works entry, the Prancing Horse shield was initially painted out, but it reappeared for the race.

TECHNICAL SPECIFICATION

ENGINE
front, longitudinal, V12 (60°)

Bore and stroke	79x74.5 mm
Unitary cubic capacity	365.17
Total cubic capacity	4382.0
Valve gear	single overhead camshaft
Number of valves	two per cylinder
Compression ratio	13:1
Fuel feed	three Weber 40IF4C carburettors
Ignition	double, four magnetos
Coolant	water
Lubrication	dry sump
Maximum power	400 hp at 7500 rpm
Specific power	91.2 hp/litre

TRANSMISSION
Rear-wheel drive

Clutch	multi-disc
Gearbox	en block with differential four speeds + reverse

BODY
Single-seater

CHASSIS

Chassis	longitudinal and cross members
Front suspension	independent, double wishbones, transverse semi-elliptic spring, hydraulic dampers
Rear suspension	De Dion axle, transverse semi-elliptic spring, hydraulic dampers
Brakes	drum
Steering	worm and sector
Fuel tank	-
Tyres front/rear	6.00-16/8.00-18

DIMENSIONS AND WEIGHT

Wheelbase	2500 mm
Track front/rear	1270/1250 mm
Length	-
Width	-
Height	-
Kerb weight	829 kg

PERFORMANCE

Top speed	325 km/h
Power to weight ratio	2.05 kg/hp

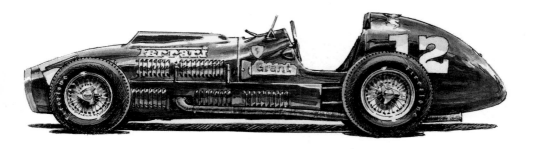

Ferrari 375 Indy   1952

The 1951 375 F1 was the car with which Maranello achieved its objective of developing a V12 4.5 litre engine: it won the Prancing Horse's first F1 race driven by Jose Froilan Gonzalez at Silverstone, followed by the Alberto Ascari wins at the Nürburgring and Monza. Ferrari even came close to winning the world championship with the car at the end of the season. Although yet another change to the regulations, which had previously scuppered the small 500 F2 cars, also stopped the potent 375 F1 from furthering its world championship quest, its racing career continued as a Ferrari entry for the 1952 500 Miles of Indianapolis. But the F1 car's mechanics had to be much revised before it became the 375 Indy, with the adoption of new Weber 40IF4C carburettors, which increased its power to 400 hp at 7,500 rpm. As a result, it was necessary to strengthen the Indy car's chassis and suspension, as well as lengthen the wheelbase. In that configuration, Ferrari's Indianapolis car took to the track for the first time on 6 April 1952 at the Circuito del Valentino for the Grand Prix of Turin and won, driven by Gigi Villoresi.

But once it got to the States and the legendary Brickyard oval, the 375 showed it was not up to that kind of competition. Of the four 375s sent to the United States – one for Alberto Ascari entered by Luigi Chinetti's North American Racing Team and the rest for other American teams - only the Milanese driver was able to qualify, but on the ninth row of the grid. After 41 laps, a broken hub ended Ascari's race, even though he had shown he could keep pace with his opponents. The 375 Indy reappeared in 1958 at the 500 Kilometres of Monza: NART entered the car again, this time for American Harry Schell, whose performance was poor.

Vignale used a number of styling devices on the Ferrari 225 S barchettas, like the three oval air vents along the sides and the small intakes at the sides of the radiator grill, which then became regular characteristics of Maranello's cars bodied by the company. The picture shows the 225 S of Mario and Franco Bornigia on the starting ramp of the 1952 Mille Miglia, from which they retired just before Rome.

TECHNICAL SPECIFICATION

ENGINE
front, longitudinal, V12 (60°)

Bore and stroke	70x58.8 mm
Unitary cubic capacity	226.28
Total cubic capacity	2715.46
Valve gear	single overhead camshaft
Number of valves	two per cylinder
Compression ratio	8.5:1
Fuel feed	three Weber 36DCF carburettors
Ignition	single, two distributors
Coolant	water
Lubrication	dry sump
Maximum power	210 hp at 7200 rpm
Specific power	77.3 hp/litre

TRANSMISSION
Rear-wheel drive

Clutch	single dry disc
Gearbox	en bloc with engine Five speeds + reverse

BODY
Two-seater sports saloon/barchetta

CHASSIS

Chassis	longitudinal and cross members
Front suspension	independent, double wishbones, transverse semi-elliptic spring, hydraulic dampers
Rear suspension	live axle, double longitudinal semi-elliptic springs. hydraulic dampers
Brakes	drum
Steering	worm and sector
Fuel tank	-
Tyres front/rear	5.50-16 all round

DIMENSIONS AND WEIGHT

Wheelbase	2250 mm
Track front/rear	1278/1250 mm
Length	-
Width	-
Height	-
Kerb weight	850 kg

PERFORMANCE

Top speed	230 km/h
Power to weight ratio	4.04 kg/hp

Ferrari 225 S

1952

While the four-cylinder engine was competing in Formula One, work continued on updating the V12 two-litre, the cubic capacity of which was increased in successive stages to 2,700 cc and then 2,900 cc. The 225 Sport (2,715.46 cc) was the first car to emerge from the revision and made its debut in the 1952 Giro di Sicilia in both open and closed versions, the two bodied by Vignale, for Giovanni Bracco, Vittorio Marzotto, Piero Taruffi and Gigi Villoresi. The new cars were put to a tough test over 1,088 kilometres of that difficult route and did not finish. Later, at the Mille Miglia, no fewer than seven 225 Ss came under starter's orders, but they did no better in an event won by the experimental Ferrari 250 S of Bracco and Alfonso Rolfo.

The car's first important result was chalked up by a 225 S driven by Vittorio Marzotto at the Grand Prix of Monaco, the first and only time in its history the event was for sports racing cars. The Italian aristocrat won in a Vignale 225 S barchetta, which continued to race throughout 1952 and scored other significant victories, not least in the Coppa delle Dolomiti with Paolo Marzotto. The feverish activity at Maranello in that period had, in the meantime, led to the successful development of the three-litre V12 unit, which sparked off new models that dictated the progressive withdrawal of the 225 S from works competition. But the car did continue to race with private teams and drivers. Another important motor racing episode was also linked to the 225 S: on 19 October 1952 Alberto Ascari, accompanied by Gilera world motorcycle champion Umberto Masetti, drove the car on a number of demonstration laps at the new Imola racing circuit to check the quality of the vehicle, the first time a Rossa had been taken to the banks of the River Santerno.

The 1952 Mille Miglia took place over a difficult route, made even more treacherous by rain. Despite such conditions, Giovanni Bracco and Alfonso Rolfo in a 250 S managed to beat the powerful Mercedes-Benz 300 SLs just where the route was at its most demanding – on the Futa and Raticosa passes. Bracco was uncatchable on those slippery hairpins and went down in motor racing history for his gritty victory.

TECHNICAL SPECIFICATION

ENGINE
front, longitudinal, V12 (60°)

Bore and stroke	73x58.8 mm
Unitary cubic capacity	246.10
Total cubic capacity	2953.21
Valve gear	single overhead camshaft
Number of valves	two per cylinder
Compression ratio	9:1
Fuel feed	three Weber 36DCF carburettors (three Weber 36IF4C – 250 S Le Mans)
Coolant	water
Lubrication	dry sump
Ignition	single, one coil and two distributors
Maximum power	230 hp at 7500 rpm
Specific power	77.9 hp / litre

TRANSMISSION
Rear-wheel drive

Clutch	single dry disc
Gearbox	en bloc with engine Five speeds + reverse

BODY
Two-seater sports saloon

CHASSIS

Chassis	"Tuboscocca" tubular trellis
Front suspension	independent, double wishbones, transverse semi-elliptic spring, hydraulic dampers
Rear suspension	live axle, double longitudinal semi-elliptic springs, hydaulic dampers
Brakes	drum
Steering	worm and sector
Fuel tank	150 litres
Tyres front/rear	5.50-16 / 6.00-16

DIMENSIONS AND WEIGHT

Wheelbase	2250 mm
Track front/rear	1278 / 1250
Length	-
Width	-
Height	-
Kerb weight	850 kg

PERFORMANCE

Top speed	250 km/h
Power to weight ratio	3.7 kg/hp

Ferrari 250 S   1952

Among the 27 Ferraris that competed in the 1952 Mille Miglia, number 611 driven by Giovanni Bracco and Alfonso Rolfo was the sports saloon built on rolling chassis 0156 ET by Vignale and looked no different from its contemporary 225 Ss – but it was powered by a new concept V12, the cubic capacity of which had been increased to almost three-litres (2,953.21 cc). That engine, which had new 73 mm diameter pistons, was the latest evolution of the glorious Gioachino Colombo V12 engine design project. Once again, the Mille Miglia was considered the best test bed on which to measure the performance and reliability of the new unit. As it turned out, the engine was severely tested, not only by the length of the event but also by the competitiveness of its adversaries. Mercedes-Benz had, in fact, fielded an impressive team for the 19th Mille Miglia of three 300 SL coupés for Rudolf Caracciola, Hermann Lang and Karl Kling. But the quality of the new Ferrari and especially Bracco's driving soon showed how it was going to be: by the Ravenna control, the 250 S had already distanced itself from the rest, but at mid-race it had dropped to third, unable to match the pace of the potent German cars on the interminable straights of the Adriatic coast. The outcome of the hard-fought battle between Ferrari and Mercedes was decided on the roads of the Futa and Raticosa passes, where Bracco cut his way back up through the field and wrote an epic page in the history of motor racing.
Bracco's 4'40" behind Kling's Mercedes at the Florence control was transformed into 1'10" lead over the German at Bologna, resulting in the Biella driver scoring an extraordinary victory and Ferrari its fifth consecutive Mille Miglia win, the first of a series that 12-cylinder three-litre Ferrari 250s would deliver in the years to come.

Eugenio Castellotti and Ivo Regosa about to start the 1953 Mille Miglia from the Viale Rebuffone ramp in Brescia, at the wheel of a Ferrari 340 Mexico entered by Scuderia Guastalla. After a modest beginning that meant 14th overall by the Ravenna control, by which time he had averaged 153.504 km/h after 1h58"26', the sports saloon dropped out with mechanical problems before Pescara.

TECHNICAL SPECIFICATION

ENGINE
front, longitudinal, V12 (60°)

Bore and stroke	80x68 mm
Unitary cubic capacity	341.80
Total cubic capacity	4101.66
Valve gear	single overhead camshaft
Number of valves	two per cylinder
Compression ratio	8:1
Fuel feed	three Weber 40DCF carburettors
Ignition	single, two distributors
Coolant	water
Lubrication	dry sump
Maximum power	280 hp at 6600 rpm
Specific power	68.3 km/litre

TRANSMISSION
Rear-wheel drive	
Clutch	multi-disc
Gearbox	en bloc with engine five forward speeds and reverse

BODY
Two-seater sports saloon/barchetta

CHASSIS
Chassis	longitudinal and cross members
Front suspension	independent, double wishbones, transverse semi-elliptic spring, hydraulic dampers
Rear suspension	live axle, longitudinal semi-elliptic springs, double hydraulic dampers
Brakes	drum
Steering	worm and sector
Fuel tank	150 litres
Tyres front/rear	5.50-16/6.50-16

DIMENSIONS AND WEIGHT
Wheelbase	2600 mm
Track front/rear	1278/1250 mm
Length	-
Width	-
Height	-
Kerb weight	900 kg

PERFORMANCE
Top speed	280 km/h
Power to weight ratio	3.2 kg/hp

Ferrari 340 Mexico   1952

The Taruffi-Chinetti victory and the Ascari-Villoresi second place driving 212 Inters in the 1951 Carrera Panamericana generated a lot of publicity and encouraged other major constructors to compete in the punishing Mexican marathon. At the start of the 1952 event were Mercedes-Benz, who had sent three 300 SL sports saloons to the country, supported by a legion of men and tons of equipment, Gordini, Porsche, Lancia and, of course, Ferrari. As well as 212 Inters and the 250 S in which Giovanni Bracco won the Mille Miglia, Maranello competed with three sports saloons and a roadster, all with Vignale bodies on rolling chassis powered by the 340 America's 4,100 cc engine, with new Weber 40DCF carburettors. The involvement of the four 340 Mexicos, entered and run entirely by the Prancing Horse's U.S. importer Luigi Chinetti and Scuderia Guastalla, was financed by the Sinclair lubricants company. Designer Giovanni Michelotti pushed the concept for the 212 Inter even further and penned assertive and exuberant shapes for the cars, which included an unusual radiator grill with headlights recessed between the central area, and prominent wings, which terminated in two rounded stub tails. The result of all Maranello's efforts was anything but positive. Ascari, Villoresi and Piccato all came to an halt along the way with technical problems and of the four Mexicos only the one driven by Chinetti-Lucas placed well in third, behind the two Mercedes-Benz of Karl Kling and Hermann Lang. After returning to Italy, one of the Mexicos was driven by Eugenio Castellotti and Ivo Regosa in the 1953 Mille Miglia but they, too, were forced out with mechanical trouble during an early stage of the race.

Paolo Marzotto and Marino Marini, the latter entered under the pseudonym Zignago, on the starting ramp of the 1953 Mille Miglia in the new Ferrari 250 MM sports saloon designed by Pinin Farina. The crew turned in an outstanding performance, holding third behind Giannino Marzotto and Juan Manuel Fangio for much of the race. But a few kilometres from the end, their car burst into flame and was burnt out in a few minutes.

TECHNICAL SPECIFICATION

ENGINE
Front, longitudinal, V12 (60°)

Bore and stroke	73x58.8 mm
Unitary cubic capacity	246.10
Total cubic capacity	2953.21
Valve gear	single overhead camshaft
Number of valves	two per cylinder
Compression ratio	9:1
Fuel feed	three Weber 36IF4C carburettors
Ignition	single, two distributors
Coolant	water
Lubrication	damp sump
Maximum power	240 hp at 7200 rpm
Specific power	81.3 hp/Litre

TRANSMISSION
Rear-wheel drive

Clutch	multi-disc
Gearbox	en bloc with engine four gears + reverse

BODY
Two-seater sports saloon/barchetta

CHASSIS

Chassis	longitudinal and cross members
Front suspension	independent, double wishbones, transverse semi-elliptic spring, hydraulic dampers
Rear suspension	live axle, double longitudinal semi-elliptic springs, hydraulic dampers
Brakes	drum
Steering	worm and sector
Fuel tank	150 litres
Tyres front/rear	6.40-15 or 6.00-16 all round

DIMENSIONS AND WEIGHT

Wheelbase	2420 mm (sports saloon)
Track front/rear	1300/1320 mm (sports saloon)
Length	3990 mm (sports saloon)
Width	1600 mm (sports saloon)
Height	1260 mm (sports saloon)
Kerb weight	900 kg (barchetta 850)

PERFORMANCE

Top speed	250 km/h
Power to weight ratio	3.7 kg/hp (barchetta 3.5)

Ferrari 250 MM   1953

The experimental 250 S prototype in which Giovanni Bracco and Alfonso Rolfo won the 1952 Mille Miglia and was entered for both that year's 24 Hours of Le Mans and the Carrera Panamericana, spawned a new family of grand tourers developed around the three-litre, V12 engine. A chassis with a 250 S power unit made its debut at the 1952 Paris Motor Show, still without a name. Pinin Farina interpreted Ferrari's ideas for the project by creating an extraordinarily innovative body, which appeared at the following year's Geneva show and immediately made designs by other carrozzieri seem old. The clean and essential lines of the 250 MM – the name commemorated Ferrari's recent victory in the Mille Miglia – had lost all the excesses of previous bodies, starting with the radiator grill aperture, which was smaller and not chromed. The slightly dihedral flanks terminated in a compact wraparound tail, surmounted by a panoramic rear window. The open version of the car by Vignale also broke new ground with certain styling elements, like headlights recessed into the body and chrome oval air vents at the sides, which eventually becoming regular features on the body builder's barchettas of subsequent years.

The 250 MM made its racing debut in the 1953 Giro di Sicilia in the hands of privateer: Paolo Marzotto, who held the lead until Enna, before being overtaken by Gigi Villoresi in a 340 MM to win: the Milanese driver also took the Grand Prix of the Autodromo at Monza in a 250 MM on 29 June. The car's motor racing career was a long one: "old" champion Clemente Biondetti took fourth in the 1954 Mille Miglia in a Morelli-bodied barchetta version of the 250 MM.

The Ferrari-Abarth 166 MM being pushed out of the Turin racer's workshops by Abarth test driver Garrone. Bodied by the Austro-Italian firm in 1953, the 166 was perhaps one of the most extravagant yet innovative creations ever built on a Ferrari rolling chassis: it was a barchetta with a highly advanced design and was extremely light in plain aluminium panels, which were interchangeable using self-tightening screws.

TECHNICAL SPECIFICATION

ENGINE
Front, longitudinal, V12 (60°)

Bore and stroke	60x58.8 mm
Unitary cubic capacity	166.25
Total cubic capacity	1995.02
Valve gear	single overhead camshaft
Number of valves	two per cylinder
Compression ratio	9.5:1
Fuel feed	three Weber 32IF4C carburettors
Ignition	single, two magnetos
Coolant	water
Lubrication	damp sump
Maximum power	160 hp at 7200 rpm
Specific power	80.2 hp/Litre

TRANSMISSION
Rear-wheel drive

Clutch	single dry disc
Gearbox	en bloc with engine five speeds + reverse

BODY
Two-seater barchetta/sports saloon

CHASSIS

Chassis	longitudinal and cross members
Front suspension	independent, double wishbones, transverse semi-elliptic spring, hydraulic dampers
Rear suspension	live axle, double semi-elliptic springs, anti-roll bar. hydraulic dampers
Brakes	drum
Steering	worm and sector
Fuel tank	90 litres
Tyres front/rear	6.40-15 all round

DIMENSIONS AND WEIGHT

Wheelbase	2250 mm
Track front/rear	1270/1250 mm
Length	4180 mm
Width	1495 mm
Height	1212 mm
Kerb weight	545 kg

PERFORMANCE

Top speed	230 km/h
Power to weight ratio	3.4 hp/litre

Ferrari-Abarth 166 MM/53   1953

Between 1952 and 1953, the 12-cylinder, 1,995.02 engine that had powered the Ferrari 166 experienced a second coming. Fitted with new Weber 32IF4C carburettors that increased its power to 160 hp at 7,200 rpm, the car spawned a second series of Ferrari 166 Mille Miglias called the MM/53, which successfully competed once more in the Sport category. Most of them were bodied by Vignale as either barchettas and sports saloons, in line with the Turin atelier's traditions of the day, but others were some of the most characteristic ever built on a Ferrari chassis. That year, Pinin Farina created the elegant dual-tone 166 MM/53 racer, which was nothing other than a 250 MM of slightly reduced scale, - wheelbase 2,250 mm against the 2,420 mm of the 250 - but in the spring of 1953 Carlo Abarth became the creator of a really extreme rendition of the car. At the request of Scuderia Guastalla, the Austrian built a special body for the car that was made up of a series of modular aluminium panels, fixed to a light, trellis-like structure with boxed elements that were also in the light alloy. The body weighed just 54.4 kg, including seats and framework.

The end product was extraordinarily modern, because Abarth had solved the problem of quickly replacing the car's body panels damaged during a race. That extravagant looking car made its debut in that year's Targa Florio driven by Giulio Musitelli, but he went off and did not finish. The Vignale 166 MM/53 body design was much more conventional and comprised features already used by the Turin body shop for the open two-seater Ferrari 250 MM in previous years.

Alberto Ascari in a 553 F2 during practice for the Grand Prix of Italy at Monza, in which the car was not driven by the world champion but by Umberto Maglioli and Piero Carini. Ascari's working relationship with Ferrari was coming to an end, as he and Gigi Villoresi had signed contracts with Lancia on 21 January 1954 to compete in Formula One and Sport category events.

TECHNICAL SPECIFICATION

ENGINE
Front, longitudinal, four cylinders in line

Bore and stroke	93x73.5 mm
Unitary cubic capacity	499.27
Total cubic capacity	1997.11
Valve gear	twin overhead camshafts
Number of valves	two per cylinder
Compression ratio	13:1
Fuel feed	two Weber 52DCOA3 carburettors
Ignition	double, two magnetos
Coolant	water
Lubrication	dry sump
Maximum power	180 hp at 7200 rpm
Specific power	90 hp/litre

TRANSMISSION
Rear-wheel drive

Clutch	multi-disc
Gearbox	en bloc with differential five speeds + reverse

BODY
Single-seater

CHASSIS

Chassis	tubular trellis
Front suspension	Independent, double wishbones, transverse semi-elliptic spring, hydraulic dampers
Rear suspension	De Dion axle, transverse semi-elliptic spring, Houdaille dampers
Brakes	drum
Steering	worm and sector
Fuel tank	160 litres (two lateral tanks)
Tyres front/rear	5.25-16/6.50-16

DIMENSIONS AND WEIGHT

Wheelbase	2160 mm
Track front/rear	1278/1250 mm
Length	3988 mm
Width	1427 mm
Height	1020 mm
Kerb weight	600 kg

PERFORMANCE

Top speed	260 km/h
Power to weight ratio	3.3 kg/hp

Ferrari 553 F2 1953

This single-seater was the link between the glorious 500 F2 with its four-cylinder, two-litre engine and the subsequent 1954 555 Supersqualo Formula One car and had its cubic capacity increased to 2.5 litres. It was designed by Aurelio Lampredi and, like the 500 F2, boasted a four-cylinder, but bored out to 93 mm to produce a total rating of 1,997.11 cc. Apart from that, the car confirmed itself to be an original single-seater in every way, starting with its denomination. For the first time, that only mirrored its unitary cubic capacity – 499.27 cc, rounded up to 500 cc in this case - with the initial digit of its designation: the rest stood for 1952, the year in which it was built.

Equally innovative was its chassis, the structure of which was a tubular trellis in place of the traditional longitudinal and cross members. Aurelio Lampredi was the first to come up with one feature that would be made famous by Vittorio Jano's Lancia D50 of 1954: the Ferrari engineer placed one of the 553 F2's two fuel tanks on each side of the cockpit; creating two bulges in the bodywork that earned the car the name squalo or shark. That new arrangement helped in the development of a tail that was especially low and tapered, it no longer being hampered by a bulky fuel tank.

The sporting life of this single-seater lasted for just one Grand Prix, though. Two 553 F2s were assigned to Umberto Maglioli and Piero Carini for the last race of the 1953 world championship, which took place at Monza on 13 September – but both cars retired.

The obligation to use normally aspirated 2,500 cc engines for Formula One cars from 1954 brought the 553 F2's career to an abrupt halt, but Ferrari did derive the subsequent 555 from the defunct car and that racer, nicknamed not surprisingly the Supersqualo, competed for the 1954 Formula One World Championship, together with the 625.

The Ferrari 625 TF built by Vignale in 1953, photographed (left) in the body stylist's own courtyard, was one of the last bodies by the Turin atelier for Maranello. Only one example of the car was produced (chassis number 0302 TF) and had a 2,498.32 cc, four-cylinder in-line engine that generated 220 hp. The car was bought by racing driver Franco Cornacchia for Scuderia Guastalla of Milan.

TECHNICAL SPECIFICATION

ENGINE
Front, longitudinal, four cylinders in line

Bore and stroke	94x90 mm
Unitary cubic capacity	624.58
Total cubic capacity	2498.32
Valve gear	twin overhead camshaft
Number of valves	two per cylinder
Compression ratio	9:1
Fuel feed	two Weber 50DCOA3 carburettors
Ignition	double, two magnetos
Coolant	water
Lubrication	dry sump
Maximum power	220 hp at 7000 rpm
Specific power	88 hp/litre

TRANSMISSION
Rear-wheel drive

Clutch	multi-disc
Gearbox	en block with differential four speeds + reverse

BODY
Two-seater barchetta/sports saloon

CHASSIS

Chassis	longitudinal and cross members
Front suspension	independent, double wishbones, lower transverse semi-elliptic spring, hydraulic dampers
Rear suspension	De Dion axle, push rods, transverse semi-elliptic spring, hydraulic dampers
Brakes	drum
Steering	worm and sector
Fuel tank	-
Tyres front/rear	5.25-16/6.00-16

DIMENSIONS AND WEIGHT

Wheelbase	2250 mm
Track front/rear	1278/1284 mm
Length	-
Width	-
Height	-
Kerb weight	730 kg

PERFORMANCE

Top speed	240 km/h
Power to weight ratio	3.3 kg/hp

Ferrari 625 TF   1953

The excellent results achieved by the four-cylinder in-line engines designed by Aurelio Lampredi and installed in the 500 F2 and 625 F1 encouraged Ferrari to experiment with that configuration on closed wheel cars, a sector in which the monopoly of those potent and reliable 12-cylinder engines had never been questioned until that moment.

The four-cylinder Ferrari Sport made its first appearance at the VI Grand Prix dell'Autodromo at Monza on 29 June 1953, driven by Mike Hawthorn. The barchetta was so similar to its contemporary Vignale 250 MM roadster, the design of which it followed almost completely, that it passed by almost unobserved. But in place of the 60° 12-cylinder engine was a 2.5-litre, 2,498.32 cc four-cylinder, derived directly from the two-and-a-half litre that powered the 625 F1 car. Despite the fact that the Monza track's interminable straights did not enable the little barchetta to perform at its best, having been conceived for medium-fast circuits, the fourth place scored by Mike Hawthorn was considered an encouraging result and meant the continued use of the four-cylinder unit in sports car events.

In the spring of 1953 Carrozzeria Vignale, which had just about reached the end of its working relationship with Ferrari, built one single sports saloon version of the car, which featured all the styling elements that had been seen on its previous models: they included headlights recessed into the front of the car with Plexiglas fairing, chromed oval air vents down the sides and even the ample triangular air vents in the rear wings for the dissipation of hot air from the rear axle area. The car had a rather long nose, contrasting with its rounded, stubby tail.

At Monza on 29 June 1953, Alberto Ascari competed in the VI Grand Prix dell'Autodromo at Monza with this 735 S barchetta, bodied by the Carrozzeria Autodromo di Modena. The Milanese driver held the lead in the unusual looking car, trailed by the Lancia D 23 of Jose Froilan Gonzalez and Felice Bonetto, before having to retire after a collision with a lapped competitor.

TECHNICAL SPECIFICATION

ENGINE
Front, longitudinal, four cylinders in line

Bore and stroke	102x90 mm
Unitary cubic capacity	735.41
Total cubic capacity	2941.66
Valve gear	twin overhead camshaft
Number of valves	two per cylinder
Compression ratio	9:1
Fuel feed	two Weber 50DCOA carburettors
Ignition	double, one distributor
Coolant	water
Lubrication	dry sump
Maximum power	225 hp at 6800 rpm
Specific power	76.5 hp/litre

TRANSMISSION
Rear-wheel drive

Clutch	multi-disc
Gearbox	en bloc with differential five speeds + reverse

BODY
Two-seater barchetta

CHASSIS

Chassis	longitudinal and cross members
Front suspension	independent, double wishbones, transverse semi-elliptic spring, hydraulic dampers
Rear suspension	De Dion axle, transverse semi-elliptic spring, hydraulic dampers
Brakes	drum
Steering	worm and sector
Fuel tank	-
Tyres front/rear	5.25-16/7.00-16

DIMENSIONS AND WEIGHT

Wheelbase	2250 mm
Track front/rear	1278/1284 mm
Length	-
Width	-
Height	-
Kerb weight	750 kg

PERFORMANCE

Top speed	260 km/h
Power to weight ratio	3.3 kg/hp

Ferrari 735 S   1953

Alberto Ascari was on the starting grid at Monza on 29 June 1953 for the VI Grand Prix dell'Autodromo at the wheel of a Ferrari with a four-cylinder, in-line engine, the same race in which Britain's Mike Hawthorn competed in a 625 TF. The Ascari car's power unit was derived from the 625 F1, but its cubic capacity had been increased to 2,941.66 cc. The car was called the 735 S, after its unitary cubic capacity. As well as an increase in bore to 102 mm, the model had been given the new five-speed gearbox, which formed an en bloc unit with the differential.

The shape of the 735 S was created by Carrozzeria Autodromo di Modena, which had already bodied the 166 MM/53, and that gave the little barchetta a somewhat sleek, low line. It had a droop snoot nose, its radiator grill inclined at almost 45°, small chromed air vents along the flanks - as in the case of the Vignale Ferraris from which it had also inherited rounded headlights that were recessed into the body.

Ascari managed to put up the fastest time of 2'05"9 in qualifying, ahead of the Lancia D 23 of Jose Froilan Gonzalez and another Ferrari 250 MM driven by Gigi Villoresi. At the drop of the flag, Ascari shot into the lead and stayed there until he was involved in a disastrous collision while lapping a Ferrari 250 MM back marker driven by Bianca Maria Piazza. The impact sent him flying off the track and out of the race, which was won by Gigi Villoresi and his Ferrari 250 MM, ahead of Felice Bonetto in a Lancia.

The use of the four-cylinder engine for sports category cars, which was meant to test the 625 TF against the 735 S, was further consolidated at the end of 1953, when Maranello began to assiduously install two-litre versions in a series of new concept cars called the 500 Mondial.

Vittorio Marzotto waiting to start the XXI Mille Miglia in 1954. The 500 Mondial barchetta, chassis number 0404 MD, with which he came second in a generous race behind Alberto Ascari's Lancia D24, was one of the first bodied by Carrozzeria Scaglietti. Pinin Farina also built numerous barchetta bodies on the Ferrari 500 Mondial rolling chassis.

TECHNICAL SPECIFICATION

ENGINE
Front, longitudinal, four cylinders in line

Bore and stroke	90x78 mm
Unitary cubic capacity	496.21
Total cubic capacity	1984.85
Valve gear	twin overhead camshafts
Number of valves	two per cylinder
Compression ratio	9.2:1
Fuel feed	two Weber 45DCOA3 carburettors
Ignition	double, two magnetos or two coils
Coolant	water
Lubrication	dry sump
Maximum power	170 hp at 7000 rpm
Specific power	85.6 hp/litre

TRANSMISSION
Rear-wheel drive

Clutch	multi-disc
Gearbox	en bloc with differential five speeds + reverse

BODY
Two-seater barchetta/sports saloon

CHASSIS

Chassis	longitudinal and cross members
Front suspension	independent, double wishbones, transverse semi-elliptic spring, hydraulic dampers
Rear suspension	De Dion axle, transverse semi-elliptic spring, hydraulic dampers
Brakes	drum
Steering	worm and sector
Fuel tank	145 litres
Tyres front/rear	5.20-16/6.00-16

DIMENSIONS AND WEIGHT

Wheelbase	2250 mm
Track front/rear	1278/1284 mm
Length	3750 mm (sports saloon)
Width	1520 mm (sports saloon)
Height	1250 mm (sports saloon)
Kerb weight	720 kg

PERFORMANCE

Top speed	235 km/h
Power to weight ratio	4.2 kg/hp

Ferrari 500 Mondial   1953

After Ferrari's 1953 exploits with the 625 TF and the 735 S, the installation of four-cylinder in-line engines in sports category cars continued at the end of that year and included the 500 Mondial. Alberto Ascari and Gigi Villoresi gave the little four-cylinder Ferrari barchetta its debut on 20 December 1953 in the 12 Hours of Casablanca, a round in the world sports car championship for covered wheel cars. The engine was derived directly from that of the world championship-winning 500 F2, but had a lower compression ratio of 9.2:1 and was named the 500 Mondial to mark the world titles won by Ascari. The car came a distant second behind another Ferrari – the much more powerful 375 MM, which sported a 4,522.94 cc V12 engine As with the succession of similar cars built in 1954, that first Mondial was bodied by Carrozzeria Scaglietti of Modena, still a company of artisans, which began its prolific working relationship with Ferrari by creating the body for that very car. Afterwards, Scaglietti fashioned bodies for almost all of Ferrari's sports racing cars of the late Fifties. Due to its remarkable handling and a overall weight kept down to 720 kg, positive results were not long in coming and did so as early as the 1954 season, the most important of which being Vittorio Marzotto's second place driving a Scaglietti 500 Mondial barchetta in the year's Mille Miglia. The race was won by Alberto Ascari in a Lancia D 24 after the Milanese driver had signed for the Turin manufacturer at the start of the season.

As well as the two coupés, that year Pinin Farina also built numerous barchettas on the 500 Mondial rolling chassis. The small four-cylinder engines continued to be raced until the mid-Fifties: Jean Guichet and Alfredo Vaccari competed in the XXIV Mille Miglia with two Mondials in 1957.

One of the first 340 MMs bodied by Pinin Farina in 1952 for the French racing driver Pierre Boncompagni. With this model, the Turin atelier again offered clean and essential lines, like those that had already graced the 250 MM. He created a car of great equilibrium and elegance and reconfirmed himself as an extraordinary interpreter of Maranello's cars. The 340 MM barchettas built by Vignale were no less vibrant.

TECHNICAL SPECIFICATION

ENGINE
Front, longitudinal, V12 (60°)

Bore and stroke	80x68 mm
Unitary cubic capacity	341.80
Total cubic capacity	4101.66
Valve gear	single overhead camshaft
Number of valves	two per cylinder
Compression ratio	8:1
Fuel feed	three Weber 40DCF carburettors
Ignition	single, two magnetos
Coolant	water
Lubrication	dry sump
Maximum power	300 hp at 6600 rpm
Specific power	73.1 hp / litre

TRANSMISSION
Rear-wheel drive

Clutch	multi-disc
Gearbox	en bloc with engine five gears + reverse

BODY
Two-seater barchetta/sports saloon

CHASSIS

Chassis	longitudinal and cross members
Front suspension	indipendent, double wishbones, transverse semi-elliptic spring, hydraulic dampers
Rear suspension	live axle, longitudinal semi-elliptic springs, hydraulic dampers
Brakes	drum
Steering	worm and sector
Fuel tank	150 litres
Tyres front/rear	6.00-16/7.50-16

DIMENSIONS AND WEIGHT

Wheelbase	2500 mm
Track front/rear	1325/1320 mm
Length	-
Width	-
Height	-
Kerb weight	1000 kg

PERFORMANCE

Top speed	270 km/h
Power to weight ratio	3.3 kg/hp

Ferrari 340 MM   1953

The year 1953 was important to sports racing cars, because the events restricted to covered wheel racers were woven into a championship on which FIA conferred world status for the first time. As a result, car manufacturers' interest in that kind of competition grew considerably. To meet the new challenge, Ferrari decided to "rejuvenate" not only the 166 and 250 MM, but also the 340 (4,101.66 cc) series, with the introduction of a new model also called an MM. The new generation four-litre engines, which were generating 300 hp by that time, showed their effectiveness from their debut in the Giro di Sicilia, won by Villoresi-Cassani in a renewed 340 Vignale. Even more important was the Marzotto-Crosara win in the Mille Miglia, which was also a round in the new sports car world championship. That day, the Marzotto 340 MM Vignale, with which a Touring version also competed, beat the works Alfa Romeo 6C 3,000s and Lancia D20s. After those brilliant results, Ferrari concentrated all its efforts on the 24 Hours of Le Mans, which it had not won since 1949. Pinin Farina built two sports saloons on 340 chassis for the occasion, almost identical to the 250 MM displayed at the Geneva Motor Show. The two cars were assigned to Nino Farina-Mike Hawthorn and Giannino-Paolo Marzotto, to which a NART 340 MM barchetta was added for Tom Cole-Luigi Chinetti. Despite this deployment of strength, only the Marzotto brothers finished - in fifth place. The 4.5-litre works Ferrari 375 MMs did no better but, regardless, it was this new car that Ferrari decided to enter for future sports car events, and that brought the brief career of the 340 MM to an end: it was never entered as a works car again.

The first Ferrari 375 MM chassis number 0364 AM bodied by Pinin Farina was known as the Kimberley, after wealthy industrialist Jim Kimberley, who had commissioned it. The car had ample, shell-shaped front wings, which was repeated in the deep sculpture of the rear mudguards. A car of tremendous personality and elegance, about 15 two-seater 375 MM barchettas were built.

TECHNICAL SPECIFICATION

ENGINE
Front, longitudinal, V12 (60°

Bore and stroke	84x68 mm
Unitary cubic capacity	376.8
Total cubic capacity	4522.94
Valve gear	single overhead camshaft
Number of valves	two per cylinder
Compression ratio	9:1
Fuel feed	three Weber 40IF4C or 42DCZ carburettors
Ignition	double, two magnetos
Coolant	water
Lubrication	dry sump
Maximum power	340-350 hp at 7000 rpm
Specific power	75-2-77.4 hp/litre

TRANSMISSION
Rear-wheel drive

Clutch	multi-disc
Gearbox	en bloc with engine four gears + reverse

BODY
Two-seater roadster/sports saloon

CHASSIS

Chassis	longitudinal and cross members
Front suspension	independent, double wishbones, transverse semi-elliptic spring, Houdaille dampers
Rear suspension	live axle, longitudinal semi-elliptic springs, Houdaille dampers
Brakes	drum
Steering	worm and sector
Fuel tank	180 litres
Tyres front/rear	6.00-16/7.50-16

DIMENSIONS AND WEIGHT

Wheelbase	2600 mm
Track front/rear	1325/1320 mm
Length	4190 mm
Width	1635 mm
Height	1090 mm
Kerb weight	900 kg

PERFORMANCE

Top speed	240-275 km/h
Power to weight ratio	2.6 kg/hp

Ferrari 375 MM   1953

The inexhaustible vitality of Ferrari's V12 engine showed itself once again at the 1953 24 Hours of Le Mans, in which Maranello entered an experimental sports saloon bodied by Pinin Farina. The car was similar in appearance to the 340 MM, which also competed at the Sarthe circuit that year and was driven by the established crew of Ascari-Villoresi. Called the 375 MM, the car was fitted from the outset with the tried and tested 4,500 cc twelve cylinder, directly derived from its single-seater namesake. But the 375 MM did not last long and retired with a broken transmission, its Achilles heel throughout the season. However, Ferrari decided to persevere, placing all his bets on the new model – and it was a winning decision. The contribution of the car in 1953 was a determining factor in Ferrari's conquest of the sport car world championship as a result of victories by Farina-Hawthorn in Belgium's 24 Hours of Spa-Francorchamps and Ascari, who was paired with Farina once more, in the 1,000 Kilometres of the Nürburgring at the wheel of a Vignale barchetta. The extraordinary performance of the 4.5-litre V12 proved to be the model's secret weapon: it dredged up 350 hp at 7,000 rpm for a top speed that touched 280 km/h. Once again, Pinin Farina designed an exquisite barchetta body of clean and flowing lines for the 375 MM's rolling chassis the following year and that car, with its front wings cut into a shell shape, was christened the Kimberley, after the president of the Sports Car Club of America who commissioned it. In 1954, the Ferrari 375 MM was joined by an even more potent version of the car called the 375 Plus, the V12 power unit of which had been increased to almost five litres. This model was also offered with both open and closed bodies and became another Ferrari winner in the 1954 sports car world championship.

Imposing, elegant and aerodynamic at the same time, the Pinin Farina-bodied Ferrari 375 MM Coupé commissioned in 1954 by film director Roberto Rossellini for his wife, actress Ingrid Bergman, was attractive for many of its ultra-modern styling details. Note the sculpting of its flanks, which play host to the engine compartment air vents, the pop-up optical group combined with small sidelights, recessed into the wings.

TECHNICAL SPECIFICATION

ENGINE
Front, longitudinal, V12 (60°)

Bore and stroke	84x68 mm
Unitary cubic capacity	376.8
Total cubic capacity	4522.94
Valve gear	single overhead camshaft
Number of valves	two per cylinder
Compression ratio	9:1
Fuel feed	three Weber 40IF4C or Weber 42DCZ carburettors
Ignition	double, two magnetos
Coolant	water
Lubrication	dry sump
Maximum power	340-350 hp at 7000 rpm
Specific power	75.2-77.4 hp/litre

TRANSMISSION
Rear-wheel drive

Clutch	multi-disc
Gearbox	en bloc with engine four speeds + reverse

BODY
Two-seater coupé

CHASSIS

Chassis	longitudinal and cross members
Front suspension	independent, double wishbones, transverse semi-elliptic spring, Houdaille dampers
Rear suspension	live axle, longitudinal semi-elliptic springs, Houdaille dampers
Brakes	drum
Steering	worm and sector
Fuel tank	180 litres
Tyres front/rear	6.00-16/7.50-16

DIMENSIONS AND WEIGHT

Wheelbase	2600 mm
Track front/rear	1325/1320 mm
Length	4320 mm
Width	1525 mm
Height	1320 mm
Kerb weight	1090 kg

PERFORMANCE

Top speed	240-275 km/h
Power to weight ratio	3.1 kg/hp

Ferrari 375 MM Coupé   1953

The 375 MM's important 1953 victories had inevitable repercussions on production and inspired Ferrari to assign the task of creating a number of road car grand tourers of the model to his by now well-established partner, Pinin Farina. In designing that body, the Turin atelier delved deep into its creative ability to style some of the most fascinating sports saloons ever to come out of the Ferrari workshops. The first 375 MM grand tourers retained all the majesty and austerity of the racing version's line, but adopted chromed bumper bars and pop-up headlights recessed into the dual-tone body: none of which was sufficient to tone down the sporting character of a car that was born to race. A vocation confirmed once more by the V12, which, despite losing a few horse power, still put out 340, 350 hp for a top speed of around 280 km/h. Only its interior made the 375 MM coupé a car of luxurious class, with its high-quality leather trim. The 375 "family" also included an aerodynamic version, commissioned by film director Roberto Rossellini for his wife, actress Ingrid Bergman. The film star's car was unveiled at the 1954 Paris Motor Show and was the model on which Pinin Farina introduced highly modern styling features, which later appeared on subsequent Ferraris, like pop-up headlights and air vent slats in the flanks. No less oriented towards future production was the last 375 MM sports saloon, which appeared at the 1955 Turin show and had new concept elliptical-shaped radiator, chromed side air vent grills, through which engine compartment heat flowed, and air outlets below the rear window, all styling items that would become regulars on the 250 grand tourers in the years to come.

In 1953 and 1954, Pinin Farina designed bodies for 15 coupés and just one cabriolet on the 250 Europa chassis, presented at the New York Auto Show in 1955. Another three coupés were built by Vignale, which, as well as the first example displayed at the 1953 Paris Motor Show, produced another two in 1954. Ferrari inaugurated a long series of grand touring cars of 250 designation with the Europa.

TECHNICAL SPECIFICATION

ENGINE
Front, longitudinal, V12 (60°)

Bore and stroke	68x68 mm
Unitary cubic capacity	246.95
Total cubic capacity	2963.4
Valve gear	single overhead camshaft
Number of valves	two per cylinder
Compression ratio	8:1
Fuel feed	three Weber 36DCF carburettors
Ignition	single, one distributor
Coolant	water
Lubrication	damp sump
Maximum power	200 hp at 6300 rpm
Specific power	67.5 hp/litre

TRANSMISSION
Rear-wheel drive

Clutch	multi-disc
Gearbox	en block with engine five gears + reverse

BODY
Two-seater coupé/cabriolet

CHASSIS

Chassis	longitudinal and cross members
Front suspension	indipendent, double wishbones, transverse semi-elliptic spring, hydraulic dampers
Rear suspension	live axle, semi-elliptic springs and double longitudinal push rods, hydraulic dampers
Brakes	drum
Steering	worm and sector
Fuel tank	140 litres
Tyres front/rear	7.10-15 all round

DIMENSIONS AND WEIGHT

Wheelbase	2800 mm
Track front/rear	1325/1320 mm
Length	-
Width	-
Height	-
Kerb weight	1150 kg

PERFORMANCE

Top speed	218 km/h
Power to weight ratio	5.75 kg/hp

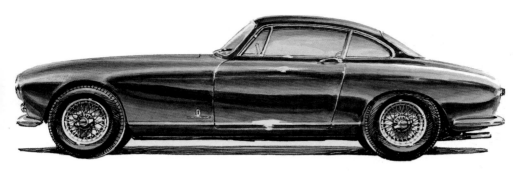

Ferrari 250 Europa   1953

The 1953 Paris Motor Show was the event at which a new grand tourer called the 250 Europa made its public entrance. The car took the place of the 212 Inter and, as its name suggested, was mainly destined for European markets. It seemed normal to entrust the design of that first example to Carrozzeria Vignale, who had come up with the best interpretation of the 212's body. But next to Pinin Farina's 375 America, which was unveiled at the same time, the Vignale body seemed dated, so much so that Pinin Farina was given the job of bodying the remaining examples of the car. And the Turin stylist did not disappoint with his sports saloon powered by Maranello's 2,963.4 cc V12. For his 250 Europas, the first in a long and successful line of 250s, Pinin Farina once again offered sober and elegant lines similar to those of the 375, designing various models that differed from each other through a number of styling elements, like the rear panoramic window and the radiator grill profile, with or without chromed edging, sometimes slightly recessed to give the car extra sleekness. At the 1954 New York Auto Show, Pinin Farina presented the only cabriolet version (0311 EU) of the 250 Europa, the basic design of which remained close to that of the 212 Inter, seen at the Big Apple's show the previous year. Exploiting the opportunities offered by the 2,800 mm wheelbase, the Europa cabriolet was even more svelte and streamlined, an impression further underscored by the panel surfaces, which had no air intakes or apertures that could interfere with the cabrio's cleanliness of shape. Even the door handles were recessed into the car's body so as not to create protrusions.

The 1953 Paris Motor Show: the 375 America was officially presented as the 342 America's successor. As well as the elegance of its shape, Ferrari seemed to be putting its money on performance, as shown on the small publicity panel in front of the car. It says: "Ferrari 375 America 12-cylinder, 240 km/h". Such high performance was the work of the 4,522 cc V12 engine, which put out 300 hp at 6,500 rpm.

TECHNICAL SPECIFICATION

ENGINE	
Front, longitudinal, V12 (60°)	
Bore and stroke	84x68 mm
Unitary cubic capacity	376.84
Total cubic capacity	4522.09
Valve gear	single overhead camshaft
Number of valves	2 per cylinder
Compression ratio	8:1
Fuel feed	three Weber 40DCF carburettors
Ignition	single, one coil and two distributors
Coolant	water
Lubrication	dry sump
Maximum power	300 hp at 6500 rpm
Specific power	66.3 hp/litre
TRANSMISSION	
Rear-wheel drive	
Clutch	multi-disc
Gearbox	en bloc with engine four gears + reverse
BODY	
Two-seater coupé	

CHASSIS	
Chassis	longitudinal and cross members
Front suspension	independent, double wishbones, transverse semi-elliptic spring, Houdaille dampers
Rear suspension	live axle, longitudinal semi-elliptic springs, Houdaille dampers
Brakes	drum
Steering	worm and sector
Fuel tank	140 litres
Tyres front/rear	7.10-15 all round
DIMENSIONS AND WEIGHT	
Wheelbase	2800 mm
Track front/rear	1325/1320 mm
Length	-
Width	-
Height	-
Kerb weight	1150 kg
PERFORMANCE	
Top speed	240 km/h
Power to weight ratio	3.8 kg/hp

Ferrari 375 America   1953

It would have been extremely difficult for the American market to remain indifferent to a car like the 375 MM, which blended a racing car's power and performance with the luxury of a high class grand tourer of elegant line and refined interior.

Launched and promoted in the United States as always by Luigi Chinetti, Maranello's North American importer, the Pinin Farina-bodied 375 America was given its first public airing by Ferrari at the 1953 Paris Motor Show with a 2,800 mm wheelbase, like that of the Ferrari 250 Europa. Compared to the earlier closed version of the 375 MM, the lines of the new car had become even softer and more harmonious, a shape that was decidedly more in accordance with a luxurious coupé than a racing car. Nothing about this sober grand tourer was excessive or disproportionate, starting with the grey-blue livery chosen for its preview, the traditional radiator grill already used by Pinin Farina for the 342 America and underlined here by rather large chromium edging all the way to the rear end in which the rear window, boot and door sills blended together in complete harmony.

Less sober and essential but still ingenious in its way was Pinin Farina's interpretation on the 375 America, which first came under the public gaze at the 1955 Turin Motor Show. On that occasion, the carrozziere displayed an extravagant coupé created especially for Gianni Agnelli, a car that had a rectangular radiator grill, a panoramic windscreen and ample glass surfaces set into the roof group, its rear fins integrated into the same, all of which had already been seen on the 375 MM built for Ingrid Bergman and Roberto Rossellini. Vignale and Ghia also constructed bodies for the 375 America in 1954/55, although with less positive results than those of Pinin Farina.

Mike Hawthorn drove the 553 F1 single-seater to its one and only victory in the Grand Prix of Spain at Barcelona's Pedralbes circuit on 24 October 1954. That was a bleak season for Maranello, whose cars only scored two victories in a championship entirely dominated by the Mercedes-Benz W196 of Juan Manuel Fangio, who was able to win six Grands Prix as well as the world title.

TECHNICAL SPECIFICATION

ENGINE
Front, longitudinal, four cylinders in line

Bore and stroke	100x79.5 mm
Unitary cubic capacity	624.39
Total cubic capacity	2497.56
Valve gear	twin overhead camshafts
Number of valves	two per cylinder
Compression ratio	13.1
Fuel feed	two Weber 50DCOA3 carburettors
Ignition	double, two magnetos
Coolant	water
Lubrication	dry sump
Maximum power	260 hp at 7500 rpm
Specific power	104.1 hp/Litre

TRANSMISSION
Rear-wheel drive

Clutch	multi-disc
Gearbox	en bloc with differential four gears + reverse

BODY
Single-seater

CHASSIS

Chassis	tubular trelliss
Front suspension	independent, double wishbones, transverse semi-elliptic spring, Houdaille dampers
Rear suspension	De Dion axle, transverse semi-elliptic spring, Houdaille dampers
Brakes	drum
Steering	worm and sector
Fuel tank	180 litres (two lateral, one rear)
Tyres front/rear	5.25-16/7.00-16

DIMENSIONS AND WEIGHT

Wheelbase	2160 mm
Track front/rear	1278/1250 mm
Length	3988 mm
Width	1427 mm
Height	1020 mm
Weight in running order	590 kg

PERFORMANCE

Top speed	280 km/h
Power to weight ratio	2.3 kg/hp

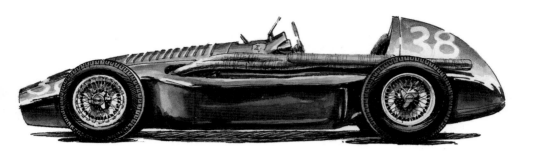

Ferrari 553 F1 1954

After its fleeting appearance, still in the guise of an F2 car, at the 1953 Grand Prix of
Monza, the 553 became a fully fledged F1 racer in early 1954, with the adoption of
a 2.5-litre four-cylinder in-line engine (bore and stroke equal to 100x79.5 mm) that
produced a power output of 260 hp at 7,500 rpm. Externally, it was similar in shape
to the 1953 F2 car, from which it took perhaps its most characteristic element of fuel
tanks located to the sides of the cockpit, which earned it the name "Squalo".
At the end of 1954, another tank was installed in the tail so that its rear end went
back to being of rather generous proportions, and no longer as aerodynamic, in line
with earlier versions. Jose Froilan Gonzalez gave the car its debut as an F1 single-
seater at the 1954 Grand Prix of Siracusa, a non-championship event from which the
Argentinean driver retired. In fact, that was the first of the car's long
series of retirements, caused by chronic unreliability and roadholding problems that
made its handling erratic on the track. So Maranello had to wait until the Grand Prix
of Spain at Barcelona, the last race of 1954, to see the 553 with its improved suspension finally win in the hands of Mike Hawthorn, ahead of Luigi Musso in a Maserati
250 F and a Mercedes-Benz W196 driven by Juan Manuel Fangio, the real dominator of the season. The Balcarce driver won six of the nine rounds in the world championship – two with Maserati – to take his second world title at the end of the year
with 42 points, 17 more than his second placed fellow countryman, Gonzalez. The
other star cars of the Grand Prix that day were the new Lancia D 50s, which were
given their debut after almost a year of testing and tuning.

The Mercedes-Benz W196s of Juan Manuel Fangio, Stirling Moss and André Simon dropped out of the 1955 Grand Prix of Monaco, because they were not suited to the Monte Carlo circuit. That was also the case with Alberto Ascari's Lancia D 50, which ended up in the sea at the harbour kink – without injury to the driver – when he was leading. Maurice Trintignant unexpectedly found himself in the number one spot in a Ferrari 625 F1 and took Maranello's only victory of the season.

TECHNICAL SPECIFICATION

ENGINE
Front, longitudinal, four cylinders in line

Bore and stroke	94x90 mm
Unitary cubic capacity	624.58
Total cubic capacity	2498.32
Valve gear	twin overhead camshafts
Number of valves	two per cylinder
Compression ratio	13:1
Fuel feed	two Weber 50DCOA3 carburettors
Ignition	double, two magnetos
Coolant	water
Lubrication	dry sump
Maximum power	250 hp at 7200 rpm
Specific power	100.1 hp/litre

TRANSMISSION
Rear-wheel drive

Clutch	multi-disc
Gearbox	en bloc with differential four speeds + reverse

BODY
Single-seater

CHASSIS

Chassis	tubular trellis
Front suspension	independent, double wishbones, transverse semi-elliptic spring, Houdaille dampers
Rear suspension	Di Dion axle, transverse lower semi-elliptic spring, Houdaille dampers
Brakes	drum
Steering	worm and sector
Fuel tank	180 litres
Tyres front/rear	5.25-16/7.00-16

DIMENSIONS AND WEIGHT

Wheelbase	2160 mm
Track front/rear	1278/1250 mm
Length	3988 mm
Width	1427 mm
Height	1020 mm
Weight in running order	600 kg

PERFORMANCE

Top speed	270 km/h
Power to weight ratio	2.4 kg/hp

Ferrari 625 F1   1954

The lack of performance of the 553 F1 was compensated for in part in 1954 by the presence of the 625 F1, which competed for the world championship that year and was a logical evolution of the glorious 500 F2, as it also adopted a four-cylinder in-line engine increased to 2.5 litres as permitted by the new technical regulations that came into force from the start of the '54 season. The car also took its external shape from the 500 F2, being a compact and with the traditional cockpit set back close to the tail, inside which was the fuel tank. But compared to its victorious predecessor, winner of two world championships in 1952/3, the results achieved by the 625 F1 were anything but as successful. The 625 F1 was in difficulty due to Alberto Ascari moving to Lancia in 1954, the constant increase in the competitiveness of Maserati with the new 250 F and especially due to the return of Mercedes-Benz, with their W196 in both open and covered wheel versions - depending on the typology of the different tracks - and drivers the calibre of Juan Manuel Fangio, Stirling Moss and Karl Kling: in 1954 and 1955, the German team won nine out of a possible 16 races. Although its victories were numerous in non-championship races, those that counted toward the title numbered just two and were scored at the 1954 Grands Prix of Great Britain by Jose Froilan Gonzalez and the 1955 Grand Prix of Monaco by Maurice Trintignant. All the other races saw the relentless success of Mercedes-Benz and its number one driver Juan Manuel Fangio, who won both world championships with 10 victories in those two seasons, two of them at the wheel of the Maserati.

One of the five Ferrari 750 Monzas that competed in the 1955 Mille Miglia from 30 April-1 May was driven by Piero Carini, who made the 15th control at Ravenna but had to retire before Pescara. That day, the best of the 750 Monzas was driven by Sergio Sighinolfi, who came sixth overall, after a persistently steady climb up the results table, in 11h 33'27".

TECHNICAL SPECIFICATION

ENGINE
front, longitudinal, four cylinders in line

Bore and stroke	103x90 mm
Unitary cubic capacity	749.90
Total cubic capacity	2999.62
Valve gear	twin overhead camshafts
Number of valves	two per cylinder
Compression ratio	9.2:1
Fuel feed	two Weber 58DCOA3 carburettors
Ignition	double, two distributors
Coolant	water
Lubrication	dry sump
Maximum power	250 hp at 6000 rpm
Specific power	83.4 hp/litre

TRANSMISSION
Rear-wheel drive

Clutch	multi-disc
Gearbox	en bloc with differential five gears + reverse

BODY
Two-seater barchetta

CHASSIS

Chassis	longitudinal and cross members
Front suspension	independent, double wishbones, transverse semi-elliptic spring, hydraulic dampers
Rear suspension	De Dion axle, transverse semi-elliptic spring, hydraulic dampers
Brakes	drum
Steering	worm and sector
Fuel tank	145 litres
Tyres front/rear	5.25-16/6.00-16

DIMENSIONS AND WEIGHT

Wheelbase	2250 mm
Track front/rear	1278/1284 mm
Length	-
Width	-
Height	-
Kerb weight	760 kg

PERFORMANCE

Top speed	265 km/h
Power to weight ratio	3.04 kg/hp

Ferrari 750 Monza   1954

From 1954, the installation of the three-litre (2,999.62 cc) four-cylinder engine in sports racing cars was systematic and continuous at Ferrari. The 750 was the first step towards a new typology of barchetta, the strong points of which were agility and lightness of structure. Creation of the small "sport" body was assigned to Pinin Farina, who styled the first example with a view to it competing in the II Grand Prix Supercortemaggiore at Monza on 27 June 1954. Umberto Maglioli and Mike Hawthorn were at the wheel of the car with its low and structured line, droop snoot nose, fairly stubby tail, also distinguishable by a number of other features, including a longitudinal white stripe. It did not take long for the 750 to show what it could do: the two drivers were first across the finish line, ahead of another Ferrari 750 campaigned by Jose Froilan Gonzalez and Maurice Trintignant. The second-placed car was bodied by Scaglietti and had a longer nose than the winner, its driving position on the right and set a little further back, almost up against the tail and surmounted by a faired headrest. In time, the small Modena carrozzeria turned out to be the best interpreter of the 750, which was later called the 750 Monza in view of its debut victory at the northern Italian circuit.

Those barchettas brought Ferrari other prestigious successes in both hillclimbs and races in the Italian Championship. The 750 Monza competed effectively in World Sport Car Championship races, along side other more powerful Ferraris, scoring points that helped the Scuderia win the 1954 title. The following season, still in their definitive Scaglietti body shape, the Monzas were swamped by the all-conquering power of the Mercedes-Benz 300 SLRs, as much the unrivalled dominator of the sports car category as the W196 was in Formula One.

The 250 Monza on rolling chassis number 0420 M, bodied in 1954 by Pinin Farina. The Turin atelier gave the car a shape already seen on the 500 Mondial, the chassis of which was retained by the car. Another two examples were bodied by Scaglietti along the lines of the 750 Monza. Cornacchia-Gerini came third in the II 1954 Grand Prix Supercortemaggiore at Monza in one of these cars.

TECHNICAL SPECIFICATION

ENGINE
front, longitudinal, V12 (60°)

Bore and stroke	73x58.8 mm
Unitary cubic capacity	246.16
Total cubic capacity	2953.2
Valve gear	single overhead camshaft
Number of valves	two per cylinder
Compression ratio	9:1
Fuel feed	three Weber 36IF4C carburettors
Ignition	single, two magnetos
Coolant	water
Lubrication	dry sump
Maximum power	240 hp at 7200 rpm
Specific power	81,3 hp/litre

TRANSMISSION
Rear-wheel drive

Clutch	multi-disc
Gearbox	en bloc with differential four gears + reverse

BODY
Two-seater barchetta

CHASSIS

Chassis	longitudinal and cross members
Front suspension	independent, double wishbones, transverse semi-elliptic spring, hydraulic dampers
Rear suspension	De Dion, transverse semi-elliptic spring, hydraulic dampers
Brakes	drum
Steering	worm
Fuel tank	-
Tyres front/rear	5.50-16 / 6.00-16

DIMENSIONS AND WEIGHT

Wheelbase	2250 mm
Track front/rear	1278 / 1284 mm
Length	-
Width	-
Height	-
Kerb weight	850 kg

PERFORMANCE

Top speed	250 km/h
Power to weight ratio	3.5 kg/hp

Ferrari 250 Monza   1954

The two main areas of Ferrari production in the mid-Fifties were the 12-cylinder, three-litre engines installed in the sport racing and grand touring cars and the four-cylinder in-line units for the small, agile 750 Monza barchettas and Formula One single-seaters. The two joined forces in a single car in 1954, the name of which betrayed this unusual marriage of car and engine: the 250 Monza. The new model, which was to compete in the sports racer category, was built on a 750 Monza rolling chassis in which was installed a 60° V12 with three Weber 36IF4C carburettors, instead of the traditional four-cylinder in-line unit. The first two 250 Monzas bodied by Pinin Farina in 1954 reiterated the external shape of the 500 Mondial barchetta, with one of which Maurice Trintignant and Luigi Piotti won the 12 Hours of Hyères - not a round in the World Sports Car Championship.

A few weeks later, the same day in which the 750 Monza appeared for the first time at the Grand Prix Supercortemaggiore, Franco Cornacchia and Gerino Gerini came third in a Carrozzeria Scaglietti 250 Monza, behind two Maranello four-cylinders. The Modena body builder "dressed" another 750 in 1954, but despite a promising start, the union between the Monza chassis and the glorious Ferrari V12 power plant was taken no further. The motor sport career of the 250 Monza continued until 1956 with various entries in the Mille Miglia, but the car's results were poor. In fact, Musitelli-Drago were forced to retire their car in the early stages of the 1954 race, but in 1955 Erasmo Simeoni managed to get a 250 Monza up to 15th overall: in 1956, Dos Santos-Araujo came 79th but were over the time/limit.

One of the obvious differences between the 375 MM barchetta and the Plus version was the latter's generous bulge at the rear, which housed the 180 litre fuel tank. Ferrari scored two important victories with this car of exceptional power – 330 hp – one in the 24 Hours of Le Mans driven by Froilan Gonzalez-Maurice Trintignant and the other in the Carrera Panamericana with Umberto Maglioli at the wheel.

TECHNICAL SPECIFICATION

ENGINE
front, longitudinal, V12 (60°)

Bore and stroke	84x74.55 mm
Unitary cubic capacity	412.8
Total cubic capacity	4954.3
Valve gear	single overhead camshaft
Number of valves	two per cylinder ·
Compression ratio	9.2:1
Fuel feed	three Weber 46DCF3 carburettors (42DCZ - cabrio)
Ignition	double, two magnetos
Coolant	water
Lubrication	dry sump
Maximum power	330 hp at 6000 rpm
Specific power	68.6-70.6 hp/litre

TRANSMISSION
Rear-wheel drive

Clutch	multi-disc
Gearbox	en bloc with differential four gears + reverse

BODY
Two-seater barchetta/sports saloon/cabriolet

CHASSIS

Chassis	longitudinal and cross members
Front suspension	independent, double wishbones, transverse semi-elliptic spring, hydraulic dampers
Rear suspension	De Dion axle, transverse semi-elliptic spring, double dampers
Brakes	drum
Steering	worm and sector
Fuel tank	180 litres
Tyres front/rear	6.00-16/7.00-16

DIMENSIONS AND WEIGHT

Wheelbase	2600 mm
Track front/rear	1325/1284 mm
Length	4187 mm (barchetta)
Width	1624 (barchetta)
Height	1091 (barchetta)
Kerb weight	900 kg

PERFORMANCE

Top speed	280 km/h
Power to weight ratio	2.7 kg/hp

Ferrari 375 Plus 1954

In 1954, an even more powerful 4,954.3 cc, 12-cylinder engine was installed in some of the 375 MMs, which did so well in the 1953 World Sports Car Championship. It was the latest evolution of a unit the origins of which harked back to 1950, when it powered an F1 car in 4.5-litre guise. Pinin Farina almost fully reproduced the shape of the 375 MM for the Ferrari 375 Plus. The car put out about 350 hp and competed for the 1954 world championship. Unlike its older sister, it had a bulge in the rear bodywork to accommodate a bigger fuel tank and a spare wheel. Given the stress placed on the Plus by its potent V12 power unit, its chassis was substantially modified by the adoption of a De Dion rear axle.

The debut of the Ferrari 375 Plus was not one of the best, however, as its power turned out to be anything but docile in races like the Giro di Sicilia and the Mille Miglia, so it was often in difficulty. But when Silverstone, the Le Mans and the Carrera Panamericana came along, the 375's almost 350 hp made all the difference. Jose Froilan Gonzalez won at the British circuit and the Argentinean teamed up with Maurice Trintignant to give Ferrari victory in the Sarthe marathon for the first time since 1949. Umberto Maglioli was the victor on the interminable straights of the Mexican Carrera. and, once again, the World Sports Car Championship ended up in Maranello. This success inspired Pinin Farina to build an extraordinarily elegant cabriolet on the 375 Plus chassis for a famous customer, ex-King Leopold III of the Belgians.

The sobriety of shape and refined elegance of line exuded by the first of the 250 Europas in 1953 were fully confirmed again by Pinin Farina in the GTs, which were built the following year. The 1954 V12 Ferrari 250 Europa GT was to withstand the test of time, due to the difference in many of the cars' details and various aesthetic approaches.

TECHNICAL SPECIFICATION

ENGINE
front, longitudinal, V12 (60°)

Bore and stroke	73x58.8 mm
Unitary cubic capacity	246.1
Total cubic capacity	2953.2
Valve gear	single overhead camshaft
Number of valves	two per cylinder
Compression ratio	8.5:1
Fuel feed	three Weber 36DCZ3 carburettors
Ignition	single, two distributors
Coolant	water
Lubrication	dry sump
Maximum power	220 hp at 7000 rpm
Specific power	74.5 hp/litre

TRANSMISSION
Rear-wheel drive

Clutch	multi-disc
Gearbox	en bloc with engine four gears + reverse

BODY
Two-seater sports saloon/coupé

CHASSIS

Chassis	longitudinal and cross members
Front suspension	independent, double wishbones, transverse semi-elliptic spring, anti-roll bar, Houdaille dampers
Rear suspension	live axle, longitudinal semi-elliptic springs, Houdaille dampers
Brakes	drum
Steering	worm and sector
Tyres front/rear	6.00-16 all round

DIMENSIONS AND WEIGHT

Wheelbase	2600 mm
Track front/rear	1354/1349 mm
Length	-
Width	-
Height	-
Kerb weight	1050 kg

PERFORMANCE

Top speed	230 km/h
Power to weight ratio	4.8 hp/litre

Ferrari 250 Europa GT   1954

First seen at the 1954 Paris Motor Show, from the outside the 250 Europa GT seemed a simple update of the previous year's 250 Europa, but in reality, it was a car with a wealth of new features. They ranged from the first appearance of the letters GT and extended to the car's V12 engine of almost three litres (2,953.2 cc), derived from the 12-cylinder designed by Gioachino Colombo. Between 1954 and 1956, Ferrari followed that coupé of clean and sober Pinin Farina design with the first series of 250 GTs of various different bodies and finishes, but all with that great elegance, aimed at an elite but sporting clientele. Pinin Farina introduced several styling features that would become regulars on Ferrari GTs, including the elliptically-shaped radiator grill that was smaller than those of previous models, air vents located at the edge of the rear window and more outlets between the front wing and the door. On the sports saloon (pictured) the designer also brought back the rear fins first seen on the aerodynamic 375 MM, built on chassis 0403 GT in 1955. The performance of the V12 was anything but "touristic", the first series being accredited with 220 hp, which increased between 1956 and 1958 to 240 hp at 7000 rpm.

Maranello began semi-standard production with the Ferrari 250 GT, eventually making 130 of the cars in their various forms. The legend of the 250 GT was definitively consolidated as it was campaigned by many gentlemen drivers and was built in one-off examples commissioned by prestigious customers, including Prince Bernhard of the Netherlands and Liliana de Réthy, wife of ex-King Leopold III of the Belgians.

As was the practice in those days, sports racers and single-seaters were test driven at the Aerautodromo of Modena, often under the watchful eye of Enzo Ferrari himself (photo, background, behind car). Nino Farina gave the 555 F1 – derived from the 1954 553 – its debut, but the outstanding performance of the Mercedes-Benz W196 stood in the way of the 555 bringing home significant results.

TECHNICAL SPECIFICATION

ENGINE
front, longitudinal, four cylinders in line

Bore and stroke	100x79.5 mm
Unitary cubic capacity	624.39
Total cubic capacity	2497.56
Valve gear	twin overhead camshaft
Number of valves	two per cylinder
Compression ratio	13:1
Fuel feed	two Weber 50DCOA3 carburettors
Ignition	double, two magnetos
Coolant	water
Lubrication	dry sump
Maximum power	260 hp at 7200 rpm
Specific power	104.1 hp/litre

TRANSMISSION
Rear-wheel drive

Clutch	multi-disc
Gearbox	en bloc with differential four gears + reverse

BODY
Single-seater

CHASSIS

Chassis	tubular trellis
Front suspension	independent, double wishbones, coil springs, anti-roll bar Houdaille dampers
Rear suspension	De Dion axle, transverse semi-elliptic spring, Houdaille dampers
Brakes	drum
Steering	worm and sector
Fuel tank	180 litres (two laterals, one rear)
Tyres front/rear	5.50-16/7-00-16

DIMENSIONS AND WEIGHT

Wheelbase	2160 mm
Track front/rear	1270/1250 mm
Length	3988 mm
Width	1427 mm
Height	1020 mm
Kerb weight	590 kg

PERFORMANCE

Top speed	280 km/h
Power to weight ratio	2.2 kg/hp

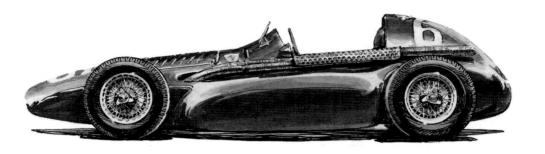

Ferrari 555 F1 1955

Despite the modest results it achieved in 1954, the 553 continued to race for Ferrari the following season. The car, which by that time had been re-named the 555 "Supersqualo", had a radically revised chassis and suspension. The lateral fuel tanks had been among the 1954 trouble makers, so they were joined by an additional tank in the tail of the car. But these substantial modifications did not bring the improvements hoped for and the car's performance remained mediocre. The various drivers who alternated at the Supersqualo's wheel were unable to do better than score a few modest results: they included a third by Nino Farina at the Grand Prix of Spa-Francorchamps, another third by Eugenio Castellotti at Monza and a fourth by Paul Frére in the Grand Prix of Belgium - the only ones worthy of note.

The evolution of the 555 ground to a halt after the Grand Prix of Italy, last round in the F1 world championship, in which Ferrari's top-placed driver was Eugenio Castellotti at third with 12 points, to the 40 of title winner Juan Manuel Fangio. On the single-seater front, Maranello was going through a period of profound creative crisis and its cars were never a threat to the dominance of the Mercedes-Benz W196, the unquestioned masters of the Formula One World Championship that year. But Lancia's retirement from the motor sport in 1955 and the eight D50s with which the Turin company had competed in the first half of the championship being handed over to Ferrari, was a vital boost for the Prancing Horse. Handled by Fiat, the operation brought a switch of Lancia technicians to Maranello, including Vittorio Jano, father of the D50 and its V8 engine, which signalled new and prolific prospects in technological development for the Scuderia.

When Mercedes-Benz officially retired from racing in 1955, Juan Manuel Fangio, who was always careful to secure the best available F1 car for himself, had no choice but to sign for the Prancing Horse. The Argentinean won the world title again in 1956 in a D50, thanks in part to the help of his team mate Peter Collins; Fangio won three championship counters, including the British GP at Silverstone (photo).

TECHNICAL SPECIFICATION

ENGINE		**CHASSIS**	
front, longitudinal, V8 (90°)		*Chassis*	tubular trellis
		Front suspension	independent,
Bore and stroke	73.6x73.1 mm		double wishbones,
	(76x68.5 mm in 1956)		transverse
Unitary cubic capacity	310.75		semi-elliptic spring,
Total cubic capacity	2485.98		Houdaille dampers
Valve gear	twin overhead camshafts	*Rear suspension*	De Dion axle, transverse
Number of valves	two per cylinder		semi-elliptic spring,
Compression ratio	11.9:1		Houdaille dampers
Fuel feed	four Solex 40PII carburettors	*Brakes*	drum
Ignition	double, two magnetos	*Steering*	worm and sector
Coolant	water	*Fuel tank*	190 litres
Lubrication	dry sump	*Tyres front/rear*	5.50-16/7.00-16
Maximum power	265 hp at 8000 rpm		
Specific power	106.6 hp/litre		
		DIMENSIONS AND WEIGHT	
TRANSMISSION		*Wheelbase*	2280 mm
Rear-wheel drive		*Track front/rear*	1270/1270 mm
Clutch	multi-disc	*Length*	3850 mm
Gearbox	en bloc with the differential	*Width*	1448 mm
	five gears + reverse	*Height*	962 mm
		Weight in running order	640 kg
BODY			
Single-seater		**PERFORMANCE**	
		Top speed	280 km/h
		Power to weight ratio	2.4 hp/kg

Ferrari-Lancia D 50   1955

The tragic death at Monza on 26 May 1955 of Alberto Ascari while trying out the Ferrari Sport of his friend Eugenio Castellotti and Lancia's difficult financial situation in the mid-Fifties, spelt the end of motor racing for the Turin firm during the course of the season. Thanks to a joint operation by Fiat and the president of the Automobile Club of Italy, all of Lancia's F1 material was assigned to Ferrari in July 1955, including eight D50s, the cars' engineers, technicians and drivers. Designed by Vittorio Jano in 1953, the single-seater was powered by a 2,500 cc, 90° V8 engine, as required by the regulations. Jano had used a number of extraordinarily innovative techniques when creating the racer, like lateral fuel tanks either side of the central body of the car.

The career of the D50 as a Lancia works car was a very short one: it began at the end of 1954 with its debut at the Grand Prix of Spain and ended in mid-1955, when Ascari plummeted into Monte Carlo harbour during the Grand Prix of Monaco. Despite its precarious reliability, in that span of time the D50 scored two victories, one at the Turin and the other at Naples - both non-championship events - confirming its enormous potential. After Lancia disappeared from the scene and its cars' were handed to Ferrari, the D50s enjoyed a new lease of life. In 1956, in the hands of fine drivers like Musso, Castellotti, Collins and Fangio, it won five Grands Prix, took the Argentinean to his fourth world championship and brought the title back to Ferrari again – but not without bitter disputes that saw Fangio leave Maranello at the end of the season and return to Maserati.

After consolidating a long period of experience with 12-cylinder engines and an intense involvement with four cylinder in line units, Ferrari used the latter as a launch pad to the six cylinder, another in line power plant, which went into the 118 and 121 LM that competed in sports car racing in 1955. Driving one of those cars, Umberto Maglioli and Luciano Montefferaio (photograph) came third in that year's Mille Miglia, behind the unbeatable Mercedes-Benz 300 SLRs.

TECHNICAL SPECIFICATION

ENGINE
front, longitudinal, six cylinders in line

Bore and stroke	94x90 mm
	(102x90 mm 121 LM)
Unitary cubic capacity	624.58
	(725.41 121 LM)
Total cubic capacity	3747.48 (4412.49 121 LM)
Valve gear	twin overhead camshafts
Number of valves	two per cylinder
Compression ratio	8:1 (8.5:1 121 LM)
Fuel feed	three Weber 58DCOA3
	carburettors
Ignition	double, two distributors
Coolant	water
Lubrication	dry sump
Maximum power	280 hp at 7000 rpm
	(330 hp at 6000 rpm 121 LM)
Specific power	74.7 hp/litre (74.8 121 LM)

TRANSMISSION
Rear-wheel drive

Clutch	multi-disc
Gearbox	en bloc with differential
	five gears + reverse

BODY
Two-seater barchetta

CHASSIS

Chassis	longitudinal and cross members
Front suspension	independent, double wishbones, coil springs, hydraulic dampers
Rear suspension	De Dion axle, transverse semi-elliptic spring, hydraulic dampers
Brakes	drum
Steering	worm and sector
Fuel tank	-
Tyres front/rear	5.50-16/7.50-16

DIMENSIONS AND WEIGHT

Wheelbase	2400 mm
Track front/rear	1278/1284 mm
Length	-
Width	-
Height	-
Kerb weight	850 kg

PERFORMANCE

Maximum speed	270 km/h
Power to weight ratio	3 kg/hp (2.6 121 LM)

Ferrari 118 LM and 121 LM   1955

Starting with the four-cylinder, 1,984.85 cc engine from the 500 Mondial as a base, Aurelio Lampredi designed the first six-cylinder engine in Ferrari's history in 1954. It was designated the 306 S but the unit remained a prototype and never found a real purpose in life. Regardless, that power plant was the start of a unique construction-al theme that led Lampredi to design two other six-cylinder, in-line engines of 3.7 and 4.4 litres respectively. The former inspired the design and construction of the Ferrari 118 LM and the latter powered the 121 LM. Both cars' were bodied by Car-rozzeria Scaglietti and neither differed much from the 750 Monza, although their wheelbase was lengthened to 2,400 mm. Both the 118 and the 121 LM competed in sports car races in 1955, but, like other Maranello barchettas, they came up against the crushing superiority of the Mercedes-Benz 300 SLRs.

After an unfortunate debut in the 1000 Kilometres of Buenos Aires, first round in the year's World Sports Car Championship - in which the 118 LM driven by Jose Froilan Gonzalez and Maurice Trintignant was disqualified - Piero Taruffi and Umberto Maglioli took the first two places in the Giro di Sicilia in LMs. Three 118s and a lone 121 LM made their debut in the next Mille Miglia driven by Eugenio Castellotti but, despite the 330 horse power of the car's six-cylinder, 4.4-litre power plant, nothing could tame the Mercedes-Benz of Stirling Moss and Juan Manuel Fangio, who took the first two places in that order in the Brescia-Rome-Brescia marathon.

The brief appearance of the six cylinder engines in the 118 and 121 LMs, which soon concluded their motor racing careers at the end of the '55 season, was only the first act in a technical performance that would shortly lead Ferrari to use that engine architecture again for a prolific generation of cars called Dinos.

The Ferrari 410 S chassis number 0596 CM was also at scrutineering for the 1957 Mille Miglia, entered by Swedish driver Sture Nottrop with Tom Brahmer (picture). But even though the car was assigned a number – 521 - it did not compete. The motor racing career of the 410 S was so limited that it was only entered once as a works car.

TECHNICAL SPECIFICATION

ENGINE
front, longitudinal, V12 (60°)

Bore and stroke	88x68 mm
Unitary cubic capacity	413.58
Total cubic capacity	4961.57
Valve gear	single overhead camshaft
Number of valves	two per cylinder
Compression ratio	8.5:1
Fuel feed	three Weber 42DCZ4 carburettors
Ignition	single, four coils
Coolant	water
Lubrication	dry sump
Maximum power	380 hp at 6200 rpm
Specific power	76.6 hp / litre

TRANSMISSION
Rear-wheel drive

Clutch	multi-disc
Gearbox	en bloc with differential five gears + reverse

BODY
Two-seater barchetta

CHASSIS

Chassis	longitudinal and cross members
Front suspension	independent, double wishbones, coil springs, hydraulic dampers
Rear suspension	De Dion axle, transverse semi-elliptic spring, hydraulic dampers
Brakes	drum
Steering	worm and sector
Fuel tank	120-155 litres
Tyres front/rear	6.50-16 / 7.50-16

DIMENSIONS AND WEIGHT

Wheelbase	2420 mm
Track front/rear	1455 mm
Length	-
Width	-
Height	-
Kerb weight	1200 kg

PERFORMANCE

Top speed	280 km/h
Power to weight ratio	3.2 hp/kg

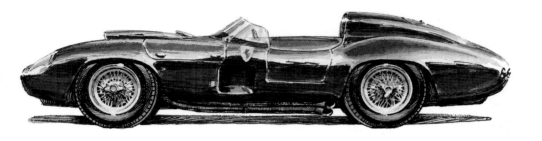

Ferrari 410 S   1955

By 1955, the development and tuning of new sports racing cars had almost reached fever pitch at Maranello. As well as the four-cylinder 750 and 860 Monza and the six-cylinder 118 and 121 LMs in preparation for that year's Carrera Panamericana –which was expected to be held in November - Ferrari also built a potent barchetta with a V12 engine of almost five litres (4,961.57 cc) called the 410 S. That power unit, which had delivered an amazing 380 hp on the test bench, had a new ignition system. For the first time, the new arrangement had four coils and 24 spark plugs, of which 12 were located outside the cylinder banks and could be reached through two trapdoors, one in each wing. To withstand the inevitable stress the potent engine would generate, it was necessary to strengthen the chassis and install a De Dion rear axle. The planned debut of the car at the 1955 Carrera Panamericana did not happen, because the Mexican marathon did not take place. The following year, two 410 Ss were entered for the 1000 Kilometres of Buenos Aires, one for Juan Manuel Fangio-Eugenio Castellotti and the other for Luigi Musso-Peter Collins. But, unfortunately, despite the remarkable performance of the engine, the transmission could not take the stress and neither car lasted the distance. The two cars were sold to two privateers, John Edgar and Sture Nottorp as early as the 12 Hours of Sebring. Meanwhile, Carrozzeria Scaglietti built another two 410 S barchettas with single ignition for Scuderia Parravano and a sports saloon similar to the 250 GT Competizione for French driver Michel-Paul Cavallier.

The 410 SA (Superamerica), the first example of which was unveiled at the 1956 Brussels Motor Show, was Ferrari's top grand tourer of the Fifties. Powered by a 4,963 cc V12 engine, it was a car for which Pinin Farina broke new stylistic ground that was not without some extravagant excesses, as can be seen with the 1956 Superfast coupé shown in the picture.

TECHNICAL SPECIFICATION

ENGINE		CHASSIS	
front, longitudinal, V12 (60°)		Chassis	longitudinal and cross members
Bore and stroke	88x68 mm	Front suspension	independent,
Unitary cubic capacity	413.6		double wishbones,
Total cubic capacity	4963		coil springs,
Valve gear	single overhead camshaft		anti-roll bar Houdaille
Number of valves	two per cylinder		dampers
Compression ratio	8.5:1 (9:1 1958)	Rear suspension	live axle, longitudinal
Fuel feed	three Weber 40 DCF		semi-elliptic springs,
	carburettors		Houdaille dampers
	(three 42 DCF 1958)	Brakes	drum
Ignition	double, one coil, two	Steering	worm and sector
	distributors	Fuel tank	100 litres
Coolant	water	Tyres front/rear	6.50-16 all round
Lubrication	dry sump		
Maximum power	340 at 6000 rpm	DIMENSIONS AND WEIGHT	
	(360-400 hp at 7600 rpm	Wheelbase	2800 mm
1958)			(2600 in 1958)
Specific power	68.5 hp/litre (72.5-80.6 1958)	Track front/rear	1455/1450 mm
		Length	4700 mm (4500 in 1958)
TRANSMISSION		Width	1690 mm
Rear-wheel drive		Height	1115 mm
Clutch	multi-disc	Kerb weight	1250 kg (1320 in 1958)
Gearbox	en bloc with engine		
	four gears + reverse	PERFORMANCE	
		Top speed	220-260 km/h
BODY			(230-295 in 1958)
Two-seater coupé		Power to weight ratio	3.7 kg/hp (3.3 in 1958)

Ferrari 410 SA and 410 Superfast   1956

Ferrari showed a new concept chassis at the 1955 Paris Motor Show, with longitudinal members that passed over the rear axle, from which a new grand tourer to replace the 375 coupé took shape. It was called the 410 Superamerica and made its debut at the 1956 Brussels Motor Show. That first Pinin Farina coupé already flaunted its grand tourer character, and was a car aimed at an exclusive clientele. In effect, the 410 SA was the most advanced blend of high performance, with its 4,963 cc, V12 engine that generated 340 hp at 6,000 rpm, a car of great refinement and class. For the 410 S, Pinin Farina adopted a number of styling features already seen on the 250 GT, including the panoramic rear window, slatted air vents on the sides and the elliptically shaped radiator grill, which was accentuated on this car and was able to confer a blend of elegance and unique personality on the coupé at the same time.

Of the Superamerica's different kinds of body produced between 1956 and 1959 in both long (2,800 mm) and short (2,600 mm) wheelbase, the most unusual was the 410 Superfast, which was exhibited at the 1956 Paris Motor Show. Pinin Farina created a white and grey dual-tone two-seater coupé with a satin finish in the lower area and rear bumper bars that terminated with two particularly prominent fins.

As well as the Turin stylist, who designed the most successful interpretation of that model, Ghia and Boano built 30 410 SA bodies between them. The most extreme was a coupé by Ghia for an American customer, closely followed by a sports saloon, both of them loaded with design features in vogue in the United States in the mid-Fifties.

Gino Munaron's works Ferrari 500 TR at a time control during the XXIV and last Mille Miglia in 1957. As well as coming eighth overall and winning his class, Munaron became the up to 2000 cc Sport category champion of Italy. Early sponsorship began to appear during the period, as the "Idriz" legend shows on the car's front wing.

TECHNICAL SPECIFICATION

ENGINE
front, longitudinal, four cylinders in line

Bore and stroke	90x78 mm
Unitary cubic capacity	496.21
Total cubic capacity	1984.85
Valve gear	twin overhead camshafts
Number of valves	two per cylinder
Compression ratio	8.5:1
Fuel feed	two Weber 40DCO3 carburettors
Ignition	double, two distributors
Coolant	water
Lubrication	dry sump
Maximum power	190 hp at 7400 rpm
Specific power	95.8 hp/litre

TRANSMISSION
Rear-wheel drive

Clutch	multi-disc
Gearbox	en bloc with engine four gears + reverse

BODY
Two-seater barchetta

CHASSIS

Chassis	longitudinal and cross members
Front suspension	independent, double wishbones, coil springs, hydraulic dampers
Rear suspension	live axle, coil springs, hydraulic dampers
Brakes	drum
Steering	worm and sector
Fuel tank	120 litres
Tyres front/rear	5.50-16/6.00-16

DIMENSIONS AND WEIGHT

Wheelbase	2250 mm
Track front/rear	1308/1250 mm
Length	-
Width	-
Height	-
Kerb weight	680 kg

PERFORMANCE

Top speed	245 km/h
Power to weight ratio	3.6 kg/hp

Ferrari 500 TR   1956

Ferrari's prolific string of four cylinder in-line engines of the mid-Fifties contributed to expanding the already extensive range of sports racing cars with the 500 TR, which replaced the 500 Mondial in 1954. The new car inherited the same mechanics and cubic capacity of 1,984.85 cc, but the important new feature was in the barchetta's denomination: while the 500 referred, as always, to the unitary cubic capacity of 496.21 cc, TR stood for Testa Rossa a point driven home by the cylinder head, which was painted in red. Ferrari also gave the car a new two-disc dry clutch, a four speed synchronised gearbox and coil springs in place of the transverse semi-elliptic units for the front and rear suspension. Almost all the 500 TRs were built by Carrozzeria Scaglietti, in line with basics already established for Ferrari sports racers of the period: the 500 TR was an agile and light two-seater barchetta of soft yet determined line. Only three of them were built by Carrozzeria Touring of Milan and they were almost identical to the Scaglietti cars. In 1956, the 500 TRs joined the 750, 860 Monza and 290 MM in the sports car world championship. They were always entered by privateers, but campaigned by able drivers, who scored good placings and a few class wins, contributing to yet another world title - Ferrari's third in four years. It was in the Italian championship that the Prancing Horse's "small car" achieved its most significant results. Competing against the battle hardened Maserati A6GCS and 200 S of drivers like Francesco Giardini, Luigi Bellucci and Odoardo Govoni, they won the up to 2,000 cc Sport category in 1956 with Franco Cortese and in 1957 driven by Gino Munaron, who also won his class in that year's Mille Miglia.

Eugenio Castellotti and his Ferrari 290 MM wait for the off in the 1956 Mille Miglia on the famous Viale Rebuffone ramp. The young driver from Lodi, northern Italy, was to score an epic victory in torrential rain in the Brescia-Rome-Brescia marathon. It was one of his most prestigious successes in a career that ended abruptly in a tragic accident in which he lost his life on the Modena circuit on 14 March 1957.

TECHNICAL SPECIFICATION

ENGINE
front, longitudinal, V12 (60°)

Bore and stroke	73x69.5 mm
Unitary cubic capacity	290.88
Total cubic capacity	3490.61
Valve gear	single overhead camshaft (290 S twin-cam)
Number of valves	two per cylinder
Compression ratio	9:1
Fuel feed	three Weber 36IR4/C1 (290 S six Weber 42DCN)
Ignition	single, four distributors
Coolant	water
Lubrication	dry sump
Maximum power	320 hp at 7300 rpm (290 S 330 hp at 8000 rpm)
Specific power	91.7 hp/litre (290 S 94.6)

TRANSMISSION
Rear-wheel drive

Clutch	multi-disc
Gearbox	en bloc with differential four gears + reverse

BODY
Two-seater barchetta

CHASSIS

Chassis	longitudinal and cross members
Front suspension	independent, double wishbones, coil springs, hydraulic dampers
Rear suspension	De Dion axle, transverse semi-elliptic spring, hydraulic dampers
Brakes	drum
Steering	rack
Fuel tank	-
Tyres front/rear	6.50-16/7.00-16

DIMENSIONS AND WEIGHT

Wheelbase	2350 mm
Track front/rear	1310/1286 mm
Length	-
Width	-
Height	-
Kerb weight	880 kg

PERFORMANCE

Top speed	280 km/h
Power to weight ratio	2.7 kg/hp (290 S 2.6)

Ferrari 290 MM and 290 S   1956

After the brief appearance of the 410 S, Maranello went back to developing the 12-cylinder engine for a sports racing car called the 290 MM, coming up with a 3,490.61 cc unit with its bore and stroke increased to 73 x 69.5 mm. The car was decidedly conventional as far as the gearbox and chassis were concerned. The 'box was a four speed and the chassis' steel tube layout was anchored to two integrated long members. Externally, the Carrozzeria Scaglietti body was not much different than the "smaller" 860 Monza's, if one dismisses a long exhaust pipe that ran under the length of the right flank and which was not on the four-cylinder car, and the air intake on the bonnet which, unlike on the 860 Monza's, looked like it had been abruptly cut off, without joining the body.

Abstaining from the first two rounds in the World Sports Car Championship, the 290 MM made its first public racing appearance in the Giro di Sicilia, in which the two cars driven by Eugenio Castellotti and Luigi Musso were unable to finish. But it was Castellotti who made the name of the new car at the following Mille Miglia with a most extraordinary performance in his yellow-nosed 290 MM: the race took place in extremely bad weather, with strong winds, heavy rain and even hail lashing the open top car from start to finish. The man from Lodi still won with an impressive performance at an average speed of 137.442 km/h, beating Juan Manuel Fangio in a similar car by over half-an-hour. Making its final bid for the last few points that would win the world title for Maranello in a year in which the Maserati 300 S was the 290 MM's fiercest rival, the Ferrari took first and second in the Grand Prix of Sweden driven by Trintignant-P. Hill and Collins-von Trips respectively. The 290 MM, which competed with an even more powerful 330 hp version called the 290 S, also won the 1000 Kilometres of Buenos Aires again in 1957.

This Scaglietti 860 Monza roadster competed in the XXIII Mille Miglia in the hands of Peter Collins, the talented works driver, and Louis Klemantaski, an outstanding photographer, and was distinguishable from Maranello's other entries by its green painted nose. Klemantaski photographed the entire race, taking memorable sequences of pictures from the car's cockpit.

TECHNICAL SPECIFICATION

ENGINE
front, longitudinal, four cylinders in line

Bore and stroke	102x105 mm
Unitary cubic capacity	857.98
Total cubic capacity	3431.93
Valve gear	twin overhead camshafts
Number of valves	two per cylinder
Compression ratio	8.5:1
Fuel feed	two Weber 58DCOA3 carburettors
Ignition	double, two coils
Coolant	water
Lubrication	dry sump
Maximum power	280 hp at 6000 rpm
Specific power	81.6 hp/litre

TRANSMISSION
Rear-wheel drive

Clutch	multi-disc
Gearbox	en bloc with differential four gears + reverse

BODY
two-seater barchetta

CHASSIS

Chassis	longitudinal and cross members
Front suspension	independent, double wishbones, coil springs, hydraulic dampers
Rear suspension	De Dion axle, transverse semi-elliptic spring, hydraulic dampers
Brakes	drum
Steering	worm and sector
Fuel tank	-
Tyres front/rear	6.00-16/7.00-16

DIMENSIONS AND WEIGHT

Wheelbase	2350 mm
Track front/rear	1246/1310 mm
Length	-
Width	-
Height	-
Kerb weight	860 kg

PERFORMANCE

Top speed	260 km/h
Power to weight ratio	3.1 kg/hp

Ferrari 860 Monza   1956

In an attempt to stem Mercedes-Benz' supremacy, against which neither the 750 Monza nor the 118 or 121 LM were able to put up any viable resistance, during the course of 1955 Maranello increased its efforts to add further versions of those two barchettas that were more reliable and powerful. One of them was the 857 S, with a 3,421.20 cc, four-cylinder in line engine the power of which was upped to 280 hp at 5,800 rpm and lowered into a 750 Monza chassis. The car made its debut at the 1955 Tourist Trophy, but it did not do well, much less give the German cars opposition. The following year, a new team of technicians started work on that engine, among them Vittorio Bellentani, Alberto Massimino and Andrea Fraschetti, who joined Ferrari's technical department run by Aurelio Lampredi. The new power unit had its bore and stroke increased to 102x105 mm and generated 280 hp to become the basis of the Scaglietti-bodied 860 Monza. In 1956, with Mercedes-Benz out due to their manifest superiority at the end of the previous year, the 290 MM joined the 850 Monza and, as well as winning races on the African continent in Dakar and Agadir, also won the Giro di Sicilia with Peter Collins-Louis Klemantaski and the 12 Hour International of Florida at Sebring driven by Juan Manuel Fangio-Eugenio Castellotti. The 860 Monza also performed well in the Mille Miglia, taking second and third places overall (Collins and Luigi Musso) behind Castellotti's 290 MM. In spite of the Maserati 300 S's victory in the 1000 Kilometres of the Nürburgring and the D-Type Jaguar's win in the 24 Hours of Le Mans, Ferrari still managed to take the sports car world title again in 1956.

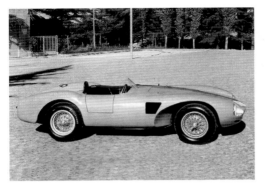

The 1956 24 Hours of Le Mans regulations permitted the entry of prototypes of no more than 2.5 litres or cars with bigger engines of which more than 50 examples had been built. That is how Ferrari came to construct three Touring bodied barchettas on the three 500 TR rolling chassis, previously seen at Monza, for the French event and powered by the 2.5 litre 625 F1 engine.

TECHNICAL SPECIFICATION

ENGINE
front, longitudinal, four cylinders in line

Bore and stroke	94x90 mm
Unitary cubic capacity	624.58
Total cubic capacity	2498.32
Valve gear	twin overhead camshafts
Number of valves	two per cylinder
Compression ratio	9:1
Fuel feed	two Weber 42DCOA carburettors
Ignition	double, two distributors
Coolant	water
Lubrication	dry sump
Maximum power	225 hp at 6200 rpm
Specific power	90.1 hp / litre

TRANSMISSION
Rear-wheel drive

Clutch	multi-disc
Gearbox	en bloc with engine four gears + reverse

BODY
Two-seater barchetta

CHASSIS

Chassis	longitudinal and cross members
Front suspension	independent, double wishbones, coil springs, hydraulic dampers
Rear suspension	live axle, coil springs, hydraulic dampers
Brakes	drum
Steering	worm and sector
Fuel Tank	140 litres
Tyres front/rear	5.50-16 / 6.00-16

DIMENSIONS AND WEIGHT

Wheelbase	2250 mm
Track front/rear	1308 / 1250 mm
Length	-
Width	-
Height	-
Kerb weight	700 kg

PERFORMANCE

Top speed	250 km/h
Power to weight ratio	3.1 kg/hp

Ferrari 625 LM   1956

After a number of years out of the picture, Carrozzeria Touring was back working with Maranello, alternating with Scaglietti and bodying a number of sports racing cars, among them three 500 TRs in 1956. The cars raced on 24 June of that year in the IV Grand Prix Supercortemaggiore at Monza. The three were driven by Fangio-Castellotti, von Trips-Herrmann and Collins-Hawthorn, who won and took the 2,000 cc class. The mechanics of the cars were transformed so that they could compete in the year's 24 Hours of Le Mans under the denomination 625 LM.

Following the horrific carnage of the 1955 French marathon in which Francois Levegh's Mercedes-Benz killed 81 spectators as well as the driver, the Automobile Club de l'Ouest brought out new regulations for the 1956 event that imposed a 2.5 litre limit on sports prototypes, of which less than 25 examples had been built. That stopped Ferrari entering both the 860 Monza (3,431 cc) and the 290 MM (3,491 cc) and meant a car had to be specially built for the race. So Maranello installed 2.5- litre 625 F1 engines in the three 500 TRs, reducing the compression ratio from 12:1 to 9:1 and replaced the single-seater's 50 mm carburettors with two 42 DCOA units. But the new 625 LM was unable to hold the 3.4-litre D-Type Jaguars, which were admitted because their manufacturer declared it had built more than 50 examples of the model. The British racers won, but of the three 625 LMs only the one driven by Olivier Gendebien and Maurice Trintignant finished – third.

The long wheelbase (2,600 mm) Ferrari 250 GT Competizione was also known as the 250 Tour de France, to mark the series of victories the Prancing Horse had chalked up in the French event. The car was one of the most successful Ferraris and its successes included the Gendebien-Bianchi win in the 1957 Tour, plus Gendebien's over 2,000 cc class win (picture) in that year's Mille Miglia.

TECHNICAL SPECIFICATION

ENGINE
front, longitudinal, V12 (60°)

Bore and stroke	73x58.8 mm
Unitary cubic capacity	246.1 cc
Total cubic capacity	2953.2 cc
Valve gear	single overhead camshaft
Number of valves	two per cylinder
Compression ratio	8.5:1
Fuel feed	three Weber 36DCZ3 carburettors
Ignition	single, two distributors
Coolant	water
Lubrication	dry sump
Maximum power	240-260 hp at 7000 rpm
Specific power	81.2-88 hp/litre

TRANSMISSION
Rear-wheel drive

Clutch	multi-disc
Gearbox	en bloc with engine four gears + reverse

BODY
Two-seater sports saloon

CHASSIS

Chassis	longitudinal and cross members
Front suspension	independent, double wishbones, transverse semi-elliptic spring, anti-roll bar, Houdaille dampers
Rear suspension	live axle, longitudinal semi-elliptic springs and pushrods, Houdaille dampers
Brakes	drum
Steering	worm and sector
Fuel tank	100 litres
Tyres front/rear	6.00-16 all round

DIMENSIONS AND WEIGHT

Wheelbase	2600 mm
Track front/rear	1354/1349 mm
Length	4400 mm
Width	1650 mm
Height	1280 mm
Kerb weight	1145 kg

PERFORMANCE

Top speed	250 km/h
Power to weight ratio	4.8-4.4 kg/hp

Ferrari 250 GT Competizione   1956

In the mid-Fifties, the 250 Europa and 250 GT sports saloons were the best high performance grand tourers on the market and their sales success encouraged Ferrari to begin the production of the Competizione version of the model. The intention was to build a new car, which, while conserving the rigor and formal simplicity already expressed in touring models, could successfully be used on the track by an increasing number of sporting customers. With that presupposition, the first 250 GT Competiziones started to take shape in 1956 - better known as the Tour de France, a race won by Ferrari each year from 1956 to 1964 – at Carrozzeria Scaglietti, which had turned into a talented interpreter of Enzo Ferrari's ideas. The "Tour de France" immediately established itself as an extremely fascinating, no nonsense sports saloon, with its elliptically shaped radiator grill framed between two bumper guards, its bonnet-mounted air intake to make room for the inlet trumpets, its air vent slats on the rear pillars and the Plexiglas fairing later used for the headlights. This racing grand tourer was powered, naturally, by the 2,953.2 V12 and in racing the long wheelbase (LWB) 250 was unbeatable, winning an impressive number of national and international events on circuits, roads and hillclimbs in the hands of both the top professionals of the day and gentleman drivers.

With the 1959 24 Hours of Le Mans in mind, a short wheelbase (2,400 mm) Tour de France was built and called the 250 GT Interim, which gave a preview of the shape and acted as a test bed for the body of the 250 SWB, which appeared in 1959.

One of the Ferrari 500 TRCs built by Scaglietti in 1957. To meet new sporting regulations, all barchettas had to have a tonneau cover "in canvas or other flexible material, demountable by hand and without the use of any tools" that covered the cockpit; during pre-race scrutineering; cars also had to have a hood.

TECHNICAL SPECIFICATION

ENGINE
front, longitudinal, four-cylinders in line

Bore and stroke	90x78 mm
Unitary cubic capacity	496.21 cc
Total cubic capacity	1984.85 cc
Valve gear	twin overhead camshaft
Number of valves	two per cylinder
Compression ratio	9:1
Fuel feed	two Weber 40DCO3 carburettors
Ignition	double, two coils
Coolant	water
Lubrication	dry sump
Maximum power	190 hp at 7400 rpm
Specific power	95.8 hp/litre

TRANSMISSION
Rear-wheel drive

Clutch	multi-disc
Gearbox	en bloc with engine four gears + reverse

BODY
Two-seater barchetta

CHASSIS

Chassis	longitudinal and cross members
Front suspension	independent, double wishbones, coil springs, hydraulic dampers
Rear suspension	live axle, coil springs, hydraulic dampers
Brakes	drum
Steering	worm and sector
Fuel tank	120 litres
Tyres front/rear	5.50-16/6.00-16

DIMENSIONS AND WEIGHT

Wheelbase	2350 mm
Track front/rear	1308/1250 mm
Length	-
Width	-
Height	-
Kerb weight	680 kg

PERFORMANCE

Top speed	245 km/h
Power to weight ratio	3.6 kg/hp

Ferrari 500 TRC   1957

Ferrari built a second 500 TR series at the end of 1956. The car incorporated a number of modifications, which were necessary for it to conform to the new regulations for the extended C-section of the Sporting Code that subdivided and classified the different typologies of vehicle allowed to compete. From 1957, cars entered in the Sport category had to have a cockpit with a minimum width of 120 mm, able to accommodate a possible passenger; each side of the car required a rigid door and, during scrutineering, had to wear a hood. It was also obligatory to fit a windscreen that extended to the passenger side of the car. Scaglietti built a body for the 500 TRC that produced a lower, sleeker car than the TR, with a greater inclination of the radiator grill, a higher bonnet and wings plus more accentuated curves in correspondence with each tyre. Overall, the 500 TRC appeared altogether more compact, despite a slightly longer wheelbase of 2,350 mm, and was attractive. The dual-tone livery also contributed to making the fascinating little four-cylinder more alluring and assertive, characterised by a strip that ran low down on the car from the rear to kick up to the bonnet and continue down the other side. The 500 TRC was not raced as a works car, but by private teams and sporting customers in Italian national and world championships events for sports category cars. Gaetano Starrabba and Franco Cortese came seventh overall in the 1958 Targa Florio and won the event's up to 2000 cc class driving a 500 TRC.

The 250 GT Cabriolet by Pinin Farina appeared for the first time at the 1957 Geneva Motor Show as an experimental pre-series car and was even more clean and elegant of line; that is why the model became one of the most coveted and sought-after Ferraris by the elite of the mid-Fifties. The 250 in the picture, with its faired headlights, is one of the first 1957 cars, which was followed by a second series in 1959.

TECHNICAL SPECIFICATION

ENGINE
front, longitudinal, V12 (60°)

Bore and stroke	73x58.8 mm
Unitary cubic capacity	246.10 cc
Total cubic capacity	2953.2 cc
Valve gear	single overhead camshaft
Number of valves	two per cylinder
Compression ratio	8.5:1
Fuel feed	three Weber 36DCF carburettors
Ignition	single, one distributor
Coolant	water
Lubrication	dry sump
Maximum power	220 at 7000 rpm
Specific power	74.5 hp/litre

TRANSMISSION
Rear-wheel drive

Clutch	multi-disc
Gearbox	en bloc with engine four gears + reverse

BODY
Two-seater roadster/cabriolet

CHASSIS

Chassis	longitudinal and cross members
Front suspension	independent, double wishbones, coil springs, Anti-roll bar, Houdaille dampers
Rear suspension	live axle, longitudinal semi-elliptic springs, Houdaille dampers
Brakes	drum
Steering	worm and sector
Fuel tank	90 litres
Tyres front/rear	6.00-16 all round

DIMENSIONS AND WEIGHT

Wheelbase	2600 mm
Track front/rear	1354/1349 mm
Length	-
Width	-
Height	-
Kerb weight	-

PERFORMANCE

Top speed	220 km/h
Power to weight ratio	-

Ferrari 250 GT Cabriolet — 1957

The 250 GT range was graced in 1957 with a number of cabriolets, all designed by Pinin Farina and cars that contributed in a determinate manner to further bolstering the legend and creating yet more fascination for this extraordinary series of grand tourers, as always built around Ferrari's evergreen 2,953.2 cc V12 engine. The Turin designer was able to imbue the car's body with even greater styling features than those that were already a part of the closed 250s, blending the ingenious new attributes knowledgeably with many stylistic features introduced on the 410 Superamerica and Superfast. The first prototype cabriolet was exhibited at the 1957 Geneva Motor Show. Boasting an alternation of straight surfaces and graphic angles, underlined and emphasised by chromium plated profiles and bumper bars, the car was assertive and elegant at the same time. It was soon painted black for private ownership, instead of the show car's red with beige interior: one of its owners was works Ferrari racing driver Peter Collins, who acquired a 250 GT cabrio for his private use. The first real series was the cabriolet, production of which began during the second half of 1957, was preceded by other one-off versions in which the concepts expressed by the show model were refined and occasionally softened. Among those "intermediate" bodies were the racing roadster, with a faired headrest and a tonneau cover on the passenger side; another was commissioned by the Aga Khan for his future wife. To render his gift even more valuable, the head of the Ismaili Muslim sect had a large, heart-shaped precious stone set into the car's dashboard in place of one of the instruments. The cabriolet was one of the last of the first series, which was succeeded by series two in the summer of 1959. Between the spring of 1957 and the summer of 1959, Pinin Farina built 40 250 GTs in either roadster or cabriolet form.

Derived from the Ferrari-Lancia D50 that won the 1956 Formula One World Championship, the 1957 Ferrari 801 retained its predecessor's 90° V8 engine, which was given more power, but the car was unable to repeat the results of the previous year. Mike Hawthorn, Peter Collins and Luigi Musso had to be content with just a few placings – a second in Germany, a third in Britain and a fourth in Monaco – without being able to win a single race, much less the title.

TECHNICAL SPECIFICATION

ENGINE
front, longitudinal, V8 (90°)

Bore and stroke	80x62 mm
Unitary cubic capacity	311.65 cc
Total cubic capacity	2493.2 cc
Valve gear	twin overhead camshafts
Number of valves	two per cylinder
Compression ratio	11.5:1
Fuel feed	four Solex 40PII carburettors
Ignition	double, two magnetos
Coolant	water
Lubrication	dry sump
Maximum power	285 hp at 8800 rpm
Specific power	114.3 hp/litre

TRANSMISSION
Rear-wheel drive

Clutch	en block with differential
Gearbox	five gears + reverse

BODY
Single-seater

CHASSIS

Chassis	tubular trellis
Front suspension	independent, double wishbones, coil springs, anti-roll bar, Houdaille dampers
Rear suspension	De Dion axle, transverse semi-elliptic spring, Houdaille dampers
Brakes	drum
Steering	worm and sector
Fuel tank	200 litres (two lateral, one rear)
Tyres front/rear	5.50-16/7.00-16

DIMENSIONS AND WEIGHT

Wheelbase	2280 mm
Track front/rear	1305/1334 mm
Length	3850 mm
Width	1448 mm
Height	962 mm
Weight in running order	650 kg

PERFORMANCE

Top speed	280 km/h
Power to weight ratio	2.4 kg/hp

Ferrari 801 F1 $\qquad$ 1957

The Ferrari-Lancia D50 in which Juan Manuel Fangio won the 1956 Formula One World Championship was radically revised at the end of that same year. The mechanics, especially the chassis and body, were all modified so much that the car was given a new model number: it became the 801, the first digit standing for the number of cylinders and the last for Formula One. Increasing bore and stroke to 80 x 62 mm took the power output to 285 hp at 8,800 rpm.

As well as at the sides, a fuel tank was also installed in the tail of the 801 and that contributed to a substantial improvement in weight distribution. But despite such radical modifications, the car's results were rather disappointing: it took the win in three non-title races - Peter Collins in the Grands Prix of Siracusa and Naples, and Luigi Musso in Reims - but none in the Formula One World Championship. That in a year in which Juan Manuel Fangio and his works Maserati 250 F were dominant, earning the Argentinean his fifth world championship, his fourth in succession. Fangio won the '57 crown by taking victory in four Grands Prix out of a possible eight. But the revelation of the year was Vanwall, a British team that first competed in Formula One in 1954 and was headed by brass bearing manufacturer Sir Guy Anthony (Tony) Vandervell. Thanks to his number one driver Stirling Moss, who had made his mark in earlier British "assemblers'" cars, Vanwall won three times – once each at Britain's Aintree, Pescara and Monza in Italy – and that gave Moss second place in the world drivers' championship.

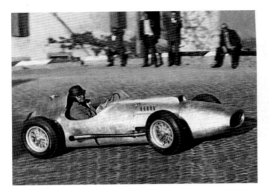

24 April 1957: the Dino 156 F2 single-seater first turned a wheel on the roads of Maranello, driven by test driver Martino Severi. Still with unpainted bodywork, the car was powered by a new concept 65° 1,489.35 cc engine. There was no way Enzo Ferrari could miss his new car's maiden run, so there he is in our picture, on the right wearing dark glasses and sitting on a low wall.

TECHNICAL SPECIFICATION

ENGINE
front, longitudinal, V6 (65°)

Bore and stroke	70x64.5 mm
Unitary cubic capacity	248.22
Total cubic capacity	1489.35
Valve gear	twin overhead camshafts
Number of valves	two per cylinder
Compression ratio	10:1
Fuel feed	three Weber 38DCN carburettors
Ignition	double, two magnetos
Coolant	water
Lubrication	dry sump
Maximum power	180 hp at 9000 rpm
Specific power	120.9 hp/litre

TRANSMISSION
Rear-wheel drive

Clutch	multi-disc
Gearbox	en bloc with differential four gears + reverse

BODY
Single-seater

CHASSIS

Chassis	tubular trellis
Front suspension	independent, double wishbones, coil springs, Houdaille dampers
Rear suspension	De Dion axle, transverse semi-elliptic spring, Houdaille dampers
Brakes	drum
Steering	worm and sector
Fuel tank	150 litres
Tyres front/rear	5.50-16/6.50-16

DIMENSIONS AND WEIGHT

Wheelbase	2160 mm
Track front/rear	1270/1250 mm
Length	-
Width	-
Height	-
Kerb weight	512 kg

PERFORMANCE

Top speed	240 km/h
Power to weight ratio	2,8 kg/hp

Dino 156 F2 1957

Alfredo Ferrari died after a long illness on 30 June 1956. The "total" son, as Enzo Ferrari himself referred to the young man, had obtained an engineering degree in Switzerland and had immediately shown great enthusiasm for and dedication to engines. When it was time to design a 1,500 cc power unit for a Formula Two single-seater, Dino, as everyone usually called him, was prodigious in the advice he gave. His father wrote, "I remember with how much insistence, with which arguments and with how much competent attention Dino observed and discussed all the memorandums that I took home to him every day from Maranello. Finally, a selection was made in favour of a V6 for reasons of mechanical yield and bulk. That is how the famous 156 was born...". The Dino 156 F2 was built the following year around that 65° V6 of 1,489.35 cc with its twin overhead camshafts, testing of which began in the winter of 1956. The car made its racing debut in the 1957 Grand Prix of Naples, where Luigi Musso drove it to a promising third place. Different from the 801 for the fairing of its engine cover air intake, the new car won its first race at Reims, France, driven by Maurice Trintignant, ahead of a rear-engined Cooper. That was the first of a string of victories chalked up by the Dino 156 until 1960. The V6 F2 was continually updated during that period. In '60, the inclination of the unit's cylinder banks was changed from 65° to 60°, the number of its camshafts was reduced from two to one and it was given new bore and stroke values (73x58.8 mm) to produce a total cubic capacity of 1,476.60. The Dino engine sparked off a new line of six cylinder units in various configurations of between 1,500 and 3,000 cc, which powered F1 and F2 single-seaters and sports racing cars, as well as a series of grand tourers, right up to the start of the Seventies.

One of the best Ferrari drivers between 1950 and the early Sixties was, certainly, Wolfgang von Trips, who did well at the wheel of both single-seaters and sports racing cars. He competed in the 1957 Mille Miglia with a 315 S barchetta (photograph) with which he took second place behind the winner, Piero Taruffi. The German driver died in a dramatic accident at Monza in 1961.

TECHNICAL SPECIFICATION

ENGINE
front, longitudinal, V12 (60°)

Bore and stroke	76x69.5 mm
Unitary cubic capacity	315.28
Total cubic capacity	3783.40
Valve gear	twin overhead camshafts
Number of valves	two per cylinder
Compression ratio	9:1
Fuel feed	six Weber 42DCN carburettors
Ignition	double, two distributors
Coolant	water
Lubrication	dry sump
Maximum power	360 hp at 7800 rpm
Specific power	95.1 hp/litre

TRANSMISSION
Rear-wheel drive

Clutch	multi-disc
Gearbox	en bloc with differential Four gears + reverse

BODY
Two-seater barchetta

CHASSIS

Chassis	tubular trellis
Front suspension	independent, double wishbones, coil spring, hydraulic dampers
Rear suspension	De Dion axle, transverse semi-elliptic springs, hydraulic dampers
Brakes	drum
Steering	rack
Fuel tank	-
Tyres front/rear	6.00-16/7.00-16

DIMENSIONS AND WEIGHT

Wheelbase	2350 mm
Track front/rear	1296/1310 mm
Length	-
Width	-
Height	-
Kerb weight	880 kg

PERFORMANCE

Top speed	290 km/h
Power to weight ratio	2.4 kg/hp

Ferrari 315 S   1957

Ferrari not only competed in the 1957 World Sports Car Championship with the 290 MM – a tuned 290 S - but also with the 315 S, its V12 engine increased to 3,783.40 cc (bore and stroke 76x69.5 mm). The car, with a body by the usual Scaglietti, was not much different externally from the 290 MM, of which it retained the imposingly rounded shape typical of Ferrari sports racers of the period. The first two 315 Ss were sent to the 12 Hours of Sebring on 23 March for Peter Collins-Maurice Trintignant and Alfonso De Portago-Luigi Musso. But both were slowed by brake and tyre problems and finished a modest sixth and seventh. For the Mille Miglia, third round in the world championship, Ferrari entered a host of Scaglietti-bodied 250 GTs as well as two 315 Ss for Wolfgang von Trips of Germany and Italian Piero Taruffi, plus another two sports cars with the power of their V12s upped to four litres. Their most dangerous opponent was a Maserati 450 S driven by Stirling Moss and Denis Jenkinson, whose race came to an abrupt end after just 12 kilometres due to a simple accelerator cable break. With the Maserati out of contention, Ferrari had no more real opposition and Piero Taruffi won the last Mille Miglia with a time of 10h 27'47", ahead of von Trips. The 315 S also came third in the 1000 Kilometres of the Nürburgring and fifth in the 24 Hours of Le Mans. Despite Maserati's ever increasing competitiveness, which was, however, too often hampered by unreliability, Ferrari once again won the World Sports Car Championship at the end of 1957 with a total of 41 points, scored both by the 315 S and the 335 S, the two of them powered by the four-litre V12.

After the 1956 experience, Peter Collins and Louis Klemantaski competed in the Mille Miglia again in 1957, this time in a 335 S barchetta. Klemantaski recorded his experiences once more with a series of striking pictures taken during the event, but the crew's race came to an end at Parma, where their transmission broke while they were in the lead.

TECHNICAL SPECIFICATION

ENGINE
front, longitudinal, V12 (60°)

Bore and stroke	77x72 mm
Unitary cubic capacity	335.27 cc
Total cubic capacity	4023.32 cc
Valve gear	twin overhead camshafts
Number of valves	two per cylinder
Compression ratio	9:1
Fuel feed	six Weber 42DCN carburettors
Ignition	double, two coils
Coolant	water
Lubrication	dry sump
Maximum power	390 hp at 7400 rpm
Specific power	96.9 hp/litre

TRANSMISSION
Rear-wheel drive

Clutch	multi-disc
Gearbox	en block with differential four gears + reverse

BODY
Two-seater barchetta

CHASSIS

Chassis	tubular trellis
Front suspension	independent, double wishbones, coil springs, hydraulic dampers
Rear suspension	De Dion axle, coil springs, hydraulic dampers
Brakes	drum
Steering	rack
Fuel tank	-
Tyres front/rear	6.00-16/7.00-16

DIMENSIONS AND WEIGHT

Wheelbase	2350 mm
Track front/rear	1296/1310 mm
Length	-
Width	-
Height	-
Kerb weight	880 kg

PERFORMANCE

Top speed	300 km/h
Power to weight ratio	2.3 kg/hp

Ferrari 335 S   1957

After the 12 Hours of 12 Hours of Sebring, Ferrari made further effort to increase the power output of the 12-cylinder engine that had already been installed in the 290 MM and the 315 S, taking it up to 390 hp with a total cubic capacity of 4,023.32. The unit was lowered into the 335 S and raced for the first time in the Mille Miglia from 12-13 May, together with the 315 S. Scaglietti bodied two cars for the occasion that were almost identical to the 315 and they were assigned to Peter Collins-Louis Klemantaski and Alfonso De Portage-Ed Nelson. The incredible power of the V12 in that configuration enabled Collins to impose a remarkable pace on the marathon, which meant he beat the record set for part of the race by Stirling Moss in 1955 driving a Mercedes-Benz 300 SLR, reaching Siena after 6h 47'48" at an average of 161.992 km/h. Unfortunately, a broken transmission put an end to the Collins-Klemantaski performance at Parma. The second 335 S driven by De Portago-Nelson was always up among the leaders, but about 10 kilometres from the finish, a tyre blowout caused the car to charge off the road and into a group of spectators, killing nine onlookers and the crew. That dramatic accident spelt the end for the Mille Miglia, which became a regularity race for a few years before disappearing from the scene completely. After that disaster, the 335S still took two second places, one at the 1000 Kilometres of the Nürburgring and the other at the Grand Prix of Sweden, plus a 1-2 in the Grand Prix of Venezuela in Caracas, which assured Ferrari of its fourth World Sports Car Championship. The three surviving 335 Ss were sold to private teams in 1958 and three new ones were built. They competed for the entire year, during which they were modified somewhat and ended up looking rather like the new 250 Testa Rossa.

The short wheelbase version (2,400 mm) of the Ferrari 250 GT California was unveiled at the 1960 Geneva Motor Show. The newcomer differed from the 1958 car due to its faired optical group, front and rear bumper bar guards and more "muscular" wings. About 100 examples of this extraordinary model were built and is, perhaps, the most assertive looking roadster ever produced by an Italian manufacturer.

TECHNICAL SPECIFICATION

ENGINE		CHASSIS	
front, longitudinal, V12 (60°)		Chassis	longitudinal and cross members
Bore and stroke	73x58.8 mm	Front suspension	independent,
Unitary cubic capacity	246.10 cc		double wishbones,
Total cubic capacity	2953.2 cc		coil springs,
Valve gear	single overhead camshaft		Houdaille dampers
Number of valves	two per cylinder	Rear suspension	live axle, longitudinal
Compression ratio	8.5:1 (9.6:1 in 1960)		semi-elliptic springs,
Fuel feed	three Weber 36 DCL3		Houdaille dampers
	carburettors	Brakes	drum (discs in 1959)
	(three Weber 40DCL6 in 1960)	Steering	worm and sector
Ignition	single, one coil	Fuel tank	90-136 litres (100-120 litres
Coolant	water		in 1960)
Lubrication	dry sump	Tyres front/rear	6.00-16 all round
Maximum power	240-280 hp at 7000 rpm		
		DIMENSIONS AND WEIGHT	
TRANSMISSION		Wheelbase	2600 mm (2400 in 1960)
Rear-wheel drive		Track front/rear	1354/1349 mm
Clutch	multi-disc		(1378/1374 in 1960)
Gearbox	en bloc with engine	Length	4400 mm (3950 in 1960)
	four gears + reverse	Width	1650 mm
		Height	1400 mm (1370 in 1960)
BODY		Kerb weight	1000/1075 kg
Two-seater roadster			(1050 in 1960)
		PERFORMANCE	
		Top speed	268 km/h
		Power to weight ratio	4.2 kg/hp (3.7 in 1960)

Ferrari 250 GT California   1957

The fascinating 250 cabriolet designed by Pinin Farina at the end of the Fifties and powered by the potent Ferrari three-litre V12 was even more elegant than the 250 GT California, which debuted in December 1957. Luigi Chinetti encouraged Maranello to produce an open model expressly for the U.S. market and the Scaglietti body transformed the desires of the American importer into reality. The roadster had tremendous grace and cleanliness of line, already well received in the latest Pinin Farina creations, which knowingly blended with a certain angularity and sobriety of a racing car. The installation of the V12 engine from the Tour de France sports saloon, also built by Scaglietti, further underlined the California's sporting vocation, as did the creation of a steel alloy bodyshell, with moving parts in aluminium. In addition, some examples were bodied entirely in the alloy for racing.

Another version joined the early models with optical groups under Plexiglas fairing in 1958. It had a protruding lights minus fairing, bordered by more pronounced wings. A second restyling in 1959 brought in new lateral air vents, chrome headlight surrounds and a different air intake on the bonnet. Disc brakes were also fitted to these Californias in 1959.

The 250 California appeared as a short wheelbase car (2,400 mm against the first version's 2,600 mm) on its SWB chassis at the 1960 Geneva Motor Show and had been given an even more powerful V12 engine, which pushed out 280 hp at 7,000 rpm. Undoubtedly among the most fascinating Ferraris ever built, California production continued until 1962.

The 250 Testa Rossa, as it appeared on the day of its presentation at Maranello, 22 November 1957. Ferrari competed with the car, bodied by Scaglietti and powered by the evergreen three-litre V12, in the Sport category in which the Testa Rossa remained Ferrari's top car until 1961, scoring an extraordinary sequence of victories.

TECHNICAL SPECIFICATION

ENGINE	
front, longitudinal, V12 (60°)	
Bore and stroke	73x58.8 mm
Unitary cubic capacity	246.1 cc
Total cubic capacity	2953.21 cc
Valve gear	single overhead camshaft
Number of valves	two per cylinder
Compression ratio	9.8:1
Fuel feed	six Weber 38DCN carburettors
Ignition	single, two distributors
Coolant	water
Lubrication	dry sump
Maximum power	300 hp at 7000 rpm
Specific power	101.6 hp/litre

TRANSMISSION	
Rear-wheel drive	
Clutch	multi-disc
Gearbox	en bloc with engine four gears + reverse

BODY
Two-seater barchetta

CHASSIS	
Chassis	tubular trellis
Front suspension	independent, double wishbones, coil springs, Houdaille dampers
Rear suspension	live axle, coil springs, Houdaille dampers
Brakes	drum (disc in 1959)
Steering	worm and sector
Fuel tank	140 litres
Tyres front/rear	5.50-15/6-00-16

DIMENSIONS AND WEIGHT	
Wheelbase	2350 mm
Track front/rear	1308/1300 mm
Length	-
Width	-
Height	-
Kerb weight	800 kg

PERFORMANCE	
Top speed	270 km/h
Power to weight ratio	2.6 kg/hp

Ferrari 250 Testa Rossa 1957

When the 250 Testa Rossa competed in its first race, the 1000 Kilometres of the Nür-burgring on 26 May 1957, nobody could ever have guessed that the car, entered almost incognito and dressed in the livery of a private American team, would become one of the most successful Ferraris in the manufacturer's history. Compared to other Maranello sports cars, all powered by engines of over three litres, the new-born hid a derivative of the 250 GT's 2,953.21 cc V12 under its bonnet: in fact, since 1958, motor racing regulations had obliged sports racing cars to use three-litre engines. The Testa Rossa looked very much like the 500 TR, but at 2,350 mm its wheelbase was longer: the need to house the aspiration trumpets of the six twin-choke Weber carburettors made it necessary to accentuate the protrusion of the bon-net. After first appearing at the 1957 24 Hours of Le Mans, for which one car was assigned to Gendebien-Trintignant, 1958 became the Testa Rossa's first real season of racing successes: its initial wins were chalked up by Phil Hill and Peter Collins in the 1000 Kilometres of Buenos Aires and the 12 Hours of Sebring, ahead of other TRs; the Targa Florio went to Musso-Gendebien and the 24 Hours of Le Mans to Gendebien, this time paired with Phil Hill.

But 1959 was tougher for the Testa Rossa and its new disc brakes as the car was up against an extremely competitive opponent in the Aston Martin DBR1, which took the sports car championship. The Ferrari was only able to win at Sebring that year, but in 1960, the car won the 1000 Kilometres of Buenos Aires and the 24 Hours of Le Mans again and was first past the flag in 1961 at Sebring and the 4 Hours of Pescara. That extraordinary record was completed in 1962 by victories once more at Sebring and Le Mans.

Suitably modified, the cars of Indianapolis and Formula One clashed on two occasions at the end of the Fifties, at Monza on both occasions. In 1957 and 1958, the circuit hosted the 500 Miles, a sort of Italian version of Indianapolis, in which Ferrari entered this four-litre car in 1958 for Luigi Musso, who came third.

TECHNICAL SPECIFICATION

ENGINE
front, longitudinal, V12 (60°)

Bore and stroke	77x72 mm
Unitary cubic capacity	335.27
Total cubic capacity	4023.32
Valve gear	twin overhead camshafts
Number of valves	two per cylinder
Compression ratio	9.9:1
Fuel feed	six Weber 42DCN carburettors
Ignition	double, two magnetos
Coolant	water
Lubrication	dry sump
Maximum power	415 hp at 8000 rpm
Specific power	103.2 hp/litre

TRANSMISSION
Rear-wheel drive

Clutch	multi-disc
Gearbox	en bloc with differential four gears + reverse

BODY
Single-seater

CHASSIS

Chassis	tubular trellis
Front suspension	independent, double wishbones, coil springs, hydraulic dampers
Rear suspension	De Dion axle, transverse semi-elliptic spring, hydraulic ampers
Brakes	*drum*
Steering	-
Fuel tank	204 litres
Tyres front/rear	6.70-16/8.00-16

DIMENSIONS AND WEIGHT

Wheelbase	2300 mm
Track front/rear	1296/1310 mm
Length	-
Width	-
Height	-
Kerb weight	-

PERFORMANCE

Top speed	320 km/h
Power to weight ratio	-

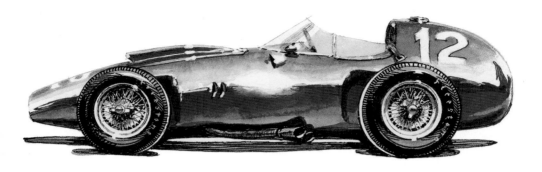

Ferrari 412 MI   1958

The 500 Miles of Indianapolis became part of the Formula One World Championship from 1950 and continued to be so until 1960. With the exception of 1952, when Ferrari entered a 375 in the American race in NART colours for Alberto Ascari, no F1 team really competed at the Brickyard during that decade, because the event required cars especially built for the fabled Indiana circuit.

The American single seaters, powered by either four-cylinder Offenhauser engines or an eight-cylinder Novis, met up with the cars of the Old Continent for the first time at Monza 29 June 1957, when the north Italian circuit hosted a unique 500 Miles event of its own. Put together by the Automobile Club of Italy and the organisation that ran the Indianapolis circuit, the race set the American drivers of the day against those of Formula One – or tried to do so. That year, the European racers boycotted the event, because they considered it too fast and dangerous; but it still took place and was won by Jimmy Brian in a 4.2-litre Dean Van Lines Special. Despite the previous year's boycott, the 500 Miles of Monza was held again in 1958 and that was when the grid was packed with the best American and European drivers. For instance, Ferrari entered Luigi Musso in a 412 MI single-seater, powered by a four-litre engine. Phil Hill also started the race in a Dino 246 F1 with a three-litre power plant, as did Harry Shell in an old 375 Indy, exhumed by Luigi Chinetti and entered in NART colours. Stirling Moss competed in a Maserati 420/m/58 sponsored by Eldorado, the ice-cream manufacturer. After having put up the fastest qualifying lap time of 281.077 km/h, Musso came third in a 500 Miles of Monza won by American Jim Rathmann.

The picture shows Luigi Musso at the wheel of the 246 F1 during the Grand Prix of Argentina, first round in the 1958 world championship. That day, the Roman driver came second behind the Cooper-Climax of Stirling Moss, a result that was repeated at Monte Carlo. After a seventh in Holland and a retirement in Belgium, Musso went to Reims holding third place in the championship, but was tragically killed at the French circuit.

TECHNICAL SPECIFICATION

ENGINE
front, longitudinal, V6 (65°)

Bore and stroke	85x71 mm
Unitary cubic capacity	402.88 cc
Total cubic capacity	2417.33 cc
Valve gear	twin overhead camshaft
Number of valves	two per cylinder
Compression ratio	9.8:1
Fuel feed	three Weber 42DCN carburettors
Ignition	double, one magneto
Coolant	water
Lubrication	dry sump
Maximum power	280 hp at 8500 rpm
Specific power	115.8 hp/litre

TRANSMISSION
Rear-wheel drive

Clutch	multi-disc
Gearbox	en bloc with differential four gears + reverse

BODY
Single-seater

CHASSIS

Chassis	tubular trellis
Front suspension	independent, double wishbones, coil springs, anti-roll bar, telescopic dampers
Rear suspension	De Dion axle, transverse semi-elliptic spring, two pushrods, Houdaille dampers
Brakes	drum
Steering	worm and sector
Fuel tank	160 litres
Tyres front/rear	5.50-16/6.50-16

DIMENSIONS AND WEIGHT

Wheelbase	2160 mm
Track front/rear	1240/1240 mm
Length	4030 mm
Width	1500 mm
Height	980 mm
Kerb weight	560 kg

PERFORMANCE

Top speed	280 km/h
Power to weight ratio	2.0 kg/hp

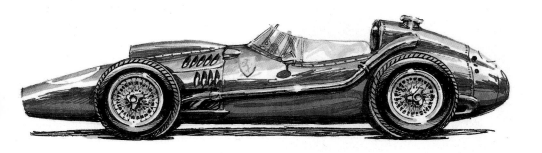

Ferrari 246 F1   1958

Through successive evolutionary stages, the cubic capacity of the 65° V6 engine that had powered the first Dino 156 F2 in 1957 was increased to 2,417.33 cc and, in that configuration, was installed in the single-seater that competed for the 1958 Formula One World Championship – the 246 F1. The first step towards the unit's 2.5-litre limit was a 1,877.78 cc version, which was immediately increased to 1,983.72 cc, and that went into the 196 F1, which was given its race debut at Modena at the end of 1957. At the start of the following year, the power output of the V6 had climbed to 2,195.15 cc and then reached its definitive 2.4 litres. In the meantime, the Formula One picture evolved rapidly: 1958 saw the firm establishment of the British assemblers, with Vanwall, a car that revealed itself to be of great quality, winning no fewer than six Grands Prix, driven by Stirling Moss and Tony Brooks. The rear engined Cooper-Climax won the opening round of the championship in Argentina. Compared to those light and agile little cars, the 246 F1, which put out 280 hp at 8,500 rpm, was conceptually overtaken and strained to compete with the little newcomers. Even so, Mike Hawthorn still managed to bring the world title back to Maranello, stealing the march on Moss by one point, despite only one single victory – in the Grand Prix of France. Hawthorn was further helped by turning in five fastest laps, for each of which the regulations of the day allotted one point to the driver who put up the quickest time during a GP. The return of the Prancing Horse to the summit of F1 was, however, marked by a series of deaths: Luigi Musso was killed in an accident at Reims and Peter Collins died at the Nürburgring. Mike Hawthorn lost his life in a road accident at the wheel of his own Jaguar on 22 January 1959.

Production of the Ferrari 250 GT Coupé started in the summer of 1958 was preceded by the construction of a number of one-off cars. The prototype, which first appeared in early 1958, was followed by a 250 GT (photograph), chassis number 0853 GT, and was sold to a prestigious client: Prince Bertil of Sweden. That one-of-a- kind included a number of styling features later built into the production cars, like the heavily inclined rear window.

TECHNICAL SPECIFICATION

ENGINE
front, longitudinal, V12 (60°)

Bore and stroke	73x58.8 mm
Unitary cubic capacity	246.1 cc
Total cubic capacity	2953.2 cc
Valve gear	single overhead camshaft
Number of valves	two per cylinder
Compression ratio	9:1
Fuel feed	three Weber 36DCZ3 carburettors
Ignition	single, two distributors
Coolant	water
Lubrication	dry sump
Maximum power	240 at 7000 rpm
Specific power	81.3 hp/litre

TRANSMISSION
Rear-wheel drive

Clutch	multi-disc
Gearbox	en bloc with engine
	four gears + reverse

BODY
Two-seater coupé

CHASSIS

Chassis	longitudinal and cross members
Front suspension	independent, double wishbones, transverse semi-elliptic spring, anti-roll bar Houdaille dampers (telescopic – 1960)
Rear suspension	live axle, semi-elliptic springs and longitudinal push rods. Houdaille dampers
Brakes	drum (disc in 1960)
Steering	worm and sector
Fuel tank	100 litres
Tyres front/rear	6.00-16 all round

DIMENSIONS AND WEIGHT

Wheelbase	2600 mm
Track front/rear	1354/1349
Length	4400 mm
Width	1650 mm
Height	1400 mm
Kerb weight	1230 kg

PERFORMANCE

Top speed	200-250 km/h
Power to weight ratio	5.1 kg/hp

Ferrari 250 GT Coupé   1958

The Ferrari 250 GT Coupé Pinin Farina II, which revived a model launched in 1954 and was shown for the first time in Milan in 1958, went from artisan-type construction to semi-industrialised production. The 335 cars built between 1958 and 1960 represented an extraordinary leap forward in Maranello's manufacturing capability, especially for a company that usually produced just under 100 cars a year up until that moment, either as one-offs or a few examples of a single model on request. To fit in with this change of direction, the coupé was designed from the outset along lines that would result in greater simplicity than the Ferraris previously built by Pinin Farina, who had also made elegance and simplicity inescapable elements. After the first two experimental prototypes, each with a panoramic rear window, the definitive 250 GT Coupé emerged as an extremely classical car, with a traditionally long and narrow radiator grill, protruding optical groups and a windscreen that more or less had the inclination of the rear window, all of which gave the car great equilibrium. The flanks, the lower part of which had a light dihedral line, were devoid of any other disturbing elements. As with the previous 250 grand tourer, the 1958 coupé was also powered by the 2,953.2 cc V12 engine fed by three Weber 36DCZ3 carburettors and generated around 240 hp. Given its touring vocation and not being a car destined to become a racer, the 250 GT Coupé, was fitted with disc brakes from 1960. Its rear suspension had telescopic dampers of a new conception, rather than the traditional Houdailles, to make it safer and more comfortable to drive. The car with the Superfast tail displayed at the 1961 London Motor Show brought the 250 GT Coupé series to a close.

A mechanic working on the 256 F1 single-seater, photographed in the pits of the Aer-autodromo di Modena. Derived from the 1958 246 F1, this car did not have a long motor sport life and produced rather poor results. Its opponents were the light and agile cars of the British assemblers, Cooper and Lotus prominent among them, who were ahead of Ferrari, having opted for cars with central-rear engines.

TECHNICAL SPECIFICATION

ENGINE
front, longitudinal, V6 (65°)

Bore and stroke	86x71 mm
Unitary cubic capacity	412.42 cc
Total cubic capacity	2474.54 cc
Valve hear	twin overhead camshaft
Number of valves	two per cylinder
Compression ratio	9.8:1
Fuel feed	three Weber 42 DCN carburettors
Ignition	double, one magneto
Coolant	water
Lubrication	dry sump
Maximum power	295 hp at 8600 rpm
Specific power	119.2 hp/litre

TRANSMISSION
Rear-wheel drive

Clutch	multi-disc
Gearbox	en bloc with differential five gears + reverse

BODY
Single-seater

CHASSIS

Chassis	tubular trellis
Front suspension	independent, double wishbones, coil springs, anti-roll bar, telescopic dampers
Rear suspension	De Dion axle, push rods, coil springs, telescopic dampers
Brakes	drum
Steering	rack
Fuel tank	150 litres
Tyres front/rear	5.50-16/7.00-16

DIMENSIONS AND WEIGHT

Wheelbase	2200 mm
Track front/rear	1240/1300 mm
Length	4030 mm
Width	1500 mm
Height	980 mm
Weight in running order	560 kg

PERFORMANCE

Top speed	280 km/h
Power to weight ratio	1.9 kg/hp

Ferrari 256 F1 1959

After having suffered a series of driver deaths at the end of 1958 with the loss of Luigi Musso, Peter Collins and Mike Hawthorn, Scuderia Ferrari found it necessary to recruit new blood, so it engaged Tony Brooks and Cliff Allison of Britain, Jean Behra of France and Dan Gurney of the U.S.A., names that inaugurated a new era in the Formula One team. But there were not so many new developments on the technical front, an area in which the Prancing Horse limited itself to updating the 246 F1, the previous year's world championship winner, with the adoption of new disc brakes, a five-speed gearbox and new concept suspension. The cubic capacity of the 65° V6 power unit was upped to 2,474.54 by increasing the diameter of the pistons to 86 mm. The outside appearance of the new 256 F1 clearly showed its close relationship to the 1958 car, which, with the exception of a number of air vents down the sides, an exhaust pipe that ran low down along the left side and a small cupola in Plexiglas on the bonnet that sheltered the carburettor trumpets, faithfully took on the look of the 246 F1. The new developments introduced by the British assemblers in 1959 were of an entirely different level: after their catholic predecessors HWM, Cooper Bristol and Vanwall, the Brits came to Formula One with Cooper and Lotus both brandishing single-seaters powered by Coventry Climax engines, accompanied by the BRMs. Between 1959 and 1960, those agile and fast cars whose strongpoint was their engines, located stoically at the rear, won 14 races out of a possible 19, leaving Ferrari with just two Grand Prix victories by Tony Brookes in France and Germany in 1959 and at Monza in 1960 with Phil Hill. In the meantime, Richie Ginther gave the rear-engined 246 P its debut at Monaco in 1960, a sign that Ferrari, too, believed it was time to "put the horse behind the cart".

In 1960, Pinin Farina designed and built this hard top 250 GT on 2,400 mm wheelbase rolling chassis number 1,737 GT of the 250 Spider California, the car having been commissioned by a French client. This one-off creation, the body of which echoed numerous features of the 400 Superamerica, did not have much in common with the "production" 250 GT Cabriolet, all designed with an extraordinary cleanliness of line and a formal equilibrium of great elegance.

TECHNICAL SPECIFICATION

ENGINE		CHASSIS	
front, longitudinal, V12 (60°)		*Chassis*	longitudinal and cross members
Bore and stroke	73x58.8 mm	*Front suspension*	independent,
Unitary cubic capacity	246.1 cc		double wishbones,
Total cubic capacity	2953.2 cc		coil springs,
Valve gear	single overhead camshaft		anti-roll bar, Houdaille
Number of valves	two per cylinder		dampers
Compression ratio	8.8:1	*Rear suspension*	live axle, longitudinal
Fuel feed	three Weber 36 DCF		semi-elliptic springs,
	carburettors		Houdaille dampers
Ignition	single, two distributors	*Brakes*	disc
Coolant	water	*Steering*	worm and sector
Lubrication	dry sump	*Fuel tanks*	90 litres
Maximum power	240 hp at 7000 rpm	*Tyres front/rear*	6.00-16 all round
Specific power	81.3 hp / litre		
		DIMENSIONS AND WEIGHT	
TRANSMISSION		*Wheelbase*	2600 mm
Rear-wheel drive		*Track front/rear*	1354 / 1349 mm
Clutch	multi-disc	*Length*	4700 mm
Gearbox	en bloc with engine	*Width*	1690 mm
	four gears + reverse	*Height*	1330 mm
		Kerb weight	1200 kg
BODY			
Two-seater roadster/cabriolet		PERFORMANCE	
		Top speed	250 km/h
		power to weight ratio	5.0 kg/hp

Ferrari 250 GT Spider 1959

After the early roadsters built between 1957 and 1958, Pinin Farina went back to the open top car theme in 1960 with the 250 Cabriolet GT II series, which, as had been the case with the coupé version, was made using semi-industrial standards, resulting in about 200 examples being produced between 1959 and 1962. Here once again, Pinin Farina designed a car of sober lines and tremendous equilibrium to create the new roadster, which was introduced at the 1959 Paris Motor Show – a car that would be made in small number. The previous version's Plexiglas fairing had disappeared from the headlights, which were now in a more advanced position to produce an aesthetic feature that made the nose of the car yet more compact and even handed. The windscreen was less inclined and a feint dihedral line ran through the flanks of the 250 GT Spider to unite the two wings. The elegance of the car's exterior counterbalanced that of the interior, in which could be found seats in leather and carpeting on the floor. The car now measured 4.7 metres in length and was almost 1.7 metres wide. Maranello had also paid much attention to the 250 GT Spider's driving and riding comfort, for which reason it had installed rather ample seats, adopted a scaled down steering so that the driver only needed to make three-and-a-quarter turns from one lock to lock – and made the instruments more easily readable and the principal controls easily accessible. The 250 Cabriolet II series could also be ordered with a demountable rigid hard top.

Good performance was assured for the II series by the three-litre (2,953.2 cc) power unit of classical 60° V12 configuration, which produced 240 km/h at 7,000 rpm and a top speed that came close to 250 km/h. The Pinin Farina formulation of the 250 GT hard top built for a French client in 1960 was much different. That car was given the shape of the 400 Superamerica roadster and was unveiled by the Turin stylist at the Brussels Motor Show.

Externally rather similar to the 1959-60 250 Testa Rossa, the Dino 196 S powered by the two-litre V6 differs from the 250 not only because of its less powerful engine, but also due to its smaller dimensions in both the wheelbase (2,250 mm) and track. The car's motor sport results did not match those of the glorious Testa Rossa: it managed only a few victories in the Italian championship and placings in the world series.

TECHNICAL SPECIFICATION

ENGINE		CHASSIS	
front, longitudinal, V6 (65°) (60° - 246 S)		Chassis	tubular trellis
		Front suspension	independent,
Bore and stroke	77x71 mm (85x71 – 246 S)		double wishbones,
Unitary cubic capacity	330.62 cc (402.88 – 246 S)		coil springs,
Total cubic capacity	1983.72 cc (2417.33 – 246 S)		telescopic dampers
Valve gear	twin overhead camshafts	Rear suspension	De Dion axle, coil springs,
	(single – 246 S)		telescopic dampers Brakes disc
Number of valves	two per cylinder	Steering	worm and sector
Compression ratio	9:1 (9.8:1 – 246 S)	Fuel tank	160 litres
Fuel feed	three Weber 42 DCN	Tyres front/rear	5.50-16 / 6.00-16
	carburettors		
Ignition	double, two distributors	DIMENSIONS AND WEIGHT	
Coolant	water	Wheelbase	2250 mm (2160 – 246 S)
Lubrication	dry sump	Track front/rear	1240/1200 mm
Maximum power	195 hp at 7800 rpm		(1245/1205 – 246 S)
	(245 hp at 7800 rpm – 246 S)	Length	-
Specific power	100.9 hp/litre (101.4 – 246 S)	Width	-
		Height	-
TRANSMISSION		Kerb weight	640 kg
Rear-wheel drive			
Clutch	multi-disc	PERFORMANCE	
Gearbox	en bloc with differential	Top speed	250 km/h
	four gears + reverse	Power to weight ratio	3.2 kg/hp (2.6 – 246 S)

BODY
Two-seater barchetta

Dino 196 S and 246 S   1959

The positive results racked up by the Formula Two Dino 156 with its 1.5-litre, V6 engine and the 246 Formula One version, induced Ferrari to experiment with the same engine typology for sports racing cars. The first time the 1,983.72 cc, 65° V6 from the 196 F2 was lowered experimentally into the sports barchetta was in 1957: the car made its debut in the 1958 Glover Trophy at Goodwood, where Peter Collins drove it to an encouraging third.

After that first appearance, the definitive version of the Scaglietti-bodied Dino 196 S appeared at Modena in March 1959. The barchetta, which looked like the 250 Testa Rossa from the outside, was powered by a new concept narrower 60° V6 and only had one overhead camshaft for each cylinder bank: it also had a new lubrication system with a geared pump. This narrower engined car was given its maiden outing at Monza in the Coppa Sant'Ambroeus, which it won, with Giulio Cabianca at the wheel. But after that excellent start to its career, the rest of the Dino's season proved extremely difficult at both the national level, where it first crossed swords with the lighter and more reliable Maserati 200 S, and internationally, at which the works Porsche 718 RSK literally outclassed the little sports car from Maranello. A new Dino was unveiled at the end of 1959 and appeared no different from its lack-lustre predecessor, but its engine power had been increased to 2.4 litres, which earned it the denomination 246 S: the newcomer's bore and stroke were also increased to 85 x 71 mm. The best result the 246 S could manage was second to the Joachim Bonnier-Hans Herrmann Porsche 718 RS60 in the 1960 Targa Florio, an event that extolled the virtues of the small, compact Ferrari, driven by Wolfgang von Trips and Phil Hill.

The Sixties Ferrari grand tourer par excellence was, without doubt, the 250 GT sports saloon, better known as the SWB or short wheelbase (2,400 mm). The car was born to race and, judging by the results it chalked up, born to win. An all-aluminium body - at least for the early examples - disc brakes and a three-litre V12 engine that put out 280 hp were the main characteristics of this thoroughbred Ferrari.

TECHNICAL SPECIFICATION

ENGINE
front, longitudinal, V12 (60°)

Bore and stroke	73x58.8 mm
Unitary cubic capacity	246.1 cc
Total cubic capacity	2953.2 cc
Valve gear	single overhead camshaft
Number of valves	two per cylinder
Compression ratio	9.2:1 (9.7:1 – 250 SWBL)
Fuel feed	three Weber 36DCL carburettors (40DCL6 – 250 SWBL)
Ignition	single, two distributors
Coolant	water
Lubrication	dry sump
Maximum power	240 – 280 hp at 7000 rpm
Specific power	81.2 – 94.8 hp/litre

TRANSMISSION
Rear-wheel drive	
Clutch	multi-disc
Gearbox	en bloc with engine four gears + reverse

BODY
Two-seater sports saloon

CHASSIS
Chassis	longitudinal and cross members
Front suspension	independent, double wishbones, coil springs, anti-roll bar, Houdaille dampers
Rear suspension	live axle, longitudinal semi-elliptic springs and push rods, Houdaille dampers
Brakes	disc
Steering	worm and sector
Fuel tank	120 litres
Tyres front/rear	6.00-16 all round

DIMENSIONS AND WEIGHT
Wheelbase	2400 mm
Track front/rear	1354/1349 mm
Length	4150 mm
Width	1690 mm
Height	1260 mm
Kerb weight	960 kg (aluminium body) 1100 kg (steel body)

PERFORMANCE
Top speed	268 km/h
Power to weight ratio	4.0 – 3.9 kg/hp

Ferrari 250 SWB 1959

The prolific 250 grand tourer series was enriched in 1959 by another model of a sporting ability that was even more startling: it was the 250 GT sports saloon, better known as the SWB or short wheelbase, built on the 250 GT chassis and with the distance between its front and rear axles cut to 2,400 mm. The new car, which provided room inside for two seats and not much else, was of compact and rounded line and substantially different from the shape of the Tour de France car. All of those things gave the SWB great equilibrium, making it look elegant and assertive at the same time. Two series of the car were produced between 1959 and 1962. One had an aluminium body and was built by Carrozzeria Scaglietti: its kerb weight was only 960 kg and was designed expressly for racing. The other was in steel and called the Lusso, a model that had a more refined finish both internally and externally.

The evergreen 60° V12 three-litre engine was also dropped into this new car, while a new development of historical importance was the installation of four disc brakes, the first time they had ever been fitted in the place of drums to a Ferrari. The sporting qualities of the car soon became evident. In the early Sixties, the 250 SWB, which was being campaigned both by gentlemen drivers and established champions, scored an extraordinary sequence of victories in races valid for national and international championships. Among the races it won in the 1960-61 season were the Tour de France (Willy Mairesse-Georges Berger), the 1960 Intereuropa Cup at Monza (Carlo Mario Abate) and the 1961 Tourist Trophy by Stirling Moss, who drove an SWB entered by Rob Walker. An interesting body was built by Bertone on short wheelbase chassis number 1,739 GT in 1962: the carrozziere gave his version of the SWB a front end similar to that of the 156 F1, with a split radiator grill.

This car was of radically different conception to all other Ferraris up to that moment. The Pinin Farina Superfast II was built on the 400 Superamerica chassis and launched at the 1960 Turin Motor Show: the picture shows the version that went on sale. The car's shape was especially aerodynamic and embodied stylistic features never previously seen. The Superfast II was a forerunner of the 400 SA Coupé, which made its debut at the 1961 Geneva show.

TECHNICAL SPECIFICATION

ENGINE
front, longitudinal, V12 (60°)

Bore and stroke	77x71 mm
Unitary cubic capacity	330.6 cc
Total cubic capacity	3967.4 cc
Valve gear	single overhead camshaft
Number of valves	two per cylinder
Compression ratio	9.8:1
Fuel feed	three Weber 46DCF3 carburettors
Ignition	single, one coil, two distributors
Coolant	water
Lubrication	dry sump
Maximum power	340 hp at 7000 rpm
Specific power	85.7 hp/litre

TRANSMISSION
Rear-wheel drive

Clutch	multi-disc
Gearbox	en bloc with engine four forward speeds and reverse

BODY
Two-seater cabriolet/coupé

CHASSIS

Chassis	longitudinal and cross members
Front suspension	independent, double wishbones, coil springs, anti-roll bar Houdaille dampers
Rear suspension	live axle, longitudinal semi-elliptic springs Houdaille dampers
Brakes	disc
Steering	worm and roller
Fuel tank	100 litres (120 – cabriolet)
Tyres front/rear	6.50-15 all round

DIMENSIONS AND WEIGHT

Wheelbase	2600 mm (2420 – cabriolet)
Track front/rear	1395/1387 mm (1380/1375 - cabriolet)
Length	4670 mm (4300 – cabriolet)
Width	1680 mm (1770 – cabriolet)
Height	1300 mm (1310 – cabriolet)
Kerb weight	1280 kg (1200 – cabriolet)

PERFORMANCE

Top speed	265 km/h
Power to weight ratio	4.9 kg/hp (4.6 cabriolet)

Ferrari 400 Superamerica   1960

The name of this Ferrari can be considered a declaration of intent: the almost bespoke construction of cars of exceptional power, aimed at a small clientele. That was the inspirational philosophy of the Superamerica. Unveiled in 1960 with a four-litre, 12-cylinder engine boasting a bore and stroke of 77 x 71 mm, the car put out 340 hp at 7,000 rpm and remained in production until the mid-Sixties: but it never spawned a real family of cars, rather a small series and, on some occasions, one-off examples.

After the first two Superamericas - an unusual coupé especially bodied in 1959 for Giovanni Agnelli and a cabriolet similar to the open top 250 GT sent to the 1960 Brussels Motor Show – it was with the experimental Superfast II (Turin, 1960) that Pinin Farina designed a new body for the Ferrari grand tourer and broke new ground on the car styling front. The 400's highly aerodynamic line started from the radiator grill of oval shape at the extremity of the tapered front end, which had pop-up headlights, and extended towards the sloping rear, where there was an ample wraparound panoramic rear window. That first prototype gave rise to a small series of cars, whereas actual construction of the 400 SA did not begin until 1961. The "production" car retained the general imposition of the aerodynamic coupé, from which it differed only in a few details, such as the front window deflectors and the fixed headlights, which were either faired or in a forward position. While Pinin Farina was intent on further refining the aerodynamic prototype shown in Turin in 1960 to create a Superfast III and then a Superfast IV with twin faired headlamps, production of the 400 Superamerica continued until the end of 1963, with final deliveries to customers being made in January 1964.

The first 2+2 grand tourer from Maranello appeared at the 1960 Paris Motor Show. Developed around the classic three-litre 12-cylinder, the 250 GT 2+2 was only modified slightly while in production until 1963: for instance, there were different positions of the indicator lights for the various series. Confirmation that the body shape created by Pinin Farina in 1960 was equilibrated and elegantly sober.

TECHNICAL SPECIFICATION

ENGINE
front, longitudinal, V12 (60°)

Bore and stroke	73x58.8 mm
Unitary cubic capacity	246.1
Total cubic capacity	2953.2
Valve gear	single overhead camshaft
Number of valves	two per cylinder
Compression ratio	8.8:1
Fuel feed	three Weber 36DCL carburettors
Ignition	single, two distributors
Coolant	water
Lubrication	dry sump
Maximum power	240 hp at 7000 rpm
Specific power	81.3 hp/litre

TRANSMISSION
Rear-wheel drive

Clutch	multi-disc
Gearbox	en bloc with engine four gears + reverse

BODY
2+2 coupé

CHASSIS

Chassis	longitudinal and cross members
Front suspension	independent, double wishbones, coil springs, anti-roll bar, hydraulic dampers
Rear suspension	live axle, longitudinal semi-elliptic springs and push rods hydraulic dampers
Brakes	disc
Steering	worm and sector
Fuel tank	100 litres
Tyres front/rear	6.50-15 all round

DIMENSIONS AND WEIGHT

Wheelbase	2600 mm
Track front/rear	1354/1394 mm
Length	4700 mm
Width	1710 mm
Height	1340 mm
Kerb weight	1280 kg

PERFORMANCE

Top speed	230 km/h
Power to weight ratio	5.3 kg hp

Ferrari 250 GT 2+2   1960

The search for maximum driving comfort and the qualities of habitability that were first instilled into the 250 GT and cabriolet were also built into the 250 GT 2+2, introduced at the 1960 Paris Motor Show. While adopting the same rolling chassis as the coupé version (2,600 mm), room was made in this model for two more seats by moving the engine 20 centimetres forward. As always, Pinin Farina gave this luxurious Ferrari "family car", which was also called the GTE after the 128 E engine that powered it, a classically elegant body. It had a narrower radiator grill than the previous 250s and its headlights were recessed into the wings in line with the body, the clean surfaces of which were only interrupted by a chromium strip in the centre of the bonnet and a suggestion of a rib that ran horizontally along both flanks. The sloping roof group blended into a rather short tail, which boasted the particularly original feature of three tiers of rear lights on either side of a boot that could hold the luggage of four occupants. The three tiers of lights gave way to just one on either side on the last of the 250 GT 2+2s. The high class grand tourer pedigree was also reflected in the car's Connolly leather interior and instruments with chrome surrounds. The car's livery majored on metallic colours in place of the traditional red, which was not much suited to the grand tourers of motorists with little sporting ability. About 1,000 2+2s were built before the model went out of production in the autumn of 1963. The following year, though, Ferrari did supply two of the cars to the Flying Squad in Rome, both black and with police markings along the sides.

The 1961 Formula One season saw Scuderia Ferrari return to the top with a revolutionary car designed by Carlo Chiti: the 156 F1, which had a 1,500 cc, V6 engine in the rear. American Phil Hill, (pictured winning the Grand Prix of Belgium at Spa-Francorchamps) also secured the world title for himself during the season's last race at Monza, a Grand Prix marred by von Trips' death.

TECHNICAL SPECIFICATION

ENGINE		CHASSIS	
rear, longitudinal, V6 (65° - 120°)		*Chassis*	tubular trellis
		Front suspension	independent,
Bore and stroke	81x48.2 mm (73x58.8 - 120°)		double wishbones,
Unitary cubic capacity	249.40 cc (246.1 – 120°)		coil springs,
Total cubic capacity	1496.43 cc (1476.60 – 120°)		telescopic dampers
Valve gear	twin overhead camshafts	*Rear suspension*	independent, deformable
Number of valves	two per cylinder		quadrilaterals, coil springs,
Compression ratio	9.8:1		telescopic dampers
Fuel feed	three Weber 42 DCN	*Brakes*	disc
	carburettors	*Steering*	rack
	(two Weber 40IF3C – 120°)	*Fuel tank*	75 litres (two lateral)
Ignition	double, two distributors	*Tyres front/rear*	5.50-15/6.00-15
Coolant	water		
Lubrication	dry sump	DIMENSIONS AND WEIGHT	
Maximum power	200 hp at 10500 rpm	*Wheelbase*	2320 mm (2300 – 1962)
	(190 hp at 9500 rpm – 120°)	*Track front/rear*	1200/1200 mm
Specific power	133.7 hp/Litre (128.7 – 120°)	*Length*	4060 mm
		Width	1400 mm
TRANSMISSION		*Height*	1000 mm
rear-wheel drive		*Kerb weight*	420 kg (470 – 120°)
Clutch	multi-disc		
Gearbox	en bloc with differential	PERFORMANCE	
	five gears + reverse	*Top speed*	260 km/h
	(six gears – 1962)	*Power to weight ratio*	2.1 kg/hp (2.5 – 120°)
BODY			
Single-seater			

Ferrari 156 F1 1961

For the 1961 season, the International Federation banned Formula One cars from using superchargers and imposed a 1.5-litre limit on total cubic capacity, a measure for which Ferrari was well prepared. It had successfully developed a 1,489.35 cc, 65° V6 in the 156 F2 as early as 1957, so Maranello started with that power unit and moulded it into a new F1 engine of the same concept, which was duly installed in the 156. In parallel, engineer Carlo Chiti was made technical head of the Racing Department and put in hand the creation of another V6 motor, but this time with a 120° angle between its cylinder banks that lowered the car's centre of gravity. Both the 65° and 120° versions were located behind the driver in an almost central position within the tubular structure of the car, in line with the design concept introduced by the British assemblers a few years earlier. The fuel tanks were positioned to the sides of the cockpit and the radiator went into the car's nose, cooled by two oval air intakes that typified the 156. The car was extremely competitive, enabling its drivers to win a number of Grands Prix – Wolfgang von Trips was first in Holland and then Britain, Giancarlo Baghetti, who was making his debut in a championship GP, won in France, and Phil Hill in Italy, where he also became world champion. That was 10 September 1961, a day marred by the death of von Trips and 13 spectators: the German went off at the Parabolica on the second lap after a collision with Jim Clark's Lotus. The 156 F1 also competed for the title the following year, but without winning a Grand Prix.

The 246 SP was the first Ferrari with its engine/gearbox behind the cockpit, in line with the similarly powered 156 F1, from which the covered wheeler also inherited the unique front air intakes. This photograph of the car was taken during its press presentation and shows the stubby tail, which had obviously been carefully developed to optimise aerodynamics.

TECHNICAL SPECIFICATION

ENGINE
rear, longitudinal, V6 (65°)

Bore and stroke	85x71 mm
Unitary cubic capacity	402.88
Total cubic capacity	2417.33
Valve gear	twin overhead camshafts
Number of valves	two per cylinder
Compression ratio	9.8:1
Fuel feed	three Weber 42DCN carburettors
Ignition	double, one coil
Coolant	water
Lubrication	dry sump
Maximum power	275 hp at 7500 rpm
Specific power	113.8 hp/litre

TRANSMISSION
Rear-wheel drive

Clutch	multi-disc
Gearbox	en bloc with engine five gears + reverse

BODY
Two-seater barchetta

CHASSIS

Chassis	tubular trellis
Front suspension	independent, double wishbones, coil springs, hydraulic dampers
Rear suspension \	independent, double wishbones, coil springs, hydraulic dampers
Brakes	disc
Steering	-
Fuel tank	-
Tyres front/rear	5.50-15/6.50-15

DIMENSIONS AND WEIGHT

Wheelbase	2320 mm
Track front/rear	1310/1300 mm
Length	-
Width	-
Height	-
Kerb weight	590 kg

PERFORMANCE

Top speed	270 km/h
Power to weight ratio	2.1 kg/hp

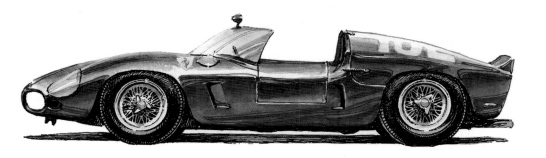

Ferrari 246 SP

1961

Once Enzo Ferrari had lifted the ban on rear engines, Maranello quickly extended the technology to its single-seaters and sports racing cars. Unveiled in February 1961, the 246 SP was the first determined application of that technique, its engine lodged inside the tubular trellis chassis. On top of that truly revolutionary new development, the 246 SP and its 65°, 2,417.33 cc V6 engine were much admired for their aerodynamics, which gave the car an assertive yet elegant look: like the 156 F1, the 246 SP was designed by engineer Carlo Chiti. Its nose had the double oval air intakes, above which were faired optical groups. The windscreen ran around the whole cockpit, linking up with the rear end, which was slightly sloped and had a highly original stubby tail: it was the first time a Ferrari had adopted such feature, which was quickly extended to all its closed wheel cars. The new sports prototype made its debut at the 12 Hours of Sebring in March 1961. Before it went off the track and out of the race, the 246 SP showed it was competitive in the hands of Richie Ginther and Wolfgang von Trips. Its handling qualities really came out on tortuous circuits, like the Madonie mountain roads of the Targa Florio, and the twists, turns and undulations of the Nürburgring's 1,000 kilometres. In Sicily, Olivier Gendebien and von Trips beat the Porsches - as did Willy Mairesse and Pedro Rodriguez in 1962 – while only bad weather kept the Ferrari from certain victory on the German circuit. Together with the Testa Rossa 60/61, the points contribution of the 246 SP helped bring yet another world constructors' championship to Maranello.

The 196 SP was one of a group of cars developed by Maranello to race in 1962 and was unveiled to the press on 24 February of the same year. Externally, the car was identical to the 286 and 248 SP, both of which were also on display in the factory courtyard that day. The difference between the three cars was, obviously, in their engines – the six-cylinder 2 and 2.9-litre for the former and a 2.5 V8 for the latter.

TECHNICAL SPECIFICATION

ENGINE
rear, longitudinal, V6 (60°)

Bore and stroke	77x71 mm (90x75 – 286 SP)
Unitary cubic capacity	330.62 (477.15 – 286 SP)
Total cubic capacity	1983.72 (2862.90 – 286 SP)
Valve gear	single overhead camshaft
Number of valves	two per cylinder
Compression ratio	9.8:1 (9.5:1 – 286 SP)
Fuel feed	three Weber 42 DCN carburettors
Ignition	single, one coil, two distributors
Coolant	water
Lubrication	dry sump
Maximum power	210 hp at 7500 rpm (260 hp at 6800 rpm – 286 SP)
Specific power	105.9 hp/litre (90.8 – 286 SP)

TRANSMISSION
Rear-wheel drive

Clutch	multi-disc
Gearbox	en bloc with engine five gears + reverse

BODY
Barchetta

CHASSIS

Chassis	tubular trellis
Front suspension	independent, double wishbones, coil springs, hydraulic dampers
Rear suspension	independent, double wishbones, coil springs, hydraulic dampers
Brakes	disc
Steering	rack
Fuel tank	-
Tyres front/rear	5.25-15 all round (5.50-15/7.00-15 – 286 SP)

DIMENSIONS AND WEIGHT

Wheelbase	2320 mm
Track front/rear	1240/1200 mm
Length	-
Width	-
Height	-
Kerb weight	600 kg

PERFORMANCE

Top speed	240 km/h (290 – 286 SP)
Power to weight ratio	2.8 kg/hp (2.3 – 286 SP)

Ferrari 196 SP and 286 SP   1962

On 24 February 1962, Ferrari put on an amazing show of vitality by not only unveiling to the press the revised 156 F1 and a sports saloon destined to make its impression on a whole motor racing era and beyond – the 250 GTO – but no fewer than four sports racing cars, which all looked the same but were really powered by different engines. Among them was the 196 SP, with a 1,983.72 cc, 60° V6 single overhead cam engine. Aesthetically, the 196 SP was more or less identical to the 246 SP, an updated '62 version of which was presented on the same day. As with the 246 Sport, the 196 SP had a body that resulted from advanced aerodynamic research: it had a nose that ended in the shape of a wedge and the usual oval air intakes, its windscreen and stubby tail even lower and more tapered. Just above the nose was a small, rectangular intake that channelled air to the radiator. The collection of cars being given their press launch also included a 286 SP identical to the 196, except for its 2.9 litre V6 engine. The most suitable territory for the 196 SP's debut was the Targa Florio's tortuous Madonie road circuit, on which Giancarlo Baghetti and Lorenzo Bandini came second, behind the Ricardo Rodriguez-Olivier Gendebien-Willy Mairesse 246 Sport.

The category in which the 196 SP scored its best results was the European Hillclimbing Championship, the little sports car wearing the colours of the Scuderia Sant'Ambroeus that year and driven by Lodovico Scarfiotti. The power, handling and weight distribution of the 196 were best highlighted by hillclimbs: those qualities enabled Scarfiotti to win three events and gave Ferrari its first European title in that motor sport discipline, breaking Porsche's four-year grip on the championship.

Eight cylinder Ferrari engines were never up to much, at least not until the mid-Seventies. Seen at Maranello for the first time in the D50 single-seaters inherited from Lancia in 1955, that kind of power unit was taken up again in 1960 by Carlo Chiti, who designed a 90° V8 of 2,458.70 cc for the 248 GT. The eight-cylinder for the 248 and 268 SPs was based on that unexploited design.

TECHNICAL SPECIFICATION

ENGINE
rear, longitudinal, V8 (90°)

Bore and stroke	77x66 mm (77x71 – 268 SP)
Unitary cubic capacity	307.33 (330.62 – 268 SP)
Total cubic capacity	2458.70 (2644.96 – 268 SP)
Valve gear	single overhead camshaft
Number of valves	two per cylinder
Compression ratio	9.8:1 (9.6:1 – 268 SP)
Fuel feed	four Weber 40IF2C carburettors
Ignition	single, one distributor
Coolant	water
Lubrication	dry sump
Maximum power	250 km/h at 7400 rpm (260 hp at 7500 rpm – 268 SP)
Specific power	101.7 hp/litre (98.3 – 268 SP)

TRANSMISSION
Rear-wheel drive

Clutch	multi-disc
Gearbox	en bloc with engine five gears + reverse

BODY
Two-seater barchetta

CHASSIS

Chassis	tubular trellis
Front suspension	independent, double wishbones, coil springs, hydraulic dampers
Rear suspension	independent, double wishbones, coil springs, hydraulic dampers
Brakes	disc
Steering	-
Fuel tank	-
Tyres front/rear	5.50-15 / 7.00-15

DIMENSIONS AND WEIGHT

Wheelbase	2320 mm
Track front/rear	1310 / 1300 mm
Length	-
Width	-
Height	-
Kerb weight	660 kg

PERFORMANCE

Top speed	290 km/h
Power to weight ratio	2.6-2.5 kg/hp

Ferrari 248 SP and 268 SP   1962

Another Ferrari sports racing car was there for the press to see in the Prancing Horse's courtyard on 24 February 1962. It had a 90°, 2,458 cc V8 engine fed by four Weber 401F2C carburettors, was called the 248 SP and looked identical to the 196 and 286 SPs. Turning to an eight-cylinder power plant was something new for Ferrari, if we consider that the only engine of like architecture up until that time had been designed by Vittorio Jano for the Lancia D50, eight of which arrived at Maranello in 1955 with Jano himself, technicians and a host of spares. In 1962, the 248 SP joined a substantial entry of Ferrari sports racing cars. The 248 SP bowed in wearing NART colours at the 12 Hours of Sebring on 24 March and driven by Fukp-Ryan, but it did not do well and came 13th. After that disappointing first outing, the car was given a new 2,645 cc V6 engine and under its new name of 248 SP, it underwent qualifying for the 24 Hours of Le Mans equipped with a generous roll bar and driven by Lorenzo Bandini. The 268 SP did not produce good results during its motor racing lifetime; that was not always due to its erratic reliability, it often suffered more than its fair share of plain bad luck. One or the other or both thwarted the efforts of Phil Hill at the Targa Florio, the Rodriguez brothers at the 1000 Kilometres of the Nürburgring and Giancarlo Baghet-ti-Lodovico Scarfiotti in the 24 Hours of Le Mans. The car's career that did not last long and came to an end as 1962 drew to a close.

Armed with its experience of the 246, 196, 286, 248 and 268 SP earlier in the Sixties, Ferrari went back to developing its glorious 12-cylinder in 1965, installing it in a centre-rear position - at last - in a new family of sports racers all identified by the letter P. They were soon to add further lustre to an already glorious list of impressive results and imbue the Ferrari image with even greater fascination, right through to the early Seventies.

The Ferrari 250 GTO competed in its first race at the 12 Hours of Sebring on 24 March 1962, a month to the day after it had been given its press preview. The new car immediately displayed its exceptional qualities: Phil Hill and Olivier Gendebien took a North American Racing Teams liveried car – chassis 3387 GT – to second overall in Florida and victory in the GT category.

TECHNICAL SPECIFICATION

ENGINE
front, longitudinal, V12 (60°)

Bore and stroke	73x58.8 mm
Unitary cubic capacity	246.1
Total cubic capacity	2953.21
Valve gear	single overhead camshaft
Number of valves	two per cylinder
Compression ratio	9.7:1
Fuel feed	six Weber 38DCN carburettors
Ignition	single, one coil, two distributors
Coolant	water
Lubrication	dry sump
Maximum power	295 – 302 hp at 7500 rpm
Specific power	99.9 – 102.3 hp/litre

TRANSMISSION
Rear-wheel drive

Clutch	single dry disc
Gearbox	en bloc with engine five gears + reverse

BODY
Two-seater barchetta

CHASSIS

Chassis	longitudinal and cross members
Front suspension	independent, double wishbones, coil springs, anti-roll bar, coil springs, hydraulic dampers
Rear suspension	live axle, longitudinal semi-elliptic springs, hydraulic dampers
Brakes	disc
Steering	worm and lever
Fuel tank	133 litres
Tyres front/rear	6.00-15.00 / 7.00-15.00

DIMENSIONS AND WEIGHT

Wheelbase	2400 mm
Track front/rear	1354 / 1350 mm
Length	4400 mm
Width	1675 mm
Height	1245 mm
Kerb weight	900 kg

PERFORMANCE

Top speed	280 km/h
Power to weight ratio	3.05-3.0 kg/hp

Ferrari 250 GTO   1962

The Ferrari 250 GTO (Gran Turismo Omologata) is, perhaps, one of the cars that contributed most to consolidating the Ferrari legend, one that brings together in a single entity the charisma of a grand tourer and the performance of a sports racer. It was developed to meet new 1962 regulations that meant the title of world champion constructor would no longer be assigned on the basis of points amassed by sports prototype cars, but grand tourers. Ferrari had already begun work on a high performance GT towards the end of 1961, starting with the short wheelbase chassis of the 250 SWB (2,400 mm) and combining it with the 60° V12 engine from the 250 Testa Rossa. The development team was led by engineer Giotto Bizzarrini and they built a prototype that autumn with a body in plain aluminium. The car was tested with good results at Monza by Stirling Moss and at the Modena Aerautodromo by Willy Mairesse. The new sports racing saloon, which was unveiled to the press in its definitive form in February 1962, immediately attracted a lot of attention and admiration for its clean, aerodynamic shape: it had a prominent, droop snoot of a nose and a stubby tail, styling elements of considerable eminence. After being driven to an extraordinary second place at the 12 Hours of Sebring by Phil Hill-Olivier Gendebien, the GTO showed itself to be a winner in all conditions. The car's list of results is among the most impressive to have been achieved by a Ferrari, and includes two victories in the Tourist Trophy in 1962 with Innes Ireland and in 1963 with Graham Hill; two in the Tour de France driven by Jean Guichet in 1963 and Lucien Bianchi in 1964, plus many others, among them a host of class wins in the principal endurance races of the early Sixties, always hot on the heels of the most powerful overall winners. The GTO showed it was no less effective in hill-climbs, which it often won in the hands of Edoardo Lualdi.

The 250 Gran Turismo Lusso bowed in at the 1962 Paris Motor Show and was a car the luxurious interior of which befitted the sobriety and elegance of the exterior of the Pininfarina body. The 250 GTL in the photograph is the car Battista Pininfarina designed for his personal use, which, unlike the production version, had no air intake on the bonnet.

TECHNICAL SPECIFICATION

ENGINE
front, longitudinal, V12 (60°)

Bore and stroke	73x58.8 mm
Unitary cubic capacity	246.1
Total cubic capacity	2953.21
Valve gear	single overhead camshaft
Number of valves	two per cylinder
Compression ratio	9.2:1
Fuel feed	three Weber 36DCS carburettors
Ignition	single, two distributors
Coolant	water
Lubrication	dry sump
Maximum power	250 hp at 7500 rpm
Specific power	84.7 hp/litre

TRANSMISSION
Rear-wheel drive

Clutch	single dry disc
Gearbox	en bloc with engine four gears + reverse

BODY
Two- seater sports saloon

CHASSIS

Chassis	longitudinal and cross members
Front suspension	independent, double wishbones, coil springs, anti-roll bar, hydraulic dampers
Rear suspension	live axle, longitudinal semi-elliptic springs and push rods, hydraulic dampers
Brakes	disc
Steering	worm and sector
Fuel tank	114 litres
Tyres front/rear	185-15 all round

DIMENSIONS AND WEIGHT

Wheelbase	2400 mm
Track front/rear	1395/1387 mm
Length	4410 mm
Width	1750 mm
Height	1290 mm
Kerb weight	1020-1310 kg

PERFORMANCE

Top speed	240 km/h
Power to weight ratio	4.0-5.2 kg/hp

Ferrari 250 GTL 1962

The Ferrari 250 Gran Turismo Lusso was one of the finest Ferrari sports saloon body designs ever created by Carrozzeria Pininfarina. Into that car, which was unveiled at the 1962 Paris Motor Show, went all the experience gathered by the atelier when creating Fifties grand tourers in terms of style. It was further enhanced by the new features introduced on the SWB and GTO, giving birth to a car of extraordinary elegance and equilibrium. The prominent nose of the GTL owes much to the earlier grand tourers, with the traditional long and narrow oval radiator grill framing round fog lights set into the body and underlined by an unusual three-element chrome bumper bar. The cleanly designed flanks without any form of decoration; clear reference to the sports racing Ferraris, could be found at the rear of the 250 GTL, with its stubby tail and the mirror gently recessed in relation to the line of the boot. The adoption of round optical groups of one or two elements was also a clear reference to the SWB and more in general to the sports racers of those years, with which the 250 GTL also shared the fact that it was built in the workshops of Carrozzeria Scaglietti. The car's 2,400 mm short wheelbase chassis was similar to that of the GTO as was the engine for both the Tipo 168, fed in this case by three Weber 36 DCS carburettors instead of the GTO's six. Not many modifications were made to the 250 GTL between 1962 and 1964, except for the face lifted frontal area in line with that of the a one-off example of the 400 Superamerica, which was exhibited at the 1963 London Motor Show, with headlights faired in Plexiglas. Even though it was not designed for racing, the GTL did compete in a number of events in 1963/4: Taormina-Tacci, for example, took 13th overall in just such a car in the 1964 Targa Florio.

Winner of seven motorcycle world championships with MV Agusta, John Surtees moved into Formula One in 1962 and did well at the wheel of a Lola. He became a Ferrari works driver in 1963, after which he soon confirmed he was a driver of undoubted talent in the Maranello cars: fourth at Monte Carlo (picture), third in Holland, second in Britain and first in Germany, ending the season with fourth place in the drivers' world championship table with 22 points.

TECHNICAL SPECIFICATION

ENGINE
rear, longitudinal, V6 (120°)

Bore and stroke	73x58.8 mm
Unitary cubic capacity	246.1
Total cubic capacity	1476.60
Valve gear	twin overhead camshafts
Number of valves	two per cylinder
Compression ratio	9.8:1
Fuel feed	Bosch direct injection
Ignition	double, two distributors
Coolant	water
Lubrication	dry sump
Maximum power	205 hp at 10,500 rpm
Specific power	138.9 hp/litre

TRANSMISSION
Rear-wheel drive	
Clutch	multi-disc
Gearbox	en bloc with engine five gears + reverse

BODY
Single-seater

CHASSIS
Chassis	tubular trellis
Front suspension	independent, double wishbones, coil springs, hydraulic dampers
Rear suspension	independent, double wishbones, coil springs, two push rods, hydraulic dampers
Brakes	disc
Steering	rack
Fuel tank	two laterals, 121 litres
Tyres front/rear	5.50-15/6.50-15

DIMENSIONS AND WEIGHT
Wheelbase	2380 mm
Track front/rear	1330/1380 mm
Length	3900 mm
Width	790 mm
Height	810 mm
Weight in running order	460 kg

PERFORMANCE
Top speed	260 km/h
Power to weight ratio	2.2 kg/hp

Ferrari 156 F1 1963

Scuderia Ferrari entered a revised version of the 156 F1 for the 1962 Grand Prix of Germany. Driven by Lorenzo Bandini, it had completely modified suspension and a new concept chassis with a slightly longer wheelbase of 2,380 mm. There were also substantial visual differences between the old car raced in 1961/2 and the new: the twin air intakes in the nose gave way to one – still oval – and traditional spoked wheels made way for light alloy rims. The 120° V6 engine group was retained and installed in the rear of the car, inside the chassis's tubular structure; fuel feed was, for the first time, by Bosch direct injection with a high pressure pump. The first real racing season for the 156 was in 1963, a year in which numerous new developments took place in the team. Britain's John Surtees, a seven times world motorcycle champion with MV Agusta, arrived from Lola and he took on the role of number one driver in a team with Lorenzo Bandini and Willy Mairesse. But despite the undoubted ability of the drivers and the quality of the cars, the 1963 season was under the inexorable domination of the Lotus 25, powered by a 1.5 litre Coventry Climax engine. The all-conquering Lotus was the first car in the history of Formula One to have riveted panels, incorporated fuel tanks and a front suspension that had its springs located inside the body. The Lotus 25 was the car in which Jim Clark won seven out of a possible 10 Grands Prix and the 1963 world championship. The Scotsman exhibited a disconcerting supremacy and an exceptional driving ability, leaving victory for John Surtees and his Ferrari in only the Grand Prix of Germany at the Nürburgring and the non-championship Mediterranean event.

The first of the new family of V12 rear-engined Ferrari prototypes was the 1963 250 P, which immediately showed its winning ways and enabled the Prancing Horse to become world champion constructor for the ninth time since 1953. Among the Scuderia's successes that year was victory in the 24 Hours of Le Mans by Lodovico Scarfiotti and Lorenzo Bandini (picture).

TECHNICAL SPECIFICATION

ENGINE
front, longitudinal, V12 (60°)

Bore and stroke	73x58.8 mm
Unitary cubic capacity	246.1
Total cubic capacity	2953.2
Valve gear	single overhead camshaft
Number of valves	two per cylinder
Compression ratio	9.5:1
Fuel feed	six Weber 38DCN carburettors
Ignition	single, one coil, two distributors
Coolant	water
Lubrication	dry sump
Maximum power	310 hp at 7500 rpm
Specific power	104.9 hp/litre

TRANSMISSION
Rear-wheel drive

Clutch	multi-disc
Gearbox	en bloc with engine five gears + reverse

BODY
Two-seater barchetta

CHASSIS

Chassis	tubular trellis
Front suspension	independent, double wishbones, helicoidal springs, hydraulic dampers
Rear suspension	independent, double wishbones, coil springs, hydraulic dampers
Brakes	disc
Steering	rack
Fuel tank	-
Tyres front/rear	5.50-15/7.00-15

DIMENSIONS AND WEIGHT

Wheelbase	2400 mm
Track front/rear	1350/1340 mm
Length	4015 mm
Width	1670 mm
Height	1080 mm
Kerb weight	760 kg

PERFORMANCE

Top speed	290 km/h
Power to weight ratio	2.4 kg/hp

Ferrari 250 P 1963

By this time, the installation of a power unit in the mid-rear position in both the Formula One 156 F1 single-seater and the various categories of sports racer like the 246, 196 and 248 SP had become a matter of course at Maranello, with the creation of purpose-built, increasingly light and resistant chassis that could host an engine in that position. Now, it was time to use that system for the glorious V12. The 1963 250 P was the meeting point between the two technologies and it became the first Ferrari sports racer with a rear engined 12-cylinder power unit. In November 1962, Maranello started testing a new prototype, which comprised the chassis of the 246 SP with a longer, 2,400 mm wheelbase and the three-litre V12 Testa Rossa power plant. Testing continued until March the following year, when the new 250 P was officially unveiled at Monza. The car's soft, sinuous lines echoed the curves of the Ferrari barchettas of the period and boasted a substantial roll bar behind the cockpit – first tests of that safety device were carried out on the 268 SP – and a series of unusual features for a prototype, from the wraparound glass windscreen to the blue cloth upholstery. Right from its maiden race in the 12 Hours of Sebring on 23 March, the 250 P turned in performances of an extraordinary level in terms of both power and reliability. The car took first and second places in the Florida classic, driven by Mike Parkes-Umberto Maglioli and Lodovico Scarfiotti-Nino Vaccarella respectively. That year, Enzo Ferrari could allow himself the luxury of entering cars of the typology best suited to the kind of race and circuit, assigning the 250 P the task of defending the Prancing Horse's honour in long endurance races. Scarfiotti and Lorenzo Bandini won the 24 Hours of Le Mans in the car and John Surtees-Willy Mairesse the 1000 Kilometres of the Nürburgring.

To celebrate the 30th anniversary of the 250 GTO in 1992, a memorable gathering took place at Ferrari's Fiorano track, where all the lucky owners of that extraordinary grand tourer were assembled. That day, a number of rare examples of the car's "big sister" returned to the track: the 330 LMB, built around an almost four-litre (3,967.44 cc), V12 engine in 1963, of which Carrozzeria Scaglietti constructed just four cars.

TECHNICAL SPECIFICATION

ENGINE
front, longitudinal, V12 (60°)

Bore and stroke	77x71 mm
Unitary cubic capacity	330.62
Total cubic capacity	3967.44
Valve gear	single overhead camshaft
Number of valves	two per cylinder
Compression ratio	9.2:1
Fuel feed	six Weber 42DCN carburettors
Ignition	single, one distributor
Coolant	water
Lubrication	dry sump
Maximum power	400 hp at 7500 rpm
Specific power	100.8 hp/litre

TRANSMISSION
Rear-wheel drive	
Clutch	multi-disc
Gearbox	en bloc with engine five gears + reverse

BODY
Two-seater sports saloon

CHASSIS
Chassis	longitudinal and cross members
Front suspension	independent, double wishbones, coil springs, hydraulic dampers
Rear suspension	live axle, longitudinal semi-elliptic springs, hydraulic dampers
Brakes	disc
Steering	worm and sector
Fuel tank	120 litres
Tyres front/rear	6.00-15/7.00-15

DIMENSIONS AND WEIGHT
Wheelbase	2500 mm
Track front/rear	1422/1414 mm
Length	-
Width	-
Height	-
Kerb weight	950 kg

PERFORMANCE
Top speed	280 km/h
Power to weight ratio	2.4 kg/hp

Ferrari 330 LMB 1963

Together with the 250 P, Ferrari also presented a new sports saloon called the 330 LMB at Monza in March 1963, but this car was equipped with an almost four-litre (3,967.44 cc) version of the V12 engine. Only four examples of that car were built by Carrozzeria Scaglietti. This was the distillation of an experiment that had already been carried out on a number of 1962 GTOs, which had also been given the most powerful of the Ferrari V12s. Seen from the outside, the 330 LMB could be considered a marriage between a 250 GTO, which inspired its tapered nose, small oval radiator grill and faired headlights, and the 250 GTL, from which it took its almost identical stubby rear end, in this case with an even more accentuated spoiler. The flanks bore GTO-type air vents, both in the proximity of the front and rear wings, above which were two apertures faired in rectangular fashion, among other things. These were made necessary by the need to house wider tyres inside the wheel housings.

Like the 250 P, the 330 LMB made its debut at the 1963 12 Hours of Sebring, driven by Mike Parkes and Lorenzo Bandini, but the car went off and that put an early end to its race.

The best results achieved by this sports saloon were chalked up in 1963 and include a third place overall at Bridgehampton, USA, with Dan Gurney and a fifth at the 24 Hours of Le Mans by Jack Sears-Mike Salmon in chassis number 4725 SA, entered by Maranello Concessionaires Ltd. A second 330 LMB also competed at Le Mans that day – it was the car that came third at Bridgehampton – driven by Dan Gurney and Jim Hall, but it did not finish. Lorenzo Bandini took eighth place and a class win in the Guards Trophy at Brand Hatch, England in one of the cars.

In 1965, a Ferrari 250 LM driven by Jochen Rindt and Masten Gregory won the 24 Hours of Le Mans and contributed to Maranello becoming the World Sports Car Champions once again. Yet, as far as its outside appearance was concerned, the car was neither a sports racer nor a prototype. It was conceived to take the place of the 250 GTO in the GT category, for which its failure to be homologated left no choice but to pit it directly against the prototypes.

TECHNICAL SPECIFICATION

ENGINE
rear, longitudinal, V12 (60°)

Bore and stroke	77x58.8 mm
Unitary cubic capacity	273.8
Total cubic capacity	3285.7
Valve gear	single overhead camshaft
Number of valves	two per cylinder
Compression ratio	9.7:1
Fuel feed	six Weber 38DCN carburettors
Ignition	single, two coils
Coolant	water
Lubrication	dry sump
Maximum power	320 hp at 7500 rpm
Specific power	97.4 hp/litre

TRANSMISSION
Rear-wheel drive

Clutch	single dry disc
Gearbox	en bloc with engine five gears + reverse

BODY
Two-seater sports saloon

CHASSIS

Chassis	tubular trellis
Front suspension	independent, double wishbones, coil springs, hydraulic dampers
Rear suspension	independent, double wishbones, coil springs, hydraulic dampers
Brakes	disc
Steering	worm and sector
Fuel tank	130 litres
Tyres front/rear	5.50-15/7.00-15

DIMENSIONS AND WEIGHT

Wheelbase	2400 mm
Track front/rear	1350/1340 mm
Length	4090 mm
Width	1700 mm
Height	1115 mm
Kerb weight	850 kg

PERFORMANCE

Top speed	235-295 km/h
Power to weight ratio	2.7 kg/hp

Ferrari 250 Le Mans   1963

After the victories of the GTO, Ferrari went on the hunt for a worthy successor and devised a revolutionary car, which looked more like a prototype than a grand tourer from the outside: it was called the 250 Le Mans. The car first appeared in public at the 1963 Paris Motor Show. That "road going" version of the 250 P, from which it inherited both its wheelbase of 2,400 mm and its three-litre engine installed only in the example shown in Paris, actually seemed like a concept car. Pininfarina gave the 250 LM a particularly engaging shape of great equilibrium. He took his lead from the classically low and aerodynamic front end, to which he added the amply inclined windscreen like that of the GTO/64 and continued with a roll bar that was an integral part of the engine cover, inserted into which was a narrow, vertical rear window. The sports saloon ended with a stubby tail that was very much a part of the Ferrari sports racing cars of those years.

But the 250 Le Mans, of which 33 were built between 1964/5, 31 of them with the 3.3-litre engine, was denied GT category homologation, at least for international competition, and that meant it was obliged to compete against the prototypes, - and it acquitted itself outstandingly well. The racing career of the Le Mans is studded with numerous successes: it won the 1964 12 Hours of Reims, the Swiss mountain Grand Prix, the 1965 500 Kilometres of Spa, the Circuito of Mugello and, most significant of all, the 24 Hours of Le Mans. Pininfarina also built a 250 Le Mans called "berlinetta speciales" or special sports saloons for road use. Exhibited at the Geneva Motor Show in NART colours, that car boasted a roof group divided into two that could be taken off and was hinged in the centre: it also had an ample rear window in Plexiglas similar to others built into the period's Porsche prototypes – but the car never went into production.

Ferrari wrote some of the most significant pages in its history at the 24 Hours of Le Mans, one of which was certainly on the 1964 event, in which this 275 P (photograph) was driven by Umberto Maglioli and Giancarlo Baghetti, but the car went out after an accident on the 68th lap. The other 275 P won the event in the hands of Jean Guichet and Nino Vaccarella, ahead of the two 330 Ps of Graham Hill-Joachim Bonnier and John Surtees-Lorenzo Bandini.

TECHNICAL SPECIFICATION

ENGINE
rear, longitudinal, V12 (60°)

Bore and stroke	77x58.8 mm (77x71 – 330 P)
Unitary cubic capacity	273.8 (330.6 – 330 P)
Total cubic capacity	3285.72 (3967.44 – 330 P)
Valve gear	single overhead camshaft
Number of Valves	two per cylinder
Compression ratio	9.7:1 (9.8:1 – 330 P)
Fuel feed	six Weber 38DCN carburettors
Ignition	single, one distributor
Coolant	water
Lubrication	dry sump
Maximum power	320 hp at 7700 rpm (370 hp at 7300 rpm – 330 P)
Specific power	97.4 hp/litre (93.3 – 330 P)

TRANSMISSION
Rear-wheel drive

Clutch	multi-disc
Gearbox	en bloc with engine five gears + reverse

BODY
Two-seater barchetta

CHASSIS

Chassis	tubular trellis
Front suspension	independent, double wishbones, coil springs, dampers
Rear suspension	independent, double wishbones, coil springs, dampers
Brakes	disc
Steering	-
Fuel tank	-
Tyres front/rear	5.50-15/7.00-15

DIMENSIONS AND WEIGHT

Wheelbase	2500 mm
Track front/rear	1350/1340 mm
Length	4160 mm (4015 – 330 P)
Width	1675 mm (1670 – 330 P)
Height	1055 mm (1080 – 330 P)
Kerb weight	755 kg

PERFORMANCE

Top speed	300 km/h
Power to weight ratio	2.3 kg/hp (2.04 – 330 P)

Ferrari 275 P and 330 P 1964

In 1964, Ferrari had two different versions built of the illustrious GTO, but neither attained the success of their forebear's sports racer and 250 P derivatives in the 1963 grand touring category. The two new cars' chassis and appearance were similar to their redoubtable progenitor, but were an interesting step forward in terms of performance. The first was the 275 P with a 3.3-litre (bore and stroke 77 x 58.8 mm) version of the V12, the power output of which was estimated at around 320 hp; the second was the 330 P, driven by an engine of almost four litres (3,967.44 cc) that generated 370 hp at 7,300 rpm. The new power plants had also been installed in a number of 250 Ps in 1963. The body of the 330 P - built like all the sports racers by Scaglietti - incorporated a number of new features: both the windscreen and roll bar were more inclined, while the ample rear engine cover was of almost the same shape as the 250 LM's, a revolutionary GT that Ferrari was constructing at the time.

The more or less complete domination of Ferrari closed wheel cars in 1962/63 was repeated during the 1964 season. The 275 P took the first two places in the 12 Hours of Sebring, crewed by Mike Parkes-Umberto Maglioli and Ludovico Scarfiotti-Nino Vaccarella and won the 1000 Kilometres of the Nürburgring with Scarfiotti-Vaccarella, who took the 24 Hours of Le Mans with Jean Guichet, ahead of two 330 Ps. The four-litre version won the Tourist Trophy again, as well as the 1000 Kilometres of Paris. To complete a triumphant season for Maranello, the 250 Le Mans produced its first significant results with victories in the 12 Hours of Reims and the Swiss Mountain Grand Prix (Sierre-Montana-Crans), a foretaste of the Prancing Horse's coming dominance in events for sports racing cars.

The year 1964 saw the definitive consecration of John Surtees, whom the British fans nicknamed "Big John": he won the Formula One World Championship at the wheel of a Ferrari 158 F1, just one point ahead of Graham Hill's BRM. The season saw Surtees, pictured here during the Grand Prix of Germany at the Nürburgring, climb to the top of the podium twice – at the Nürburgring and Monza – while Lorenzo Bandini won at Zeltweg, Austria.

TECHNICAL SPECIFICATION

ENGINE
rear, longitudinal, V8 (90°)

Bore and stroke	67x52.8 mm
Unitary cubic capacity	186.15
Total cubic capacity	1489.23
Valve gear	twin overhead camshafts
Number of valves	two per cylinder
Compression ratio	10.5:1
Fuel feed	Bosch direct injection
Ignition	double, one coil, two distributors
Coolant	water
Lubrication	dry sump
Maximum power	210 hp at 11000 rpm
Specific power	141.0 hp/litre

TRANSMISSION
Rear-wheel drive

Clutch	multi-disc
Gearbox	en bloc with engine five gears + reverse

BODY
Single-seater

CHASSIS

Chassis	monocoque, aluminium panels riveted to tubular structure
Front suspension	independent, double wishbones, coil springs, inboard coaxial hydraulic dampers
Rear suspension	independent, double wishbones, coil springs, two pushrods, coaxial dampers
Brakes	disc
Steering	rack
Fuel tanks	two, lateral, 125 litres
Tyres front/rear	5.00-13/7.00-13

DIMENSIONS AND WEIGHT

Wheelbase	2380 mm
Track front/rear	1350/1350 mm
Length	3950 mm
Width	697 mm
Height	768 mm
Kerb weight	468 kg

PERFORMANCE

Top speed	270 km/h
Power to weight ratio	2.2 kg/hp

Ferrari 158 F1 1964

If 1962/63 delivered a wealth of success to Maranello in the sports car and grand tourer categories, the same could be said of Formula One, in which the 156 had shown the
way but was unable to beat either the BRMs or the revolutionary Lotus 25. Things
changed in 1964, when Ferrari broke new ground and came up with the 158, which
was innovative in the areas of both its mechanics and chassis. The choice of engine
was made in favour of a 90° V8 of 1,489.23 cc, boasting Bosch direct fuel injection and
able to put out over 200 hp at almost 11,000 rpm. But the most important new development of all concerned the chassis, with which Ferrari showed it had learnt the les-
sons taught by the English assemblers: the 158 had a monocoque chassis made of a
series of aluminium panels that were riveted to an integrated body architecture of
steel tubes. Inside that structure, the driver sat in an almost reclined position, with the
engine group at his back performing a load-bearing function. That construction
afforded the optimisation of weight distribution and the maximum limitation of bulk:
the 158 was only 76.8 centimetres high and had a kerb weight of just 468 kg. Ferrari
also gave the car new, five-spoke magnesium wheels and, from 1965, the body was
made entirely of glass fibre. The advantages of such innovation did not take long to
register. John Surtees won the Grands Prix of Germany and Italy with consistent
drives and took the last round in the F1 world championship in Mexico to win the
drivers' Formula One World Championship, the sixth for Maranello. Team mate
Lorenzo Bandini, who had won in Austria with the 156, played a determining role in
that championship-winning GP: he collided with Graham Hill, Big John's rival for the
title, and so put Hill and his BRM out of the race and the title chase.

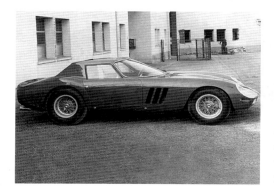

The 1964 version of the GTO had an even more assertive and aerodynamic shape, even if it was less equilibrated compared to the previous model, with its windscreen heavily inclined and the roof group line continuing backwards to an ample roll bar, as on its prototype contemporaries. The results achieved by the GTO/64 came up to expectations, although the car was unable to repeat the scintillating performance of its glorious predecessor.

TECHNICAL SPECIFICATION

ENGINE
front, longitudinal, V12 (60°)

Bore and stroke	73x58.8
Unitary cubic capacity	246.1
Total cubic capacity	2953.2
Valve gear	single overhead camshaft
Number of valves	two per cylinder
Compression ratio	9.7:1
Fuel feed	six Weber 38DCN carburettors
Ignition	single, two distributors
Coolant	water
Lubrication	dry sump
Maximum power	295-302 hp at 7500 rpm
Specific power	99.9-102.3 hp/kg

TRANSMISSION
Rear-wheel drive

Clutch	multi-disc
Gearbox	en bloc with engine five gears + reverse

BODY
Two-seater sports saloon

CHASSIS

Chassis	longitudinal and cross members
Front suspension	independent, double wishbones, coil springs, anti-roll bar, coil springs, telescopic dampers
Rear suspension	live axle, longitudinal semi-elliptic springs, semi-elliptic springs, telescopic dampers
Brakes	disc
Steering	worm and lever
Fuel tank	133 litres
Tyres front/rear	5.50-16/7.00-15

DIMENSIONS AND WEIGHT

Wheelbase	2400 mm
Track front/rear	1354/1350 mm
Length	4210 mm
Width	1760 mm
Height	1140 mm
Kerb weight	900 kg

PERFORMANCE

Top speed	280 km/h
Power to weight ratio	3.05 kg/hp

Ferrari 250 GTO / 64   1964

At the end of 1963, when Maranello was already working on the 250 Le Mans project, Pininfarina was given the task of designing a new "dress" for the 250 GTO, which had covered itself with glory during 1962/63. The Turin carrozziere created a low and streamlined body of highly aerodynamic line for a car with a wider track than the earlier version and, overall, a more assertive if less harmonious and elegant appearance. The ample nose, with its optical groups still faired in Perspex, was even more compressed and boasted two air intakes, one for the long, narrow radiator and the other open at the centre of the bonnet for the engine. The most significant new feature, however, was in the central-rear area of the car, in which Pininfarina used a number of new techniques that were also later transferred to the 250 Le Mans. They included a much inclined windscreen and a roof group that dropped sharply on its way to the rear until it blended with the tail by means of a sort of roll bar. The designer also gave the GTO/64 a stubby tail, which was emphasised by a rather pronounced spoiler. The engine was unchanged and remained the 2,953.2 cc, 60° V12.

In all, Sergio Scaglietti built seven GTO/64s, four by re-bodying '62 cars and three completely new. The later version of the GTO was often campaigned by private teams and gentlemen drivers, who achieved brilliant results, including the many hillclimb victories by Edoardo Lualdi, two class wins in two Targa Florios – in 1964 with Corrado Ferlaino and in '65 with Clemente Ravetto – as well as numerous victories in categories that counted towards the world constructor's championship, plus overall wins in the 500 Kilometres of Spa (Mike Parkes) and the 1000 Kilometres of Paris (Pedro Rodriguez-Jo Schlesser), both in 1964.

The 275 GTB designed by Pininfarina and introduced at the 1964 Paris Motor Show strongly reaffirmed the technology of locating the 12-cylinder engine in the front of the car, as can be seen from that elegant sports saloon's enormous bonnet. The 275 GTB, which was to become one of the most classical and sought after Ferraris, was joined by a 275 GTS which was, at least as far as its body design was concerned, more conventional and shared little with the closed version.

TECHNICAL SPECIFICATION

ENGINE
front, longitudinal, V12 (60°)

Bore and stroke	77x58.8 mm
Unitary cubic capacity	273.8
Total cubic capacity	3285.7
Valve gear	single overhead camshaft
Number of valves	two per cylinder
Compression ratio	9.2:1
Fuel feed	three Weber 40DFI carburettors
Ignition	single, two coils, two distributors
Coolant	water
Lubrication	dry sump
Maximum power	280 hp at 7500 rpm (260 at 7000 – 275 GTS)
Specific power	88.2 hp/litre (79 – GTS)

TRANSMISSION
Rear-wheel drive

Clutch	single dry disc
Gearbox	en bloc with differential five gears + reverse (transaxle – 1966)

BODY
Two-seater coupé/roadster

CHASSIS

Chassis	tubular trellis
Front suspension	independent, double wishbones, coil springs, anti-roll bar, telescopic dampers
Rear suspension	independent, double wishbones, coil springs, anti-roll bar, telescopic dampers
Brakes	disc
Steering	worm and roller
Fuel tank	86 litres
Tyres front/ rear	205 HR 14 all round (185 HR 14 all round GTS)

DIMENSIONS AND WEIGHT

Wheelbase	2400 mm
Track front/rear	1377/1393 mm
Length	4325 mm (4370 – GTS)
Width	1725 mm (1675 – GTS)
Height	1245 mm (1250 – GTS)
Kerb weight	1100 kg (1120 – GTS)

PERFORMANCE

Top speed	250 – 265 km/h (225 – 240 – GTS)
Power to weight ratio	3.9 kg/hp (4.3 – GTS)

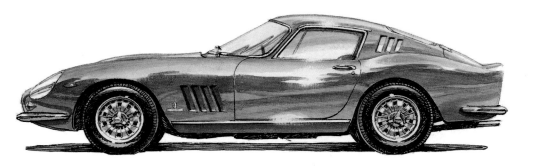

Ferrari 275 GTB and GTS 1964

If Ferrari showed itself to be in the lead with its mid-Sixties Formula One and sports racing cars and in line with the machinery of other key European manufacturers, it revealed itself to be more conservative in the grand tourer segment, protective and proud at the same time, unwilling to veer from the traditional 12 cylinder sports saloon, with its power plant located up front. That tradition was forcefully repeated in the 275 GTB, unveiled at the 1964 Paris Motor Show. The car was of short wheelbase chassis (2,400 mm) and with its potent 3,285.7 cc 12 cylinder engine, offered itself as the new top-of-the-range Ferrari: it was the first Maranello production car with independent suspension on all four wheels. In reality, though, the opinions expressed by the motoring press were not all in agreement that the car should be projected as the latest in a long line of outstanding Pininfarina creations. Many thought the 275 GTB was disproportionate by virtue of its extremely long front, an impression that was accentuated by its rakishly inclined windscreen, which terminated with a generous radiator grill and faired headlights. The roof group, with its rear window ensconced in the centre, and the stubby tail that ended with the suggestion of a spoiler blended one into the other with extraordinary equilibrium. On that sports saloon of sculptural beauty were introduced modern alloy rims with central hub nuts in place of the traditional spoked wheels. Of the 275 GTB, 453 cars were produced. The closed version of the car was much more catholic, in that the 275 GTS seemed simpler and more conventional, with less headlight fairing and windscreen inclination. The car had an essential and clean line, decorated with only some ornate moulding that ran along the length of the flanks and appeared again on the bonnet and boot. The sports saloon generated 280 hp and the GTS 260. Later, the roadster was given lateral air vents, the same kind that graced the 250 GTE but were later replaced with the slatted variety.

Maranello unveiled another coupé-type 2+2 grand tourer at the end of 1963, having installed a 3,967.4 cc, V12 engine in a GTE chassis. The prototype, used by Enzo Ferrari as his personal transport, led to the 330 GT 2+2, which was bodied by Pininfarina and introduced at the 1964 Brussels Motor Show. The aesthetic peculiarity of that car was its double optical groups, a feature that was dropped for the second series of the model.

TECHNICAL SPECIFICATION

ENGINE
front, longitudinal, V12 (60°)

Bore and stroke	77x71 mm
Unitary cubic capacity	330.62
Total cubic capacity	3967.4
Valve gear	single overhead camshaft
Number of valves	two per cylinder
Compression ratio	8.8:1
Fuel feed	three Weber 40DCZ/6 carburettors
Ignition	single, two coils, two distributors
Coolant	water
Lubrication	dry sump
Maximum power	300 hp at 7000 rpm
Specific power	72.9 hp/litre

TRANSMISSION
Rear-wheel drive

Clutch	single dry disc
Gearbox	en bloc with engine Four gears + reverse (five + reverse – 1965)

BODY
2+2 coupé

CHASSIS

Chassis	tubular trellis
Front suspension	independent, double wishbones, coil springs anti-roll bar, telescopic dampers
Rear suspension	live axle, semi-elliptic springs, longitudinal push rods, coil springs, anti-roll bar, telescopic dampers
Brakes	disc
Steering	worm and roller
Fuel tank	90 litres
Tyres front/rear	205 HR 15 all round

DIMENSIONS AND WEIGHT

Wheelbase	2650 mm
Track front/rear	1405/1400 mm
Length	4840
Width	1715 mm
Height	1365 mm
Kerb weight	1380 kg

PERFORMANCE

Top speed	245 km/h
Power to weight ratio	4.6 hp/kg

Ferrari 330 GT 2+2   1964

Over a thousand Ferrari GT 2+2s were produced, so the car was a major sales success for Maranello and opened a new market segment at the same time – the grand touring "station wagon". The company went back to that theme at the end of 1963, bringing out another 2+2 designed around a new concept chassis with a 2,650 mm wheelbase and a four-litre (3,967.4 cc) V12 engine in a front-longitudinal position, linked at first to a four and then five speed and reverse gearbox. Enzo Ferrari tested the first example of the new grand tourer and used the 330 GT as his personal car for some time.

The unfailing Pininfarina designed a sober and essentially bodied grand tourer, devoid of excesses and without any new, ground breaking features. The first series of the 330 GT 2+2, which was unveiled at the 1964 Brussels Motor Show, incorporated a number of elements already seen on the 275 GTS, including the shape of the front air intake, the vents located on the flanks just beyond the wings and the same kind of rear optical groups. The hallmark feature of that grand tourer was the double front head-lights, enclosed in a chrome spinner. That oddity did not curry much favour, and had been replaced by the more catholic singles when the second series of the car came out in mid-1965. Repeating the procedure already used for the 275 GTS, the lateral air vents were updated with three-element slats, which appeared increasingly on Ferraris from that moment on. The Borrani spoked wheels also made way for alloy rims of more modern design, as had been the case with the 275 GTB. Production of the 330 GT 2+2 came to an end in 1967, after 1,080 cars had been built.

The 1964 Ferrari 500 Superfast broke away from the traditional layout of Ferrari GTs, in much the same way as the first generation of Superfasts did: they were built by Pininfarina as one-offs or in small runs between 1960 and 1963. The new version was imposing both for its dimensions – it had a 2,650 mm wheelbase - its performance, powered as it was by a five-litre (4,963 cc) engine that put out 400 hp.

TECHNICAL SPECIFICATION

ENGINE
front, longitudinal, V12 (60°)

Bore and stroke	88x68 mm
Specific cubic capacity	413,5
Total cubic capacity	4963
Valve gear	single overhead camshaft
Number of valves	two per cylinder
Compression ratio	8.8:1
Fuel feed	six Weber 40DC3 carburettors (three Weber 40DCZ/6 – II series)
Ignition	single, two coils, two distributors
Coolant	water
Lubrication	dry sump
Maximum power	400 hp at 6500 rpm
Specific power	80.6 hp/litre

TRANSMISSION
Rear-wheel drive

Clutch	single dry disc
Gearbox	en bloc with engine four gears + overdrive + reverse (five + reverse – II series)

BODY
2+2 coupé

CHASSIS

Chassis	longitudinal and cross members
Front suspension	independent, double wishbones, coil springs, anti-roll bar, telescopic dampers
Rear suspension	live axle, longitudinal semi-elliptic springs, coil springs, telescopic dampers
Brakes	disc
Steering	worm and roller
Fuel tank	100 litres
Tyres front/rear	205-15 all round

DIMENSIONS AND WEIGHT

Wheelbase	2650 mm
Track front/rear	1405/1397 mm
Length	4820 mm
Width	1780 mm
Height	1280 mm
Kerb weight	1400 kg

PERFORMANCE

Top speed	280 km/h
Power to weight ratio	3.5 hp/kg

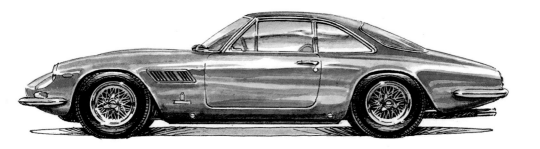

Ferrari 500 Superfast   1964

When the 400 Superamerica went out of production at the end of 1963, Ferrari found itself without a top-of-the-range car, one that could be offered to the most exclusive and carefully selected clientele. To fill that gap, the company introduced a grand tourer at the 1964 Geneva Motor Show that attracted a great deal of motoring press attention for both the choice of its mechanics and its admirable lines, penned once more by Pininfarina.

A new five-litre (4,963 cc) V12 engine that could put out 400 hp at 6,500 rpm was lowered into a 330 GT 2+2 chassis: the car's speedometer was calibrated to 300 km/h and the big V12 took its new charge up to a top speed of about 280 km/h, with acceleration to match.

Pininfarina built 36 bodies for this potent Ferrari combination – plus another with a 330 GT engine. Outwardly, it displayed an imposing, sculptured form, starting with the very long nose that culminated in an oval shaped radiator grill, accentuated by double chrome bumper bars; the cleanliness and essentiality of the car's lines continued at the rear, which narrowed progressively to a stubby tail, where the double bumpers were repeated once again. The quality of the interior was no less refined, with adjustable seats in Connolly leather – as was the gear lever surround – with much of its interior finished by hand: the car also boasted a stereo unit and an air conditioner. The 500 Superfast was built from 1964 to 1966 in two small production runs, during which few aesthetic modifications were made: one of the few involved the lateral air intakes, which were given three slatted elements in place of the more classical 250 GT 2+2 type. Of greater importance was the installation of a new five-speed synchronised gearbox in second series models, which took over from the previous four-speed unit.

After the open wrangling between Ferrari and the motor sport Federation over the lack of homologation of the 250 Le Mans in the grand tourer category, Enzo Ferrari was quick to announce his team's withdrawal from motor racing at the end of 1964. At that year's Grand Prix of Mexico, he fielded his cars in Scuderia NART's white and blue colours: they included a 512 F1 for Lorenzo Bandini, who came third behind John Surtees.

TECHNICAL SPECIFICATION

ENGINE
rear, longitudinal, V12 (180°)

Bore and stroke	56x50.4 mm
Unitary cubic capacity	124.135
Total cubic capacity	1489.63
Valve gear	twin overhead camshafts
Number of valves	two per cylinder
Compression ratio	9.8;1
Fuel feed	Lucas indirect injection
Ignition	single, one coil, two distributors (double – 1965)
Coolant	water
Lubrication	dry sump
Maximum power	220 hp at 12000 rpm
Specific power	147.7 hp/litre

TRANSMISSION
Rear-wheel drive

Clutch	multi-disc
Gearbox	en bloc with engine five gears + reverse

BODY
Single-seater

CHASSIS

Chassis	monocoque with riveted aluminium panels

Front suspension	independent, double wishbones, coil springs, Inboard coaxial dampers
Rear suspension	independent, double wishbones, coil springs, two pushrods, inboard coaxial dampers
Brakes	disc
Steering	rack
Fuel tank	140 litres (two lateral, one rear)
Tyres front/rear	5.50 or 6.00-13/7.00-13

DIMENSIONS AND WEIGHT

Wheelbase	2400 mm
Track front/rear	1350/1350 mm
Length	3950 mm
Width	697 mm
Height	768 mm
Weight in running order	490 kg

PERFORMANCE

Top speed	270 km/h
Power to weight ratio	2.2 kg/hp

Ferrari 512 F1 1964

Ferrari went ahead with the development of a 1.5-litre V12 engine, which had an inclination between the cylinder banks of 180 °, in parallel with the V8 158 F1 project. The 12-cylinder unit was installed in a single-seater called the 512 F1, a car given its racing debut by Lorenzo Bandini as early as the 1964 Grand Prix of Mexico. The new single-seater's significant developments were threefold: the engine had two overhead camshafts for each cylinder bank and Lucas indirect injection; the monocoque chassis's aluminium panels were riveted to a skeleton of steel tubes; and the external shape faithfully followed that of the 158 F1, so that the only differences that set the two cars apart were represented by the number of engine air intakes – eight, of course, for the cylinders of one and twelve for the other.

The motor racing career of the 512 F1 was rather short, because of the new regulations due to come into force at the start of the 1966 season, which called for normally aspirated three-litre engines. That outlawed the 512 F1 before it could be fully exploited. Not surprisingly, the car was no Maranello history maker as far as results were concerned, if we exclude its second place in the 1965 Grand Prix of Monaco. That was the year of Jim Clark's absolute domination in the Lotus 33, yet another extraordinary design by the ingenious Colin Chapman: the Scot won the world championship and scored six victories in six races. Even when the unbeatable Clark-Lotus duo was unable to win, the BRMs of Graham Hill and Jackie Stewart won the Grands Prix of Monaco, Monza and Watkins Glen. The last round in the 1965 title chase in Mexico went to Richie Ginther in the 12-cylinder Honda, giving the Japanese manufacturer, which had been competing directly in F1 since 1964, its first GP win.

Lightness and agility united with a flexible and potent engine were, without doubt, the qualities of the Dino 166 P, which competed for the World Sports Car Championship in 1965. It was not by chance that the Dino driven by Bandini-Vaccarella came fourth overall in the 1000 Kilometres of the Nürburgring that year, heading several prototypes. At the end of the event, the incredulous race officials had the car's V6 engine dismantled to verify its effective cubic capacity.

TECHNICAL SPECIFICATION

ENGINE
rear, longitudinal, V6 (65°)

Bore and stroke	77x57 mm
	(86x57 – 206 SP)
Unitary cubic capacity	265.4 (331.1 – 206 SP)
Total cubic capacity	1592.57 (1986.60 – 206 SP)
Valve gear	single overhead camshaft
	(twin cam – 206 SP)
Number of valves	two per cylinder
Compression ratio	9.8:1 (12.5:1 – 206 SP)
Fuel feed	three Weber 40DCN2
	carburettors
Ignition	double, one coil, two
	distributors
Coolant	water
Lubrication	dry sump
Maximum power	180 hp at 9000 rpm
	(205 hp at 8800 rpm – 206 SP)
Specific power	113 hp/litre (103.1 – 206 SP)

TRANSMISSION
Rear-wheel drive

Clutch	multi-disc
Gearbox	en bloc with engine
	five gears + reverse

BODY
Two-seater sports saloon/barchetta

CHASSIS

Chassis	tubular trellis
Front suspension	independent,
	double wishbones,
	coil springs,
	telescopic dampers
Rear suspension	independent,
	double wishbones,
	coil springs,
	telescopic dampers
Brakes	disc
Steering	rack
Fuel tank	-
Tyres front/rear	5.50-13/6.50-13
	(5.50-13/7.00-13 – 206 SP)

DIMENSIONS AND WEIGHT

Wheelbase	2280 mm
Track front/rear	1350/1350 mm
Length	3820 mm
Width	1570 mm
Height	960 mm (800 – 206 SP)
Kerb weight	586 kg (532 – 206 SP)

PERFORMANCE

Top speed	260 km/h
Power to weight ratio	3.3 kg/hp (2.5 – 206 SP)

Dino 166 P and 206 SP 1965

In 1965, the family of six-cylinder Dinos made way for a new member called the 166 P, which was unveiled at Maranello in February. The little sports racer, the first to carry the name Dino on its bodywork, retraced the soft and sinuous shape of the 330 P2 and had extensive glass surfaces that included a wraparound windscreen, the lateral windows and the back of the roof group, below which was the engine in its central-longitudinal position.

The power plant, derived directly from that of the 1961 156 F1, appertained to the first generation of Dino units, with four overhead camshafts and cylinder banks inclined at a 65° angle. Recourse to a body made entirely of aluminium contributed to keeping the car's weight down to less than 600 kg, ensuring qualities of handling and agility that would make the Dino perform best on medium-fast road routes, circuits and in hillclimbs.

The 1.6-litre 166 P made its first foray into racing at the 1965 1000 Kilometres of Monza, in which its Baghetti-Biscaldi crew were soon forced to retire before they could really show the new car's worth. As well as an incredible fourth overall in the 1000 Kilometres of the Nürburgring driven by Bandini-Vaccarella and victory at Vallelunga, the Dino chalked up its best results in the 1965 European Hillclimb Championship, in which Ludovico Scarfiotti won four of the series' five rounds – the Trento-Bondone, Cesana-Sestrière, Freiburg-Schauinsland and Ollon-Villars. It was with an open top Dino, powered by a different two-litre, six-cylinder engine, able to produce around 200 hp at 8,800 rpm, that the Italian gave Maranello its second European hillclimb title in three years.

Lorenzo Bandini and Sicily's Nino Vaccarella were the unquestioned protagonists of the 1965 Targa Florio. They drove a memorable race at the wheel of a Ferrari 275 P2 barchetta, the qualities of which were perfect for the tortuous roads of the Madonie Mountains. The two established a new lap record for the 72 kilometre route of 39'21" at an average 109.874 km/h and won, beating the Porsche 904/8 being driven by Colin Davis and Gerhard Mitter.

TECHNICAL SPECIFICATION

ENGINE
rear, longitudinal, V12 (60°)

Bore and stroke	77x58.8 mm
	(77x71 – 330 P2)
Unitary cubic capacity	273.8
	(330.62 - 330 P2)
Total cubic capacity	3285.72 (3967.44 – 330 P2)
Valve gear	twin overhead camshafts
Number of valves	two per cylinder
Compression ratio	9.5:1
Fuel feed	six Weber 40DCN2
	carburettors
Ignition	double, one coil
Coolant	water
Lubrication	dry sump
Maximum power	350 hp at 8500 rpm
	(410 at 8000 – 330 P2)
Specific power	106.5 hp
	(103.3 – 330 P2)

TRANSMISSION
Rear-wheel drive

Clutch	multi-disc
Gearbox	en bloc with engine
	five gears + reverse

BODY
Two-seater barchetta

CHASSIS

Chassis	tubular trellis
Front suspension	independent,
	double wishbones,
	coil springs
	telescopic dampers
Rear suspension	independent,
	double wishbones,
	coil springs,
	telescopic dampers
Brakes	disc
Steering	rack
Fuel tank	-
Tyres front/rear	5.50-15/5.00-15
	(5.50-15/6.50-15 – 330 P2)

DIMENSIONS AND WEIGHT

Wheelbase	2400 mm
Track front/rear	1400/1370 mm
Length	4260 mm
Width	1675 mm
Height	1040 mm
Kerb weight	790 kg (820 – 330 P2)

PERFORMANCE

Top speed	300 km/h
Power to weight ratio	2.2 kg/hp (2.0 – 330 P2)

Ferrari 275 P2 and 330 P2   1965

As their designations suggest, the Ferrari 275 P2 and 330 P2 were natural evolutions of the P prototypes raced in 1964. Although ostensibly boasting the same V12 engines, more muscle was extracted from both, with the 275's 3,285.72 cc power plant now generating 350 hp and the 3,967.44 unit of the 330 putting out over 400 hp. The chassis were considerably improved: as with the single-seaters, Maranello opted for a trellis of steel tubes to which aluminium panels were riveted, so lightening and strengthening the barchettas.

The P2's body shape was substantially the same as that of the previous year's prototypes, retaining the sinuous and rounded profile of the mudguards, the ample wraparound windscreen that blended into the arched aerodynamic wing at the rear, becoming an integral part of the abundant engine cover, which could be removed completely to provide the best access to the power unit.

Despite the status of Maranello's adversaries, with Ford committing itself more and more to the World Sports Car Championship with muscular cars driven by eight cylinder motors of up to even seven litres, the Prancing Horse decorously kept its head when faced with such an American onslaught. The 275 P2 still took the 1000 Kilometres of Monza plus an epic victory in the Targa Florio through Lorenzo Bandini and local idol Nino Vaccarella, the "flying headmaster", while the 330 won on the tormented Nürburgring circuit, driven by reigning British F1 world champion John Surtees and Italian Lodovico Scarfiotti.

Those successes, to which should also be added others by the 250 Le Mans and the 365 P, brought Ferrari yet another sports car world title, a successful opening in the first act of its protracted battle with Ford, a company that had become the Prancing Horse's toughest opponent.

The 24 Hours of Le Mans has always been ideal terrain on which to try new technical developments and aerodynamics on racing cars: The 1966 French classic was no different, with the Ferrari 365 P sporting a new engine cover that was more profiled and had a long tail. The body of the sports saloon entered for Le Mans wearing NART's colours and driven by Bob Bondurant-Masten Gregory was built in the Drogo workshops at Modena.

TECHNICAL SPECIFICATION

ENGINE
rear, longitudinal, V12 (60°)

Bore and stroke	81x71 mm
Unitary cubic capacity	365.86
Total cubic capacity	4390.35
Valve gear	single overhead camshaft
Number of valves	two per cylinder
Compression ratio	9.5:1
Fuel feed	six Weber 38DCN carburettors
Ignition	single, one coil
Coolant	water
Lubrication	dry sump
Maximum power	380 hp at 7200 rpm
Specific power	86.5 hp/litre

TRANSMISSION
Rear-wheel drive

Clutch	multi-disc
Gearbox	en bloc with engine five gears + reverse

BODY
Two-seater barchetta

CHASSIS

Chassis	tubular trellis
Front suspension	independent, double wishbones, coil springs, telescopic dampers
Rear Suspension	independent, double wishbones, coil springs telescopic dampers
Brakes	disc
Steering	rack
Fuel tank	-
Tyres front/rear	5.50-15/7.00-15

DIMENSIONS AND WEIGHT

Wheelbase	2400 mm
Track front/rear	1400/1370 mm
Length	4160 mm
Width	1675 mm
Height	1055 mm
Kerb weight	800 kg

PERFORMANCE

Top speed	300 km/h
Power to weight ratio	2.1 kg/hp

Ferrari 365 P   1965

The strength with which to stand up to Ferrari came increasingly from Ford and, in 1965, led Maranello to enter the 365 P2 in which was installed a 12-cylinder engine with just one overhead camshaft and a total cubic capacity of 4,390.35 cc, as well as the 275 and 330 P2. The new sports racer, which was not substantially different from the Scuderia's other prototypes, was especially built for private entrants, who raced it during the 1965 and 1966 seasons.

The 365 P made its first public appearance in Scuderia Filipinetti colours at the 1965 1000 Kilometres of Monza, where Tommy Spychiger-Herbert Muller took it to second place, until a dramatic accident, in which Spychiger was killed, brought the car's race to an end. After that horrific debut, the 365 P went on to take seventh place in the 24 Hours of Le Mans and to win the 12 Hours of Reims, in the NART livery of Ferrari's American importer Luigi Chinetti; the winning drivers were Pedro Rodriguez-Jean Guichet, ahead of a sister car entered by Britain's Maranello Concessionaires driven by John Surtees-Mike Parkes. At the end of the season, Mexican Rodriguez took another second place in the car at the 500 Kilometres of Bridgehampton.

Another three 365 Ps were built for the 1966 season for Scuderias Francorchamps and Filipinetti, plus one for driver David Piper. The cars took on a body shape that was substantially the same as that of the new 330 P3, with a large wraparound windscreen and kept the protruding air intakes at the front of the rear mudguards. That season, which saw the almost unchallenged domination of the Ford Mark IIs and the Porsche 906s, the best the 365 P could do was a fourth place on 5-6 February in the 24 Hours of Daytona, driven by Pedro Rodriguez and Mario Andretti.

In a year dominated by the Brabham-Repcos of driver-constructor Jack Brabham, who became world champion at the end of the season, Ferrari's only F1 victories were scored by John Surtees in the Grand Prix of Belgium and Lodovico Scarfiotti in the Italian GP at Monza (photograph). After severe disagreements with Ferrari sports director Eugenio Dragoni, Surtees left Maranello in mid-season.

TECHNICAL SPECIFICATION

ENGINE
rear, longitudinal, V12 (60°)

Bore and stroke	77x53.5 mm
Unitary cubic capacity	249.1
Total cubic capacity	2989.56
Valve gear	twin overhead camshafts
Number of valves	two per cylinder
Compression ratio	11.8:1
Fuel feed	Lucas indirect injection
Ignition	single or double, one coil, two distributors
Coolant	water
Lubrication	dry sump
Maximum power	360 hp at 10,000 rpm
Specific power	120.4 hp/litre

TRANSMISSION
Rear-wheel drive

Clutch	multi-disc
Gearbox	en bloc with engine five gears + reverse

BODY
Single seater

CHASSIS

Chassis	monocoque with riveted aluminium panels
Front suspension	independent, double wishbones, inboard springs/dampers
Rear suspension	independent, double wishbones, two pushrods, telescopic dampers
Brakes	disc
Steering	rack
Fuel tank	158 litres (two laterals)
Tyres front/rear	5.50-14/7.00-15

DIMENSIONS AND WEIGHT

Wheelbase	2400 mm
Track front/rear	1450/1435 mm
Length	3830 mm
Width	760 mm
Height	870 mm
Weight in running order	548 kg

PERFORMANCE

Top speed	300 km/h
Power to weight ratio	1.5 kg/hp

Ferrari 312 F1 1966

Ferrari 312 F1   1966

Formula One rules were changed for the umpteenth time in 1966 and, as a result, dictated the use of either normally aspirated 3,000 cc or 1,500 cc supercharged engines, all with a minimum weight of 500 kg.

Ferrari took up the challenge with a car that sparked off a series of single-seaters, which Maranello continued to campaign until the early Seventies: it was the 312 F1 galvanised by a three-litre, 60° V12 power plant derived from that of the P2 prototype, with an unchanged bore of 77 mm and stroke decreased to 53.5 mm. So it was a rather conventional car, married to the traditional, tried and tested 12- cylinder and the same monocoque chassis as the 158 and 512. Among the most attractive aesthetic elements of the car were, without doubt, the exhaust pipes, which were painted white: they snaked out of the banks of the 12 cylinder in groups of three and came together in two terminals, one for each side of the car.

The 1966 season was no less difficult and tormented for Ferrari than the previous one: after just a single Grand Prix victory at Watkins Glen, Jim Clark's Lotus was overtaken in the championship table by the Brabham, powered by an eight-cylinder Repco engine. The car was driven by Jack Brabham, boss of the young British-based team, who had won four Grands Epreuves and the world title by the end of the season. The Prancing Horse had to be content with two victories, the first by John Surtees at the Grand Prix of Spa-Francorchamps, and the second by Lodovico Scarfiotti in the Italian GP at Monza: Surtees left the team after his win in Belgium, due to antagonism between him and the Scuderia's sports director, Eugenio Dragoni. The two and four-wheel world champion moved to Cooper-Maserati in time to win the season's last Grand Prix, in Mexico.

The Dino 206 S of 1966 suffered from the same problem as the 250 Le Mans: in fact, Ferrari was unable to build the 50 examples of the car needed for its homologation in the Sport category and the Dino was forced to compete against the big prototypes. But the car still performed competitively and, among other placings, took two seconds, one at the Targa Florio and the other at the 1000 Kilometres of the Nürburgring.

TECHNICAL SPECIFICATION

ENGINE
rear, longitudinal, V6 (65°)

Bore and stroke	86x57 mm
Unitary cubic capacity	331.10
Total cubic capacity	1986.61
Valve gear	twin overhead camshafts
Number of valves	two per cylinder
Compression ratio	10.8:1
Fuel feed	three Weber 42DCN2 carburettors – Lucas injection
Ignition	double, one coil
Coolant	water
Lubrication	dry sump
Maximum power	218 hp at 9000 rpm
Specific power	109.7 hp / litre

TRANSMISSION
Rear-wheel drive

Clutch	multi-disc
Gearbox	en bloc with engine five gears + reverse

BODY
Two-seater sports saloon/ barchetta

CHASSIS

Chassis	tubular trellis
Front suspension	independent, double wishbones, coil springs, telescopic dampers
Rear suspension	independent, double wishbones, coil springs, telescopic dampers
Brakes	disc
Steering	rack
Fuel tank	-
Tyres front/rear	5.50-13 / 6.50 or 7.00-13

DIMENSIONS AND WEIGHT

Wheelbase	2280 mm
Track front/rear	1392 / 1414 mm
Length	3875 mm
Width	1780 mm
Height	985 mm
Kerb weight	580 kg

PERFORMANCE

Top speed	260 km/h
Power to weight ratio	2.4 kg/hp

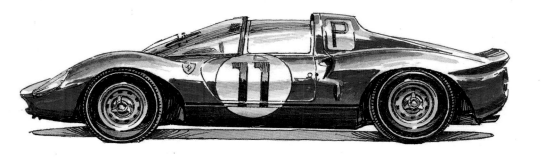

Dino 206 S   1966

On a grey day in 1966, Ferrari introduced its new sports racing car to the press, the Dino 206 S, as well as its new prototype stable mate, the 330 P3, both of splendidly soft and sinuous lines and built at Modena by Carrozzeria Drogo. The renewed Dino, equipped with a 65° V6 fed at first by three Weber 42DCN carburettors and later by Lucas fuel injection, immediately attracted attention for the fascination and compactness of its shape. It had inherited much of its external appeal from the previous 166 P, with its considerable glass surfaces and classical ring-shaped rear wing, which blended into the engine cover.

Maranello intended to build at least 50 of the little sports racers so that it could be granted the homologation the car needed to compete in the Sport category. But Ferrari could not even manage 20, which meant the Dino 206 S had to compete directly against the much more powerful prototypes – and it acquitted itself well. In fact, the 206 S became a bit of a giant killer as it turned in some respectable results against the more potent machines. That was the case in the 1000 Kilometres of the Nürburgring, for instance, in which works drivers Lodovico Scarfiotti and Lorenzo Bandini and the Chinetti-entered Pedro Rodriguez-Richie Ginther came second and third, behind the Joachim Bonnier-Phil Hill Chaparral. On other occasions, only a generous dose of bad luck sent potentially good results up in smoke: in the 1000 Kilometres of Monza and the Targa Florio, which both took place in pouring rain, it was the poor performance of the windscreen wipers that neutered the efforts of the 206 S drivers. But the little car really showed what it was made of on tortuous tracks and hillclimbs. Scarfiotti was a key player once again in the European Hillclimbing Championship, although he had to make do with second place this time, behind Porsche's Gerhard Mitter.

Despite the exceptional power of the 420 hp 12-cylinder engine in such a light chassis, not to mention the quality of the drivers involved – Parkes, Bandini, Surtees – the Ferrari 330 P3 was only able to beat the eight cylinder, seven-litre Ford GT40 on a few occasions. Two of them were at Monza and Spa, but that was not enough to give Ferrari the constructors' championship.

TECHNICAL SPECIFICATION

ENGINE
rear, longitudinal, V12 (60°)

Bore and stroke	77x71 mm
Unitary cubic capacity	330.62
Total cubic capacity	3967.44
Valve gear	twin overhead camshafts
Number of valves	two per cylinder
Compression ratio	11.4:1
Fuel feed	Lucas indirect injection
Ignition	double, coil
Coolant	water
Lubrication	dry sump
Maximum power	420 hp at 8200 rpm
Specific power	106 hp / litre

TRANSMISSION
Rear-wheel drive

Clutch	multi-disc
Gearbox	en bloc with engine
	five gears + reverse

BODY
Two-seater sports saloon / barchetta

CHASSIS

Chassis	tubular trellis
Front suspension	independent, double wishbones, coil springs, telescopic dampers
Rear suspension	independent, double wishbones, coil springs, telescopic dampers
Brakes	disc
Steering	rack
Fuel tank	-
Tyres front/rear	5.50-15 / 7.00-15

DIMENSIONS AND WEIGHT

Wheelbase	2400 mm
Track front/rear	1462 / 1431 mm
Length	4170 mm
Width	1780 mm
Height	950 mm
Kerb weight	720 kg

PERFORMANCE

Top speed	310 km / h
Power to weight ratio	1.7 kg / hp

Ferrari 330 P3 1966

Next to the Dino 206 S at the press presentation in February 1966 was the car with which Ferrari renewed its challenge against Ford in the International Sport and Proto-type Championship: the 330 P3. But even before it hit the track to show what it could do, the car attracted a great deal of attention for the extraordinary beauty of its shape, created by Drogo. In profile, the body was a continuous curved line, from the front to the progression of its considerable wraparound windscreen, the teardrop air intakes inside the actual doors, to the rear wing. That fascinating prototype, made even more aggressive by modern magnesium alloy rims, was equipped with a 3,967.44 cc, 60° V12 engine derived from that of the P2, with the new Lucas indirect fuel injection. The gear-box, with its five forward speeds and reverse, was not made at Maranello but was acquired in Germany. That was a detail symptomatic of the economic and social situa-tion in Italy during the period: trade union agitation that went on throughout the land did not even have mercy on Ferrari, from whose factories just three examples of the new prototype emerged, with chassis numbers 0844, 0846 and 0848.

Absent from the 24 Hours of Daytona on 5 February, the P3 played out the first act of its Ford challenge at the 12 Hours of Sebring, where the American cars took the four top places: the sole Maranello barchetta, entered for Bob Bondurant and Mike Parkes, was forced to retire. The Ford Mark IIs and the GT40s continued to do well for the rest of the season, winning the 24 Hours of Le Mans, among other things, a race that had not slipped though Ferrari's fingers since 1959. The 330 P3 was able to outrace the Fords on just two occasions: at the 1000 Kilometres of Monza, won by Mike Parkes and John Surtees, and at Spa-Francorchamps with Parkes and Lodovico Scarfiotti.

While the 275 GTS could not, in any way, be considered as elegant as the GTB – at least as far as looks went – one could not say the same thing about the GTB/4, which came along two years later. The topless version of that model (photograph) was needed by the American importer Luigi Chinetti, for which reason it was called the 275 GTS/4 NART, and turned out to be equally assertive, if not even more svelte than the sports saloon. Ten cars were built.

TECHNICAL SPECIFICATION

ENGINE
front, longitudinal, V12 (60°)

Bore and stroke	77x58.8 mm
Unitary cubic capacity	273.8
Total cubic capacity	3285.7
Valve gear	twin overhead camshafts
Number of valves	two per cylinder
Compression ratio	9.2:1
Fuel feed	six Weber 40DCN carburettors
Ignition	double, two distributors
Coolant	water
Lubrication	dry sump
Maximum power	300 hp at 8000 rpm
Specific power	91.2 hp/litre

TRANSMISSION
Rear-wheel drive

Clutch	single dry disc
Gearbox	en bloc with differential five gears + reverse

BODY
Two-seater sports saloon/roadster

CHASSIS

Chassis	tubular trellis
Front suspension	independent, double wishbones, coil springs, anti-toll bar, telescopic dampers
Rear suspension	independent, double wishbones, coil springs, anti-roll bar, telescopic dampers
Brakes	disc
Steering	worm and roller
Fuel tank	94 litres
Tyres front/rear	205 HR 14 all round

DIMENSIONS AND WEIGHT

Wheelbase	2400 mm
Track front/rear	1400/1420
Length	4410 mm
Width	1725 mm
Height	1200 mm (1245 – 275 GTS/4)
Kerb weight	1050 kg (1115 – 275 GTS/4)

PERFORMANCE

Top speed	260 km/h (240 – GTS/4)
Power to weight ratio	3.5 kg/hp (3.8 – 275 GTS/4)

Ferrari 275 GTB/4 and GTS/4   1966

When a 275 GTB of such length and prominence made its first appearance at the 1964 Paris Motor Show, one could have imagined it capable of just about anything – except a motor racing career. On the contrary, two years later Carrozzeria Scaglietti began to build racing bodies for a number of 275s called the 275 GTC, which hid all the principal new developments of an engine with new 40 DFI3 carburettors and the valves of the 250 Le Mans. The body, which had longer wings, was made of thinner aluminium and all its glass surfaces were, in fact, in Plexiglas.

Those sports racing saloons concluded the first series of single camshaft 275 GTBs, which was succeeded at the 1966 Paris Motor Show by an updated version of the car with a revised quadruple overhead camshaft V12 engine, from which the denomination GTB/4 came: the car had six 40DCN carburettors in place of the previous model's three 40DC2s as well as a dry sump lubrication system. From the appearance point of view, the GTB/4 was not significantly different from the GTB, if one makes an exception of the new model's more bulbous bonnet to accommodate the six carburettors, plus a few details of which the most significant was greater profiling of the nose and front wings and more wraparound chrome bumper bars. Using the rolling and mechanics of the GTB/4 as its base, in 1967 Ferrari's United States importer Luigi Chinetti gave Pininfarina the task of designing a small number of roadsters – around 10 of them – all of which were built at Carrozzeria Scaglietti in Modena and specifically aimed at the North American market: that is how the 275 GTS/4 NART came about. The imposing and elegant lines of the 275 GTB acquired even more assertiveness and dash once it had lost its roof group, but the success of the GTS/4 was limited to the U.S.

From the union of the 3,67.4 cc V12 power unit of the 330 GT 2+2 with the 2,400 mm short wheelbase chassis of the 275 GTB came the 1966 330 GTC (pictured). Carrozzeria Pininfarina used more of the styling features of the Superfast range for this model, which was further updated with other new developments introduced on the 275 GTB and GTS: the replacement of spoked wheels with new alloy rims was particularly successful.

TECHNICAL SPECIFICATION

ENGINE
front, longitudinal, V12 (60°)

Bore and stroke	77x71 mm
Unitary cubic capacity	330.6
Total cubic capacity	3967.4
Valve gear	single overhead camshaft
Number of valves	two per cylinder
Compression ratio	8.8:1
Fuel feed	three Weber 40DFI carburettors
Ignition	single, two coils, two distributors
Coolant	water
Lubrication	dry sump
Maximum power	300 hp at 7000 rpm
Specific power	75.5 hp / litre

TRANSMISSION
Rear-wheel drive

Clutch	single dry disc
Gearbox	en bloc with differential five gears + reverse

BODY
Two-seater coupé/roadster

CHASSIS

Chassis	tubular trellis
Front suspension	independent, double wishbones, coil springs, anti-roll bar, telescopic dampers
Rear suspension	independent, double wishbones, coil springs, anti-roll bar, telescopic dampers
Brakes	disc
Steering	worm and roller
Fuel tank	90 litres
Tyres front/rear	205 HR 14 all round

DIMENSIONS AND WEIGHT

Wheelbase	2400 mm
Track front/rear	1401 / 1417 mm
Length	4400 mm (4430 – GTS)
Width	1675 mm
Height	1300 mm (1250 – GTS)
Kerb weight	1300 kg (1200 – GTS)

PERFORMANCE

Top speed	245 km / h (235 – GTS)
Power to weight ratio	4.3 kg / hp (4 – GTS)

Ferrari 330 GTC and GTS　　　　1966

Confirming once again its inexhaustible and prolific ability to create, Pininfarina once again interpreted Ferrari's requirements with panache. During the second half of the Sixties, Maranello decided to continue fashioning elegant, high class grand tourers, readying the 330 GTC for the 1966 Geneva Motor Show and, for the next Paris show, a GTS version of the car. Both took their lead from the chassis and the 2,400 mm short wheelbase of the 275 GTB, around which the Turin stylist penned a coupé that embodied all the experience the Prancing Horse had gained from the realisation of its previous cars. The nearest point of reference was, evidently, the 330 GT 2+2 from which the GTC took its soft and equilibrated lines. A radiator grill inspired by that of the 500 Superfast was added, with its small oval air intake for the radiator, underlined by double chrome bumper bars and headlights set into the wings, without their Plexiglas fairing. The three-element slatted air vents on the flanks of the car, just beyond the mudguards, and alloy rims instead of the spoked variety all found their way to the 330 GTC.

The roadster, however, was a logical evolution of the 275 GTS seen a year earlier, from which the new car took its sides and the shape of the rear end, with the same kind of chrome bumper bars and optical groups.

Both new versions were equipped with a 3,967.4 cc, 60° V12 power plant, which developed 300 hp at 7,000 rpm. A few years after the 330 GTC went out of production, Luigi Chinetti commissioned Zagato to design a coupé convertible in 1974, a one-off; but only a series of photographs remain of the car today, taken in front of the Arco della Pace in Milan. To build the car, with its harsh, angular lines, Zagato used a damaged 330 GTC rolling chassis

The extreme Ferraris - the ones with engines of extraordinary power derived from the 4,390.35 cc 12-cylinder unit of the 365 P – have a shape of equal militancy and elegance, of which the 365 California is certainly one. Bodied by Pininfarina in 1966, only 14 of these cars were built, the first of which was unveiled at the Geneva Motor Show. About one 365 California was produced each month, as the attention that had to be paid to detail was considerable.

TECHNICAL SPECIFICATION

ENGINE		CHASSIS	
front, longitudinal, V12 (60°)		*Chassis*	longitudinal and cross members
Bore and stroke	81x71 mm	*Front suspension*	independent,
Unitary cubic capacity	365.86		double wishbones,
Total cubic capacity	4390.35		coil springs,
Valve gear	single overhead camshaft		anti-roll bar, telescopic
Number of valves	two per cylinder		dampers
Compression ratio	8.8:1	*Rear suspension*	live axle, semi-elliptic
Fuel feed	three Weber 40 DFI carburettors		springs and longitudinal pushrods, coil springs,
Ignition	single, two distributors		anti-roll bar, telescopic
Coolant	water		dampers
Lubrication	dry sump	*Brakes*	disc
Maximum power	320 hp at 6600 rpm	*Steering*	power, worm and roller
Specific power	72.2 hp/litre	*Fuel tank*	100 litres
		Tyres front/rear	205 HR 15 all round
TRANSMISSION			
Rear-wheel drive		DIMENSIONS AND WEIGHT	
Clutch	multi-disc	*Wheelbase*	2650 mm
Gearbox	en bloc with engine	*Track front/rear*	1405/1400 mm
	five gears + reverse	*Length*	4900 mm
BODY		*Width*	1780 mm
Roadster		*Height*	1330 mm
		Kerb weight	1320 kg
		PERFORMANCE	
		Top speed	245 km/h
		Power to weight ratio	4.1 kg/hp

Ferrari 365 California   1966

While pressing on with production of models of which up to 1,000 examples and more were built, in the mid-Sixties Maranello continued to commission Pininfarina to build small numbers of exclusive cars to be sold to an elite clientele and on which styling experiments were carried out with a view to extending successful results to cars produced in bigger production runs. That was the case with the 365 California unveiled at the 1966 Geneva Motor Show and of which only 14 examples were built. On that roadster, which took shape around the 2,650 mm wheelbase chassis of the 330 GT 2+2 and the 60° 4390.35 cc V12 engine derived from that of the prototype 365 P, the Turin stylist designed a taut, clean and essential body that was further emphasised by its length of almost five metres. The rather wide (178 cm) and flat nose had the traditional radiator grill of the Superfast type, in this case with its headlights recessed and faired. Meanwhile, the cleanliness of the flanks with a heavily dihedral profile remained uninterrupted by superfluous features: even the door handles were set into air channels, across which ran a small, straight metal strip. The styling feature introduced on the car's tail was significant, with the boot slightly lower than the wings and the adoption of fairly unusual optical groups, which appeared on the car for the first time. The name California also confirmed that Ferrari wished to stupefy, using once more - after the 250 roadster – the denomination for an unusual open top car, destined to leave its indelible mark on Ferrari production. It was not by chance that the 365 California was exhibited at the key motor shows from 1966 to 1967, including the '66 Geneva and the '67 New York.

As well as competing for the Formula Two championship, the Dino single-seater raced in the Tasman Cup series from 1968. The cars used for those events were, in reality, powered by 2.4 litre (246 T / FL) six-cylinder engines. Chris Amon (picture) was one of the drivers who competed in that championship and, after two victories in '68, won the title the following year, with Jochen Rindt second in the points table.

TECHNICAL SPECIFICATION

ENGINE
rear, longitudinal, V6 (65°)

Bore and stroke	86x45.8 mm
	(79.5x53.5 1968)
Unitary cubic capacity	266.04
Total cubic capacity	1596.25
Valve gear	twin overhead camshafts
Number of valves	three per cylinder (four in 1968)
Compression ratio	11:1
Fuel feed	Lucas indirect injection
Ignition	double, one distributor (single, one distributor – 1968)
Coolant	water
Lubrication	dry sump
Maximum power	200 hp at 10,000 rpm (225 hp at 11,000 rpm 1968 and 232 – 1969)
Specific power	125.3 hp / litre (141 – 1968 and 145.3 – 1969)

TRANSMISSION
Rear-wheel drive

Clutch	multi-disc
Gearbox	en bloc with engine five gears + reverse

BODY
Single-seater

CHASSIS

Chassis	semi-monocoque
Front suspension	independent, double wishbones, coil springs, telescopic dampers
Rear suspension	independent, double wishbones, coil springs, telescopic dampers
Brakes	disc
Steering	-
Fuel tank	100 litres (110 – 1968)
Tyres front/rear	5.50-9.50-13 / 6.00-1200-13

DIMENSIONS AND WEIGHT

Wheelbase	2220 mm
Track front/rear	1405 / 1425 mm
Length	-
Width	-
Height	840 mm
Kerb weight	425 kg (430 – 1968)

PERFORMANCE

Top speed	265 km / h
Power to weight ratio	2.1 kg / hp (1.9 – 1968)

Dino 166 F2 1967

In a traditional meeting with his closest collaborators on 6 January 1967 to plan the coming year's programme, Enzo Ferrari astounded them all with a request that seemed impossible to meet, to say the least: he wanted them to built an F2 car to display at the Racing Car Show in Turin from 25 February – 5 March of the same year. That sparked off the mad race against time that led to the construction of the Dino 166 F2, which was built and ready in a record few weeks to make its appearance at the show. The little car was conceived around a 65° V6 engine with three valves per cylinder that was extraordinarily compact: as stipulated by the regulations, only power units derived from one of which at least 500 had been produced could be homologated for the Formula Two championship. That was made possible by Ferrari reaching an agreement with Fiat to use the engine the company installed in a coupé and Bertone roadster.

Having circumvented the regulation in that way, the Dino took to the track in the summer of 1967, but difficulties linked to there being only three valves per cylinder meant the technicians had to create a new four valve version of the unit. The little Dino did not become competitive until the end of 1968, when Ernesto Brambilla won the first race with it at Hockenheim, Germany, and did so again in Rome. Brambilla and Andrea De Adamich also drove the car to three victories out of the four races that made up Argentina's Temporada, but the Dino 166 F2's real glory year - powered by a 2.4 litre six cylinder engine, though - was 1969, when Chris Amon won the Tasman Cup with it on New Zealand and Australian circuits, beating Jochen Rindt's F2 Lotus and team mate Derek Bell's Dino in the process.

After being defeated by Ford in the 1966 International Constructors' Championship, the year in which the American giant also won the prestigious 24 Hours of Le Mans, Maranello did not take long to react: the 330 P4, an evolution of the P3, made its debut in 1967 and that car brought the title back to Ferrari. The Prancing Horse's most memorable victory of the year was in the 24 Hours of Daytona, where the Ferraris crossed the finish line three abreast to take the first three places.

TECHNICAL SPECIFICATION

ENGINE
rear, longitudinal, V12 (60°)

Bore and stroke	77x71 mm
Unitary cubic capacity	330.62
Total cubic capacity	3967.44
Valve gear	twin overhead camshafts
Number of valves	three per cylinder
Compression ratio	11:1
Fuel feed	Lucas indirect injection six Weber 40 DCN2 carburettors (412 P)
Ignition	double, one distributor
Coolant	water
Lubrication	dry sump
Maximum power	450 hp at 8000 rpm (420 hp at 8200 rpm – 412 P)
Specific power	113.4 hp/litre (105.8 – 412 P)

TRANSMISSION
Rear-wheel drive

Clutch	multi-disc
Gearbox	en bloc with engine five gears + reverse

CHASSIS

Chassis	tubular with aluminium reinforcing elements
Front suspension	independent, double wishbones, coil springs telescopic dampers
Rear suspension	independent, double wishbones, coil springs telescopic dampers
Brakes	disc
Steering	rack
Fuel tank	-
Tyres front/rear	10.15-15/12.15-15

DIMENSIONS AND WEIGHT

Wheelbase	2400 mm
Track front/rear	1488/1450 mm
Length	-
Width	-
Height	-
Kerb weight	792 kg

PERFORMANCE

Top speed	320 km/h
Power to weight ratio	1.8 kg/hp (1.9 – 412 P)

Ferrari 330 P4 and 412 P 1967

The third act in the Ferrari - Ford challenge took place in 1967 when Maranello entered the P4, the most extreme version of its P series, for the World Sports Car and Prototype Championship: Ford countered with an update of its GT40. The 330 P4 began to rise from the ashes of the P3 at the end of 1966, with greater effort put into making its four-litre, 12-cylinder more powerful. The version of the engine lowered into the P4 had a new head of three valves per cylinder and an updated Lucas injection system that increased power output to 450 hp at 8,000 rpm. The transmission was also radically revised, while the external shape of the car was still the 330 P3's, even though the new racer had a longer wheelbase and was bulkier than its predecessor. The most substantial difference from the appearance standpoint was in the P4's rims, which were of a new star design. At the same time, the 1966 P3 was re-bodied by Drogo in the style of the P4, was given the new designation of 412 P and passed on to private entrants as a replacement for the 365 P.

On its debut in the 1962 24 Hours of Daytona, the P4 wrote yet another and even more legendary page in the history of the Prancing Horse, inflicting a crushing defeat on Ford on their home ground. The Ferraris took the Florida event's first three places: the two P4s driven by Lorenzo Bandini-Chris Amon and Mike Parkes-Ludovico Scarfiotti plus a 412 P crewed by Pedro Rodriguez-Jean Guichet crossed the finish line three abreast. Bandini and Amon also won the 1000 Kilometres of Monza. Ford and Ferrari only crossed swords again at Le Mans, where the American manufacturer took its revenge and won with a GT40 Mark IV driven by Dan Gurney and A.J. Foyt, who led the two P4s of Scarfiotti and Willy Mairesse across the line, but Ferrari still won the constructors' trophy. The umpteenth change in regulations at the end of 1967 meant that the cubic capacity of the prototypes was limited to three litres from the start of the 1968 season and that brought the P4's career to a grinding halt.

In 1967, the road that led to the construction of the 206 GT, the first Dino road car, was an extremely long and tortuous one. The little sports saloon, with its soft and rounded lines, was undoubtedly elegant but it had been preceded by a number of designs and prototypes built by Pininfarina between 1965 and 1967. The car exhibited at the '67 Turin Motor Show already had all the characteristics of the one that eventually went into production. That first series of Dino 206 GTs added up to about 150 cars.

TECHNICAL SPECIFICATION

ENGINE			CHASSIS	
rear, transverse V6 (65°)			*Chassis*	tubular
			Front suspension	independent,
Bore and stroke	86x57 mm			double wishbones,
Unitary cubic capacity	331.10			coil springs,
Total cubic capacity	1986.6			adjustable dampers
Valve gear	twin overhead camshafts		*Rear suspension*	independent,
Number of valves	two per cylinder			double wishbones,
Compression ratio	9:1			coil springs
Fuel feed	three Weber 40DCNF3			adjustable dampers
	carburettors		*Brakes*	disc
Ignition	single, one distributor		*Steering*	rack
Coolant	water		*Fuel tank*	62 litres
Lubrication	dry sump			(two rear laterals)
Maximum power	180 hp at 8000 rpm		*Tyres front/rear*	185 VR 14 all round
Specific power	90 hp/litre			
			DIMENSIONS AND WEIGHT	
TRANSMISSION			*Wheelbase*	2280 mm
Rear-wheel drive			*Track front/rear*	1425/1400 mm
Clutch	single dry disc		*Length*	4150 mm
Gearbox	en bloc with engine		*Width*	1700 mm
	five gears + reverse		*Height*	1115 mm
			Kerb weight	1180 kg
BODY				
Two-seater sports saloon			PERFORMANCE	
			Top speed	230 km/h
			Power to weight ratio	6.55 kg/hp

Dino 206 GT   1967

The Dino 206 GT went into production at the end of 1968 after a rather long and complex gestation period, both from the styling and mechanical points of view. On the design side, the car was preceded by six different prototypes, built by Pininfarina between the 1965 Paris Motor Show and the 1967 Frankfurt exhibition, in which the numerous new features progressively delineated the little sports saloon until the production blueprint was achieved. The 1,986.6 cc, 65° V6 engine was located in a transverse position, immediately behind the back of the driver, and that demanded another look at weight distribution, including the fuel tanks' position on both sides of the power plant and the radiant mass.

Pininfarina penned a soft, rounded, compact and much equilibrated shape for the car on a wheelbase of just 2,280 mm, which was built entirely of aluminium at Carrozzeria Scaglietti in Modena. The Turin stylist included some features in his design that had graced its earlier cars: they included the elegant air intakes on the dihedral flanks, headlights without fairing but recessed into the wings, the rear window in a vertical position and in depression between two agile pieces of fairing that linked with the engine cover and boot, both of which were slightly lower than the rear wings. The stubby tail housed rounded optical groups and projected the Dino 206 GT along the same lines as Ferrari sports cars of the first half of the Sixties. The design of the alloy wheels was also new, with a three-pointed central hub nut. The two-litre version of the Dino, which the first Maranello illustrated catalogue kept well away from the "real" Ferraris, saying it was "small, quick, safe...almost a Ferrari" stayed on in production until April 1969, one month after the presentation of the 246 version in March in Geneva.

The presence of a 2+2 grand tourer in the Maranello catalogue was, by this time, a regular affair. The 330 GT 2+2 went out of production in 1967, but was immediately followed by the 365 GT, which was given its debut at the Paris Motor Show that same year. Powered by a 4,390.3 cc 12-cylinder engine up front, the car soon made a name for itself as one of high class and elegance with an impressive performance generated by its 320 hp.

TECHNICAL SPECIFICATION

ENGINE
front, longitudinal, V12 (60°)

Bore and stroke	81x71 mm
Unitary cubic capacity	365.8
Total cubic capacity	4390.3
Valve gear	single overhead camshaft
Number of valves	two per cylinder
Compression ratio	8.8:1
Fuel feed	three Weber 40FI carburettors
Ignition	double, one coil, two distributors
Coolant	water
Lubrication	dry sump
Maximum power	320 hp at 6600 rpm
Specific power	72.8 hp / litre

TRANSMISSION
Rear-wheel drive

Clutch	single dry disc
Gearbox	en bloc with engine five gears + reverse

BODY
2+2 coupé

CHASSIS

Chassis	tubular trellis
Front suspension	independent, double wishbones, coil springs, anti-roll bar, telescopic dampers
Rear suspension	independent, double wishbones, coil springs, anti-roll bar, telescopic dampers
Brakes	disc
Steering	rack
Fuel tank	100 litres
Tyres front/rear	205 VR 15 all round

DIMENSIONS AND WEIGHT

Wheelbase	2650 mm
Track front/rear	1440/1472
Length	4980 mm
Width	1785 mm
Height	1345 mm
Kerb weight	1480 kg

PERFORMANCE

Top speed	245 km/h
Power to weight ratio	4.6 kg/hp

Ferrari 365 GT 2+2   1967

The series of prestige 2+2 Ferraris was enriched by a newcomer at the 1967 Paris Motor Show: it was the 365 GT 2+2, which represented the highest expression of the grand tourer in that car segment. The body shape of the new range leader, which was almost five metres long, remained faithful to concepts already expressed by Pininfarina with the Superfasts. That was especially true of the radiator grill, which was made even more sculptural, with its air intake a perfect elliptical shape, recessed between two chromium bumpers, within which were the side and fog lights. Both the ample engine compartment and the car's flanks had clean and sober surfaces, devoid of all interference and a distinctive characteristic of numerous Ferrari models. The rear pillars were of original line and linked with the wings, a feature Pininfarina had used for a one-off version of the 330 GTC Speciale for Princess de Réthy. The sharply cut off sectional rear end hosted two optical groups, each of which was made up of three round, horizontally displaced lights. The car's extremely severe yet elegant exterior was counterbalanced by the equally high-class interior, with seats and door panels upholstered in Connolly leather. The traditionally spartan concept Ferraris was turned on its head as far as optional equipment was concerned: the 365 GT 2+2 had power steering, air conditioning, a heated rear window and a radio, all of which made it one of the most extensively accessoried grand tourers in the history of the Prancing Horse. Although weighing a total of 1,480 kg, on the performance front the car's 4,390 cc V12 still put out 320 hp at 6600 rpm. It remained in production until 1971 during which time a total of 801 examples were built.

The 1968 and 1969 Formula One seasons were among the most troubled in the history of the Prancing Horse: despite continuous modification, the 312 F1 was almost never reliable and seldom came up with the performance necessary to fight the British teams on equal terms. The "garagisti" were joined by the French Matra squad in 1969, their cars powered by an eight cylinder Ford Cosworth engine, a combination that took the world title that year, driven by Jackie Stewart.

TECHNICAL SPECIFICATION

ENGINE
rear, longitudinal, V12 (60°)

Bore and stroke	77x53.5 mm
Unitary cubic capacity	249.1
Total cubic capacity	2989.56
Valve gear	twin overhead camshafts
Number of valves	three per cylinder (4 – 1967)
Compression ratio	11.8:1
Fuel feed	Lucas indirect injection
Ignition	double, one coil, two distributors (single, 1-2 distributors 1968-1969)
Coolant	water
Lubrication	dry sump
Maximum power	390 hp at 10,000 rpm (410 hp at 10,600 rpm – 1967) (436 hp at 11,000 rpm – 1969)
Specific power	130.4 hp/litre (137.1 – 1967), (145.8 – 1969)

TRANSMISSION
Rear-wheel drive

Clutch	multi-disc
Gearbox	en bloc with engine five gears + reverse

BODY
Single-seater

CHASSIS

Chassis	monocoque with riveted aluminium panels
Front suspension	independent, double wishbones, inboard coil springs/dampers
Rear suspension	independent, double wishbones, two longitudinal pushrods, telescopic dampers
Brakes	disc
Steering	rack
Fuel tank	160-182 litres (two laterals)
Tyres front/rear	4.75-10.30-15/5.00-10.00-13.00 or 6.00-12.30-15, 6.00-13.50-15.00

DIMENSIONS AND WEIGHT

Wheelbase	2400 mm
Track front/rear	1550/1560 mm
Length	4050 mm (4060 – 1969)
Width	720 mm (738 – 1969)
Height	850 mm (910 – 1969)
Weight in running order	507 kg (530 – 1969)

PERFORMANCE

Top speed	310 km/h
Power to weight ratio	1.2-1,3 kg/hp

Ferrari 312 F1 1968

For Ferrari, 1967 was a year of transition, at least in Formula One. The three-litre 12-cylinder engine was being further evolved and, during a first stage, generated 390 hp. That went up to 410 hp at 10,600 rpm from the Grand Prix of Italy by the adoption of 48 valves. But still the Scuderia did not win a single round in the world championship, which ended with the title going to Brabham-Repco for the second successive year, this time driven by New Zealander Denny Hulme. To make things worse, the imbalance of the team contributed to the death of Lorenzo Bandini at Monte Carlo, where he was trapped in the burning wreckage of his Ferrari for a long time, and Mike Parkes' serious accident at Spa, which ended his motor racing career.

So in 1968, Ferrari had to engage new drivers and, as well as Chris Amon, took on a young Belgian driver named Jacky Ickx, who immediately showed his driving talent by winning the Grand Prix of France at Rouen in the pouring rain. But that was Maranello's only world championship win in 1968, when the Scuderia went back to racing the 312 F1 without making substantial modifications to either the chassis or engine. The most significant new development of the season was the team's introduction of aerodynamic appendages during practice for the Grand Prix of Belgium, which took their place at the front and rear of the car over the course of the season. The last year in which the 312 F1 competed for the Formula One World Championship was in 1969, when it once again confirmed its mediocre performance capability, even though the power output of its engine had been increased to 436 hp at 11,000 rpm. The best the car could do was take third place in the hands of Jacky Ickx in Holland and sixth and fifth in both the Italian and United States Grands Prix with Pedro Rodriguez at the wheel. All of which contributed a total of just seven points to the Scuderia's position in the constructors' championship.

Having set competition in the Sport Proto-type category to one side for a year, Ferrari decided to change direction in 1968 and go CAN-AM (Canadian American Challenge Cup) motor racing, which was open to sports racing cars of unlimited cubic capacity – Group 7. Maranello's direct involvement in the North American series was even greater in 1969, with the development of a car espe-cially for the series that was much like the 312 P – the 612 CAN-AM (photograph).

TECHNICAL SPECIFICATION

ENGINE		CHASSIS	
rear, longitudinal, V12 (60°)		Chassis	semi-monocoque
		Front suspension	independent,
Bore and stroke	92x78 mm		double wishbones,
Unitary cubic capacity	518.13		coil springs,
Total cubic capacity	6222.36		telescopic dampers
Valve gear	twin overhead camshafts	Rear suspension	independent,
Number of valves	four per cylinder		double wishbones,
Compression ratio	10.5:1		coil springs,
Fuel feed	Lucas indirect injection		telescopic dampers
Ignition	single, one distributor	Brakes	disc
Coolant	water	Steering	rack
Lubrication	dry sump	Fuel tank	-
Maximum power	620 hp qt 7000 rpm	Tyres front/rear	490-1390-15/600-1550-15
	(640 hp at 7700 rpm – 1969)		
		DIMENSIONS AND WEIGHT	
TRANSMISSION		Wheelbase	2450 mm
Rear-wheel drive		Track front/rear	1603/1590 mm
Clutch	multi-disc	Length	4200 mm (3720 – 1969)
Gearbox	en bloc with engine	Width	2240 mm (2140 – 1969)
	four gears + reverse	Height	890 mm
		Kerb weight	700 (680 – 1969)
BODY		PERFORMANCE	
Two-seater barchetta		Top speed	340 km/h
		Power to weight ratio	1.1 kg/hp (1.06 – 1969)

Ferrari 612 CAN-AM 1968

After the historic decision not to compete in the 1968 World Sports Car and Prototype Championship, Maranello seemed to be aiming almost exclusively at Formulas One and Two. The 330 P4, the 412 P for private entrants had also been made redundant by new regulations introduced for sports racers, and it was as a result of that difficult situation that Luigi Chinetti floated the idea of transforming one of the 412 Ps into a CAN-AM car. The Canadian American Challenge Cup was a series of races that took place in the United States and was for Group 7 cars, which were of unlimited cubic capacity and had an overall weight of no more than 700 kg. More than cars, the machines were real "monsters" that could generate around 500 hp. The first Ferrari CAN-AM car appeared in 1967: it was a 412 P modified for Chinetti, plus two semi-official 330 P4s that were renamed 350 CAN-AM.

The cars' cubic capacity was taken to 4,176 to produce a power output of 480 hp, but the Ferraris only achieved the occasional, rather modest placings in the hands of Chris Amon and Jonathan Williams. The CAN-AM project was revived again in 1968 but it was seriously late, so that the new 6.2-litre 12-cylinder 612 could not be tested until October at Monza. The car, which had a flat and imposing shape, was a forerunner of the 312 P, and was only raced by Chris Amon in the last CAN-AM event of the season, the Stardust Grand Prix in Las Vegas on 10 November. There was much anticipation and excitement among American motor racing enthusiasts, who were being bombarded with repeated McLaren victories, to see and hear the car from Maranello, but their enthusiasm was short lived. Amon became involved in a multi-car pile up on the first lap of the race and had to retire immediately.

The Ferrari 612 CAN-AM turned in more consistent and competitive performances in 1969 and was often able to finish up among the leaders with good placings, but it never really gave the McLarens cause for concern: they dominated the series and continually reconfirmed themselves the unquestioned kings of CAN-AM.

Pininfarina had already done it once. Led an earlier operation in the mid-Sixties that meant the Superfast range radically changed the kind of cars Ferrari built up until that time. The Turin stylist did it again in 1968 with the 365 GTB/4, known to the enthusiasts as the Daytona, which made its debut that year. He had designed a revolutionary car, which boasted elements of styling that are with us right up to the present day.

TECHNICAL SPECIFICATION

ENGINE
front, longitudinal, V12 (60°)

Bore and stroke	81x71 mm
Unitary cubic capacity	365.8
Total cubic capacity	4390.3
Valve gear	twin overhead camshafts
Number of valves	two per cylinder
Compression ratio	9.3:1
Fuel feed	six Weber 40DCN 20 carburettors
Ignition	single, two distributors
Coolant	water
Lubrication	dry sump
Maximum power	352 hp at 7500 rpm
Specific power	80.1 hp/litre

TRANSMISSION
Rear-wheel drive

Clutch	single dry disc
Gearbox	en bloc with differential five gears + reverse

BODY
Two-seater sports saloon

CHASSIS

Chassis	tubular trellis
Front suspension	independent, double wishbones, coil springs, anti-roll bar, telescopic dampers
Rear suspension	independent, double wishbones, coil springs, anti-roll bar, telescopic dampers
Brakes	disc
Steering	worm and roller
Fuel tank	100 litres
Tyres front/rear	G70-200 VR 15 all round

DIMENSIONS AND WEIGHT

Wheelbase	2400 mm
Track front/rear	1440/1425 mm
Length	4425 mm
Width	1760 mm
Height	1245 mm
Kerb weight	1280 kg

PERFORMANCE

Top speed	280 km/h
Power to weight ratio	3.6 kg/hp

Ferrari 365 GTB/4 «Daytona» 1968

When the 275 GTB/4 left the scene in 1968, it was a question of replacing it with a car that was up to such a glorious past. But when the 365 GTB/4 made its entrance at the Paris Motor Show and was dubbed the Daytona to mark the splendid success of the 330 P4 at the Florida circuit the year before, it was clear that Ferrari had outdone itself and exceeded all expectations, changing pace once again on anything it had previously offered. If, on the one hand, Maranello reconfirmed its loyalty to the traditional 4,390.3 cc V12 engine in the front longitudinal position at a time when mid-engines were the latest fashion as far as sporting grand tourers were concerned, on the other the Daytona bore a body of an absolutely new shape. Once again, the man who interpreted the intentions of the Prancing Horse so admirably was Pininfarina, who penned a grand tourer that was innovative in the sum total of all its parts: the traditional radiator grill had made way for a much revised droop snoot covered with a large strip of Plexiglas. Underneath were housed the optical groups that gravitated to the sides of the wings, incorporating the indicator lights on the way. The transparent strip was, however, quickly replaced by more traditional pop up lights. The 365 GTB/4 then continued with a long bonnet, slightly raised at the rear to blend in with the windscreen. Starting from the apex of the 'screen pillar, the line of the 365 GTB/4 continued in a single arc, descending towards the rear of the car where the back end hosted the traditional optical groups, comprising pairs of circular elements. The flanks of the Daytona were crossed by a profound and straight groove that linked up with the rear wing and then continued on beyond the rear mudguard, dividing the car into two opposing shells. That feature has remained a constant on almost all Ferraris, right up to the present day.

Pininfarina designed an open version of the 365 GTB/4 Daytona, which was given its first public airing at the 1969 Frankfurt Motor Show. As had already happened with the 275 GTB/4 NART, the roadster version of this car also appeared more assertive and captivating than the sports saloon. The Turin stylist chose yellow as the colour for the car's unveiling, with traditional spoked wheels, which were then replaced by the more modern five element alloy rims.

TECHNICAL SPECIFICATION

ENGINE
front, longitudinal, V12 (60°)

Bore and stroke	81x71 mm
Unitary cubic capacity	365.8
Total cubic capacity	4390.3
Valve gear	twin overhead camshafts
Number of valves	two per cylinder
Compression ratio	9.3:1
Fuel feed	six Weber 40DCN20 carburettors
Ignition	single, two distributors
Coolant	water
Lubrication	dry sump
Maximum power	352 hp at 7500 rpm
Specific power	80.1 hp/litre

TRANSMISSION
Rear-wheel drive

Clutch	single dry disc
Gearbox	en bloc with differential five gears + reverse

BODY
Roadster

CHASSIS

Chassis	tubular trellis
Front suspension	independent, double wishbones, coil springs, anti-roll bar, telescopic dampers
Rear suspension	independent, double wishbones, coil springs. anti-roll bar, telescopic dampers
Brakes	disc
Steering	worm and roller
Fuel tank	100 litres
Tyres front/rear	G70-200 VR 15 all round

DIMENSIONS AND WEIGHT

Wheelbase	2400 mm
Track front/rear	1440/1425 mm
Length	4425 mm
Width	1760 mm
Height	1245 mm
Kerb weight	1200 kg

PERFORMANCE

Top speed	260 km/h
Power to weight ratio	3.4 kg/hp

Ferrari 365 GTS/4 «Daytona» 1969

The roadster version of the Daytona was unveiled at the 1969 Frankfurt Motor Show. Even if a fleeting glance suggested a summary operation by Pininfarina of simply removing the roof group to make a kind of cut down version of the Daytona, the roadster was no less fascinating than the sports saloon. The absence of the roof had the effect of making the car look even more streamlined and assertive. That was partly due to the prominence of its nose, which was already a feature of the GTB/4 and became even more evident on the new car. This impression was further intensified by the colour chosen for the car at the German show – day glow yellow of tremendous impact, which strongly contrasted with the black leather interior. The shelving that ran horizontally along the car's flanks was also black and that emphasised even more the ideal separation between the upper and lower parts of the roadster. In addition, the 365 GTS/4 in Frankfurt was fitted with the traditional spoked wheels, which gave it a vaguely old fashioned look, to tell the truth, rather a strident one and was not in keeping with the modern lines of the car. It was not by chance that five-element Campagnolo alloy rims were soon introduced, as they had already much improved the appeal of the sports saloon.

A month later, Pininfarina also offered a hard top coupé - as in the illustration above - at the Paris Motor Show, but it remained a show car and nothing more. The car had an ample steel roll-bar rather similar to that of the Porsche 911 Targa and a removable rear window. That Daytona, which was made even more extravagant by its dual tone livery - metallic blue for the body and white for the hard top – did not have any effect on future production and remained a one-off example that was not followed up. Regardless of that pure styling exercise, the 365 GTB/4 and GTS/4 were major sales successes and are still among the most coveted Ferraris today.

The 1962 European Hillclimb Championship had been dominated by Ferrari with the Dino 166 P and then again in 1965 with the Dino 206 SP, both cars driven by Lodovico Scarfiotti. To compete for the title in 1969, Maranello built the 212 E, which was driven by Switzerland's Peter Schetty, who demolished the opposition with the car to win the Prancing Horse's third European hillclimb title.

TECHNICAL SPECIFICATION

ENGINE
rear, longitudinal, V12 (180°)

Bore and stroke	65x50 mm
Unitary cubic capacity	165.91
Total cubic capacity	1990.98
Valve gear	twin overhead camshafts
Number of valves	four per cylinder
Compression ratio	11.3:1
Fuel feed	Lucas indirect injection
Ignition	single, one distributor
Coolant	water
Lubrication	dry sump
Maximum power	290 hp at 11,500 rpm
Specific power	145.6 hp/litre

TRANSMISSION
Rear-wheel drive	
Clutch	multi-disc
Gearbox	en bloc with engine
	five gears + reverse

BODY
Two-seater barchetta

CHASSIS
Chassis	tubular trellis
Front suspension	independent,
	double wishbones,
	coil springs,
	telescopic dampers
Rear suspension	independent,
	double wishbones,
	coil springs,
	hydraulic dampers
Brakes	disc
Steering	rack
Fuel tank	30 litres
Tyres front/rear	5.50-10-13/6.00-14-13

DIMENSIONS AND WEIGHT
Wheelbase	2340 mm
Track front/rear	1485/1535 mm
Length	-
Width	-
Height	-
Kerb weight	530 kg

PERFORMANCE
Top speed	250 km/h
Power top weight ratio	1.8 kg/hp

Ferrari 212 E   1969

As if commitments to Formulas One and Two, the International Constructors' Championship, the Tasman Cup and CAN-AM were not enough, in 1969 Ferrari decided to also compete for the European Hillclimb Championship again with a car built especially for that kind of event: it was called the 212 E.

Maranello gave itself two objectives in the construction of the prototype – power, especially at low revs, and overall lightness of the structure to enable the car to be agile and handle well on the European continent's rough, narrow roads on which it would compete. The first objective was achieved by deciding on a 12-cylinder boxer engine, which meant the V between the cylinder banks was open to 180° in the two-litre (1,990.98 cc) version that generated 290 hp at 11,500 rpm, connected to a gearbox with five speeds and a reverse. The second objective was met by building a trellis chassis in tubes of various diameters that was rigid yet light, on which was placed a body that was nothing more than a series of thin plastic sheets joined together. With water and oil aboard, the car only weighed 530 kg. Great care was also taken with the 212 E's weight distribution and unsuspended mass: for example, the rear brakes were fitted close to the gearbox in an inboard position. With that car Peter Schetty, a hillclimb specialist who had been tempted away from Abarth in early 1969, faced no opposition strong enough to impede his inexorable progress. So little opposition, in fact, that Schetty won every single round in the European championship that year, to which should be added two other non-title victories at the start of the season. He established a new record on every course on which he competed with the 212 E, except the Berchtesgaden-Rossfeld due to wet asphalt. This remarkable performance leading to the conquest of the 1969 European Hillclimb Championship bolstered Ferrari in a year in which the Rosse achieved few other positive results.

For its return to sports car and prototype motor racing, in 1969 Ferrari, came up with the 312 P, a barchetta of extraordinarily low and aerodynamic line, powered by a 12-cylinder, three-litre engine. But the car won no races that year and was regularly beaten by the Porsche 908. The 312 P failed to win at the 24 Hours of Le Mans, for instance, because the drivers found it hard to settle into its cramped cockpit, especially the lanky Mike Parkes (pictured).

TECHNICAL SPECIFICATION

ENGINE
rear, longitudinal, V12 (60°)

Bore and stroke	77x53.5 mm
Unitary cubic capacity	249.12
Total cubic capacity	2989.95
Valve gear	twin overhead camshafts
Number of valves	four per cylinder
Compression ratio	11:1
Fuel feed	Lucas indirect injection
Ignition	single, Dinoplex
Coolant	water
Lubrication	dry sump
Maximum power	420 hp at 9800 rpm
Specific power	140.4 hp / litre

TRANSMISSION
Rear-wheel drive

Clutch	multi-disc
Gearbox	en bloc with engine
	five gears + reverse

BODY
Two-seater barchetta/sports saloon

CHASSIS

Chassis	semi-monocoque
Front suspension	independent,
	double wishbones,
	coil springs,
	telescopic dampers
Rear suspension	independent,
	double wishbones,
	coil springs,
	telescopic dampers
Brakes	disc
Steering	rack
Fuel tank	120 litres
Tyres front/rear	525 M13 all round

DIMENSIONS AND WEIGHT

Wheelbase	2370 mm
Track front/rear	1425 / 1400 mm
Length	4230 mm
Width	1980 mm
Height	890 mm
Kerb weight	680 kg

PERFORMANCE

Top speed	320 km/h
Power to weight ratio	1.6 kg/hp

Ferrari 312 P   1969

After a year's sabbatical, Ferrari went back to entering two works cars in the International Constructors' Championship in 1969 and brought out a new concept prototype for the purpose, which was unveiled to journalists at the Prancing Horse's traditional end-of-year press conference on 14 December 1968. Enzo Ferrari had a completely unexpected surprise up his sleeve for the occasion: he took the wraps off the 312 P, powered by a three-litre (2,989.95 cc) V12 unit, which was essential if the car was to compete under the new regulations. The car stupefied the writers with its sleek aerodynamic shape.

The most recent addition to the P generation continued with the flat, streamlined shape. Maranello had already experimented the year before with that kind of configuration in the 612 CAN-AM: an extremely low, droop snoot nose with headlights enclosed in Plexiglas fairing, a cockpit in the centre of the car's body immediately in front of the potent 12-cylinder power unit in its rear-longitudinal position. Designed by Franco Rocchi, the engine had twin overhead camshafts and was fed by a Lucas indirect injection system to generate a healthy 420 hp at 9,800 rpm.

Ferrari's difficulty in being able to operate a sports racing programme as it should be run and the calibre of its opponents - especially Porsche and its 908 - impeded the 312 P from doing well at Sebring, Monza, the Nürburgring and Le Mans, where closed cars competed. All the Prancing Horse could do was to take a lowly fourth place at Britain's Brand Hatch and a second in the 1000 Kilometres of Spa, which were slim pickings for a team with so many world titles to its credit. An umpteenth change in the regulations for 1970 called for five-litre engines in prototype cars and that meant curtains for the 312 P and its motor racing career as a works car the following year. Instead, the new regs opened up the way for cars of new conception: the 512 S and M, which were to come up against the Porsche 917, the Ferraris' most implacable adversary.

The 330 GTC was given Maranello's 4,390.3 cc 12-cylinder engine for 1969: that is how the 365 GTC began to take shape and, aesthetically, was little different from the previous 1966 model, if we exclude the absence of three-element slatted air vents at the sides and the opening of two small rectangular vents on the bonnet. The same modifications were made to the 330 GTS, which was also given the 4.4-litre engine at the end of 1968.

TECHNICAL SPECIFICATION

ENGINE
front, longitudinal, V12 (60°)

Bore and stroke	81x71 mm
Unitary cubic capacity	365.86
Total cubic capacity	4390.3
Valve gear	single overhead camshaft
Number of valves	two per cylinder
Compression ratio	8.8:1
Fuel feed	three Weber 40DFI carburettors
Ignition	single, one coil, two distributors
Coolant	water
Lubrication	dry sump
Maximum power	320 hp at 6600 rpm
Specific power	72.8 hp/litre

TRANSMISSION
Rear-wheel drive

Clutch	multi-disc
Gearbox	en bloc with differential five gears + reverse

BODY
Two-seater coupé/roadster

CHASSIS

Chassis	tubular trellis
Front suspension	independent, double wishbones, coil springs, anti-roll bar, telescopic dampers
Rear suspension	independent, double wishbones, coil springs, anti-roll bar, telescopic dampers
Brakes	disc
Steering	rack
Fuel tank	90 litres
Tyres front/rear	205/70 VR 14 all round

DIMENSIONS AND WEIGHT

Wheelbase	2400 mm
Track front/rear	1401/1417 mm
Length	4470 (4430 – 365 GTS)
Width	1670 mm (1675 – 365 GTS)
Height	1300 mm (1250 – 365 GTS)
Kerb weight	1300 kg (1200 – 365 GTS)

PERFORMANCE

Top speed	245 km/h (235 – 365 GTS)
Power to weight ratio	4.1 kg/hp (3.7 – 365 GTS)

Ferrari 365 GTC and GTS   1969

The Ferrari 330 GTC and GTS grand tourers introduced respectively at the 1966 Geneva and Paris motor shows were both reinvigorated between 1968 and 1969 by the installation of Maranello's 4,390.3 cc 12-cylinder engine, which had only been the preserve of the 365 roadster up until that time. That is how the 365 GTC took shape, as did the corresponding GTS roadster, which now had its power output increased by 20 hp from the existing model's 300 hp to 320 hp at 6,600 revolutions per minute. From the aesthetics point of view, the coupé almost fully reproduced the body shape of the 330. The new car's radiator grill was of the Superfast variety, as were the rear end and the surfaces of the flanks, which became completely smooth after having lost the three-element slatted air intakes: these were replaced with air vents on the bonnet near the windscreen. The rear of the car remained unchanged: it retained the existing optical groups and the split, two-element chromed bumper bars.

The same approach was taken with the roadster, which reiterated the shape of the 330 GTS, the only variations being localised in the rear area: compared to the previous model, the boot shape had been slightly recessed, a situation in which the profile of the boot protruded little from that of the car and had the suggestion of a barely perceptible spoiler. In this case, too, many features of the previous model were retained, including the optical groups and the shape of the chrome plated bumper bars. The 365 GTC and GTS remained in production until 1970 and generated success in both the European and overseas markets, especially the closed version. A total of 153 GTCs and 20 roadsters had been built by the time construction of the two models had come to an end. The appearance of the 365 GTB/4 Daytona at the 1968 Paris Motor Show, with its extraordinary multitude of new developments and features, had already overtaken the two older cars.

As he was committed to the World Sports Car Championship, Ignazio Giunti was not a regular member of the Ferrari Formula One team. In fact, he only competed in a few Grands Prix, among them the Belgian at Spa-Francorchamps (photograph), where he came fourth behind the Matra-Simca of Jean-Pierre Beltoise. The 312 B did not become competitive until nigh on the end of the season, during which period it won four GPs, three with Jacky Ickx and one with Clay Regazzoni.

TECHNICAL SPECIFICATION

ENGINE
rear, longitudinal, V12 (180°)

Bore and stroke	78.5x51.5 mm
Unitary cubic capacity	249.2
Total cubic capacity	2991.01
Valve gear	twin overhead camshafts
Number of valves	four per cylinder
Compression ratio	11.8 :1
Fuel feed	Lucas indirect injection
Ignition	single, Dinoplex
Coolant	water
Lubrication	dry sump
Maximum power	460 hp at 12,000 rpm
Specific power	153.7 hp/litre

TRANSMISSION
Rear-wheel drive

Clutch	multi-disc
Gearbox	en bloc with differential
	five gears + reverse

BODY
Single-seater

CHASSIS

Chassis	monocoque
Front suspension	independent,
	double wishbones,
	inboard coil
	springs/dampers
Rear suspension	independent,
	double wishbones,
	two pushrods,
	telescopic dampers
Brakes	disc
Steering	rack
Fuel tanks	200 litres (two laterals)
Tyres front/rear	9.00-22-13 / 12.50-26-15

DIMENSIONS AND WEIGHT

Wheelbase	2385 mm
Track front/rear	1565 / 1575 mm
Length	4020 mm
Width	742 mm
Height	956 mm
Weight in running order	551 kg

PERFORMANCE

Top speed	310 km/h
Power to weight ratio	1.2 kg/hp

Ferrari 312 B   1970

Only three victories in four seasons of the Formula One World Championship from 1966 to 1969, that last, catastrophic season in which the Prancing Horse plummeted to the bottom of the table having scored only seven points. An almost unheard of situation that forced Ferrari to radically change direction and design a car with both an innovative engine and chassis for 1970. The experience accumulated in 1969 with the 212 E's 12-cylinder boxer power unit was transferred to the new Formula One engine, designed and developed by Mauro Forghieri, for which he also adopted a 180° cylinder bank inclination, each one with two overhead camshafts and four valves per cylinder. There was a significant new development of the car's monocoque chassis, the integrated structure of which extended beyond the cockpit, hiding part of the power plant and making the whole rear end more rigid. The back wing was no less revolutionary, located as it was in correspondence with the car's tyres and immediately in front of the two enormous faired radiators, in a cantilevered position above the V12.

After a brief stay with Brabham, Jacky Ickx returned to Ferrari during the season and became Ignazio Giunti's team mate and then Clay Regazzoni's. But the first concrete results did not begin to emerge until the Grand Prix of Germany, by which time Jochen Rindt and his Lotus 72 already had a firm grip on the world championship. Ickx came second behind the Austrian and his Lotus at Hockenheim. But at the next Grand Prix on Rindt's home territory, the Belgian drove the 312 B to victory and was followed across the line in second place by Regazzoni to make it a Ferrari doppietta. The Swiss driver won at Monza after the accident in which world championship leader Rindt lost his life. Ickx won twice more during the closing stages of the season in Canada and Mexico, as a result of which he ended his season five points behind Jochen Rindt, who became Formula One's only posthumous world champion.

In 1970, Ferrari accepted Porsche's challenge in the World Sports Car Championship and competed with long and short tailed versions of its 512 S in the series, dependent on the kind of circuit involved. Powered by a V12 engine of almost five litres (4,993.53 cc), the Ferrari could still do little against the works Porsche 917 Ks, which dominated the season and permitted Maranello to score just one victory, in the 12 Hours of Sebring.

TECHNICAL SPECIFICATION

ENGINE
rear, longitudinal, V12 (60°)

Bore and stroke	87x70 mm
Unitary cubic capacity	416.27
Total cubic capacity	4993.53
Valve gear	twin overhead camshafts
Number of valves	four per cylinder
Compression ratio	11.5:1
Fuel feed	Lucas indirect injection
Ignition	single, one distributor
Coolant	water
Lubrication	dry sump
Maximum power	550 hp at 8500 rpm
Specific power	110.1 hp/litre

TRANSMISSION
Rear-wheel drive

Clutch	multi-disc
Gearbox	en bloc with engine
	five gears + reverse

BODY
Two-seater sports saloon/barchetta

CHASSIS

Chassis	semi-monocoque
Front suspension	independent,
	double wishbones,
	coil springs,
	dampers
Rear suspension	independent,
	double wishbones,
	coil springs,
	dampers
Brakes	disc
Steering	rack
Fuel tank	120 litres (two laterals)
Tyres front/rear	4.25-11.50-15, 6.00-14.50-15

DIMENSIONS AND WEIGHT

Wheelbase	2400 mm
Track front/rear	1518/1511 mm
Length	-
Width	-
Height	-
Kerb weight	845 kg

PERFORMANCE

Top speed	340 km/h
Power to weight ratio	1.5 kg/hp

Ferrari 512 S   1970

The new World Sports Car Championship regulations that came into force in 1968 dictated that competing cars' cubic capacity had to be limited to three litres and prototypes to five, of which 50 examples – later reduced 25 – had to have been built: a measure that pushed would-be competitors into developing and building racing cars of extraordinary power. The first to take up the challenge was Porsche, which exhibited its 12-cylinder, 4.5-litre 917 at the 1969 Geneva Motor Show –and it was a car able to generate 520 hp. As early as the end of that year, the new "monster" from Stuttgart demonstrated its impressive prowess by winning its debut appearance in the 1,000 Kilometres of Zeltweg.

Ferrari countered with the 512 S with which to compete against the German phenomenon in 1970, a car constructed around a 4,993.53 cc, 12-cylinder engine and unveiled at the 1969 Turin Motor Show in the form of a futuristic prototype designed by Pininfarina. While it displayed fewer soft and rounded lines than the 330 P4, the 512 S was another extraordinarily aggressive car, a flat and wide looking missile, its shape emphasised by an imposing engine cover that was completely detachable and widened in correspondence with the rear wings to accommodate 15-inch tyres. Both the Porsche and Ferrari had interchangeable long and short rear ends for use as dictated by the championship's various circuits.

The title went to the Porsche prototypes, after they had won no fewer than nine of the championship's 10 races – Stuttgart used the Porsche 908 to win the Targa Florio and the 1000 Kilometres of the Nürburgring – demonstrating a disconcerting supremacy in terms of both reliability and performance. Driven by Ignazio Giunti, Nino Vaccarella and Mario Andretti, the 512 S was only able to claim victory in the 12 Hours of Sebring in Florida.

Just six months after the Ferrari Dino 206 GT went on sale, the Dino 246 GT made its debut at the 1969 Geneva Motor Show. Although the cars did not look much different except in a few details, the big news was the installation of a 2.4-litre engine. One of the major contributors to the Dino's notoriety was its starring role in a well known TV series playing Roger Moore and Tony Curtis, in which the car was the unquestioned protagonist of wild car chases.

TECHNICAL SPECIFICATION

ENGINE
rear, transverse, V6 (65°)

Bore and stroke	92.5x60 mm
Unitary cubic capacity	403.20
Total cubic capacity	2419.20
Valve gear	twin overhead camshafts
Number of valves	two per cylinder
Compression ratio	9:1
Fuel feed	three Weber 40DCNF1-DCNF7 carburettors
Ignition	single, one distributor
Coolant	water
Lubrication	dry sump
Maximum power	195 hp at 7500 rpm
Specific power	80 hp / litre

TRANSMISSION
Rear-wheel drive

Clutch	single dry disc
Gearbox	en bloc with engine five gears + reverse

BODY
Two-seater coupé/roadster

CHASSIS

Chassis	longitudinal and cross members
Front suspension	independent, double wishbones, coil springs, telescopic dampers
Rear suspension	independent, double wishbones, coil springs, telescopic dampers
Brakes	disc
Steering	rack
Fuel tank	70 litres
Tyres front/rear	205/70 VR 14 all round

DIMENSIONS AND WEIGHT

Wheelbase	2340 mm
Track front/rear	1425/1400 mm
Length	4235 mm
Width	1700 mm
Height	1135 mm
Kerb weight	1080 kg

PERFORMANCE

Top speed	245 km/h
Power to weight ratio	5.5 kg/hp

Dino 246 GT and GTS 1970

The Dino 246, heir to the 206 GT, was introduced at the 1969 Geneva Motor Show. It had the same layout as the previous model, but boasted a revised 65° V6 engine of 2,419.20 cc, fed by three Weber 40DCNF1 carburettors to begin with and DCNF7s later to generate 195 hp at 7,500 rpm. The new 246 inherited the 206's five-speed and reverse gearbox and its chassis design, which was, however, 60 mm longer enabling its body to be lengthened by 85 mm. Externally, the two models looked more or less identical and could only be told apart by a few details: while the 206's petrol filler cap was on the outside and built into the left hand pillar of the rear window, the 246 GT's was hidden behind a small, round door in the same colour as the car's body. Other items that helped tell the two apart were their alloy rims: the 246 no longer had the three-pointed central wing nut, but a circular hub cap on which the Dino logo was reproduced, encircled by five wheel nuts. The sales success of the 246 GT, which stayed in production until 1974, was repeated with the GTS, which joined the coupé in the market place in 1972 and was built exclusively for sale in the United States. As well as from the absence of the small rear windows, the GTS could be distinguished from the GT by its integrated 206 S-type roll bar, on which there were three small air intakes that were essential to channelling air to the rear window when the hood was up. Once it had been taken off, the rectangular black plastic hard top could be lodged behind the seats.

Luigi Chinetti entered a Dino 246 GT for the 1972 24 Hours of Le Mans to be driven by Frenchmen Pierre Laffeach and Gilles Doncieux, who came 17th overall.

The modified 512 Ms – M for modified in the car's designation – for the 1971 World Sports Car Championship were run exclusively by private teams. Ferrari intended to develop a new sports racer called the 312 PB, which took to the track in 1971. The 512 M sports racing car scored a few reasonable placings in the world series and won a number of minor non-championship races.

TECHNICAL SPECIFICATION

ENGINE
rear, longitudinal, V12 (60°)

Bore and stroke	87x70 mm
Unitary cubic capacity	416.1
Total cubic capacity	4993.53
Valve gear	twin overhead camshafts
Number of valves	four per cylinder
Compression ratio	11.5:1
Fuel feed	Lucas indirect injection
Ignition	single, one distributor
Coolant	water
Lubrication	dry sump
Maximum power	610 hp at 9000 rpm
Specific power	122.1 hp/litre

TRANSMISSION
Rear-wheel drive

Clutch	multi-disc
Gearbox	en bloc with engine
	five gears + reverse

BODY
Two-seater sports saloon/barchetta

CHASSIS

Chassis	semi-monocoque
Front suspension	independent,
	double wishbones,
	coil springs,
	dampers
Rear suspension	independent,
	double wishbones,
	coil springs,
	dampers
Brakes	disc
Steering	rack
Fuel tank	120 litres (two laterals)
Tyres front/rear	4.25-11.50-15, 6.00-14.50-15

DIMENSIONS AND WEIGHT

Wheelbase	2400 mm
Track front/rear	1518/1511 mm
Length	-
Width	-
Height	-
Kerb weight	815 kg

PERFORMANCE

Top speed	310 km/h
Power to weight ratio	1.3 kg/hp

Ferrari 512 M   1971

To plug the gap between the Ferraris and the powerful and reliable Porsche 917s, Maranello gave the modified version of the 512 S – M for modified – its first outing at the end of the 1970 season. The car raced for the first time in the 9 Hours of Kyalami in South Africa, where it was driven by Jacky Ickx and Ignazio Giunti: the 512 M immediately took the lead and stayed there to win, ahead of the works Porsches. The M version of the 512 differed from the S in numerous details: the nose took on an even more inclined progression, with a single air intake that ran the length of its lower edge, the profile of the wings and the sides, which had become less cluttered and straight, with two ample air vents in the wheel housings just behind the water radiators. The elegant slatted cover over the 512 S's 12-cylinder power plant left room for an arched roll bar that linked with the immense "bonnet", at the centre of which was an awkward looking dynamic air intake to cool the V12.

Just when its seemed the 512 had found performance and reliability, Ferrari handed over the development and entry of the car in races to private teams, preferring to concentrate its efforts on the development of a new concept sports racer – the boxer-engined 312 PB. The best results obtained by the 512 M during the 1971 season were a victory by Loos-Pesch in the 3 Hours of Le Mans, two thirds, one by Mark Donohue and David Hobbs with a car entered by Team Penske in the 12 Hours of Sebring and the other by Sam Posey and Tony Adamowicz with a NART car in the 24 Hours of Le Mans. The decision by Ferrari to sacrifice the 512 M in favour of the new 312 PB turned out to be a winning one, because the agile and powerful 312 was often competitive in 1971, even when it came up against the five-litre prototypes, and promised even better things to come in what might turn out to be an extraordinary 1972.

The logical evolution of the 312 B was the 312 B2, but that car was unable to compete at the same level as its predecessor – especially not the way the B did towards the end of 1970 - in 1971 and 1972, the two seasons in which it raced. The picture shows Switzerland's Clay Regazzoni at the Modena circuit in 1972, conducting one of a number of tests in a 312 B2, which had a small supplementary fuel tank on its right side.

TECHNICAL SPECIFICATION

ENGINE
rear, longitudinal, V12 (180°)

Bore and stroke	80x49.6 mm
Unitary cubic capacity	249,3
Total cubic capacity	2991.8
Valve gear	twin overhead camshafts
Number of valves	four per cylinder
Compression ratio	11.5:1
Fuel feed	Lucas indirect injection
Ignition	single, Dinoplex Magneti-Marelli electronic
Coolant	water
Lubrication	dry sump
Maximum power	470 hp at 12,600 rpm
Specific power	157.1 hp/kg

TRANSMISSION
Rear-wheel drive

Clutch	multi-disc
Gearbox	en bloc with engine five gears + reverse

BODY
Single-seater

CHASSIS

Chassis	monocoque with riveted aluminium panels
Front suspension	independent, double wishbones, inboard coil springs/dampers
Rear suspension	independent, double wishbones, inboard coil springs/dampers
Brakes	disc
Steering	rack
Fuel tank	233 litres (two laterals)
Tyres front/rear	8.6-200-13, 13.5-240-15

DIMENSIONS AND WEIGHT

Wheelbase	2426 mm
Track front/rear	1523/1580 mm
Length	4020 mm
Width	742 mm
Height	956 mm
Weight in running order	560 kg (578 – 1972)

PERFORMANCE

Top speed	320 km/h
Power to weight ratio	1.2 kg/hp

Ferrari 312 B2   1971

The Ferrari 312 B2 took over from the 312 B at Monaco, after the older car had taken Mario Andretti to victory again in the opening race of the 1971 season, the Grand Prix of Kyalami in South Africa. The new car repeated the layout of its predecessor but it also brought in significant new developments. The power of the V12 boxer engine with opposed cylinders was increased to 470 hp at 12,600 rpm by modifying the bore and stroke (80x49.6 mm). While the front end of the car repeated the architecture of the 312 B, with its nose just a little flatter and squarer, the new developments were concentrated behind the cockpit, where Mauro Forghieri had designed fairing that created an angularly aerodynamic shape, which covered the mechanics and blended into the central area of the rear wing. Another new feature at the back of the car was represented by the dampers, which were located in a horizontal position. But despite those innovations, the 1971 season was not as positive as the previous one for Ferrari. Making the most of his remarkable wet weather driving ability, Jacky Ickx was able to win the Grand Prix of Holland in the rain, while no fewer than seven championship races went to the 003 Tyrrell Ford. Six Grands Prix were won for the British team by Jackie Stewart, who also became world champion at the end of the season, and one victory was scored by François Cévert.

The 312 B2's rear suspension was revised and a little more power was squeezed out of its V12 boxer engine for the 1972 season, but to hardly any effect. Once again, the car was disappointing and was able to clock up just one victory for Maranello, on the tortuous Nürburgring driven once more by Jacky Ickx. Ferrari was never able to compete for the world title on equal terms that year: the 1971 championship was dominated by Jackie Stewart's Tyrrell and the Lotus 72 of Brazilian Emerson Fittipaldi, who won the '72 world title. But Maranello's faith in the car was reconfirmed in 1973, when it became, not surprisingly, the B3.

After a whole year of development and testing carried out in 1971 World Sports Car Championship races in which Maranello's new 312 PB sports racer showed what it could do, 1972 was the year of the car's definitive consecration. Driven by a line-up of top drivers, who included Ickx, Regazzoni, Redman, Andretti, Merzario and Munari, the 312 PB won Maranello's 13th and last in a glorious series of world sports car titles.

TECHNICAL SPECIFICATION

ENGINE		CHASSIS	
rear, longitudinal, V12 (180°)		*Chassis*	simi-monocoque
		Front suspension	independent,
Bore and stroke	80x49.6 mm		double wishbones,
Unitary cubic capacity	249.3		coil springs,
Total cubic capacity	2991.80		telescopic dampers
Valve gear	twin overhead camshafts	*Rear suspension*	independent,
Number of valves	four per cylinder		double wishbones
Compression ratio	11.5:1		coil springs,
Fuel feed	Lucas indirect injection		telescopic dampers
Ignition	single, Dinoplex	*Brakes*	disc
	Magneti-Marelli electronic	*Steering*	rack
Coolant	water	*Fuel tank*	120 litres
Lubrication	dry sump	*Tyres front/rear*	8.6-20-13 / 13.5-24-15
Maximum power	450 hp at 11,000 rpm		
Specific power	150.4 hp / litre	DIMENSIONS AND WEIGHT	
		Wheelbase	2220 mm
TRANSMISSION		*Track front/rear*	1425 / 1448 mm
Rear-wheel drive		*Length*	-
Clutch	multi-disc	*Width*	-
Gearbox	en bloc with engine	*Height*	-
	five gears + reverse	*Kerb weight*	665 kg
BODY		PERFORMANCE	
Two-seater barchetta		*Top speed*	320 km / h
		Power to weight ratio	1.5 kg / hp

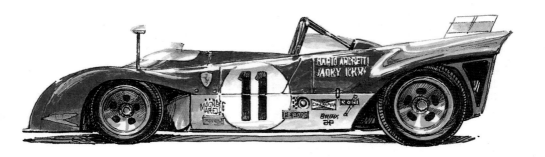

Ferrari 312 PB 1971

The five-litre sports racing cars had such a short life because the motor sport regulations for 1972 went back to admitting cars powered by three-litre engines. Ferrari was certainly not caught on the hop, having already developed the innovative 312 PB in 1971 racing. It was a car built around their 12-cylinder boxer engine, which had been used successfully by Maranello's Formula One cars for a number of years and was then lowered into a car that bore no relation to the enormous 512 S and M that preceded it. Indeed, the 312 PB was much smaller and more compact, with a 2,220 mm wheelbase, and had a semi-monocoque chassis with the 12-cylinder boxer power unit and en bloc five-speed gearbox, inclined and nestling longitudinally in the rear.

As with the 212 E, a major research effort went into the correct distribution of the 312 PB's mass and the containment of its weight to around 650 kg. The water radiators were located at the sides of the engine and the 120-litre fuel tank was in the lower left area of the barchetta to counterbalance the weight of the driver sitting on the right. The PB's speed and handling were tested in racing as early as 1971. That season, the car often started from pole position and stayed up with the leaders for a long time before it had to retire, either with mechanical trouble or due to its unlucky involvement in dramatic accidents. Ignazio Giunti died in exactly that way at the wheel of a PB in the 1971 1,000 Kilometres of Buenos Aires. The 312 PB's first win came at the end of the season in the 9 Hours of Kyalami, but the year of the car's definitive consecration was 1972. That was when the new Ferrari won the 1,000 Kilometres of Buenos Aires again, as well as similar races at Brands Hatch, Monza, Spa, Zeltweg, the 6 Hours of Daytona, the Targa Florio and at Watkins Glen. The 312 PBs also raced in 1973, but they came up against the Matra-Simca MS 670s and that was an almost unbeatable adversary, against which the Ferrari was only able to win once, in the 1,000 Kilometres of Monza, driven by Jacky Ickx and Brian Redman.

The 1971 Geneva Motor Show was the venue at which Ferrari's 365 GTC/4 was presented to the press and public. Like its 365 GTB/4 predecessor, the car was of an especially modern line, even if less ingenious than the Daytona, but still with a number of innovative styling details that included front bumpers integrated into its nose. The car in the picture with the Prancing Horse on its side was the personal transport of Sergio Pininfarina.

TECHNICAL SPECIFICATION

ENGINE
front, longitudinal, V12 (60°)

Bore and stroke	81x71 mm
Unitary cubic capacity	365.86
Total cubic capacity	4390.3
Valve gear	twin overhead camshafts
Number of valves	two per cylinder
Compression ratio	8.8:1
Fuel feed	six Weber 38DCOE carburettors
Ignition	single, one distributor
Coolant	water
Lubrication	dry sump
Maximum power	340 hp at 6800 rpm
Specific power	77.4 hp/litre

TRANSMISSION

Rear-wheel drive	
Clutch	single dry disc
Gearbox	en bloc with engine five gears + reverse

BODY
Two-seater coupé

CHASSIS

Chassis	tubular trellis
Front suspension	independent, double wishbones, coil springs, anti-roll bar, telescopic dampers
Rear suspension	independent, double wishbones, coil springs, anti-roll bar, telescopic dampers
Brakes	disc
Steering	worm and roller
Fuel tank	110 litres
Tyres front/rear	215/70 VR 15 all round

DIMENSIONS AND WEIGHT

Wheelbase	2500 mm
Track front/rear	1470/1470 mm
Length	4570 mm
Width	1780 mm
Height	1270 mm
Kerb weight	1450 kg

PERFORMANCE

Top speed	260 km/h
Power to weight ratio	4.3 kg/hp

Ferrari 365 GTC/4   1971

The 365 GTC/4 exhibited at the 1971 Geneva Motor Show represented a genealogy of Ferraris all rolled into one, as different from the high range grand tourers that went before it bearing the 365 denomination as it was from the cars that were to succeed it in the Seventies.

Designed around the traditional 4,390.3 cc 12-cylinder engine slotted into a shorter 2,500 mm wheelbase chassis, Pininfarina created a two-seater coupé with two occasional places in the back of sinuous and streamlined shape that was clearly developed in the stylist's new wind tunnel, which came into operation during that period. The most significant new feature of the 365 GTC/4 from the styling point of view was a radiator grill encircled by a broad ring that acted as bumper bars, placed at the extremity of the car's long and tapered nose. Within that were located lidded headlights and, on the bonnet, two rectangular air intakes to cool the six-cylinder power unit and its six Weber 38DCOE carburettors. As on the Daytona, the roof group surfaces, rear window and boot all blended into one before being brusquely interrupted by the tail. Seen from the side, the GTC made an impact, with its sinuous, almost wave-like profile and the pointed form of the tail lights, which made an almost perfect triangle with the pillars.

The rear end, which was slightly in depression compared to the boot profile, was given three-element circular optical groups, later to become more ubiquitous on the cars of the Prancing Horse, among them the 365 GT/4 BB. Measured against its illustrious progenitor with which it shared its five-spoke alloy rims and the engine's two overhead camshafts per cylinder bank, the 365 GTC/4 was certainly less innovative: it was not by chance that the car registered a diminished sales success. Between 1971 and 1972, Maranello produced 500 examples of this model.

The concept of a chassis comprising two opposed shells, which was an ingenious first time feature of the 1968 365 GTB/4 Daytona, was used again for the 365 GT/4 2+2, unveiled in 1972. The soft, rounded lines typical of the Ferrari grand tourers designed by Pininfarina made way for a more taut shape, characterised by live angles that were equally elegant and essential.

TECHNICAL SPECIFICATION

ENGINE	
front, longitudinal, V12 (60°)	
Bore and stroke	81x71 mm
Unitary cubic capacity	365.8
Total cubic capacity	4390.3
Valve gear	twin overhead camshafts
Number of valves	two per cylinder
Compression ratio	8.8:1
Fuel feed	six Weber 38DCOE 59/60 carburettors
Ignition	single, one distributor
Coolant	water
Lubrication	dry sump
Maximum power	340 hp at 6800 rpm
Specific power	77.4 hp/litre

TRANSMISSION	
Rear-wheel drive	
Clutch	single dry disc
Gearbox	en bloc with engine five gears + reverse

BODY
2+2 coupé

CHASSIS	
Chassis	tubular trellis
Front suspension	indipendent, double wishbones, coil springs, anti-roll bar, telescopic dampers
Rear suspension	indipendent, double wishbones, coil springs, anti-roll bar, telescopic dampers
Brakes	disc
Steering	worm and roller
Fuel tank	120 litres
Tyres front/rear	215/70 VR 15 all round

DIMENSIONS AND WEIGHT	
Wheelbase	2700 mm
Track front/rear	1470/1500 mm
Length	4800 mm
Width	1800 mm
Height	1290 mm
Kerb weight	1500 kg

PERFORMANCE	
Top speed	245 km/h
Power to weight ratio	5.3 kg/hp

Ferrari 365 GT/4 2+2   1972

Just four years after the 1968 introduction of the 365 Daytona, a car with which Ferrari changed the face of its grand tourers turned out to be no less revolutionary: it was called the 365 GT/4 2+2. Exploiting a 2,700 mm chassis right down to the last millimetre, Pininfarina brought to life a three-volume car closer to a saloon than a coupé, in which four people could travel together in comfort.

The Turin-based body stylist chose a clean and elegant line for the Ferrari 365 GT/4 2+2, distinguished by a taut and angular shape, with a massive bumper made in expanded resin, inside which was the radiator's air intake. The dominant design motif was the deep furrow - identical to the kind first seen on the original Daytona - that ran in a straight line along the entirety of both flanks, uniting the wheel housings and dividing the car perfectly into two opposing shells. There was a slatted vent in the centre of the ample and profiled bonnet that channelled air to the 65° V12 power unit. The determining role of the car's body shape was once again played by the GT/4 2+2's equally ample glass surfaces, which provided excellent visibility that was not exactly a common feature of Ferrari grand tourers.

The interior of the 2+2 was especially refined: the car's seats were upholstered in leather, and there was no lack of other optional equipment, such as a radio, air conditioner, electric windows and power steering.

With a kerb weight of 1,500 kg, the Ferrari 365 GT/4 2+2 could not claim lightness as one of its virtues, so Maranello selected its 4,390 cc V12 engine that had a veritable battery of six Weber 38DCOE carburettors, all of which helped to generate a maximum of 340 hp at 6,800 rpm that could take the car to a top speed of 245 km/h.

Ferrari's 1973 was a year of transition, as the racing department went looking for a car able to increase the competitiveness of the Scuderia. The various versions of the 312 B3 built during the course of the season were part of the search and ranged from the "snowplough" by Mauro Forghieri to the more aerodynamic example pictured here during testing by Belgium's Jacky Ickx in his last season with Ferrari.

TECHNICAL SPECIFICATION

ENGINE
rear, longitudinal, V12 (180°)

Bore and stroke	80x49.6 mm
Unitary cubic capacity	249.3
Total cubic capacity	2991.80
Valve gear	twin overhead camshafts
Number of valves	four per cylinder
Compression ratio	11.5:1
Fuel feed	Lucas indirect injection
Ignition	single, Dinoplex Magneti Marelli electronic
Coolant	water
Lubrication	dry sump
Maximum power	485 hp at 12,500 rpm
Specific power	162.1 hp/litre

TRANSMISSION
Rear-wheel drive	
Clutch	multi-disc
Gearbox	en bloc with differential five gears + reverse

SINGLE-SEATER
Body

CHASSIS
Chassis	monocoque
Front suspension	independent, double wishbones, inboard coil springs/dampers, telescopic dampers
Rear suspension	independent, double wishbones, coil springs, telescopic dampers
Brakes	disc
Steering	rack
Fuel tank	230 litres (two laterals)
Tyres front/rear	9.0-20.0-13, 14.0-26.0-13

DIMENSIONS AND WEIGHT
Wheelbase	2500 mm
Track front/rear	1625/1605 mm
Length	4335 mm
Width	2056 mm
Height	900 mm
Weight in running order	578 kg

PERFORMANCE
Top speed	325 km/h
Power to weight ratio	1.1 kg/hp

Ferrari 312 B3 1973

With the advent of the 312 B in the early Seventies, Ferrari found a satisfactory level of competitiveness in Formula One, but even so, it was unable to achieve reasonable results, if one excludes 1970. So it came as no surprise that the racing department was still hunting for a definitive shape by the end of 1972 for the following season's car. The first 312 B3 created by Mauro Forghieri remained a prototype and was never raced. It was the single-seater they nicknamed the snowplough, because of the unusual shape of its nose and the huge front wing it carried as an integral part of the bodywork: a wing so wide it partially hid the car's tyres.

The B3 that made its debut at the first Grand Prix of the season was a more traditional car, in that it had a monocoque chassis built for the first time in Great Britain, a 12-cylinder boxer engine capable of generating 485 hp at 12,500 rpm and tyres by Goodyear, a company beginning its first period of cooperation with Maranello, replacing Firestone as it did so.

But this second version of the B3 was also uncompetitive and only enabled works drivers Jacky Ickx and Arturo Merzario to score modest placings. But before the season came to an end, Forghieri made some drastic changes to the project and they resulted in important modifications that were later also transferred to the Prancing Horse's single-seaters of the future. One of the most visible was the large central air intake or scoop that was placed above the cockpit behind the driver to channel air to the engine group.

This final version of the B3 was raced for the first time during the second half of the season and was more competitive, suggesting a rosier future for Scuderia Ferrari. It then benefited from further development work with the 1974 season in mind. But 1973 still came to a close with Tyrrell and Jackie Stewart winning the drivers' world championship.

Carrozzeria Bertone did not design many cars for Ferrari: a 166 cabriolet in the early Fifties, an interesting body for the SWB chassis and, 10 years later, a concept car called the Rainbow. But in 1973, with Fiat playing a leading role, Bertone bodied a V8 2+2 that was called the Dino 308 GT/4, a car that remained in production until 1980.

TECHNICAL SPECIFICATION

ENGINE
central, transverse, V8 (90°)

Bore and stroke	81x71 mm
Unitary cubic capacity	365.86
Total cubic capacity	2926.90
Valve gear	twin overhead camshafts
Number of valves	two per cylinder
Compression ratio	8.8:1
Fuel feed	four Weber 40DCNF carburettors
Ignition	single, two distributors
Coolant	water
Lubrication	dry sump
Maximum power	255 hp at 7700 rpm
Specific power	85 hp/litre

TRANSMISSION
Rear-wheel drive

Clutch	single dry disc
Gearbox	en bloc with engine five gears + reverse

BODY
2+2 coupé

CHASSIS

Chassis	tubular trellis
Front suspension	independent, double wishbones, coil springs, dampers
Rear suspension	independent, double wishbones, coil springs, dampers
Brakes	disc
Steering	rack
Fuel tank	80 litres
Tyres front/rear	205/70 VR 14 all round

DIMENSIONS AND WEIGHT

Wheelbase	2550 mm
Track front/rear	1460/1460 mm
Length	4300 mm
Width	1710 mm
Height	1210 mm
Kerb weight	1150 kg

PERFORMANCE

Top speed	236 km/h
Power to weight ratio	4.5 kg/hp

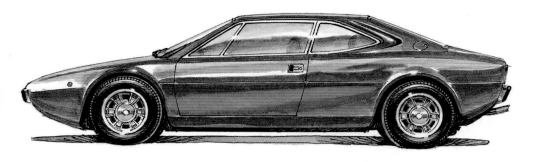

Dino 308 GT/4 1973

Pininfarina's monopoly of Ferrari car design left little leeway for other stylists and from the mid-Fifties his company penned all the grand tourers that came out of the Maranello factory – up until 1973. That year, Carrozzeria Bertone was given the chance to create a small 2+2 called the Dino 308 GT/4. It was Fiat, in whose orbit Ferrari took its place in 1969, who played a leading role in the operation, pushing hard until Bertone was given the task of bodying the car. The characteristics of the Dino 308 GT/4 included some features already expressed during the period by the body stylist from Grugliasco, Italy, on other designs for cars, like the Lamborghini Urraco and the world rally championship winning Lancia Stratos, with its transverse engine located in the centre of the car. Making its first public appearance on the Bertone stand at the 1973 Paris Motor Show, the new 2+2 coupé was of rather compact and sober shape, without the front and rear overhangs typical of Pininfarina's designs. The car was powered by a 90° V8 engine of three litres (2,926.9 cc), fed by four Weber 40DCNF carburettors: it developed 255 hp at 7,700 rpm that took the car to a maximum speed of 236 km/h. It was the location of the power unit in the centre of the car that permitted Bertone to design a 2+2 body on a chassis with a wheelbase of only 2,550 mm, but that still produced a good quantity of room and a reasonable boot for such a modestly proportioned car.

Regardless, the car's sober shape and the absence of the Prancing Horse badge from the nose of the early examples – which it was given in 1976 to meet the pressing demand for such an addition from Ferrari's importers - all turned the Dino 308 GT/4 into a Rossa of only half-hearted fascination. Even so, the car remained in production - with a sunroof for export models - until 1980, by which time a total of 2,826 examples had been built.

The move to a rear-engine was never systematic as far as Ferrari grand tourers were concerned, if we set the 250 Le Mans and the 365 P prototype to one side, as they were cars that never went into production. So in that sense, the Ferrari BB, which made its first public appearance at the 1971 Turin Motor Show and had a V12 power plant behind the cockpit, was a real change of direction for Maranello: and one from which the 365 GT/4 BB was derived in 1973.

TECHNICAL SPECIFICATION

ENGINE
central, longitudinal, V12 (180°)

Bore and stroke	81x71 mm
Unitary cubic capacity	365.8
Total cubic capacity	4390.3
Valve gear	twin overhead camshafts
Number of valves	two per cylinder
Compression ratio	8.8:1
Fuel feed	four Weber 40IF3C carburettors
Ignition	single, one distributor
Coolant	water
Lubrication	dry sump
Maximum power	380 hp at 7200 rpm
Specific power	86.6 hp/litre

TRANSMISSION
Rear-wheel drive

Clutch	single dry disc
Gearbox	en bloc with engine five gears + reverse

BODY
Two-seater sports saloon

CHASSIS

Chassis	tubular trellis
Front suspension	independent, double wishbones, coil springs stabiliser bar, telescopic dampers
Rear suspension	independent, double wishbones, coil springs stabiliser bar, telescopic dampers
Brakes	disc
Steering	rack
Fuel tank	120 litres
Tyres front/rear	215/70 VR 15

DIMENSIONS AND WEIGHT

Wheelbase	2500 mm
Track front/rear	1500/1510 mm
Length	4360 mm
Width	1800 mm
Height	1120 mm
Kerb weight	1445 kg

PERFORMANCE

Top speed	302 km/h
Power to weight ratio	3.8 hp/kg

Ferrari 365 GT/4 BB   1973

Maranello's gradual move towards a grand tourer with a mid-engine was long and tortuous, because Ferrari preferred to test that set-up on both single-seater and sports racing cars first and then adopt it for the Dino 206 and 246 GT models, which, as is well known, did not carry the Prancing Horse badge on their bodywork. For these reasons, the appearance of the BB sports saloon prototype at the 1971 Turin Motor Show with its 12-cylinder boxer engine located in the central-longitudinal position was an epoch-making break from tradition for Ferrari. The design of the body of that admirable creation was entrusted to Pininfarina and displayed all the stylistic and mechanical distinguishing marks that would become standard features on thorough-bred grand tourers in the years ahead. It all started with the 365 GT/4 BB, which was introduced at the end of 1973 and was of a shape already seen in the Turin prototype, even if with some slight modifications.

The body of the new GT was made up of two superimposed shells, which were further characterised by dual-tone colours, the lower area matt black and the rest in the livery selected for that specific model; the colour combination accentuated the low and stream-lined shape of the BB sports saloon's extraordinary assertiveness and elegance. The tapered nose with headlights set into the edges of the bodywork and other pop-up opti-cal groups, its slatted air intake that crossed the bonnet horizontally, progressed with-out features of continuity in the ample inclined and slightly wraparound windscreen; the equally ample engine cover was made up of two fins that flowed into the rear wings and were furrowed by a series of air vents that enabled the heart of the BB to be seen: a 12-cylinder boxer engine with the V of the cylinder banks opened out to 180° with a 4,390.3 cubic capacity, accredited with 380 hp and a top speed of around 302 km/h.

The 1974 312 B3 was the car with which rising star Niki Lauda stepped into the spotlight, having moved to Maranello that year on the coat tails of Clay Regazzoni after a brief period with BRM. The Austrian immediately showed a clean and successful driving style and an attitude that was always respectful of the car with which he competed, as well as being uncommonly fast. In 1974, Lauda won two Grands Prix, one at Jarama, Spain, and the other at Zandvoort, Holland.

TECHNICAL SPECIFICATION

ENGINE
rear, longitudinal, V12 (180°)

Bore and stroke	80x49.6 mm
Unitary cubic capacity	249.3
Total cubic capacity	2991.80
Valve gear	twin overhead camshafts
Number of valves	four per cylinder
Compression ratio	11.5:1
Fuel feed	Lucas indirect injection
Ignition	single, Dinoplex Magneti Marelli electronic
Coolant	water
Lubrication	dry sump
Maximum power	495 hp at 12,600 rpm
Specific power	163.7 hp/litre

TRANSMISSION
Rear-wheel drive

Clutch	multi-disc
Gearbox	en bloc with differential five gears + reverse

BODY
Single-seater

CHASSIS

Chassis	monocoque with riveted aluminium panels
Front suspension	independent, double wishbones, inboard coil, springs/dampers
Rear suspension	independent, double wishbones, coil springs, one pushrod, telescopic dampers
Brakes	disc
Steering	rack
Fuel tank	230 litres (two laterals)
Tyres front/rear	9.2-20.0-13, 14.0-26.0-13

DIMENSIONS AND WEIGHT

Wheelbase	2500 mm
Track front/rear	1606/1604 mm
Length	4335 mm
Width	2056 mm
Height	900 mm
Weight in running order	582 kg

PERFORMANCE

Top speed	325 km/h
Power to weight ratio	1.2 kg/hp

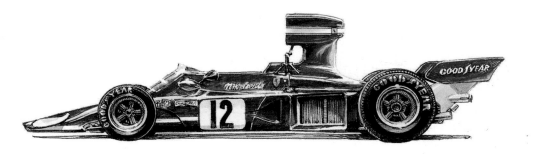

Ferrari 312 B3 1974

After spending the entire 1973 season seeking the right configuration for its Formula One car, Ferrari brought out the 312 B3 in its definitive form at the end of the year. To tell the truth, the imposition of the car's engine and chassis remained substantially unchanged - cylinder banks of the V12 power plant at an angle of 180°, its maximum power output only increased slightly from 485 hp at 12,500 rpm to 495 hp at 12,600 rpm, slotted into a monocoque structure. Significant new developments included the body, which had a unique air intake that stood high above the car, positioned immediately behind the cockpit and which would become almost the trade mark of the 312 B3. Behind the driver, there was an additional fuel tank, which was joined up to the two laterals, while the driving position was moved further towards the front axle, the pedals in close proximity with the nose itself.

A real revolution had erupted at the heart of the team: a new sports director named Luca Cordero di Montezemolo had arrived from Fiat to oversee the racing activities of the Prancing Horse, which was only involved in Formula One that year. There was also a new and a not-so-new driver situation: Clay Regazzoni had returned to Ferrari from BRM together with a young driver named Niki Lauda. A number of new technical partners also joined the team, among them Agip for the supply of fuel and Goodyear for tyres. The benefit of all those changes did not take long to make itself known: Lauda won the Grands Prix of Spain, his first victory for Ferrari, and in Holland, while Regazzoni scored points so that after the Swiss driver's win in the German GP he became the main rival to Emerson Fittipaldi and his McLaren in the race for the world title. But a drop in his Ferrari's performance meant the Swiss lost points at Watkins Glen and that gave Fittipaldi the Formula One World Championship for drivers, even though he only managed fourth in the same race.

After an 11-year wait, the drivers' world title eventually found its way back to Maranello, the merit of a revolutionary car called the 312 T, designed by Mauro Forghieri. The car was powered by a V12 boxer engine linked to a five-speed transverse gearbox from which comes the designation T and the new world champion was Niki Lauda. He won five Grands Prix and, together with points for having come third in the Grand Prix of Italy at Monza, clinched the first of his three world titles.

TECHNICAL SPECIFICATION

ENGINE		CHASSIS	
rear, longitudinal, V12 (180°)		Chassis	monoque with riveted aluminium panels
Bore and stroke	80x49.6 mm	Front suspension	independent,
Unitary cubic capacity	249.3		double wishbones,
Total cubic capacity	2991.80		inboard coil
Valve gear	twin overhead camshafts		springs/dampers
Number of valves	four per cylinder	Rear suspension	independent,
Compression ratio	11.5:1		double wishbones,
Fuel feed	Lucas indirect injection		coil springs
Ignition	single, Magneti-Marelli electronic		one pushrod, telescopic dampers
Coolant	water	Brakes	disc
Lubrication	dry sump	Steering	rack
Maximum power	495 hp at 12,200 rpm	Fuel tank	200 litres (two laterals, one central)
Specific power	165.4 hp/litre	Tyres front/rear	9.2-20.0-13, 16.2-26.0-13
TRANSMISSION			
Rear-wheel drive		DIMENSIONS AND WEIGHT	
Clutch	multi-disc	Wheelbase	2518 mm
Gearbox	en bloc with engine	Track front/rear	1510/1530 mm
	five gears + reverse	Length	4143 mm
		Width	2030 mm
BODY		Height	1275 mm
Single-seater		Weight in running order	575 kg
		PERFORMANCE	
		Top speed	330 km/h
		Power to weight ratio	6.0 kg/hp

Ferrari 312 T   1975

Even if it was presented to the press at the end of 1974, the new Ferrari Formula One
car did not race for the first time until 1 March 1975 at the Grand Prix of South Africa,
the third of the season's championship rounds. The 312 T was a rather innovative car
that required long, in-depth testing by Niki Lauda and Clay Regazzoni. The most significant new component was its transverse gearbox located in front of the rear axle: in
fact, the letter T in the car's denomination stood for the position of the 'box. The
advantages of that new development gave the car a greater concentration of its mass
- to achieve the objective at which engineer Forghieri had been aiming for a number
of years - and a better equilibrium of the car overall in terms of roadholding. There
was no hesitation in selecting the 180° V12 engine for the 312 T, its power output further increased to 495 hp at 12,200 rpm and its connection to a five-speed gearbox with
reverse. The external shape of the body was that of the B3, but with its driving position further forward and a large air intake at the rear, which was painted white.

The old B3 competed in the first two 1975 Grands Prix in Argentina and Brazil and,
after the T's troubled debut in South Africa and the subsequent auto-elimination of
Lauda and Regazzoni from the Spanish GP, the Austrian drove the car to victory three
consecutive times at Monte Carlo, Zolder and Anderstorp. There then followed other
placings and another Lauda win in France, so that he came to Monza for the Italian
GP as the leader of the driver's championship points table. And there, to the joy of the
tifosi, Regazzoni won and Lauda came third to bring the title back to Maranello, a
homecoming for which they had been waiting 11 years.

Two years after the Dino 308 GT/4 went on sale, out came the two-litre version of the car in 1975, called the Dino 208 GT/4. Bodied once more by Bertone, there was not much difference in the appearance of the new car compared to the previous model. The new Dino certainly did not excel in performance terms, with a top speed of 220 km/h from its 180 hp power output, nor did it do so in terms of body shape, which was the same as that of its older sister, the 308. The Dino 208 remained in production until 1980.

TECHNICAL SPECIFICATION

ENGINE
central, transverse, V8 (90°)

Bore and stroke	81x66.8 mm
Unitary cubic capacity	248.78
Total cubic capacity	1990.26
Valve gear	twin overhead camshafts
Number of valves	two per cylinder
Compression ratio	9:1
Fuel feed	four Weber 34DCNF carburettors
Ignition	single, two distributors
Coolant	water
Lubrication	dry sump
Maximum power	180 hp at 7700 rpm
Specific power	90.4 hp/litre

TRANSMISSION
Rear-wheel drive

Clutch	single dry disc
Gearbox	en bloc with engine five gears + reverse

BODY
2+2 coupé

CHASSIS

Chassis	tubular trellis
Front suspension	independent, double wishbones, coil springs, dampers
Rear suspension	independent, double wishbones, coil springs, dampers
Brakes	disc
Steering	rack
Fuel tank	80 litres
Tyres front/rear	197/70 VR 14 all round

DIMENSIONS AND WEIGHT

Wheelbase	2550 mm
Track front/rear	1460/1460 mm
Length	4300 mm
Width	1710 mm
Height	1210 mm
Kerb weight	1150 kg

PERFORMANCE

Top speed	220 km/h
Power to weight ratio	6.4 kg/hp

Dino 208 GT/4 1975

In Italy, cars with engines of more than two litres were hard hit by the early Seventies petrol crisis and 38% tax. It was those factors that pushed Ferrari into the sale of a "lesser" version of the Dino 308 GT/4 Bertone: the 208 GT/4 went into production in mid-1975. As its denomination suggests, the car was powered by an engine the cubic capacity of which had been dropped to 1,990,26 by a reduction in bore and stroke to 81 x 66.8 mm and an increase in the compression ratio to 9:1. The biggest change was in terms of power loss, with a drop of 80 hp compared to the three-litre car. In fact, the engine of the Dino GT/4 was accredited with a power output of only 180 hp at 7,700 rpm, which took the car to a top speed of 220 km/h and an acceleration of 0-400 metres of 16 seconds.

Carrozzeria Bertone did not change the car's dimensions, its 2,550 mm wheelbase remaining in tact: the central transverse position of the power unit also stayed the same, as did the compact and sober shape of the body it had inherited from the previous model. There were few changes of detail to create a distinction between the 208 and 308 GT/4, but there was an absence of front fog lights, the exhaust only had one terminal pipe and the tyres were of reduced dimensions at 197/70 VR 14.

The body shape was certainly not a captivating one, even if it was equilibrated and elegant. The car was a long way off the aesthetic qualities expected by Ferrari customers of the period. That and the relatively modest performance of the new Dino compared to its stable mates past and present held the 208 back and the 2+2 coupé was unable to achieve sales success: from the 468 units built in 1975, production gradually dropped to 23 produced in 1980, the last year in which the 208 GT/4 Bertone was sold.

The 308 GTB (Gran Turismo Berlinetta) introduced in 1975 marked a major change of direction for Maranello. That "small" car powered by a centrally located 90° V8 transverse engine opened up a market segment for Ferrari that had remained unexplored until that moment, having previously aimed its products at an elite clientele. Once again, Pininfarina gave a compact, clean and essential shape to the new car, one that was to stand the test of time.

TECHNICAL SPECIFICATION

ENGINE
central, transverse, V8 (90°)

Bore and stroke	81x71 mm
Unitary cubic capacity	365.86
Total cubic capacity	2926.9
Valve gear	twin overhead camshafts
Number of valves	two per cylinder (four per cylinder - Quattrovalvole)
Compression ratio	8.8:1 (9.2:1 – Quattrovalvole)
Fuel feed	four Weber 40DCNF carburettors (Bosch K-Jetronic injection – GTBi/GTSi + Quattrovalvole)
Ignition	single, one distributor
Coolant	water
Lubrication	dry sump
Maximum power	255 hp at 7700 rpm (214 hp at 6600 rpm – GTBi/GTSi) (240 hp at 7000 rpm – Quattrovalvole)
Specific power	87.1 hp/litre (73.1 GTBi/GTSi) (82 – Quattrovalvole)

TRANSMISSION
Rear-wheel drive

Clutch	single dry disc
Gearbox	en bloc with engine five gears + reverse

BODY
Two-seater sports saloon, roadster

CHASSIS

Chassis	tubular trellis
Front suspension	independent, double wishbones, coil springs, anti-roll bar, telescopic dampers
Rear suspension	independent, double wishbones, coil springs, anti-roll bar, telescopic dampers
Brakes	disc
Steering	rack
Fuel tank	80 litres (74 –GTBi/GTSi + Quattrovalvole)
Tyres front/rear	205/70 VR 14 (220/55 VR 390 – Quattrovalvole)

DIMENSIONS AND WEIGHT

Wheelbase	2340 mm
Track front/rear	1460/1460 mm
Length	4230 mm
Width	1720 mm
Height	1120 mm
Kerb weight	1300 kg (1320 – GTBi), (1330 – Quattrovalvole)

PERFORMANCE

Top speed	252 km/h (240 – GTBi/GTSi), (255 – Quattrovalvole)
Power to weight ratio	5.1 kg/hp (6.2 – GTBi/GTSi), (5.5 – Quattrovalvole)

Ferrari 308 GTB and GTS   1975

Although they only enjoyed modest sales success, the Bertone Dino 308 and 208 GT/4 deserve credit for having initiated a new series of models, all created around the 90° V8 engine in a rear-central position, which still characterise Ferrari production today. The founder of this successful and durable family of cars with which Maranello set itself the task of attracting new customers was the 308 GTB, first unveiled at the 1975 Paris Motor Show. Pininfarina designed a two-seater coupé of compact and assertive line, with a transverse engine located in the centre of the car. From the styling point of view, the Turin designer devised a perfect combination of elements that he would use in the creation of new Ferrari grand tourers for over 20 years, achieving a degree of incomparable equilibrium and exactitude. The body comprised two opposing shells, with a low and aerodynamic nose, which terminated in a narrow, rectangular radiator grill; segmented air intakes set into the car's body were placed along both flanks, between the doors and the rear end. The tail terminated abruptly and slightly inwards, playing host to round optical groups, its most prominent features. The 308 GTB soon became the most classical and coveted of Ferraris, one that blended compactness and handling with elegance and performance.

The 308 GTB and GTS remained in production until 1985 and achieved a sales success unknown to Ferrari until that time, with a total of 12,000 cars sold. The principal stages of its evolution were: the GTS derivative unveiled at the 1977 Frankfurt Motor Show; the introduction of Bosch fuel injection at the end of 1980; the adoption of four valves per cylinder technology two years later and retained until 1985.

The 312 T2 confirmed it was as competitive in 1976 as the 312 T had been in 1975, when it won the Formula One World Championship driven by Niki Lauda, with Clay Regazzoni (photograph) as his team mate. Once again, the Austrian was the undisputed protagonist of the season, but while leading the championship table at mid-season with five victories to his credit, he was involved in a dramatic accident at the Nürburgring that almost cost him his life. He concluded the season second to new world champion, James Hunt and his McLaren.

TECHNICAL SPECIFICATION

ENGINE
rear, longitudinal, V12 (180°)

Bore and stroke	80x49.6 mm
Unitary cubic capacity	249.3
Total cubic capacity	2991.80
Valve gear	twin overhead camshafts
Number of valves	four per cylinder
Compression ratio	11.5:1
Fuel feed	Lucas indirect injection
Ignition	single, Dinoplex electronic
Coolant	water
Lubrication	dry sump
Maximum power	500 hp at 12,200 rpm (512 – 1977)
Specific power	167.1 hp/litre (171 – 1977)

TRANSMISSION
Rear-wheel drive

Clutch	multi-disc
Gearbox	en bloc with differential five gears + reverse

BODY
Single-seater

CHASSIS

Chassis	monocoque with riveted aluminium panels
Front suspension	independent, double wishbones, inboard coil springs/dampers
Rear suspension	independent, double wishbones, coil springs, one pushrod, telescopic dampers
Brakes	disc
Steering	rack
Fuel tank	200 litres (two laterals, one central)
Tyres front/rear	9.2-20.0-13, 16.2-26.0-13

DIMENSIONS AND WEIGHT

Wheelbase	2560 mm
Track front/rear	1430/1450 mm
Length	4316 mm
Width	1930 mm
Height	1020 mm
Weight in running order	575 kg

PERFORMANCE

Top speed	320 km/h
Power to weight ratio	1.15 kg/hp (1.1 – 1977)

Ferrari 312 T2 1976

The first Ferrari to make a comeback brandishing the number 1 on its nose was the 312 T2. Niki Lauda had won the 1975 Formula One World Championship for drivers in a 312 and Scuderia Ferrari competed for the title with an updated version again in 1976. While the monocoque chassis and that glorious 12-cylinder opposed engine remained untouched – except for a slight power increase from 495 hp to 500 hp at 12,200 rpm – big changes were made to the body. The large air intake behind the driver was dropped after being banned for 1976 and that made it necessary to introduce the two NACA intakes on the body of the car, just in front of the windscreen. When the 312 T2 was unveiled, it had two small glass fibre "mudguards" ahead of the front tyres, but they were later banned by the Federation. The T2 made its racing debut in the Grand Prix of Spain, fourth round in the world championship, after the 312 T had dominated the season's first three races. Reigning world title holder Niki Lauda was immediately competitive and took second place at Madrid's Jarama circuit, behind James Hunt's McLaren. More victories followed in Belgium, Monte Carlo and Great Britain, all of which opened up the road to Lauda's second world championship. But his frightening accident and fire at the Nürburgring on 1 August, which almost cost the Austrian his life, eventually put an end to his title hopes that year, although not without a courageous fight. Even though he was still suffering from serious head injuries, Lauda was back racing in the Grand Prix of Italy at Monza. He was neck and neck with Hunt and his McLaren for the title as the season drew to a close, only to lose the championship by just one point to the British driver, who won a controversial last Grand Prix of the season in Japan. But Lauda beat Hunt the following year in a further updated T2 to win his momentarily elusive second world title, taking the Grands Prix of South Africa, Germany and Holland on the way to the crown.

Coming in after the 365 GT/4 2+2, the 400 GT made its debut in 1976 and continued a long line of front-engined grand tourers, this one of 4,823.2 cc. As with its predecessors, the new 2+2 was elegant, imposing and svelte of line. For the first time, a Ferrari was given and automatic gearbox – the three-speed GM Turbo Hydra-Matic – a decision not entirely appreciated or accepted by died-in-the wool Ferraristi.

TECHNICAL SPECIFICATION

ENGINE
front, longitudinal, V12 (60°)

Bore and stroke	81x78 mm
Unitary cubic capacity	401.9
Total cubic capacity	4823.2
Valve gear	twin overhead camshafts
Number of valves	two per cylinder
Compression ratio	8.8:1
Fuel feed	six Weber 40DCOE 59 or 60 carburettors (Bosch K-Jetronic injection – 400i)
Ignition	single, one distributor
Coolant	water
Lubrication	dry sump
Maximum power	340 hp at 6500 rpm (310/315 hp at 6400 rpm – 400i)
Specific power 400i)	70.5 hp/litre (64.3/65.3 –

TRANSMISSION
Rear-wheel drive

Clutch	single dry disc
Gearbox	en bloc with engine five gears + reverse (400i and 400 GT) three automatic gears + reverse (400 Automatic)

BODY
2+2 coupé

CHASSIS

Chassis	tubular trellis
Front suspension	independent, double wishbones, coil springs, anti-roll bar, telescopic dampers
Rear suspension	independent, double wishbones, coil springs, anti-roll bar, telescopic dampers
Brakes	disc
Steering	worm and roller
Fuel Tank	110 litres
Tyres front/rear	215/70 VR 15 all round

DIMENSIONS AND WEIGHT

Wheelbase	2700 mm
Track front/rear	1470/1500
Length	4810 mm
Width	1800 mm
Height	1315 mm
Kerb weight	1830 kg

PERFORMANCE

Top speed	245/250 km/h (235/245 – 400i and 400 GT)
Power to weight ratio	5.3 kg/hp (5.9/5.8 – 400i and 400 GT)

Ferrari 400 Automatic, GT and 400i 1976

The 1972 365 GT/4 was given a 4.8 litre (4,823.2 cc) engine four years later, and that laid the foundation for a new top-of-the-range Ferrari called the 400 GT. When creating this new model, Pininfarina limited itself to a number of small aesthetic changes, like adding a spoiler in the lower front area, optical groups made up of two round elements paired together instead of the 365's three element units, and the elimination of alloy rims with three point winged hub nuts and their replacement by five nuts per wheel with small, round Prancing Horse badges in the centre of each unit. But one out of place item was the huge rear vision mirror on the driver's side: it did not blend in with the cleanliness and essentiality of the car's flanks, which were crossed by the now classical moulding that linked the front and rear wings.

The 400 GT's most significant new development was on the mechanical side. The 60° V12 engine, which was initially fed by six Weber 40DCOE 59 or 60 carburettors, was given Bosch K-Jetronic direct fuel injection in 1979 and that spawned the 400i.

The importance the 400 assumed among the Ferrari grand tourers is linked most of all to the adoption by Maranello for the first time of a three speed automatic gearbox called the GM Turbo Hydra-Matic to create the Automatic derivative. But it was an innovation that was received with some perplexity by Ferrari purists. The traditional three-speed mechanical gearbox was only available in the 400 GT on request. In its various body styles, the 400 also turned out to be a grand tourer of reasonably long life, remaining in production until 1985 and becoming a sales success, especially in the United States.

Using the 1973 365 GT/4 BB as a base, in 1976 the 12-cylinder boxer engine with a 4,943 cubic capacity was installed in a new concept sports saloon called the 512 BB. Carburettors were still used for the early models, but after that Ferrari switched to electronic fuel injection and the BB soon became one of the most coveted and bewitching Ferraris of all time for two main reasons – its stylish shape and performance capability.

TECHNICAL SPECIFICATION

ENGINE
central, longitudinal, V12 (180°)

Bore and stroke	82x78 mm
Unitary cubic capacity	411.9
Total cubic capacity	4943
Valve gear	twin overhead camshafts
Number of valves	two per cylinder
Compression ratio	9.2:1
Fuel feed	four Weber 40IF3C carburettors (Bosch K-Jetronic injection – 512 BBi)
Ignition	single, one coil (single, electronic – 512 BBi)
Coolant	water
Lubrication	dry sump
Maximum power	360 hp at 6800 rpm (340 hp at 6000 rpm – 512 BBi)
Specific power	72.8 hp/litre 68.8 – 512 BBi)

TRANSMISSION
Rear-wheel drive

Clutch	multi-disc
Gearbox	en bloc with engine five gears + reverse

BODY
Two-seater sports saloon

CHASSIS

Chassis	tubular trellis
Front suspension	independent, double wishbones, coil springs, stabiliser bar, hydraulic dampers
Rear suspension	independent, double wishbones, coil springs, stabiliser bar, hydraulic dampers
Brakes	disc
Steering	rack
Fuel tank	110 litres (120 – 512 BBi)
Tyres front/rear	215/70 VR 15 all round (240/55 VR 415 – 512 BBi)

DIMENSIONS AND WEIGHT

Wheelbase	2500 mm
Track front/rear	1500/1565 mm (1510/1570 – 512 BBi)
Length	4400 mm
Width	1830 mm
Height	1120 mm
Kerb weight	1515 kg (1580 – 512 BBi)

PERFORMANCE

Top speed	302 km/h (280 – 512 BBi)
Power to weight ratio	4.2 kg/hp (4.7 – 512 BBi)

Ferrari 512 BB and BBi   1976

The same operation that transformed the 365 GT/4 2+2 into the 400 GT was carried out on the 365 GT/4 BB, which became the 512 boxer sports saloon as a result. While remaining practically the same shape from the outside, in this case, too, the car was given a 4.9-litre (4,943 cc) engine with a bore and stroke increased to 82x78 mm. Fuel was initially fed through four Weber 40IF3C carburettors – the same as those fitted to the 365 GT/4 2+2 – but in 1981, this engine, too, was given Bosch K-Jetronic injection to become the BBi. That reduced the car's power output slightly from the 360 hp generated by the carburettor version to the 340 hp of the model that was to become known as the 512 BBi. In both cases, though, the BB remained a car for the fortunate few who could afford it, in part due to its high price of Lit 28,350,000 back in 1976, but especially because of the somewhat masterful driving ability needed to dominate its exuberant power output. When Carlos Reutemann, a Ferrari works driver in 1977-78, tested the sports saloon for Italy's Quattroruote motoring magazine, he warned prospective purchasers of the car's sudden surge of power at high revs and said it was not easy to control.

From the aesthetic point of view, the 512 BB was the unchanged, clean and assertive shape of the 365 GT/4 BB, except for a few details such as a suggestion of a spoiler at the bottom of the nose, two NACA air intakes in the lower flanks just in front of the rear tyres and two instead of three element optical groups at the rear end. The petrol filler cap was on the linking fin, between the rear window pillar and the rear wing on the driver's side.

This "racing" grand tourer able to accelerate up to 300 km/h remained in production until 1984 and even today is one of the most coveted Ferraris among collectors.

The series of all-conquering single-seaters with transverse gearboxes continued in 1978 with the 312 T3. Niki Lauda moved to Brabham-Ford after a brusque farewell to Ferrari, so in came Argentinean Carlos Reutemann. He became the team mate of a young Canadian named Gilles Villeneuve, who had joined Ferrari for the last few races of 1977 and had been the talk of the Scuderia since then. But in 1978, it was Mario Andretti and his Lotus that dominated F1.

TECHNICAL SPECIFICATION

ENGINE
rear, longitudinal, V12 (180°)

Bore and stroke	80x49.6 mm
Unitary cubic capacity	249.3
Total cubic capacity	2991.80
Valve gear	twin overhead camshafts
Number of valves	four per cylinder
Compression ratio	11.5:1
Fuel feed	Lucas indirect injection
Ignition	single, Dinoplex Magneti Marelli electronic
Coolant	water
Lubrication	dry sump
Maximum power	510 hp at 12,200 rpm
Specific power	170.4 hp/litre

TRANSMISSION
Rear-wheel drive

Clutch	multiple disc
Gearbox	en bloc with differential five gears + reverse

BODY
Single-seater

CHASSIS

Chassis	monocoque with riveted aluminium panels
Front suspension	independent, double wishbones, inboard coil, springs/dampers
Rear suspension	independent, double wishbones, one pushrod, telescopic dampers
Brakes	disc
Steering	rack
Fuel tank	200 litres (two laterals, one central)
Tyres front/rear	24/55-13, 40/65-13

DIMENSIONS AND WEIGHT

Wheelbase	2560-2700 mm
Track front/rear	1620/1585 mm
Length	4250 mm
Width	2130 mm
Height	1010 mm
Weight in running order	580 kg

PERFORMANCE

Top speed	320 km/h
Power to weight ratio	1.1 kg/hp

Ferrari 312 T3   1978

The third evolution of the car that began the glorious T series with a boxer engine and a transverse gearbox was called the 312 T3. It competed for the 1978 Formula One World Championship, and as it did so, it revealed itself to be a car of highly innovative technical content.

The most important new development that season was the agreement reached with Michelin for the supply of radial ply tyres, which, while always maintaining an ample surface of support on the ground, guaranteed better roadholding, especially when cornering. The aerodynamics of the T3 had been studied and developed in every small detail in Pininfarina's wind tunnel and revised to take this new tyre industry technology into account. Revision that included the precise dissipation of internal and external air flow through the sidepods and the new concept front suspension with the spring/damper groups placed vertically in the car's architecture, right down to the least significant details, such as faired rear vision mirrors perfectly integrated into the profile of the car's body.

While Renault continued with the turbo engine, which it used for the first time in the 1977 Grand Prix of Great Britain at Silverstone, Ferrari still put its money on the power and reliability of its 12-cylinder boxer, which put out upwards of 500 hp. Even so, the 1978 season was still the year of more or less absolute domination by Mario Andretti's Lotus 79, Colin Chapman's latest creation and the first ground effect car in the history of Formula One motor racing, with its sidepods sealed to the track's surface by small flaps nicknamed mini-skirts. But Ferrari still won four Grands Prix with Carlos Reutemann in Brazil, Long Beach, Great Britain and Watkins Glen. Gilles Villeneuve, who had taken Niki Lauda's place at the end of 1977, was the revelation of the year and was able to win his home Grand Prix in Montreal at the end of the season.

On the day of its press presentation, at which there were few journalists and associated personnel, the 312 T4 was certainly not much liked for its beauty: it was graceless and angular. But once it was on the track, the car soon showed what it could do, winning its debut Grand Prix at Kyalami driven by Gilles Villeneuve. The South African was the first of six victories that led to Ferrari winning its ninth drivers' Formula One World Championship with Jody Scheckter.

TECHNICAL SPECIFICATION

ENGINE
rear, longitudinal, V12 (180°)

Bore and stroke	81x49.6 mm
Unitary cubic capacity	249.31
Total cubic capacity	2991.80
Valve gear	twin overhead camshafts
Number of valves	four per cylinder
Compression ratio	11.5:1
Fuel feed	Lucas indirect injection
Ignition	single, Dinoplex electronic Magneti Marelli
Coolant	water
Lubrication	dry sump
Maximum power	515 hp at 12,300 rpm
Specific power	172.2 hp/litre

TRANSMISSION
Rear-wheel drive

Clutch	multi-disc
Gearbox	en bloc with differential five gears + reverse

BODY
Single-seater

CHASSIS

Chassis	monocoque with riveted aluminium panels
Front suspension	independent, double wishbones, inboard coil springs/dampers
Rear suspension	independent, double wishbones, vertical coil springs/dampers
Brakes	disc
Steering	rack
Fuel tank	175-190 litres
Tyres front/rear	23/59-13, 38/68-13

DIMENSIONS AND WEIGHT

Wheelbase	2700 mm
Track front/rear	1700/1600 mm
Length	4460 mm
Width	2120 mm
Height	1010 mm
Weight in running order	500 kg

PERFORMANCE

Top speed	320 km/h
Power to weight ratio	1.1 kg/hp

Ferrari 312 T4 1979

The extraordinary results achieved by the revolutionary ground effect Lotus 79 in 1978 encouraged Maranello to take a similar technical direction for the 1979 season. The 312 T4, fourth evolution of that glorious series of transverse gearbox T cars, can be considered the first real ground effect single-seater in Ferrari's history.

The new car would win no beauty contest, for it was of angular and ungainly looking, but it made an immediate impact for its extremely well honed and advanced aerodynamics. The almost total absence of air intakes on the body itself suggested that great effort had been put into the internal dynamic flow, as had been the case with the progression of air between the body and the ground. Both the front and rear suspension systems were of the inboard type, with the spring-damper group positioned vertically on the front axle behind the chassis, and inside the gearbox group on the rear. Not yet ready to use a turbo engine, Ferrari installed the three-litre 12-cylinder boxer unit in its F1 car for the fourth consecutive year, this time with a power output of 515 hp.

While Gilles Villeneuve was reconfirmed, Carlos Reutemann moved on to Williams and along came South African Jody Scheckter to join Ferrari. He was the man best able to exploit the T4's enormous potential, often taking podium places and winning three Grands Prix in Belgium, Monaco and Monza. It was before Ferrari's homeland tifosi on the Italian track that Scheckter clinched his world championship, which was the Prancing Horse's ninth Formula One drivers' title. Gilles Villeneuve contributed in a determinate manner to bringing the world championship back to Maranello, his four victories of the season supporting his team mate's bid for the title and earning him second place in the end-of-season points table.

The 312 T5 that competed in the 1980 Formula One season was about as unreliable as its predecessors were successful. Neither Jody Scheckter, who was de-motivated after having won the 1979 world championship, nor Gilles Villeneuve were able to score a single podium finish, obtaining only modest placings. Scheckter was not even able to qualify his car before his team mate's home crowd at the Grand Prix of Canada in Montreal.

TECHNICAL SPECIFICATION

ENGINE
rear, longitudinal, V12 (180°)

Bore and stroke	80x49.8 mm
Unitary cubic capacity	249.3
Total cubic capacity	2991.80
Valve gear	twin overhead camshafts
Number of valves	four per cylinder
Compression ratio	11.5:1
Fuel feed	Lucas indirect injection
Ignition	single, Diniplex electronic
Coolant	water
Lubrication	dry sump
Maximum power	515 hp at 12,300 rpm
Specific power	172.1 hp/litre

TRANSMISSION
Rear-wheel drive

Clutch	multi-disc
Gearbox	en bloc with differential
	five gears + reverse

BODY
Single seater

CHASSIS

Chassis	monocoque with riveted
	aluminium panels
Front suspension	independent,
	double wishbones,
	inboard coil
	springs/dampers
Rear suspension	independent,
	double wishbones,
	one pushrod,
	telescopic dampers
Brakes	disc
Steering	rack
Fuel tank	185 litres
Tyres front/rear	23/59-13, 38/68-13

DIMENSIONS AND WEIGHT

Wheelbase	2700 mm
Track front/rear	1700/1751 mm
Length	4530 mm
Width	2120 mm
Height	1020 mm
Weight in running order	595 kg

PERFORMANCE

Top speed	320 km/h
Power to weight ratio	1.15 kg/hp

Ferrari 312 T5   1980

Decidedly less effective than the T4, the Ferrari 312 T5 was the last of the glorious family of F1 T cars – and was one of the most controversial in the history of the Prancing Horse. The new racer rose from the ashes of the preceding T4 project and boasted both the same monocoque chassis and its engine of 12 opposing cylinders, which had simply been given narrower heads that increased the unit's power slightly to 515 hp.

The poor performance put up by the car throughout the 1980 season was due to a series of concurrent circumstances, not all of which were of a strictly technical nature. First and foremost, Maranello knew the era of the normally aspirated engine was about to come to an end. It was precisely for that reason that all the efforts of the Racing Department were concentrated during the 1980 season on the development of a radically different new car, powered by a turbocharged engine. Not only that, but the yield of the Michelin tyres was poor and the performance of Jody Scheckter, who was basking in the glory of the world championship he had won at the end of the previous year, appeared de-motivated on more than one occasion. So much so that he was not even able to qualify his Ferrari for the Grand Prix of Canada.

The 1980 season saw Nelson Piquet win the world championship in his Brabham-Ford, after a season-long battle with the Williams-Fords of Carlos Reutemann and Alan Jones. Ferrari's best results were three fifth places, one by Scheckter at Long Beach and two by Villeneuve at Monaco and Montreal. It was Villeneuve who drove the 126 C for the first time, during qualifying for the Grand Prix of Italy, which was held at Imola that year. The coming car was powered by a turbocharged six-cylinder engine. The era of the 12-cylinder, normally aspirated power plants had drawn to a close, at least for the time being.

In a repeat of the eight-cylinder Dino operation – first marketed with a three-litre engine and later a two-litre - after the 308 GTB, Maranello unveiled the 208 in 1980. The car's body was, once again, of a soft and compact shape that had already been such a success for the 308, while the new Dino's engine was a 90° V8. In this case, too, the sports saloon was accompanied by a GTS version, a roadster equally as assertive and captivating.

TECHNICAL SPECIFICATION

ENGINE
central, transverse, V8 (90°)

Bore and stroke	68.8x71 mm
Unitary cubic capacity	248.8
Total cubic capacity	1990.6
Valve gear	twin overhead camshafts
Number of valves	two per cylinder
Compression ratio	9:1
Fuel feed	four Weber 34DCNF carburettors or Bosch K-Jetronic injection
Ignition	single, one distributor
Coolant	water
Lubrication	dry sump
Maximum power	155 hp at 6600 rpm
Specific power	77.8 hp/litre

TRANSMISSION
Rear-wheel drive

Clutch	single dry disc
Gearbox	en bloc with engine five gears + reverse

BODY
Two-seater barchetta/roadster

CHASSIS

Chassis	tubular trellis
Front suspension	independent, double wishbones, coil springs, anti-roll bar, telescopic dampers
Rear suspension	independent, double wishbones, coil springs, anti-roll bar, telescopic dampers
Brakes	disc
Steering	rack
Fuel tank	74 litres
Tyres front/rear	205/70 VR 14 all round

DIMENSIONS AND WEIGHT

Wheelbase	2340 mm
Track front/rear	1460/1460 mm
Length	4230 mm
Width	1720 mm
Height	1120 mm
Kerb weight	1305 kg (1365 – GTS)

PERFORMANCE

Top speed	215 km/h
Power to weight ratio	8.4 kg/hp (8.8 – GTS)

Ferrari 208 GTB and GTS 1980

The eight-cylinder 308 GTB and GTS followed the well-trodden path of the Dino bodied by Bertone, which was marketed first with a three-litre engine and later with a 1,990 cc unit. Maranello followed up by bring out the 298 sports saloon first and that was closely followed by the open version.

Due to the sales success already achieved by the early sports saloons, Pininfarina made no change to the aesthetic equilibrium of the preceding 308, repeating once more the same soft and voluminous shape for the two-litre version, which also conferred an unquestioned fascination on the 208. Even today, it is still not easy to tell the two models apart and it is often necessary to read the car's identification plaque near the circular optical groups at the rear end of the car under examination to conclusively identify which of the two it is.

Different power units were also installed in the 208 GTB: one was fed by four Weber 34DCNF carburettors and the other by Bosch K-Jetronic fuel injection, which gave rise to the 208 GTBi. The Quattrovalvole had, not surprisingly, four valves per cylinder,

The soft and assertive lines of the 208 were further exalted by the roadster, unveiled at the same time as the sports saloon. The open top car differed from the closed version, as it had a slatted grill that replaced the small lateral sidelights; the task of the grill was to conduct air to the rear window when the hood was closed and to hide the petrol filler cap, which was on the driver's side.

Between 1980 and 1982, Ferrari produced 160 closed 208s and 140 of the open model before the cars made way for a new coupé, which was also powered by a two-litre engine – but with the help of a turbocharger.

In 1980, Ferrari went back to using the name Mondial, which evoked the glorious barchettas of the Fifties bodied by Scaglietti and Pininfarina. It did so with a 2+2 coupé, which had its three-litre V8 engine at midships and in the transverse position and was called the Mondial 8. Initially, the car was given a tepid reception by journalists attending its unveiling at the year's Geneva Motor Show, due to its unassertive even if elegant and equilibrated shape.

TECHNICAL SPECIFICATION

ENGINE
central, transverse, V8 (90°)

Bore and stroke	81x71 mm
Unitary cubic capacity	365.8
Total cubic capacity	2926.9
Valve gear	twin overhead camshafts
Number of valves	two per cylinder (four – Quattrovalvole)
Compression ratio	8.8:1 (9.2:1 – Quattrovalvole)
Fuel feed	Bosch K-Jetronic injection
Ignition	Magneti Marelli Digiplex electronic
Coolant	water
Lubrication	dry sump
Maximum power	214 hp at 6600 rpm (240 hp at 7000 rpm – Quattrovalvole)
Specific power	73 hp/litre (82 hp/litre - Quattrovalvole)

TRANSMISSION
Rear-wheel drive

Clutch	single dry disc
Gearbox	en bloc with engine five gears + reverse

BODY
Coupé 2+2, two-seater roadster/cabriolet

CHASSIS

Chassis	tubular trellis with a unified body structure
Front suspension	independent, double wishbones, coil springs anti-roll bar, telescopic dampers
Rear suspension	independent, double wishbones, coil springs, anti-roll bar, telescopic dampers
Brakes	disc
Steering	rack
Fuel tank	84 litres (87 – Quattrovalvole)
Tyres front/rear	240/55 VR 390 all round

DIMENSIONS AND WEIGHT

Wheelbase	2650 mm
Track front/rear	1495/1535 mm
Length	4580 mm
Width	1790 mm
Height	1250 mm (1260 – Quattrovalvole)
Kerb weight	1585 kg (1490 – Quattrovalvole)

PERFORMANCE

Top speed	230 km/h, (240 – Quattrovalvole)
Power to weight ratio	7.4 kg/hp (6.2 – Quattrovalvole)

Ferrari Mondial 8 and Cabrio   1980

Even if the name suggested a car with a shape and mechanics of high order, from the moment the Ferrari Mondial 8 made its first appearance at the 1980 Geneva Motor Show it suffered criticism due to the unusual form of its Pininfarina design, which was neither assertive nor sporty, and its modest – for a Ferrari, that is - performance. Looking at the car again from a distance of well over 20 years, the Mondial seems more of a concrete attempt to marry the sporting vocation of the 208 and 308 with the formal elegance and comfort of the 2+2.

The Turin stylist, who was guilty of having designed a car of imbalance according to critics of the day, with a front that was too prominent when compared to the rear end, actually carried out his task well. The lines of the car were, effectively, of a sporting nature, especially the tapered nose that echoed the front end of the 308. The Mondial 8 became more sober and elegant of line along the flanks, which hosted two large, slatted air intakes that were to become the symbol of the whole model range. The sides connected the central part of the body through the traditional fins seen on other models, and was characterised by the abruptly cut off tail, the rear of which, embellished with circular optical groups, was in slight depression in respect of the profile of the boot.

The real Achilles heel of this Mondial was its overall weight: at 1,585 kg, far too much for a car able to put out a modest 214 hp. The eight-cylinder engine could "only" take the car to a top speed of 230 km/h. At the end of 1982, this engine, too, was given four valves per cylinder to generate another 26 hp, a move that added 10 km/h to the top speed. The cabriolet version was introduced in 1983 and was more elegant and streamlined than the coupé.

The F1 turbocharged engine, the first of which appeared in Renaults Formula One cars at the 1977 Grand Prix of Great Britain at Silverstone, had difficulty in being accepted by the other constructors. After a year of unshakable loyalty to its 12-cylinder boxer, Ferrari opted for a turbo in 1981 to power the 126 C. Thanks to the acrobatic driving style of Gilles Villeneuve, who had established himself by then as the idol of motor racing fans the world over, Ferrari won the Grands Prix of Monaco and Spain with the car.

TECHNICAL SPECIFICATION

ENGINE		CHASSIS	
rear, longitudinal, V6 (120°)		*Chassis*	monocoque with riveted aluminium panels
Bore and stroke	81x48.4 mm	*Front suspension*	independent, double wishbones, inboard coil springs/dampers
Unitary cubic capacity	249.4		
Total cubic capacity	1496.43		
Valve gear	twin overhead camshafts		
Number of valves	four per cylinder	*Rear suspension*	independent, double wishbones, one pushrod, telescopic dampers
Compression ratio	6.7:1		
Fuel feed	Lucas indirect injection two Comprex or KKK turbochargers		
		Brakes	disc
Ignition	single, Marelli electronic	*Steering*	rack
Coolant	water	*Fuel tank*	210 litres
Lubrication	dry sump	*Tyres front/rear*	22-59/13, 38-66/13
Maximum power	580 hp at 11,500 rpm		
Specific power	387.5 hp/litre	DIMENSIONS AND WEIGHT	
		Wheelbase	2719 mm
TRANSMISSION		*Track front/rear*	1761/1626 mm
Rear-wheel drive		*Length*	4468 mm
Clutch	multi-disc	*Width*	2110 mm
Gearbox	en bloc with differential five gears + reverse	*Height*	1025 mm
		Weight in running order	600 kg
BODY			
Single-seater		PERFORMANCE	
		Top speed	320 km/h
		Power to weight ratio	1.03 kg/hp

Ferrari 126 C   1981

The Ferrari 126 C made its first halting appearance in the 1980 Grand Prix of Italy, at Imola, the only time Italy's premier Grand Prix had taken place at the circuit near Bologna, driven by Gilles Villeneuve, who set a lap time with the car of 1'35"751, slower than the Canadian's time with the old T5. But the 126 C was soon to reverse that trend and become the car of the 1981 season. Ferrari's first turbocharged racer was powered by a 120° V6 engine boosted by two KKK (Kuhnle, Kopp and Kausch) turbochargers. The unit itself dated back to 1961, when Ferrari developed a Formula One engine with that architecture and special cylinder bank inclination. Compared to the 20-year-old motor, the 1981 turbo power plant had a cubic capacity of 1,496.43 and a compression ratio of 6.7:1, generating a maximum power output of 580 hp at over 11,500 rpm. Before making a final decision in favour of the turbo, Ferrari also experimented with the Comprex turbocharger, from which the letters CK and CX were derived for the 126 C.

Built around the turbocharged engine was a monocoque made up of riveted aluminium panels, its fuel tank located behind the cockpit and a five-speed gearbox with reverse once more in the transverse position, as with the Seventies T series of cars. Obviously, tuning the new engine was a rather long and delicate affair, so much so that Gilles Villeneuve and Scuderia Ferrari's new acquisition Didier Pironi were only able to put together a series of retirements in the early stages of the car's competitive life. Before the 126 C experienced another series of problems, though, Villeneuve was able to score two historic victories: the first was on the tortuous Monte Carlo city circuit – after overtaking Alan Jones's Williams in a memorable manoeuvre – that was theoretically unfavourable to the turbo's characteristics, and the second at Jarama, Spain. And that is how the era of the turbo officially began at Maranello.

The 1982 season was one of the most extraordinarily dramatic and sad in Ferrari's long history: first, Gilles Villeneuve was killed at Zolder, then an accident in Germany put an end to Didier Pironi's career. So the team was forced to recruit new drivers. They were Mario Andretti and Patrick Tambay (photograph). The Canadian won the Grand Prix of Germany at Hockenheim and was confirmed again for 1983.

TECHNICAL SPECIFICATION

ENGINE		CHASSIS	
central, longitudinal, V6 (120°)		Chassis	monocoque with riveted aluminium panels
Bore and stroke	81x48.4 mm	Front suspension	independent, double
Unitary cubic capacity	249.4		wishbones, inboard coil
Total cubic capacity	1496.43		springs/dampers
Valve gear	twin overhead camshafts	Rear suspension	independent, double
Number of valves	four per cylinder		wishbones, coil springs,
Compression ratio	6.5:1		telescopic dampers
Fuel feed	Lucas indirect injection, two	Brakes	disc
	KKK turbos	Steering	rack
Ignition	single, Marelli electronic	Fuel tank	240 litres
Coolant	water	Tyres front/rear	23-10.05/13, 26.0-15.05/15
Lubrication	dry sump		
Maximum power	580 hp at 11,000 rpm	DIMENSIONS AND WEIGHT	
Specific power	387.5 hp/litre	Wheelbase	2657 mm
		Track front/rear	1787/1644 mm
TRANSMISSION		Length	4333 mm
Rear-wheel drive		Width	2110 mm
Clutch	multi-disc	Height	1025 mm
Gearbox	en bloc with differential	Weight in running order	595 kg
	five gears + reverse		
		PERFORMANCE	
BODY		Top speed	320 km/h
Single-seater		Power to weight ratio	1 kg/hp

Ferrari 126 C2   1982

The C2, the Scuderia's second F1 car with a KKK turbocharged engine, was the first to which the modern technology, considered the norm in the sport today, was applied: it included honeycomb panels in composite material for the construction of the monocoque chassis. The aerodynamics of the C2 were further refined during long sessions in the Pininfarina wind tunnel, with the result that the car took on an even softer, rounder shape compared to the C. The new car's mechanics were unchanged, with the 120° V6 engine developing 580 hp at a slightly lower number of revolutions per minute than its predecessor. Team changes included the return of Goodyear as Maranello's tyre supplier, the introduction of wings with superimposed staggered planes that were judged to be irregular and cost Villeneuve disqualification from the Grand Prix of Long Beach.

The 1982 season went down in F1 history for the sequence of dramas that hit Scuderia Ferrari, depriving it of the world drivers' championship, which was unlikely to have slipped through its fingers. Tragedy struck for the first time on 8 May at the Zolder circuit in Belgium, where Gilles Villeneuve lost his life during qualifying after a fearful accident involving Jochen Mass and his March; disaster struck for a second time in qualifying at Hockenheim, where Didier Pironi and Alain Prost's Renault collided in heavy rain, which had hampered visibility. At the time of the accident, Pironi was heading the drivers' world championship table with 39 points, having won the Grands Prix of Imola and Holland. Now without their regular drivers, Patrick Tambay joined the team and came first in Germany, while Mario Andretti drove for the Scuderia in the last two rounds of the championship. In spite of everything, Maranello was still able to win the constructors' title, but the surprise was Finland's Keke Rosberg winning the drivers' championship in his Williams-Ford.

In line with a tradition that had been more or less consolidated at Ferrari, experience in racing found immediate application to their production cars: in this case the adoption of the turbocharger was extended to the 208 GTB and GTS. The 90° V8 engine was now fed by a KKK turbo that took its power output to 220 hp at 7,000 rpm. The sales success of that model was almost a foregone conclusion, with 687 cars built between 1982 and 1986.

TECHNICAL SPECIFICATION

ENGINE
central, transverse, V8 (90°)

Bore and stroke	68.8x71 mm
Unitary cubic capacity	248.8
Total cubic capacity	1990.6
Valve gear	twin overhead camshafts
Number of valves	two per cylinder
Compression ratio	7:1
Fuel feed	Bosch K-Jetronic injection and KKK turbocharger
Ignition	single, Marelli electronic
Coolant	water
Lubrication	dry sump
Maximum power	220 hp at 7000 rpm
Specific power	110.5 hp/kg

TRANSMISSION
Rear-wheel drive

Clutch	single dry disc
Gearbox	en bloc with engine five gears + reverse

BODY
Two-seater sports saloon/roadster

CHASSIS

Chassis	tubular trellis
Front suspension	independent, double wishbones, coil springs, anti-roll bar, telescopic dampers
Rear suspension	independent, double wishbones, coil springs, anti-roll bar, telescopic dampers
Brakes	disc
Steering	rack
Fuel tank	74 litres
Tyres front/rear	205/55 VR 390 all round

DIMENSIONS AND WEIGHT

Wheelbase	2340 mm
Track front/rear	1460/1460 mm
Length	4230 mm
Width	1720 mm
Height	1120 mm
Kerb weight	1285 kg (1295 – GTS)

PERFORMANCE

Top speed	242 km/h
Power to weight ratio	5.8 kg/hp (5.9 – GTS)

Ferrari 208 GTB and GTS Turbo   1982

The application of a turbocharger to the Formula One car's engine soon brought the first sensational victories of Gilles Villeneuve and Didier Pironi. That encouraged Ferrari to transfer the same technology to its production cars, initially selecting the small 208 GTB as its first road car to adopt a booster. The brochure for the 208 GTB turbo left no doubt about the marketing operation conducted by Maranello for that new model: initial pages showed Gilles Villeneuve testing an F1 car at Fiorano, while Didier Pironi posed next to a 208 GTB parked in front of a Scuderia Ferrari truck, used to transport the racing cars.

The Ferrari 208 GTB Turbo made its first public appearance at the 1982 Turin Motor Show: it was fitted with a KKK turbocharger without a heat exchanger and was fed by a Bosch K-Jetronic fuel injection system. The increase in power output achieved with the turbo was notable, with the maximum rising from the 155 hp of the normal version of the car to 220 hp at 7,000 rpm with the turbo. Top speed went up to 242 km/h.

As far as the car's appearance was concerned, the biggest difference between the 208 GTB and the Turbo were mainly the two NACA air intakes in front of the rear wings and different bumper bars, the front no longer protruding but now evenly integrated with the body. The same was the case with the GTS, which also made its debut in '82. As was the case with the 308, the roadster maintained the fascination and assertiveness of the closed version and was a major sales success in the United States.

The 208 GTB and GTS continued to be produced until 1986, during which time a total of 687 cars were built before Maranello moved on to the new Turbo GTB and GTS.

It was a long time before the 126 C3 made its first appearance on the track. An evolution of the C2 was used for the first half of the season and that won at Imola with Patrick Tambay and in Canada driven by new acquisition, René Arnoux. The C3 was finally ready for the Grand Prix of Great Britain, in which both drivers placed well. The car won in Germany and Holland, driven by Arnoux, to give Ferrari the world constructors' championship, instituted in 1958 and won seven times by Maranello.

TECHNICAL SPECIFICATION

ENGINE
central, transverse, V6 (120°)

Bore and stroke	81x48.4
Unitary cubic capacity	249.4
Total cubic capacity	1496.43
Valve gear	twin overhead camshafts
Number of valves	four per cylinder
Compression ratio	6.7:1
Fuel feed	Lucas indirect injection, two KKK turbochargers
Ignition	single, Marelli electronic
Coolant	water
Lubrication	dry sump
Maximum power	600 hp at 10,500 rpm
Specific power	400.9 hp/litre

TRANSMISSION
Rear-wheel drive

Clutch	multi-disc
Gearbox	en bloc with differential five gears + reverse

BODY
single seater

CHASSIS

Chassis	monocoque
Front suspension	independent, double wishbones, spring-operated links or pull rods
Rear suspension	independent, double wishbones, spring operated links or pull rods
Brakes	disc
Steering	rack
Fuel tank	220 litres
Tyres front/rear	23.5-10.05/13, 26.0-15.0/15

DIMENSIONS AND WEIGHT

Wheelbase	2600 mm
Track front/rear	1767/1666 mm
Length	4130 mm
Width	2110 mm
Height	1025 mm
Kerb weight	552 kg

PERFORMANCE

Top speed	320 km/h
Power to weight ratio	0.92 kg/hp

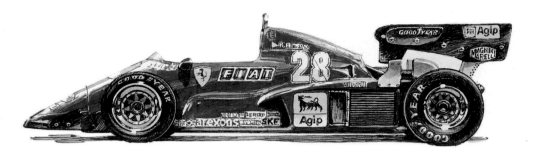

Ferrari 126 C3 1983

At the end of 1982, the Federation Internationale de l'Automobile made two radical changes to the regulations, banning in one fell swoop the use of mini-skirts, those aerodynamic flaps that provided greater adhesion of the car to the ground, and imposed the adoption of flat bottoms.

Those rule changes obliged constructors to drop projects already under development and conceive completely new kinds of cars. That was, of course, also the case at Ferrari, which, while developing the evolution of the C2, had to revert once more to the 126 C2B with which they competed in the first eight Grands Prix of the 1983 championship. That car enabled Patrick Tambay and René Arnoux, who joined the team that year, to attain brilliant results, among them victories at Imola with Tambay and in Canada with Arnoux. Ferrari had already adopted the new five-speed gearbox and different fairing for the engine group behind the driver: it also made considerable use of composite materials for the body of the 126 C3, in much the same way as McLaren was the first to develop a chassis made entirely of carbon fibre for the MP/4. The C3 raced for the first time in the Grand Prix of Great Britain and had an extremely narrow and tapered nose that broadened in correspondence with the sidepods, which contained the radiators. The car enabled Arnoux to stay in with a chance of winning the world title right up until the Grand Prix of Italy at Monza, having won in Germany and Holland and taken two second places in Austria and Italy. But the performance of the C3 suddenly nose dived during the last Grands Prix of the season and that left Alain Prost in a Renault and Nelson Piquet in the Brabham-BMW to fight it out for the championship, which eventually went to the Brazilian. But Ferrari did win the world constructors' title.

Michele Alboreto shot off the start line of the Grand Prix of Brazil, first round in the 1984 world championship, in the Ferrari 126 C4 together with Elio De Angelis in a Lotus. For the first time in years, Enzo Ferrari had selected an Italian driver to race one of his cars and Alboreto proved the right choice: he won in Belgium and fought for the world championship with honour throughout the season, even if Alain Prost and Niki Lauda in the McLaren-TAG Porsches proved unbeatable.

TECHNICAL SPECIFICATION

ENGINE
rear, longitudinal, V6 (120°)

Bore and stroke	81x48.4 mm
Unitary cubic capacity	249.4
Total cubic capacity	1496.43
Valve gear	twin overhead camshafts
Number of valves	four per cylinder
Compression ratio	6.7:1
Fuel feed	Lucas-Ferrari or Weber-Marelli indirect injection, two KKK turbos
Ignition	single, Marelli electronic
Coolant	water
Lubrication	dry sump
Maximum power	660 hp at 11,000 rpm
Specific power	441 hp/litre

TRANSMISSION
Rear-wheel drive

Clutch	multi disc
Gearbox	en bloc with differential five gears + reverse

BODY
Single-seater

CHASSIS

Chassis	monocoque in composite material
Front suspension	independent, double wishbones, spring operated links or pull rods
Rear suspension	independent, double wishbones, spring-operated links or pull rods
Brakes	disc
Steering	rack
Fuel tank	220 litres
Tyres front/rear	25.0-9.0-13, 26.0-15.0-13

DIMENSIONS AND WEIGHT

Wheelbase	2600 mm
Track front/rear	1786/1665 mm
Length	4115 mm
Width	2125 mm
Height	1080 mm
Weight in running order	540 kg

PERFORMANCE

Top speed	320 km/h
Power to weight ratio	0.8 kg/hp

Ferrari 126 C4 1984

The genealogy of the 126 C reached its fourth evolution in 1984 in the form of the 124 C4, the racing career of which is remembered not so much for its technical characteristics as for its close relationship with Michele Alboreto, who had joined the Scuderia that year. No Italian driver had competed in a Rossa since 1973 and the days of Arturo Merzario. The return of an Italian driver to Maranello was considered a sensational event by the Italian press and Alboreto enjoyed excellent credentials, having won two Grands Prix for Tyrrell-Ford.

The 126 C4 was of rather compact shape, with its low cockpit advanced to a position over the front axle and tapered sidepods in which the car's radiators were installed at a 45° angle. The engine fairing behind the driver had become lower and shorter, furrowed by two ample NACA air intakes to leave much of the V6 turbocharged engine exposed. Ferrari concentrated considerable effort on the power unit: the cylinder head and internal fluid dynamics were completely re-designed, new indirect Lucas-Marelli electronic fuel injection was fitted and a new lay-out five-speed gearbox was installed in a transverse position.

Unfortunately, the 126 C4's performance did not come up to expectations and the car often pitted with technical problems, especially the troublesome turbine. That meant Alboreto was only able to win the Grand Prix of Belgium at Zolder and take a few podium positions during the second half of the season, ending his year fourth in the drivers' championship with 30.5 points. Arnoux climbed onto the podium a number of times but did not win a Grand Prix. Indeed, the season was monopolised by the McLaren-TAG Porsches driven by Alain Prost and Niki Lauda to take the world championships by winning 12 races out of a possible 16.

The term GTO appeared on a Ferrari once more in 1984. So, as with the 1962 Gran Turismo Omologata, the 288 GTO showed it was a car of tremendous fascination and extraordinary assertiveness, able to produce a performance worthy of a racing car with its 400 hp at 7,000 rpm and a top speed of over 300 km/h. Just 272 examples of the car were built and the 288 GTO is still one of the most coveted of all Ferraris.

TECHNICAL SPECIFICATION

ENGINE
central, longitudinal, V8 (90°)

Bore and stroke	80x71 mm
Unitary cubic capacity	356.8
Total cubic capacity	2855.08
Valve gear	twin overhead camshafts
Number of valves	four per cylinder
Compression ratio	7.6:1
Fuel feed	electronic injection, two IHI turbochargers, intercooler
Ignition	Weber-Marelli electronic
Coolant	water
Lubrication	dry sump
Maximum power	400 hp at 7000 rpm
Specific power	140 hp/litre

TRANSMISSION

Rear-wheel drive	
Clutch	two-disc Borg & Beck
Gearbox	en bloc with engine five gears + reverse

BODY
Two-seater barchetta

CHASSIS

Chassis	tubular trellis
Front suspension	independent, double wishbones, coil springs, anti-roll bar, telescopic dampers
Rear suspension	independent, double wishbones, coil springs, anti-roll bar, telescopic dampers
Brakes	disc
Steering	rack
Fuel tank	120 litres (two laterals)
Tyres front/rear	255/55 VR 16, 265/50 VR 16

DIMENSIONS AND WEIGHT

Wheelbase	2450 mm
Track front/rear	1560/1560 mm
Length	4290 mm
Width	1910 mm
Height	1120 mm
Kerb weight	1160 kg

PERFORMANCE

Top speed	305 km/h
Power to weight ratio	2.9 kg/hp

Ferrari 288 GTO   1984

Two prestigious names made their comeback to the Ferrari road car stable in 1984, both irrevocably associated with Maranello's technical and sporting history. Two names that were the stuff of legends: they were the GTO and the Testarossa. Ferrari decided to build an extreme car with which to recreate the splendour of the extraordinary homologated sports saloon – a car that won three world GT championships in the Sixties – starting with the 308 GTB body shape. It is no coincidence that the origins of the new car, called the 288 GTO, are to be found in the 308 GTB Speciale, built by Pininfarina in 1977 and introduced at the Geneva Motor Show of that year. The Turin stylist dictated that the car's body should be of riveted aluminium, which made the lines of the new sports saloon even more muscular and assertive. Seven years later, that same imposition was repeated for the 288 GTO. The nose acquired a generous spoiler under the radiator grill, which hosted the optical groups; the line of the flanks had become more sinuous yet elegant as a result of the introduction of broader wings in which to house wide tyres - 255/55 VR 16 at the front and 265/50 VR 16 at the rear. The reason for selecting such tyres could only be found by analysing the car's performance capability. Powered by a 90° V8 engine fed by a Weber system of electronic injection and boosted by two IHI turbochargers, the unit generated 400 hp at 7,000 rpm, reached a top speed of 305 km/h and could accelerate from 0-100 km/h in 4.9 seconds.

The 288 GTO was produced until 1985, during which period 272 cars were built, all sold to order even before the car went into production. After having set record prices at sales by the leading auctioneers at the end of the Eighties, the 288 GTO is still one of the highest quoted Ferraris of them all and easily commands a price of 240,000 Euros, even today.

After the new GTO, Ferrari produced the remake of another of its great classics in 1984 – the Testarossa. A car of revolutionary line that had generous slatted air intakes down the entire length of its flanks and with a rather wide rear track (1,660 mm compared to 1,518 mm at the front), which was emphasised even more by the horizontal grill that ran along the whole width of the rear, incorporating the optical groups at the same time.

TECHNICAL SPECIFICATION

ENGINE
rear, longitudinal, V12 (180°)

Bore and stroke	82x78 mm
Unitary cubic capacity	411,9
Total cubic capacity	4943
Valve gear	twin overhead camshafts
Number of valves	four per cylinder
Compression ratio	9.2:1
Fuel feed	Bosch K-Jetronic injection
Ignition	Marelli Microplex electronic
Coolant	water
Lubrication	dry sump
Maximum power	390 hp at 6300 rpm
Specific power	78.9 hp/litre

TRANSMISSION

Rear-wheel drive	
Clutch	Borg & Beck bi-disc
Gearbox	en bloc with engine
	five gears + Reverse

BODY
Two-seater coupé

CHASSIS

Chassis	tubular trellis integrated with bodyshell
Front suspension	independent, double wishbones, coil springs, anti-roll bar, telescopic dampers
Rear suspension	independent, double wishbones, coil springs, anti-roll bar, telescopic dampers
Brakes	disc
Steering	rack
Fuel tank	115 litres
Tyres front/rear	255/50 VR 16 all round

DIMENSIONS AND WEIGHT

Wheelbase	2550 mm
Track front/rear	1518/1660 mm
Length	4485 mm
Width	1975 mm
Height	1135 mm
Kerb weight	1505 kg

PERFORMANCE

Top speed	290 km/h
Power to weight ratio	4.1 kg/hp

Ferrari Testarossa 1984

Ferrari's second legendary car, the extraordinary sports racer that won an impressive number of races for covered wheel cars in the Fifties and Sixties, appeared again in 1984 as a supercar designed by Pininfarina. It was called, once more, the Testarossa, but with its name written as a single word instead of the previous model's two.

A car of abnormal design and performance, the new Testarossa was born to stupefy, as was clear from the very day of its unveiling: instead of one of the traditional motor shows, Ferrari chose the stage of the famous Paris Lido nightclub for the new model's launch, a place packed with well-built dancing girls to add even more glamour to the unveiling of a glamorous car. The ballyhoo over, the car was still officially exhibited at the Paris Motor Show that year. The Testarossa was of an extreme body shape, in open contrast with the Ferrari-Pininfarina cars that had gone before. Moving from an ample front end of soft and rounded line, which curved into a slender radiator grill in the sides of which the optical groups were recessed right on the edges of the body, the car continued to widen progressively towards the back until it had broadened to a width of 1,660 mm rear track against the 1,518 of the front end. The flanks were traversed by large slatted dynamic intakes that channelled air to the laterally located radiators. The tail of the Testarossa also boasted a feature that had never been experimented with before, being covered by a horizontal grill that hid the optical groups. The performance of this new version of the legendary Ferrari racer was no less amazing, powered as it was by a 12-cylinder – it could be nothing else – 4,943 cc engine that put out 390 hp to produce a top speed of about 300 km/h.

In 1985, Pininfarina also built five Testarossa roadsters by special request, one of them commissioned by Gianni Agnelli.

It was not since Alberto Ascari's time that an Italian driver in a Ferrari had come so close to winning the Formula One World Championship. In 1985, Michele Alboreto was undoubtedly a leading contender for the title and, with two victories, one in Canada and the other in Germany, fought for the title against Alain Prost and his McLaren until mid-season. The unreliability of Alboreto's Ferrari brought the Italian's bid for glory to an end.

TECHNICAL SPECIFICATION

ENGINE		CHASSIS	
rear, longitudinal, V6 (120°)		*Chassis*	monocoque with composite materials
Bore and stroke	81x48.4 mm	*Front suspension*	independent, double wishbones, spring-loaded pushrods or pull rods
Unitary cubic capacity	249.40		
Total cubic capacity	1496.43		
Valve gear	twin overhead camshafts		
Number of valves	four per cylinder	*Rear suspension*	independent, double wishbones, spring-loaded pushrods or pull rods
Compression ratio	7:1		
Fuel feed	Weber-Marelli electronic injection, two KKK turbochargers		
		Brakes	disc
Ignition	single, Marelli electronic	*Steering*	rack
Coolant	water	*Fuel tank*	220 litres
Lubrication	dry sump	*Tyres front/rear*	25.0-10.0-13, 26.0-15-0-13
Maximum power	780 hp at 11,000 rpm		
Specific power	521.2 hp/litre		
		DIMENSIONS AND WEIGHT	
TRANSMISSION		*Wheelbase*	2762 mm
Rear-wheel drive		*Track front/rear*	1797/1663 mm
Clutch	multi-disc	*Length*	4292 mm
Gearbox	en bloc with engine five gears + reverse	*Width*	2135 mm
		Height	1080 mm
		Weight in running order	548 kg
BODY			
Single-seater		**PERFORMANCE**	
		Top speed	330 km/h
		Power to weight ratio	0.7 kg/hp

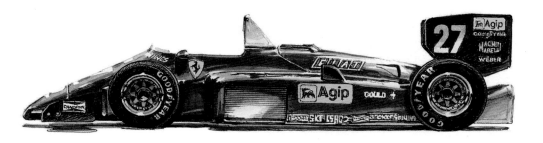

Ferrari 156/85 1985

From the day of its presentation, it was clear that the new 156/85 signalled a change in the history of Maranello single-seaters. After having led the design office of the Maranello Racing Department for 23 years and as such responsible for all the Rosse in F1 and other branches of the sport, Mauro Forghieri left Ferrari in the winter of 1984. For the first time in almost a quarter of a century was not head of the staff that penned a Prancing Horse F1 car, a role taken over by Englishman Harvey Postlethwaite.

The 156/85 was also powered by a 1.5-litre, 120° V6 unit with two KKK turbochargers placed at the sides of the engine, which delivered, at least on paper, 780 hp at 11,000 rpm. The car's aerodynamics were carefully developed with Aermacchi, who had provided a tailor made CAD-CAM programme for the purpose. The car's cockpit was further back from the nose and the sidepods, in which there were two radiators, were slimmer, especially at the rear. No new developments were indicated for either the transmission's five-speed, transverse gearbox or the suspension linkage.

Michele Alboreto was able to make the most of the car's potential, so that by mid-season he was fighting it out with Alain Prost and his McLaren for the world title, after winning the Grands Prix of Canada and Germany. Then the Ferrari suddenly lost its reliability, caused by repeated turbocharger breakages and that stopped the Italian from racking up more points in the second half, denying him a shot at the title.

Alboreto's team mate that year was the young Swede Stefan Johansson, who had taken the place of René Arnoux, but he could only manage modest placings.

In 1985, the 308 GTB and GTS sports saloon range was rejuvenated by the installation of a new engine. It was still a V8, but with its cubic capacity increased to 3,185.7 and the introduction of a number of styling improvements. They included the redesigned radiator grill, bumper colour-keyed to the body and alloy rims, which still had five spokes but were of innovative new design. The sales success of this model was no less than that of the 308.

TECHNICAL SPECIFICATION

ENGINE
central, transverse, V8 (90°)

Bore and stroke	83x73.6 mm
Unitary cubic capacity	398.2
Total cubic capacity	3185.7
Valve gear	twin overhead camshafts
Number of valves	four per cylinder
Compression ratio	9.8:1
Fuel feed	Bosch K-Jetronic injection
Ignition	Marelli Microplex electronic
Coolant	water
Lubrication	dry sump
Maximum power	270 hp at 7700 rpm
Specific power	84.8 hp/litre

TRANSMISSION
Rear-wheel drive

Clutch	single dry disc
Gearbox	en bloc with engine
	five gears + reverse

BODY
Two-seater sports saloon/roadster

CHASSIS

Chassis	tubular trellis
Front suspension	independent, double wishbones, coil springs, stabiliser bar, telescopic dampers
Rear suspension	independent, double wishbones, coil springs, stabiliser bar, telescopic dampers
Brakes	disc
Steering	rack
Fuel tank	74 litres
Tyres front/rear	205/55 VR 16, 225/50 VR 16

DIMENSIONS AND WEIGHT

Wheelbase	2350 mm
Track front/rear	1485/1465 mm
Length	4255 mm
Width	1730 mm
Height	1130 mm
Kerb weight	1265 kg (1275 – 328 GTS)

PERFORMANCE

Top speed	263 km/h
Power to weight ratio	4.7 kg/hp

Ferrari 328 GTB and GTS   1985

Ten years after the introduction of the 308 GTB at the 1975 Paris Motor Show, the car's mechanics were refreshed by the installation of a new engine that was still a 90° V8, but with its cubic capacity raised to 3,185.7, which prompted its new denominations of 328 GTB and GTS. The rejuvenation operation was particularly successful, because the new series sports saloon was accredited with 270 hp – 30 hp more than the Quattrovalvole – and a top speed of over 250 km/h, while retaining the fascination and assertiveness of the 308. As well as the new mechanical developments, a series of styling changes were made from which an even more elegant car emerged. The nose was given a new radiator grill with optical groups recessed into it, the bumpers were colour-keyed with the body, the air intake and grill on the bonnet were set closer to the pop-up headlights. The new five-spoke alloy rims were decidedly more elegant with their cleaner, more attractive design and were fitted with more generously proportioned tyres of 205/55 VR 16 on the front and 225/50 VR 16 at the rear. Exterior modifications also took into account the tail, with new fairing for the underbody, colour-keyed bumpers and the eternal circular optical groups.

The sports saloon was joined by a corresponding GTS, an equally elegant and assertive roadster, with a rigid hood and slatted air intake in place of small lateral glass surfaces at the rear. As always, the interior of the car was well finished and accessorised, with leather upholstery for both the seats and the inside door panels. The Ferrari 328 made its debut at the 1985 Frankfurt Motor Show and the production of the two models extended through to 1989, during which time 1,345 closed sports saloons and no fewer than 6,068 GTS roadsters were built.

The year 1985 was also one of change for the Mondial series, which had received such a tepid welcome in 1980: a new 3,185.7 cc engine and a number of significant aesthetic improvements gave this eight-cylinder Ferrari fresh appeal in national and foreign markets. The results of that operation were evident in both performance, with a power output of about 270 hp, and a more attractive and elegant appearance.

TECHNICAL SPECIFICATION

ENGINE
central, transverse, V8 (90°)

Bore and stroke	83x73.6 mm
Unitary cubic capacity	398.2
Total cubic capacity	3185.7
Valve gear	twin overhead camshafts
Number of valves	four per cylinder
Compression ratio	9.8:1
Fuel feed	Bosch injection
Ignition	Marelli Microplex electronic
Coolant	water
Lubrication	dry sump
Maximum power	270 hp at 7000 rpm
Specific power	84.7 hp/litre

TRANSMISSION
Rear-wheel drive

Clutch	single dry disc
Gearbox	en bloc with engine
	five gears + reverse

BODY
2+2 coupé/two-seater coupé

CHASSIS

Chassis	tubular trellis, unified body structure
Front suspension	independent, double wishbones, coil springs, anti-roll bar, telescopic dampers
Rear suspension	independent, double wishbones, coil springs, anti-roll bar, telescopic dampers
Brakes	disc
Steering	rack
Fuel tank	90 litres
Tyres front/rear	205/55 VR 16, 255/55 VR 16

DIMENSIONS AND WEIGHT

Wheelbase	2650 mm
Track front/rear	1520/1510 mm
Length	4535 mm
Width	1795 mm
Height	1235 mm (1265 – 3.2 Cabrio)
Kerb weight	1410 kg (1400 – 3.2 Cabrio)

PERFORMANCE

Top speed	250 km/h
Power to weight ratio	5.2 kg/hp

Ferrari Mondial 3.2 GTB and GTS   1985

In parallel with the 328 GTB and GTS, a similar lease of life was given to the Mondials, recipients of a 3.2 litre engine and the same styling changes previously made to the 328. That meant the Mondial 3.2 had reached the same level of performance as the 328, putting out 270 hp at 7,000 rpm, but with a top speed of "only" 250 km/h instead of the 328's 263 km/h.

From the appearance point of view, the changes were focused on the new radiator grill and the installation of Testarossa-type pop-up headlights; the bumper bar took on the colour of the car's body, but the engine cover remained unchanged. The Mondials were also given new design alloy rims, making the car look all the more elegant. The fairing under the rear bumpers was linear and essential, comprising a single piece that was also colour-keyed to the body. Double exhaust terminals exited from the rear bumper, barely protruding from the overall profile of the car.

The same body styling changes were carried out on the front and rear of the cabriolet. As was the case with the first Mondial series, the open top version was more attractive and, therefore, had a larger following than the 2+2 coupé, in part for its well-made canvas hood, which, once down, took its place behind the seats. The roadster certainly attracted attention in the North American market.

A total of 1,797 Mondial 3.2s were built between 1985 and 1989, of which 987 were coupés and 810 were cabriolets: that was the year the range was renewed once again, this time with the introduction of a transverse gearbox.

Having renewed the eight-cylinder Ferrari Mondial range and turned the 308 GTB and GTS into the 328, the next task was to do the same for the top-of-the-range grand tourer, grafting new technology onto the car and making styling changes that emerged during that period. So the Ferrari 412 was given a new, five-litre (4,943 cc) engine that increased its power output to 340 hp at 6,000 rpm.

TECHNICAL SPECIFICATION

ENGINE
front, longitudinal, V12 (60°)

Bore and stroke	82x78 mm
Unitary cubic capacity	411.9
Total cubic capacity	4943
Valve gear	twin overhead camshafts
Number of valves	two per cylinder
Compression ratio	9.6:1
Fuel feed	Bosch K-Jetronic injection
Ignition	Marelli Microplex electronic
Coolant	water
Lubrication	dry sump
Maximum power	340 hp at 6000 rpm
Specific power	68.8 hp/litre

TRANSMISSION
Rear-wheel drive

Clutch	double dry disc
Gearbox	en bloc with engine
	Three automatic gears +
	reverse or five gears + reverse

BODY
2+2 coupé

CHASSIS

Chassis	tubular trellis
Front suspension	independent, double wishbones, coil springs, stabiliser bar, telescopic dampers
Rear suspension	independent, double wishbones, coil springs, stabiliser bar, telescopic dampers
Brakes	disc
Steering	worm and roller
Fuel tank	116 litres
Tyres front/rear	240/55 VR 16 all round Or 240/55 VR 415

DIMENSIONS AND WEIGHT

Wheelbase	2700 mm
Track front/rear	1475/1510 mm
Length	4810 mm
Width	1800 mm
Height	1315 mm
Kerb weight	1805 kg

PERFORMANCE

Top speed	250 km/h (automatic) (255 – GT)
Power to weight ratio	5.3 kg/hp

280

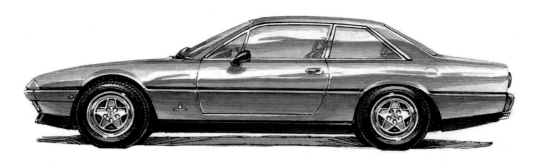

Ferrari 412 1985

In 1985, the top-of-the-range Ferraris powered by the over four-litre engine, of which the leading lights were the 365 GT/4 2+2 and the 400 GT Automatica, were renewed with the advent of the 412. The 60° V12 now had a cubic capacity of 4,943 cc, Bosch K-Jetronic fuel injection and, like the 400, was linked to either a three-speed gearbox to become the Automatica version or the traditional five-speed manual 'box. New Marelli Microplex ignition was also fitted to this luxury 2+2 and the ABS braking system became standard equipment on a production Ferrari for the first time. The shape of the 365 GT/4 and 400 was too pure and essential, almost incorruptible, to think of distorting the basic imposition. So Pininfarina limited itself to introducing a few slight, almost imperceptible changes leaving the original concept of the 400 untouched. The optical groups at the front end were brought to the fore and were no longer hidden by the grill; the bumpers took on the same colour as the body front and back; the black spoiler located in the lower area of the grill continued in ideal fashion in the sills under the doors, which were also painted black as was the fairing under the rear bumpers, from which protruded the two pairs of exhaust terminals. Being a high range car, the 412 had to have an interior and upholstery in leather, a double air conditioning plant, one for the front and the other for the back, a radio and central locking.

One of the lucky owners of the car was Michele Alboreto, who was given a 412 by Enzo Ferrari to mark the birth of his first daughter, with the comment, "Now that your family has grown, you'll need a 2+2".

The 1986 Formula One season was one of Ferrari's unhappiest: while being an extremely advanced car in every respect, from its aerodynamics to the materials used to make the bodyshell and engine, the F1/86 was hardly competitive and was chronically unreliable. Michele Alboreto and Stefan Johansson had to be content with a few modest placings and had no chance of fighting for victory.

TECHNICAL SPECIFICATION

ENGINE		CHASSIS	
rear, longitudinal, V6 (120°)		Chassis	monocoque in composite materials
Bore and stroke	81x48.4 mm	Front suspension	independent, double
Unitary cubic capacity	249.4		wishbones, spring-loaded
Total cubic capacity	1496.4		pushrods or pull rods
Valve gear	twin overhead camshafts	Rear suspension	independent, double
Number of valves	four per cylinder		wishbones, spring-loaded
Compression ratio	7.5:1		pushrods or pull rods
Fuel feed	Weber-Marelli electronic	Brakes	disc
	injection, two	Steering	rack
	Garrett turbochargers	Fuel tank	195 litres
Ignition	single, Magneti-Marelli	Tyres front/rear	25.0-10,0-13, 26.0-15.0-13
	electronic		
Coolant	water	DIMENSIONS AND WEIGHT	
Lubrication	dry sump	Wheelbase	2766 mm
Maximum power	850 hp at 11,500 rpm	Track front/rear	1807/1663 mm
		Length	4296 mm
TRANSMISSION		Width	2120 mm
Rear-wheel drive		Height	920 mm
Clutch	multi-disc	Weight in running order	548-576 kg
Gearbox	transverse, en bloc with		
	differential five gears + reverse	PERFORMANCE	
		Top speed	330 km/h
BODY		Power to weight ratio	0.6 kg/hp
Single-seater			

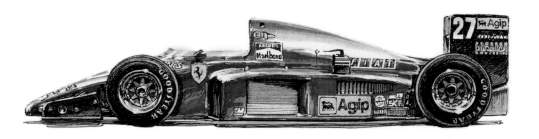

Ferrari F1/86 1986

Conceived in just three months, the F1/86 single-seater was presented as one of the most revolutionary cars Maranello had ever built, one for which the most advanced materials and technologies were used throughout. The chassis was completely new and made of composite materials with a honeycomb structure in carbon fibre and Kevlar; the spring-damper group was new, with the latter positioned horizontally at the front. Wind tunnel research on aerodynamics led to the construction of a body with an even softer and more rounded shape, compared to the 156/85. The engine cover was much admired, blending in perfectly with the hoop and the sidepods, which were higher and longer than those of previous cars, with the six-cylinder turbocharged engine enclosed in a kind of a cupola. The power unit was augmented by two Garrett turbochargers connected to a Weber-Marelli digital electronic injection system: it was credited with a power output of 850 hp at 11,500 rpm, which increased as the season wore on to over 950 hp for the unit in qualifying configuration.

Unfortunately, the cars to be driven by Michele Alboreto and Stefan Johansson were taken to Brazil without having completed the necessary track testing, so reliability problems soon came to light: the two drivers were almost always forced to retire. Their sporadic podium placings that year, especially during the second half of the season by which time the car seemed to have found some reliability, did not allow Ferrari to compete for the '86 world championship, which became a tussle between the Williams-Hondas of Nelson Piquet and Nigel Mansell, Ayrton Senna's Lotus-Renault and the McLaren-Porsche of Alain Prost, who eventually won the title at the last Grand Prix of the year in Australia.

In 1986, Ferrari's range of turbocharged cars was extended to include the GTB and GTS Turbo, developed solely for the Italian market. All the principal new developments of the period were built into those sports cars that were so similar to the 328 GTB and GTS, which had already been used for the other Prancing Horse models, including colour-keyed bumpers – the front one with a new spoiler – and the new design radiator grill.

TECHNICAL SPECIFICATION

ENGINE
central, transverse, V8 (90°)

Bore and stroke	66.8x71 mm
Unitary cubic capacity	248.83
Total cubic capacity	1990.63
Valve gear	twin overhead camshafts
Number of valves	four per cylinder
Compression ratio	7.5:1
Fuel feed	Bosch K-Jetronic injection, IHI turbocharger
Ignition	Marelli Microplex electronic
Coolant	water
Lubrication	dry sump
Maximum power	254 hp at 6500 rpm
Specific power	127.6 hp/litre

TRANSMISSION

Rear-wheel drive	
Clutch	multi-disc
Gearbox	en bloc with engine, five gears + reverse

BODY
Two-seater sports saloon/roadster

CHASSIS

Chassis	tubular trellis
Front suspension	independent, double wishbones, coil springs, anti-roll bar, telescopic dampers
Rear suspension	independent, double wishbones, coil springs, anti-roll bar, telescopic dampers
Brakes	disc
Steering	rack
Fuel tank	74 litres
Tyres front/rear	205/55 VR 16, 255/50 VR 16

DIMENSIONS AND WEIGHT

Wheelbase	2340 mm
Track front/rear	1485/1465 mm
Length	4230 mm
Width	1720 mm
Height	1120 mm
Kerb weight	1265 kg (1275 – GTS)

PERFORMANCE

Top speed	253 km/h
Power to weight ratio	4.9 kg/hp (5.0 – GTS)

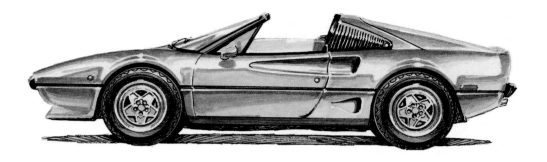

Ferrari GTB and GTS Turbo 1986

Ferrari continued to renew its model range and in 1986 came up with the GTB and GTS Turbos, in the denomination of which the model number 208 did not appear. They were in fact precisely that car, but offered in both closed and open top derivatives with a new IHI turbocharger. The blower enabled the eight-cylinder, two-litre (1,990.63 cc) engine to generate 254 hp at 6,500 rpm and to accelerate to a top speed of 250 km/h, not far off that of the 328. The GTB and GTS inherited their external shapes from the 328 and had the same radiator grill with headlights recessed into the lower nose. They also boasted the same body colour-keyed bumper bars and were given the new generation, five-spoke alloy rims, which were now characteristic of all the cars of the Prancing Horse. Apart from a slightly shorter wheelbase, reduced from 2,350 to 2,340 mm, the only means by which to tell the difference between the GTB/GTS and the 328 was by the two NACA air intakes deployed in proximity with the rear wings, the purpose of which was to channel air to the brakes. There were one or two differences in the cars' tails, where a series of discreet air vents had been opened in the GTB's and GTS's bumper bars, which were not present on the 208.

The sale of these two models continued until 1989, by which time 308 GTB and 828 GTS derivatives had been sold, once again confirming that the fascination of the eight-cylinder sports saloon and roadster inaugurated in 1975 by the 308 GTB had remained intact over time. But the two 1986 cars were the final evolution of that range of models, which, in a lifetime spanning almost 15 years, enabled Ferrari to achieve a sales success considered impossible for other models back in the mid-Seventies. The new 348 TB made its first public appearance in the autumn of 1989 at the Frankfurt Motor Show.

In his fourth year with Scuderia Ferrari, Michele Alboreto was unable to find the performance necessary to compete for the world championship. Gerhard Berger did better than the Italian, winning the last two Grands Prix of the season in Japan and Australia in a year dominated by the Williams of Nelson Piquet and Nigel Mansell, Alain Prost's McLaren and the Lotus of Ayrton Senna, who was considered a great star by this time.

TECHNICAL SPECIFICATION

ENGINE
rear, longitudinal, V6 (90°)

Bore and stroke	81x48.4 mm
Unitary cubic capacity	249.4
Total cubic capacity	1496.4
Valve gear	twin overhead camshafts
Number of valves	four per cylinder
Compression ratio	8:1
Fuel feed	Weber-Marelli digital injection,
	two Garrett turbochargers
Ignition	single, Magneti Marelli electronic
Coolant	water
Lubrication	dry sump
Maximum power	880 hp at 11,500 rpm
Specific power	588 hp/litre

TRANSMISSION
Rear-wheel drive	
Clutch	multi-disc
Gearbox	en bloc with engine six gears + reverse

BODY
Single seater

CHASSIS
Chassis	monocoque in composite materials
Front suspension	independent, double wishbones, spring-loaded pushrods or pull rods
Rear suspension	independent, double wishbones, spring-loaded push rods or pull rods
Brakes	disc
Steering	rack
Fuel tank	195 litres
Tyres front/rear	25.0-10.0-13, 26.0-15.0-13

DIMENSIONS AND WEIGHT
Wheelbase	2800 mm
Track front/rear	1797/1663 mm
Length	4280 mm
Width	2120 mm
Height	1000 mm
Weight in running order	542 kg

PERFORMANCE
Top speed	330 km/h
Power to weight ratio	0.6 kg/hp

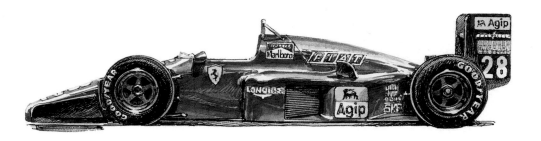

Ferrari F1/87 1987

After the disappointing results of the F1/86, the group of technicians comprising Britain's John Barnard and Harvey Postlethwaite plus Austrian Gustav Brunner decided to start from scratch again and design a new car for the 1987 season, creating a completely new F1 contender in every respect. In conceiving the F1/87, which had a lower and more streamlined nose, they concentrated in particular on the reduction of the car's mass. The sidepods were also lowered and the large hump behind the cockpit disappeared: it was replaced by a more aerodynamic and profiled fairing that flowed into the now classical Coke bottle rear end. The six-cylinder engine boasted some new developments, which included a different, 90° inclination of the cylinder banks and a six speed gearbox with reverse, which went back to a longitudinal position after 12 years of east-west Ferrari 'boxes. In producing that car, Brunner and Barnard certainly drew inspiration from the previous season's McLaren and Williams, from which they took numerous features. But despite all their efforts, the F1/87 was unable to achieve significant results on the track.

To McLaren-Porsche and Williams-Honda as principal rivals of Ferrari should be added Ayrton Senna and his Lotus-Renault in the battle for the world championship. Michele Alboreto and Gerhard Berger, Maranello's new Austrian acquisition, scored numerous podium finishes, but were rarely up there with their British-mounted rivals. It was only in the last part of the season that the F1/87 managed to find the performance it had lacked most of the season and, after having gone off and lost the Grand Prix of Portugal a few laps from the finish, Berger won the Grands Prix of Japan and Australia, breaking a spell that had bedevilled Maranello since the 1985 Grand Prix of Germany.

It was the most outlandish Ferrari of the late Eighties, the most coveted of cars, but just plain out of reach for all except the extremely well heeled, given the astronomical sums for which exotic cars were auctioned during that period. The extraordinarily aerodynamic lines of the F40, the materials from which its various components were made and, naturally, the mind-boggling performance of 0-100 km/h in 4.1 seconds, made this Rossa more like an F1 car than a grand tourer.

TECHNICAL SPECIFICATION

ENGINE
central, longitudinal, V8 (90°)

Bore and stroke	82x69.5 mm
Unitary cubic capacity	367
Total cubic capacity	2936.2
Valve gear	twin overhead camshafts
Number of valves	four per cylinder
Compression ratio	7.7:1
Fuel feed	Weber-Marelli electronic injection two IHI turbochargers
Ignition	Weber-Marelli electronic IAW
Coolant	water
Lubrication	dry sump
Maximum power	478 hp at 7000 rpm
Specific power	162.8 hp/litre

TRANSMISSION
Rear-wheel drive

Clutch	double dry disc
Gearbox	en bloc with engine five gears + reverse

BODY
Two-seater sports saloon

CHASSIS

Chassis	tubular trellis
Front suspension	independent, double wishbones, coil springs, telescopic dampers, stabiliser bar
Rear suspension	independent, double wishbones, coil springs telescopic dampers, stabiliser bar
Brakes	disc
Steering	rack
Fuel tank	60 litres (two laterals)
Tyres front/rear	245/40 ZR 17, 335/35 ZR 17

DIMENSIONS AND WEIGHT

Wheelbase	2450 mm
Track front/rear	1595/1605 mm
Length	4436 mm
Width	1970 mm
Height	1125 mm
Kerb weight	1235 kg

PERFORMANCE

Top speed	324 km/h
Power to weight ratio	2.58 kg/hp

Ferrari F 40 1987

To commemorate the 40th anniversary of the company, it was essential to build a Ferrari that was nothing short of sensational, a real racing car that could be driven on the public roads. And that is exactly what Ferrari and Pininfarina did. They created and built the F40, a car of extreme technological content and performance capability, celebrated as one of the most potent and highest performance cars ever built: one that became a true cult object to Ferrari enthusiasts.

The shape designed by Pininfarina demanded an ample boot up front, interrupted only by the optical groups and two small NACA air intakes located at the centre of the body, that sloped towards the massive grill furrowed by three dynamic intakes; the flanks literally protruded from the front compartment, proceeded straight and were crossed by air vents and NACA intakes similar to those on the 208 and 308 models, widening progressively right up until they reached their maximum quota of 1,605 mm, in correspondence with the rear wings. The enormous engine cover, which could be fully raised and was surmounted by a large back spoiler, opened up to reveal a monumental engine. The power unit could also be seen when the lid was closed, through a sizeable Plexiglas rear window that was vented to dissipate the hot air generated by this mighty motor. The heart of the F40 was a 90°, three-litre V8 boosted by two turbochargers, able to develop 478 hp at 7,000 rpm – and that produced a 0-100 km/h acceleration time of just 4.1 seconds.

Use of composite materials for the chassis, Kevlar and glass fibre for the body, small lateral windows in Plexiglas and a spartan interior made the F40 a true racing car, to be driven only by a competent, sporting clientele. The sales success of the car obliged Ferrari to extend production of that "monster" to 1992, during which period 1,337 F40s were built.

It had not been since the years of Jim Clark, the Lotus 25 and 33 that a team had monopolised the Formula One World Championship in the peremptory manner of the McLaren-Hondas of Alain Prost and Ayrton Senna, who ended up as world champion at the end of the season. The Anglo-Japanese squad won 15 Grands Prix out of a possible 16, leaving Ferrari just the Grand Prix of Italy at Monza, won by Gerhard Berger (picture) ahead of his team mate Michel Alboreto in a convincing doppietta.

TECHNICAL SPECIFICATION

ENGINE
rear, longitudinal, V6 (90°)

Bore and stroke	81x48.4 mm
Unitary cubic capacity	249.4
Total cubic capacity	1496.4
Valve gear	twin overhead camshafts
Number of valves	four per cylinder
Compression ratio	10:1
Fuel feed	Weber-Marelli electronic injection two Garrett turbochargers
Ignition	single, Magneti-Marelli static electronic
Coolant	water
Lubrication	dry sump
Maximum power	620 hp at 12,500 rpm
Specific power	414.3 hp/litre

TRANSMISSION
Rear-wheel drive

Clutch	multi-disc
Gearbox	en bloc with engine six gears + reverse

BODY
Single-seater

CHASSIS

Chassis	monocoque in composite materials
Front suspension	independent, double wishbones, spring-loaded push rods or pull rods
Rear suspension	independent, double wishbones, spring-loaded push rods or pull rods
Brakes	disc
Steering	rack
Fuel tank	150 litres
Tyres front/rear	25-10.0-13, 26-15.0-13

DIMENSIONS AND WEIGHT

Wheelbase	2800 mm
Track front/rear	1791/1673 mm
Length	4280 mm
Width	2120 mm
Height	1000 mm
Weight in running order	542 kg

PERFORMANCE

Top speed	310 km/h
Power to weight ratio	1.1 kg/hp

Ferrari F1/87-88C   1988

The 1988 season was one of transition for Formula One. The international Federation has sounded the death knell for turbocharged engines and, with effect from 1989, opened the way for normally aspirated power units with a maximum cubic capacity of 3.5 litres. For this reason, a number of teams decided to take the new route right away by fielding non-turbocharged cars in 1988. Others carried on with their turbos kept in check by a limiter valve, which restricted turbine pressure to 2.5 bar in an effort to reduce their performance and provide all competitors with a level playing field. Ferrari's Racing Department was already working on a project for a revolutionary new 1989 car, so it limited itself to competing with an updated version of its 1987 single-seater, the F1/87-88C powered by its 1.5-litre, six-cylinder turbocharged engine. The shape of the car's body was more or less unchanged: low, compact, of a sinuous and rounded line.

From the racing point of view, the 1988 season was completely dominated by the McLaren-Honda MP4/4 and the duel between its two drivers, Alain Prost and Ayrton Senna. The two won no fewer than 15 of the season's 16 Grands Prix, eight going to Senna and seven to Prost. The Brazilian won his first Formula One World Championship that year. It was only a banal misunderstanding that stopped Senna from winning the Grand Prix of Italy: Jean-Louis Schlesser in a Williams did not see the McLaren-Honda driver coming up behind him on the way out of the Monza chicane, meaning they collided and that resulted in the Brazilian being booted off the track. The race went to Gerhard Berger and his Ferrari, with Michele Alboreto in the other Rossa second, to make it what the Italians call a doppietta – the two top places on the podium. It was the first Prancing Horse victory since the death of Enzo Ferrari just under a month earlier, at the age of 90 on 14 August at his Modena home.

With the end of the turbo era, in 1989 Ferrari went back to equipping its F1 cars with the glorious 65° V12 engine, coupled to a revolutionary, electronically controlled gearbox, and operated by a small lever behind the rim of the steering wheel instead of the traditional gear lever. Nigel Mansell (picture) won the season's opening Grand Prix of Brazil, as well as the Hungarian GP, after so memorably overtaking Senna in the McLaren.

TECHNICAL SPECIFICATION

ENGINE
rear, longitudinal, V12 (65°)

Bore and stroke	84x52.6 mm
Unitary cubic capacity	291.4
Total cubic capacity	3497.96
Valve gear	twin overhead camshafts
Number of valves	five per cylinder
Compression ratio	11.5:1
Fuel feed	Weber-Marelli electronic injection,
Ignition	single, static electronic
Coolant	water
Lubrication	dry sump
Maximum power	600 hp at 12,500 rpm
Specific power	171.5 hp/litre

TRANSMISSION
Rear-wheel drive	
Clutch	multi-disc
Gearbox	en bloc with engine seven gears + reverse

BODY
Single-seater

CHASSIS
Chassis	monocoque in composite material
Front suspension	independent, double wishbones, spring-loaded push rods or pull rods
Rear suspension	independent, double wishbones, spring-loaded push rods or pull rods
Brakes	disc
Steering	rack
Fuel tank	195-205 litres (two laterals, one central)
Tyres front/rear	25-10-13, 26-15-13

DIMENSIONS AND WEIGHT
Wheelbase	2830 mm
Track front/rear	1800/1675 mm
Length	4400 mm
Width	2130 mm
Height	950 mm (1004 – GP of Mexico)
Weight in running order	505 kg

PERFORMANCE
Top speed	310 km/h
Power to weight ratio	0.8 kg/hp

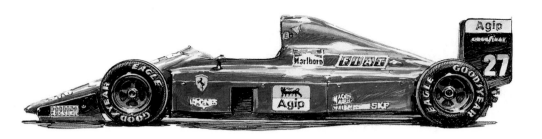

Ferrari F1/89 1989

The development of a revolutionary new Formula One car for the 1989 season started in Maranello's Racing Department in the summer of 1988, after which a laboratory car appeared at Fiorano bristling with all the new developments of the F1/89. They the included a 65° V12 engine of 3.5 litres capable of producing 600 hp at 12,500 rpm, which later rose to over 650 hp as the season wore on, and highly advanced aerodynamics fashioned right down to the smallest detail by John Barnard in a modern, purpose-built centre in Guilford, England. The external shape of the body was completely demount-able, with long sidepods that gradually sloped all the way to the tail, which was of the classic Coke bottle profile. Those were the most obvious elements that confirmed the in-depth aerodynamic research that had been carried out by the British technician.

A major new development was the revolutionary seven-speed electronic 'box, with gears that could be actioned by simply operating a small lever behind the steering wheel. It was a feature that not only enabled the driver to keep his hands on the wheel at all times, but also greatly reduced the amount of dead time between one gearchange and another.

Nigel Mansell, who had just joined Scuderia Ferrari, and Gerhard Berger had to retire many times due to teething troubles with this high technology material, which still needed a lot more development work before could deliver the necessary reliability.

But the 1989 season was still a positive one for Ferrari, with Mansell winning in Brazil and Hungary. However, Berger was involved in a frightening accident at Imola, where his car hit a wall and burst into flame. The Austrian got away with only slight-ly burnt hands and was still able to win the Grand Prix of Portugal 11 GPs later. McLaren won the title for the second successive year with Frenchman Alain Prost.

In 1989, the Mondial range was expanded by the addition of an elegant version of the car, which also had a transverse gearbox in both the saloon and cabriolet derivatives. The two cars concluded the model cycle, which began in 1980 with the Mondial 8. The newcomers were given all the principal new styling features of Ferraris of the period, although the basic imposition of sober and elegant lines that fashioned the whole series remained unaltered.

TECHNICAL SPECIFICATION

ENGINE
central, longitudinal, V8 (90°)

Bore and stroke	85x75 mm
Unitary cubic capacity	425.6
Total cubic capacity	3404.7
Valve gear	twin overhead camshafts
Number of valves	four per cylinder
Compression ratio	10.4:1
Fuel feed	Bosch M 2.5 electronic injection
Ignition	Bosch static
Coolant	water
Lubrication	dry sump
Maximum power	300 hp at 7200 rpm
Specific power	88 hp/litre

TRANSMISSION
Rear-wheel drive

Clutch	double dry disc
Gearbox	en bloc with engine five gears + reverse

BODY
Two-seater coupé/cabriolet

CHASSIS

Chassis	tubular trellis
Front suspension	independent, double wishbones, coil springs anti-roll bar, telescopic dampers
Rear suspension	independent, double wishbones, coil springs, anti-roll bar, telescopic dampers
Brakes	disc
Steering	rack
Fuel tank	96 litres (86 – Cabrio)
Tyres front/rear	205/55 ZR 16, 255/55 ZR 16

DIMENSIONS AND WEIGHT

Wheelbase	2650 mm
Track front/rear	1520/1560 mm
Length	4535 mm
Width	1810 mm
Height	1235 mm (1265 – Cabrio)
Kerb weight	1505 kg (1525 – Cabrio)

PERFORMANCE

Top speed	255 km/h
Power to weight ratio	5.0 kg/hp (5.1 – Cabrio)

Ferrari Mondial T and T Cabrio   1989

In 1989, the Ferrari Mondial range was further nurtured by two new versions of the car, the Mondial T and the Mondial T Cabrio, confirming the series as one of the most enduring of all Maranello's models – despite the tepid reception given to the first-born Mondial 8, nine years earlier.

The new T-cars' exterior had hardly been changed at all from their 3.2-litre predecessor, except for a new more sober shape with straighter lateral air intakes, door handles flush with the bodywork and colour keyed to the rest of the car. The five-spoke alloy rims were the same, as were the colour-keyed bumpers: the lower areas of the car were in matt black along the sides, the front end and the tail.

The most significant new development was concealed under the Mondial T's small engine cover, behind the cab. The 90° V8 engine was no longer in a transverse position, but was located longitudinally and was fed by a different electronic injection system called the Bosch Motronic 2.5. The cubic capacity of the unit was raised slightly to 3.4 litres (3,404.7 cc), making the Mondial Ts livelier and more muscular at high revs. The T part of the car's denomination reflected the position of the gearbox group: that was transversal, as on Ferrari's Formula One cars of the Seventies.

Production of the Mondial T and T Cabriolet was in line with the number of earlier 3.2s built at Maranello, with 842 coupés and 1,010 cabrios leaving the mythical plant for showrooms and customers.

The engine, with its cubic capacity increased to 3.4 litres, and the gearbox in a transverse position, meant the Mondial T was the link between earlier technology and a new range of models, which were to be launched at the 1989 Frankfurt Motor Show – the 348 TB and TS.

The sports saloon and roadster derivatives of the 348 made their first public appearance at the 1989 Frankfurt Motor Show. Their brief was to take the place of the 308 and 328, which had added great lustre to Maranello's image in the Eighties. The most significant new development was in the cars' external appearance, especially the new concept front end and the sides, which boasted a smaller version of the Testarossa's famous slatted air intakes.

TECHNICAL SPECIFICATION

ENGINE		CHASSIS	
central, longitudinal, V8 (90°)		*Chassis*	integral body and tubular rear chassis
Bore and stroke	85x75 mm	*Front suspension*	independent, double
Unitary cubic capacity	425.6		wishbones, coil springs,
Total cubic capacity	3404.7		anti-roll bar, telescopic
Valve gear	twin overhead camshafts		dampers
Number of valves	four per cylinder	*Rear suspension*	independent, double
Compression ratio	10.4:1		wishbones, coil springs,
Fuel feed	Bosch Motronic 2.7 injection		anti-roll bar, telescopic
Ignition	Bosch static		dampers
Coolant	water	*Brakes*	disc
Lubrication	dry sump	*Steering*	rack
Maximum power	300 hp at 7200 rpm	*Fuel tank*	95 litres
Specific power	88 hp/litre	*Tyres front/rear*	215/50 ZR 17, 255/45 ZR 17

TRANSMISSION		DIMENSIONS AND WEIGHT	
Rear-wheel drive		*Wheelbase*	2450 mm
Clutch	double dry disc	*Track front/rear*	4230 mm
Gearbox	en bloc with engine	*Length*	1502/1578 mm
	five gears + reverse	*Width*	1895 mm
		Height	1170 mm
BODY		*Kerb weight*	1395 kg
Two-seater sports saloon/cabriolet			

PERFORMANCE	
Top speed	280 km/h
Power to weight ratio	4.7 kg/hp

Ferrari 348 TB and TS   1989

At the 1989 Frankfurt Motor Show, Ferrari presented the heir to its glorious and enduring eight cylinder cars, which had brought a level of sales success to Maranello never previously achieved with other sports saloons. Much responsibility was placed squarely on the shoulders of a new model and expectations were high among the specialised press. The 348 TB and TS did not disappoint the motoring journalists, either. From the appearance point of view, with this model range Pininfarina offered once again numerous features seen on recent production Ferraris, blending them all together with great coherence and elegance. The result was a sports saloon that was compact and streamlined, with a tapered nose that embodied smaller scale examples of the Testarossa's styling features, like the optical groups recessed into the nose at the sides of the radiator grill and pop-up headlights. The 348 was also given the Testarossa's slatted side air intakes for radiator cooling, located in the lower area of the doors, as well as a more sparsely bladed area that crossed the whole tail of the car and covered the rear optical groups. The 17-inch alloy rims were of new design, with a faceted surface for the five spokes, and were now fitted with low profile tyres. The steel panel semi-integrated bodyshell was also new, combined as it was with a tubular trellis rear chassis. All of those features were also built into the TS, launched at the same time as the TB and which differed only due to its detachable black targa top.

The 348 TB and TS inherited the Mondial T's engine-gearbox group: the power unit was the 90° V8, installed in a longitudinal position and fitted with Bosch Motronic 2.7 fuel injection: the unit had a total cubic capacity of 3,404.7 that generated 300 hp at 7,200 rpm to produce a top speed of over 280 km/h and a 0-100 km/h acceleration time of 5.6 seconds. The cars' list price was around Lit 140,000,000.

Six victories in 1990: Ferrari had not won so many Formula One World Championship races or come so close to taking the world driver's title since 1979. The prime movers of this great achievement were the 641, fast and reliable throughout the year, Nigel Mansell (photograph, Monza) and Alain Prost, who were contenders for the title until the season's last race in Japan

TECHNICAL SPECIFICATION

ENGINE		CHASSIS	
rear, longitudinal, V12 (65°)		*Chassis*	monocoque in composite materials
Bore and stroke	84x52.6	*Front suspension*	independent,
Unitary cubic capacity	291.4		double wishbones,
Total cubic capacity	3497.96		spring-loaded
Valve gear	twin overhead camshafts		push rods or pull rods
Number of valves	five per cylinder	*Rear suspension*	independent,
Compression ratio	12.5:1		double wishbones,
Fuel feed	Magneti-Marelli indirect electronic injection		spring-loaded push rods or pull rods
Ignition	single, Magneti-Marelli static electronic	*Brakes*	disc
Coolant	water	*Steering*	rack
Lubrication	dry sump	*Fuel tank*	220 litres (two laterals, one central)
Maximum power	680 hp at 12,750 rpm	*Tyres front/rear*	25-10-13, 26-15-13
Specific power	194.4 hp/litre		

		DIMENSIONS AND WEIGHT	
TRANSMISSION		*Wheelbase*	2858 mm
Rear-wheel drive		*Track front/rear*	1800/1675
Clutch	three carbon fibre discs	*Length*	4460 mm
Gearbox	en bloc with engine seven gears + reverse	*Width*	2130 mm
		Height	1000 mm
		Weight in running order	503 kg

BODY		PERFORMANCE	
Single-seater		*Top speed*	310 km/h
		Power to weight ratio	0.7 kg/hp

Ferrari F1 641 1990

Reigning world champion Alain Prost signed for Ferrari at the end of 1989, bringing the world leader's number 1 to Maranello with him. Waiting for the Frenchman was the F1 641, directly derived from the F1/89 designed by John Barnard, who had already left Ferrari. Heading up the Scuderia's technical office was Pier Guido Castelli with Enrique Scalabroni, an Argentinean engineer, while Cesare Fiorio took on the role of sports director.

Like the F1/89, the new car was powered by a 3,497.96 V12 engine with a maximum output for qualifying of 710 hp at 13,800 rpm as the season progressed. The 641's aerodynamics also turned out to be extremely well conceived, with a new concept nose and low sidepods, which widened themselves progressively in correspondence with the cockpit, only to narrow again at the Coke bottle tail.

The rivalry between Prost and Ayrton Senna was worsened by the controversy that blew up between them during the conclusion of the 1989 season, after their "coming together" at Suzuka: Senna won the Japanese Grand Prix, but he was later disqualified – as a result of a protest by his French team mate, Prost. The situation between the two deteriorated even more in 1990. Senna won the first six races against Prost's five and the neck and neck result was decided once more in Japan, where the two collided at the first corner, both ending up in a sand trap. Senna and McLaren took the drivers' and constructors' championships again amid much controversy. Ferrari, who found it difficult to manage the delicate relationship between their drivers Prost and Nigel Mansell, had the consolation of having won six of the season's F1 races and to have recorded its historic 100th victory in the Formula Once World Championship in France that year.

After an excellent 1990, Scuderia Ferrari's Formula One performance fell off again the following year, this time due to its car's patchy reliability and friction inside the team, culminating at the end of the season with Alain Prost being sacked. The Frenchman had compared his 642 with a truck, because he found the car so difficult to handle. The picture shows new arrival Jean Alesi of France in Ferrari number 28

TECHNICAL SPECIFICATION

ENGINE		CHASSIS	
rear, longitudinal, V12 (65°)		*Chassis*	monocoque in composite materials
Bore and stroke	86x50.2 (88x47.9 – 643)	*Front suspension*	independent, double wishbones, spring-loaded pushrods
Unitary cubic capacity	291.6 (291.3 – 643)		
Total cubic capacity	3499.2 (3496 – 643)		
Valve gear	twin overhead camshafts	*Rear suspension*	independent, double wishbones, spring-loaded pushrods
Number of valves	five per cylinder		
Compression ratio	13:1 (13.5:1 – 643)		
Fuel feed	Weber-Marelli electronic injection	*Brakes*	disc
Ignition	single, Magneti-Marelli static electronic	*Steering*	rack
		Fuel tank	215 litres (two laterals, one central)
Coolant	water		
Lubrication	dry sump	*Tyres front/rear*	25-10-13, 26-15-13
Maximum power	720 hp at 13,800 rpm, (735 hp at 14,800 rpm – 643)		
		DIMENSIONS AND WEIGHT	
Specific power	206 hp/litre (210 hp/litre)	*Wheelbase*	2881 mm
		Track front/rear	1800/1675 mm
TRANSMISSION		*Length*	4400 mm
Rear-wheel drive		*Width*	2130 mm
Clutch	three carbon fibre discs	*Height*	1004 mm
Gearbox	en bloc with engine seven gears + reverse	*Weight in running order*	505 kg
		PERFORMANCE	
BODY		*Top speed*	320 km/h
Single-seater		*Power to weight ratio*	0.7 kg/hp (0.6 – 643)

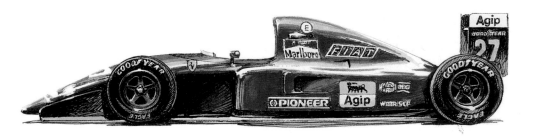

Ferrari F1 642 and F1 643   1991

There was further confirmation that the technological content and aerodynamics of Ferrari's 1989 F1 car were innovative in 1991, when Steve Nichols, the Scuderia's new technical boss, preferred to incorporate once more the basic concepts of John Barnard's design instead of coming up with a completely new single-seater himself. While the 642's nose regained the more traditional "duck bill" profile of the F1/89, the body's exterior still had those low side pods, less rounded and with an air intake also located externally at the back. The car had an usual narrowing of the body in correspondence with the tail and a voluminous air intake behind the cockpit to cool the engine. For the third consecutive year, Ferrari's F1 car was powered by the normally aspirated 12-cylinder engine, which became available in two versions during the course of the year: they were the 3,499.2 cc and the 3,496 cc respectively, both able to put out a maximum power of over 720 hp.

The first Grands Prix of the season showed Ferrari was in serious difficulty, with Alain Prost and Jean Alesi – the latter a new signing by the Prancing Horse after performing well at Tyrrell – only able to snare modest placings. It was for that reason that the new 643 was brought in as early as the Grand Prix of France: this car had modified aerodynamics, a different progression of its nose and side pods. But despite all those efforts to improve, Ferrari's results remained modest, with its drivers often on the end-of-race podium, but unable to equal the performance of either the Williams-Renaults or the McLaren-Hondas. At the end of a difficult season, Prost was sacked after the Grand Prix of Japan for having expressed himself in derogatory terms about his Ferrari. "It seems like driving a truck", he said. And he was replaced in the last race of the season in Australia by Maranello's test driver, Gianni Morbidelli.

A futuristic car, first due to the kind of materials used in the construction of the engine and monocoque and secondly because of its aerodynamic features, like the side pods separate from the car's body. But none of that was enough to boost the prospects of the team in the Formula One World Championship. Neither Jean Alesi (picture) nor Ivan Capelli was able to win a single Grand Prix in a world title chase dominated by Nigel Mansell and his Williams-Renault.

TECHNICAL SPECIFICATION

ENGINE
rear, longitudinal, V12 (65°)

Bore and stroke	88x47.9 mm (90x45.8 – GP of Imola)
Unitary cubic capacity	291.4
Total cubic capacity	3479
Valve gear	twin overhead camshafts
Number of valves	five per cylinder
Compression ratio	13.1
Fuel feed	Weber-Marelli electronic injection
Ignition	single, Magneti-Marelli static electronic
Coolant	water
Lubrication	dry sump
Maximum power	700 hp at 14,700 rpm
Specific power	200.1 hp/litre

TRANSMISSION
Rear-wheel drive

Clutch	three carbon fibre discs
Gearbox	en bloc with engine gears + reverse

BODY
Single-seater

CHASSIS

Chassis	monocoque in composite materials
Front suspension	independent, double wishbones, spring-loaded pushrods
Rear suspension	independent, double wishbones, spring-loaded pushrods
Brakes	disc
Steering	rack
Fuel tank	225 litres
Tyres front/rear	25-10-13, 26-15-13

DIMENSIONS AND WEIGHT

Wheelbase	2925 mm
Track front/rear	1810/1678 mm
Length	4350 mm
Width	2125 mm
Height	978 mm
Weight in running order	505 kg

PERFORMANCE

Top speed	320 km/h
Power to weight ratio	0.7 kg/hp

Ferrari F 92 A   1992

Scuderia Ferrari made an attempt at circumventing the kind of aerodynamics typical
of the 642 and 643 and tried to field a completely new car for 1992. It still followed the
route taken by the John Barnard design, but also come up with other bold solutions,
especially for the monocoque and the external shape of the body. The F 92 A designed
by Steve Nichols, who was also responsible for the 1988 McLaren MP4/4, together
with aerodynamics expert Jean-Claude Migeot, was indeed a evolutionary car. It had
an extremely narrow, tapered and raised nose that rested on two built-in supports at
the centre of the front wing; but the sidepods were even more innovative as they were
detached from the body of the car at the front and made the F 92 A look rather like a
fighter plane. There were also some important new developments in the underbody of
the car, where the flat bottom was detached from the monocoque to optimise the air
flow in that zone and create a kind of Venturi effect between the lower area of the car
and the ground. That season, a version of the car was also introduced with a transverse
gearbox and was called the F 92 AT, which was used from the Grand Prix of Belgium
onwards. Maximum effort was put into the development of the normally aspirated 12-
cylinder engine, which put out almost 750 hp at 15,000 rpm throughout the season.
As soon as it took to the track, the F 92 A showed that it was, unfortunately, a conceptually flawed car, one that had not only the aerodynamic problems of its predecessors, but was also afflicted by chronic unreliability. Jean Alesi and Ivan Capelli
could do nothing to compete with the burgeoning Williams-Renault of Nigel Mansell,
who clinched the world title by the Grand Prix of Hungary with six races in hand. The
best the Scuderia Ferrari drivers could do was to take two third places, with Jean
Alesi, one in Spain and the other in Canada.

While leaving the 1984 concept of the Testarossa body shape untouched, with those renowned and substantial lateral grills that spread longitudinally along the sides of the car, and the wide track of 1,530 mm at the front and 1,645 mm at the rear, the 512 TR did make its debut in 1992 with a new radiator grill and five spoke, faceted alloy rims of innovative design.

TECHNICAL SPECIFICATION

ENGINE
rear, longitudinal, v12 (180°)

Bore and stroke	82x78 mm
Unitary cubic capacity	411.9
Total cubic capacity	4943
Valve gear	twin overhead camshafts
Number of valves	four per cylinder
Compression ratio	10:1
Fuel feed	Bosch Motronic 2.7 injection
Ignition	Bosch Motronic 2.7 electronic
Coolant	water
Lubrication	dry sump
Maximum power	428 hp at 6750 rpm
Specific power	86.6 hp/litre

TRANSMISSION
Rear-wheel drive

Clutch	single dry disc
Gearbox	en bloc with engine
	five gears + reverse

BODY
Two-seater coupé

CHASSIS

Chassis	tubular trellis integrated with monocoque
Front suspension	independent, double wishbones, coil springs, anti-roll bar, hydraulic dampers
Rear suspension	independent, double wishbones, coil springs, anti-roll bar, hydraulic dampers
Brakes	disc
Steering	rack
Fuel tank	100 litres
Tyres front/rear	235/40 ZR 18, 295/35 ZR 18

DIMENSIONS AND WEIGHT

Wheelbase	2550 mm
Track front/rear	1530/1645 mm
Length	4480 mm
Width	1975
Height	1135 mm
Kerb weight	1475 kg

PERFORMANCE

Top speed	314 km/h
Power to weight ratio	4.8 kg/hp

Ferrari 512 TR   1992

Ferrari chose Los Angeles as the stage on which to unveil its new 512 TR in 1992. The car, the designation of which harked back to the boxer-engined sports saloon of the early Eighties, was powered by the same 4,943 cc, 12-cylinder engine as the earlier mould breaker, but with its output increased to 428 hp at 6,750 rpm by way of the adoption of Bosch Motronic 2.7 fuel injection. In parallel, performance went up so that the new version of the Testarossa could easily exceed 300 km/h and could accelerate from 0-100 km/h in 4.8 seconds. From the aerodynamic standpoint, the 512 TR had been extremely carefully fashioned in its lower area, where technology acquired in Formula One motor racing had had its influence.

Compared to the Eighties Testarossa, the 512 TR had a much changed front end. Pininfarina gave the car a new radiator grill similar to the 348's, with optical groups recessed into the body at the extremes of the central grill, as well as traditional pop-up headlamps. The fairing in the lower area was integrated with the rest of the car and given the same body colour. The flanks, with their long, slatted air vents, were little changed, with the exception of the external rear vision mirrors, which were no longer fixed to the door pillars but to the windscreen, a technique first used for the earlier Testarossa but soon dropped again due to high speed wind turbulence. The design of the rims in faceted alloy and 18 inches in diameter was new, and through them could be seen the self-ventilating disc brakes with ABS. The new wheels were fitted with ultra-low profile Pirelli P Zero tyres.

The Ferrari 512 TR remained in production until 1994, during which time a total of 2,280 cars were built. It was replaced by a new version called the F 512 M, many styling features of which had been changed and its performance capability further increased.

In 1992, Pininfarina returned to designing another great Prancing Horse classic, a grand tourer with a traditional 65° V12 front-mounted engine capable of absolute top performance, like many of its primogenitors. The Turin-based atelier did its job well, creating the latest in a long line of sober, elegant shapes and adding yet another Ferrari of class and incomparable fascination to an already extensive list of its outstanding creations.

TECHNICAL SPECIFICATION

ENGINE
front, longitudinal, V12 (65°)

Bore and stroke	88x75 mm
Unitary cubic capacity	456.1
Total cubic capacity	5473.9
Valve gear	twin overhead camshafts
Number of valves	four per cylinder
Compression ratio	10.6:1
Fuel feed	Bosch Motronic M 5.2 injection
Ignition	Bosch integrated Motronic 5.2 electronic
Coolant	water
Lubrication	dry sump
Maximum power	442 hp at 6250 rpm
Specific power	80.7 hp/litre

TRANSMISSION
Rear-wheel drive

Clutch	multi-disc
Gearbox	en bloc with differential six gears + reverse (four gears + reverse automatic – 456 GTA)

BODY
2+2 coupé

CHASSIS

Chassis	tubular, steel
Front suspension	independent, double wishbones, coil springs, anti-roll bar, gas-filled dampers
Rear suspension	independent, double wishbones, coil springs, anti-roll bar, gas-filled dampers
Brakes	disc
Steering	rack
Fuel tank	110 litres
Tyres front/rear	255/45 ZR 17, 285/40 ZR 17

DIMENSIONS AND WEIGHT

Wheelbase	2600 mm
Track front/rear	1585/1606 mm
Length	4763 mm
Width	1920 mm
Height	1300 mm
Kerb weight	1690 (1770 – 456 GTA)

PERFORMANCE

Top speed	over 300 km/h (over 298 – 456 GTA)
Power to weight ratio	3.8 kg/hp (4.0 – 456 GTA)

Ferrari 456 GT and GTA   1992

A sumptuous and elegant 2+2 coupé able to perform at the level of a racing car – a characteristic for ever close to Ferrari's heart - came back in no uncertain terms in the shape of the 456 GT, which was introduced at the 1992 World of Automobiles – a new name of the French show - in Paris. Making its debut in an elegant metallic blue, used for the first time to colour a Rossa, Maranello's newborn was of soft, clean lines in which the diverse body surfaces were admirably integrated with each other. That was certainly the case with the prominent front end, which flowed gracefully into the inclined windscreen and on to the boot, making its way there in an uninterrupted arc. The smooth sides were furrowed by a stark but pleasant profile, drawn from the lateral air intake exits of the engine compartment with an overall elegance and beauty of a sculpture. The rear end made itself known for its compact shape, with its tail in depression in respect of the boot, which outlined the suggestion of a spoiler, and the new round optical groups made in single units.

The elegance of the car's external shape was well matched by the 456's luxurious interior, with the creation of a sober, but at the same time cosy, appearance and a radiation of quality in an effort to offer the highest degree of comfort and habitability for all four people aboard.

A 5,473.9 cc, 12-cylinder engine with electronic fuel injection was installed in the 456 GT, in line with the best traditions of Ferrari - located up front and in a longitudinal position: it was able to propel the 2+2 coupé at over 300 km/h with its 442 hp power output. The transmission could be with either a six speed gearbox en bloc with the differential or a four speed automatic 'box from 1996 onwards, the latter mounted in a version of the car called the 456 GTA.

The second place racked up by Jean Alesi in the Grand Prix of Italy at Monza (photograph) was one of the best results achieved by the French driver for Ferrari in 1993. The season was otherwise devoid of a satisfactory return and emasculated once more by patchy reliability and a level of performance. At the end of the year, Williams' Alain Prost became world champion for the fourth time, before announcing his retirement from driving.

TECHNICAL SPECIFICATION

ENGINE		CHASSIS	
rear, longitudinal, V12 (65°)		*Chassis*	monocoque in composite materials
Bore and stroke	-	*Front suspension*	electronically controlled
Unitary cubic capacity	291.3		hydraulic,
Total cubic capacity	3497.96		double wishbones,
Valve gear	twin overhead camshafts		coil springs,
Number of valves	five per cylinder		spring-loaded pushrods
Compression ratio	13:1	*Rear suspension*	electronically controlled
Fuel feed	Weber-Marelli electronic injection		hydraulic, double wishbones, coil springs,
Ignition	single, Magneti-Marelli static electronic		spring-loaded pushrods
Coolant	water	*Brakes*	disc
Lubrication	dry sump	*Steering*	rack
Maximum power	730 hp at 14,700 rpm	*Fuel tank*	225 litres
Specific power	??????	*Tyres front/rear*	25-10-13, 26-15-13
		DIMENSIONS AND WEIGHT	
TRANSMISSION		*Wheelbase*	2930 mm
Rear-wheel drive		*Track front/rear*	1690/1605
Clutch	three carbon discs	*Length*	4350 mm
Gearbox	en bloc with engine	*Width*	1995 mm
	six gears + reverse	*Height*	995 mm
		Weight in running order	505 kg
BODY			
Single-seater		**PERFORMANCE**	
		Top speed	320 km/h
		Power to weight ratio	0.7 kg/hp

Ferrari F 93 A   1993

The excesses of the F 92 A design, a car that turned out to be mediocre in both its performance and reliability, suggested Ferrari should return to a more conventional single-seater, the development project for which was once again taken on by John Barnard, who had come back to Maranello. The 1991 93 A retained the raised nose that was part of the previous model, but bid goodbye to the air intakes that were detached from the car: they were replaced by others of larger rectangular section. The most innovative feature introduced on the 93 A gradually established itself as the car's Achilles heel as the season ground on: it was the electronically controlled front and rear suspension aka intelligent suspension, which could automatically modify the car's set-up in line with variations in aerodynamic load and track conditions. The now consolidated 3,497.96 cc normally aspirated V12 engine, one of the most powerful in F1 that year due to the adoption of new pneumatic valves, generated an output of about 730 hp at 14,700 rpm. Back with Ferrari after his four years at McLaren as Ayrton Senna's team mate, Gerhard Berger and Jean Alesi did not take long to understand that 1993 would be a lean year for them and Scuderia Ferrari. The car turned out to be unreliable both because of its difficult suspension system and repeated engine breakdowns. All of which meant the Austrian and the Frenchman could only net a few podium positions (Alesi third at Monaco and second at Monza, Berger third in Hungary) but they were never really in the running for an outright win.

After a year's sabbatical in 1992, during which he stayed well away from the F1 circus, Alain Prost won his fourth F1 world championship at the wheel of a Williams FW15C-Renault, only to announce his definitive retirement as a motor racing driver at the end of the season.

The Ferrari 348 Spider was presented first at the 1993 Geneva Motor Show and then at a special event in Rodeo Drive, Los Angeles. The car took Maranello back to the open top car in its most classical and pure form, as was the case with the 250 California and the 365 GTS/4 before it. The shape of the 348, further emphasised by the absence of a roof, seemed to be even more elegant. It was, once again, the U.S. market that took the lion's share of 348 Spider production.

TECHNICAL SPECIFICATION

ENGINE
central, longitudinal, V8 (90°)

Bore and stroke	85x75 mm
Unitary cubic capacity	425.5
Total cubic capacity	3404.7
Valve gear	twin overhead camshafts
Number of valves	four per cylinder
Compression ratio	10.4:1
Fuel feed	Bosch Motronic 2.7 injection
Ignition	Bosch static
Coolant	water
Lubrication	dry sump
Maximum power	300 hp at 7200 rpm
Specific power	88.1 hp/litre

TRANSMISSION
Rear-wheel drive

Clutch	double dry disc
Gearbox	en bloc with engine
	five gears + reverse

BODY
Two-seater roadster

CHASSIS

Chassis	integrated body and tubular rear
Front suspension	independent, double wishbones, coil springs, anti-roll bar, telescopic dampers
Rear suspension	independent, double wishbones, coil springs, anti-toll bar, telescopic dampers
Brakes	disc
Steering	rack
Fuel tank	95 litres
Tyres front/rear	215/50 ZR 17, 255/45 ZR 17

DIMENSIONS AND WEIGHT

Wheelbase	2450 mm
Track front/rear	1502/1578 mm
Length	4230 mm
Width	1895 mm
Height	1170 mm
Kerb weight	1400 kg

PERFORMANCE

Top speed	275 km/h
Power to weight ratio	4.7 kg/hp

Ferrari 348 Spider   1993

Using a similar strategy to the one set in motion for the Mondial and, years earlier, for the 365 GTS/4, Ferrari chose the 348 with which to create a pure roadster, which first appeared at the 1993 Geneva Motor Show and then at a special event in Rodeo Drive, Beverley Hills, Los Angeles. The second unveiling, attended by Ferrari president Luca Cordero di Montezemolo and Sergio Pininfarina, film stars and other well-known personalities, left no doubt as to Maranello's intentions, divining its 348 Spider with the United States market very much in mind.

While the car's mechanics came from the 348 TB and the TS – 90° 3,404.7 cc V8 engine with Bosch Motronic 2.7 fuel injection capable of producing 300 hp – the most significant work was carried out on the body: the 'shell's lateral longitudinal member and windscreen pillar areas were strengthened at the cost of a five kilos in weight over that of the range's closed version.

The 348 Spider was designed by Pininfarina using the 348 TS as a base, without the small lateral windows and, most important of all, without the anti-roll bar, which linked with the rear mudguards via two wings. In place of those characteristic components came a black hood which, once opened, was stored under a tailor made cover behind the seats: when it was used to cover the cockpit it, did so perfectly at the edge of the windscreen, with small lateral windows that raised themselves automatically to enable the hood to be properly positioned before closure. For the rest, the external shape of the 348 Spider differed little from that of the TS, except for a front spoiler: all the lower area of the car was colour-keyed with the rest of the body and was no longer matt black, as on its predecessors.

The 348 Spider continued to be produced until 1995 during which time 1,090 examples were made. By then, the open and closed versions of the F355 had already begun to dominate.

It had not been since the early Seventies and the 312 PB that Ferrari had built a closed wheel car with which to compete in the sports car category. The 333 SP, a 650 hp barchetta powered by a 65° V12 engine, was never entered for a race as a works car, but was assigned to private teams that campaigned it with success, in particular in America's IMSA World Sport Car Championship.

TECHNICAL SPECIFICATION

ENGINE
rear, longitudinal, V12 (65°)

Bore and stroke	85x58.7 mm
Unitary cubic capacity	333.1
Total cubic capacity	3997
Valve gear	twin overhead camshafts
Number of valves	five per cylinder
Compression ratio	-
Fuel feed	Weber-Marelli electronic injection
Ignition	single, Magneti-Marelli static electronic
Coolant	water
Lubrication	dry sump
Maximum power	650 hp at 15.000 rpm
Specific power	150 hp/litre

TRANSMISSION
Rear-wheel drive

Clutch	multi-disc
Gearbox	en bloc with engine five gears + reverse

BODY
barchetta

CHASSIS

Chassis	integrated, composite materials
Front suspension	independent, double wishbones, spring-loaded pushrods
Rear suspension	independent, double wishbones, spring-loaded pushrods
Brakes	disc
Steering	rack
Fuel tank	70-100 litres
Tyres front/rear	-

DIMENSIONS AND WEIGHT

Wheelbase	2750 mm
Track front/rear	1660/1572 mm
Length	4569 mm
Width	2000 mm
Height	1025 mm
Kerb weight	860 kg

PERFORMANCE

Top speed	368 km/h
Power to weight ratio	1.3 kg/hp

Ferrari F 333 SP   1993

It was with the 312 PB that Ferrari won the 1972 World Sports Car Championship and fought to the death with Matra for the title the following year, but lost it to the French company. After that, Maranello turned its attention elsewhere and did not built another sports racer for the category. If we exclude the 312 SP - a car that may have been built in 1974, but was never raced - the 365 GTB4 Daytona and the 512 BBLM, with both of which the Prancing Horse competed only sporadically, it is true to say that Ferrari concentrated all its efforts on Formula One alone.

The F 333 SP was introduced in 1993, and was a barchetta powered by a 65°, 3,997 cc V12 engine that generated more than 650 hp, a power unit that was derived from the Scuderia's F1 car. The new sports racer's integrated structure and honeycomb chassis in composite materials had the same origins, as the light body, which was completely demountable. The development of the 333 SP, which was to compete in the American IMSA championship, was expressly undertaken by Maranello so that it could assign a competitive sports racer to private scuderias and sporting clients. The car went on sale in the normal way at a list price of USD 500,000.

The racing career of the 333 SP was fairly long and successful. The car enabled the Prancing Horse to go back to the tracks on which it had competed with such distinction with its famous sports racers and prototypes in the Sixties and Seventies and win all over again. Among the new car's best remembered results are victories in the 1995 12 Hours of Sebring by Andy Evans-Fermin Velez-Eric Van der Poele, plus the IMSA drivers and constructors' championships, taking another Sebring win on the way in 1998. The F 333 SP also won a historic victory in the 24 Hours of Daytona, the MOMO entered car driven by Giampiero Moretti-Mauro Baldi-Didier Theys-Ari Luyendyk

The year 1994 was one of the most dramatic in Formula One for many seasons; one in which Ayrton Senna and Roland Ratzenberger died at the Grand Prix of San Marino. Ferrari fielded a rather complex car from the technical and aerodynamic points of view, but still the Scuderia did not bring home the results for which it hoped: Maranello did, however, win the Grand Prix of Germany at Hockenheim with Gerhard Berger after three years without a single victory.

TECHNICAL SPECIFICATION

ENGINE		CHASSIS	
rear, longitudinal, V12 (65°) (75° - GP of San Marino)		*Chassis*	monocoque in composite materials
Bore and stroke	-	*Front suspension*	independent,
Unitary cubic capacity	291.4		double wishbones,
Total cubic capacity	3497.96		spring-loaded
Valve gear	twin overhead camshafts		pushrods
Number of valves	four per cylinder	*Rear suspension*	independent,
Compression ratio	-		double wishbones,
Fuel feed	Magneti-Marelli digital		spring-loaded
	electronic injection		pushrods
Ignition	Magneti-Marelli static	*Brakes*	disc
	electronic	*Steering*	rack
Coolant	water	*Fuel tank*	200 litres
Lubrication	dry sump	*Tyres front/rear*	-
Maximum power	780 hp at 15,000 rpm		
	(800 hp at 15,250 rpm –	**DIMENSIONS AND WEIGHT**	
	GP of San Marino	*Wheelbase*	2950 mm
		Track front/rear	1690/1605 mm
TRANSMISSION		*Length*	4495.5 mm
Rear-wheel drive		*Width*	1995 mm
Clutch	three carbon fibre discs	*Height*	995 mm
Gearbox	en bloc with engine	*Weight in running order*	505 kg
	six gears + reverse		
		PERFORMANCE	
BODY		*Top speed*	320 km/h
Single-seater		*Power to weight ratio*	0.6 kg/hp

Ferrari 412 T1 and T1B   1994

After a year of transition, for 1994 Maranello went back to the car originally designed entirely by John Barnard. Like all the single-seaters penned by the British technician, the 412 had highly advanced aerodynamics, which were carefully developed down to the smallest detail in the wind tunnel. The nose was even higher than the F1 93 A's, so much so that it almost ran straight from its tip and to the arc of the cockpit. Two elegant, ogive-shaped air intakes had been built into the sidepods, which also acted as a link between the 'pods and the main body of the car. The design project, as a part of which air flow in the lower area was studied meticulously, included a fin placed almost at the height of the cockpit, which divided the air flow from the nose into two separate streams, directing them to the diffuser channels. Dropping the intelligent suspension, which was banned by FIA at the end of 1993, allowed Barnard to concentrate his efforts on the gearbox and, as a result, he created a new unit contained in a 'box made of composite materials and located in a transverse position, as the T designation suggests.

Going for such advanced technological features brought on a number of problems in a bid to find the right kind of performance, which was way down on that of the Benetton-Fords and the Williams-Renaults. Regardless, Berger and Alesi often ended up on the podium during the early part of the season. A new, modified version of the car, called the 412 T1B, came in at the Grand Prix of France, and that had additional air intakes in the sidepods: Berger drove the T1B to victory in the Grand Prix of Germany. In a year saddened by the deaths of Ayrton Senna and Roland Ratzenberger at the Grand Prix of San Marino, Michael Schumacher won the first of his Formula One World Championships.

Numerous significant styling modifications were made to the third and last evolution of the Testarossa, christened the F512 M, powered by a 4,943 cc, 180° V12 engine and unveiled at the 1994 Paris Motor Show. They ranged from the disappearance of the pop-up headlights to a new nose, the grill of which was of a more subtle shape, and optical groups recessed into the bumpers. The alloy rims were also of new design.

TECHNICAL SPECIFICATION

ENGINE
rear, longitudinal, V12 (180°)

Bore and stroke	82x78 mm
Unitary cubic capacity	412
Total cubic capacity	4943
Valve gear	twin overhead camshafts
Number of valves	four per cylinder
Compression ratio	10.4:1
Fuel feed	Bosch Motronic 2.7 injection
Ignition	Bosch static electronic injection
Coolant	water
Lubrication	dry sump
Maximum power	440 hp at 8500 rpm
Specific power	89 hp/litre

TRANSMISSION
Rear-wheel drive

Clutch	single dry disc
Gearbox	en bloc with engine five gears + reverse

BODY
Two-seater coupé

CHASSIS

Chassis	tubular trellis integrated with bodyshell
Front suspension	independent, double wishbones, coil springs, anti-roll bar, hydraulic dampers
Rear suspension	independent, double wishbones, coil springs anti-roll bar, hydraulic dampers
Brakes	disc
Steering	rack
Fuel tank	100 litres
Tyres front/rear	235/40 ZR 18, 295/35 ZR 18

DIMENSIONS AND WEIGHT

Wheelbase	2550 mm
Track front/rear	1532/1644 mm
Length	4480 mm
Width	1976 mm
Height	1135 mm
Kerb weight	1455 kg

PERFORMANCE

Top speed	315 km/h
Power to weight ratio	3.3 kg/hp

Ferrari F 512 M ·   1994

Launched at the 1994 Paris Motor Show, the Ferrari 512 M was the third evolution of the modern Testarossa, which had bowed in a decade earlier. Both the mechanics and especially the car's styling were revised. Pininfarina designed a completely new nose for the third coming of the car, with the optical groups still recessed into the bodywork, but now split into two distinct elements: headlamps and directional flashers of rectangular shape and the round front fog lights also featured. The radiator grill was in the centre of the nose, the shape of which was further modified. Significant new developments included the bonnet: the pop-up headlights were no more and were replaced by fixed units of the ellipsoidal type, and that radically modified the look of the car. Two small NACA air intakes were opened up just below the windscreen. At the rear of the 512 M, the grill that once crossed the whole tail was of reduced dimensions and framed by two pairs of small, circular back lights. The appearance of the bumpers was also renewed, as was the substantial engine cover, now all in the same colour as the rest of the body. The alloy rims were also of new design, with spokes of helicoidal progression, evidently inspired by the Mythos concept car built by Pininfarina in 1989.

The power of the Ferrari 512 M's engine was upped from the 512 TR's 428 hp to the new model's 440 hp, with a specific power of 89 hp/litre and a maximum torque of 51 kg/m at 5,500 rpm. Compared to the previous model, the new car's performance was more or less the same, with a top speed of 315 km/h, a 0-100 km/h acceleration time of 4.7 seconds and 0-1000 metres in 22.7 seconds.

Five hundred examples of the 512 M were built up to 1996 and the model was the last from Maranello to have its 12-cylinder engine located in the rear of the car.

The 1994 F 355 was a child of a well tried and tested Ferrari formula; one of small sports saloons, powered by an eight-cylinder engine located longitudinally in the rear, and was also of soft, compact design. The formula, which brought such success to the 308, was updated with more modern technology first tested in Formula One. That latest touch of magic ranged from electronic fuel injection to a flat bottom and a sequential gearbox, just like on the F1 cars.

TECHNICAL SPECIFICATION

ENGINE
rear, longitudinal, V8 (90°)

Bore and stroke	85x77 mm
Unitary cubic capacity	436.9
Total cubic capacity	3495.5
Valve gear	twin overhead camshafts
Number of valves	five per cylinder
Compression ratio	11:1
Fuel feed	Bosch Motronic 5.2 injection
Ignition	Bosch static electronic
Coolant	water
Lubrication	dry sump
Maximum power	380 hp at 8250 rpm
Specific power	108.7 hp/litre

TRANSMISSION
Rear-wheel drive

Clutch	single dry disc
Gearbox	en bloc with engine
	six gears + reverse
	(six + reverse – F 355 F1)

BODY
Two-seater coupé/GTS

CHASSIS

Chassis	integrated steel body with trellis rear chassis
Front suspension	independent, double wishbones, coil springs, anti-roll bar, gas-filled dampers
Rear suspension	independent, double wishbones, coil springs, anti-roll bar, gas-filled dampers
Brakes	disc
Steering	rack
Fuel tank	82 litres
Tyres front/rear	225/40 ZR 18, 264/40 ZR 18

DIMENSIONS AND WEIGHT

Wheelbase	2450 mm
Track front/rear	1514/1615 mm
Length	4250 mm
Width	1900 mm
Height	1170 mm
Kerb weight	1350 kg

PERFORMANCE

Top speed	295 km/h
Power to weight ratio	3.5 kg/hp

Ferrari F 355 Coupé, GTS and F 355 F1 1994

The genealogy of Maranello's eight-cylinder engine was installed in another prestigious Ferrari, as had been the case with the earlier 308, 328 and 348, all produced in sports saloon and GTS versions. Even so, the designation of the F 355 gave no indication of the number of its power unit's cylinders: in fact, the appellation simply stood for the car's 3,500 cubic capacity and the five valves of each of its cylinders. However, the F 355 was certainly a descendent of highly advanced technology that was unknown to the previous eight cylinder cars. The aerodynamic research conducted by Pininfarina was particularly refined - and not just in determining the shape of the body, which was inspired by the 348. Apart from the compact and sinuous line of the F355's exterior, distinguished by a pair of superimposed air intakes along the sides, the F 355 had a flat bottom, which ensured an optimum air flow distribution, and also guaranteed a constant interaction between the car and the ground, to the advantage of its roadholding. The cubic capacity of the F 355's eight-cylinder engine was increased to 3,495.5 for a power output of 380 hp through a gearbox with six forward speeds, which had become electronically controlled by the time of the 1997 Frankfurt Motor Show. Further confirmation of the importance of grafting experience gathered on the race track onto production cars, the F 355 F1 – the new version of the car – had a system by which gears could be changed using a small lever behind the steering wheel rim, just like on Ferrari's Formula One single-seaters. The GTS version of the F 355 maintained the same body shape, but had a detachable black roof. As was the case with the 348, a kit was also made available for the F 355 to convert it into a Challenge racer, so that it could compete on the track in the hands of sporting motorists and Ferrari concessionaires in a single marque championship that has enjoyed great success.

In his fifth year at Ferrari, Jean Alesi finally managed to achieve a long-held dream, which had so often slipped through his fingers due mainly to his cars' unreliability or plain bad luck: he won a Grand Prix in a Ferrari. Alesi scored his first success in a Rossa in Montreal, Canada, and that victory was the only positive result in a season dominated for the second successive year by a Benetton-Renault driven by Michael Schumacher.

TECHNICAL SPECIFICATION

ENGINE
rear, longitudinal, V12 (75°)

Bore and stroke	-
Unitary cubic capacity	249,7
Total cubic capacity	2997.3
Valve gear	twin overhead camshafts
Number of valves	four per cylinder
Compression ratio	12.8:1
Fuel feed	Magneti-Marelli electronic injection
Ignition	Magneti-Marelli static electronic
Coolant	water
Lubrication	dry sump
Maximum power	700 hp at 17,000 rpm
Specific power	233.5 hp/litre

TRANSMISSION
Rear-wheel drive

Clutch	three carbon fibre discs
Gearbox	en bloc with engine six gears + reverse

BODY
Single-seater

CHASSIS

Chassis	monocoque in composite materials
Front suspension	independent, double wishbones, spring-loaded pushrods
Rear suspension	independent, double wishbones, spring-loaded pushrods
Brakes	disc
Steering	rack
Fuel tank	140 litres
Tyres front/rear	-

DIMENSIONS AND WEIGHT

Wheelbase	2915 mm
Track front/rear	1690/1605 mm
Length	4380 mm
Width	1995 mm
Height	980 mm
Kerb weight	595 kg

PERFORMANCE

Top speed	310 km/h
Power to weight ratio	0.8 kg/hp

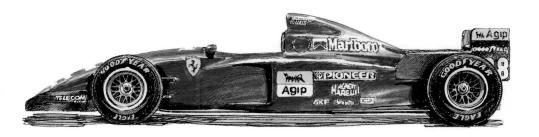

Ferrari 412 T2   1995

Changed motor sport regulations that now laid down a cubic capacity limited to three litres obliged the Maranello technicians to re-think the 12-cylinder engine for their 1995 car, which they dubbed the 412 T2. So the angle of inclination of the new F1 contender's cylinder banks was increased from its predecessor's 65° to 75°. It was able to put out 700 hp at a remarkable 17,000 revolutions per minute. The use of much advanced materials also enabled the Scuderia to reduce the cars overall weight to 595 kg and, in parallel, to diminish its bulk, very much to the advantage of best weight division and distribution, with the centre of gravity substantially advanced towards the cockpit. The external shape of the 412 T2 maintained the rather conventional imposition of the previous year's car, but with the abandonment of the raised nose in favour of a more traditional tapered profile. The sidepods were high and capacious to provide the 12-cylinder unit with the best possible air flow: for the same reason, further intakes were opened up in the rear engine cover behind the driver's back.

Both Berger and Alesi were confirmed for 1995, during which their performance was positive for the entire season, scoring numerous podium finishes and one victory, chalked up at last by Alesi in Montreal, Canada, helped along more by the retirement of Michael Schumacher and his Benetton-Ford than the Rossa's out-and-out competitiveness. But for the rest of the year, Lady Luck was less than kind to the Scuderia. At Monza, for instance, Alesi and Berger held first and second places respectively in the closing laps of the race, but they were both forced to retire with victory in sight: the Austrian due to the collapse of his car's suspension, smashed by the tiny television camera after it had detached itself form Alesi's car, on which one of the Frenchman's rear brake disc broke. So the world championship went to Schumacher again, just as he was preparing to move from Benetton-Renault to Ferrari.

By 1995, the time had come to launch the roadster version of the F 355, as was the case with the 348 two years earlier. The colour range of the new open top included out-of-the-ordinary metallic shades, which increased the fascination of the car and went well with the more refined interior colours and materials. The roadster was also offered with either a sequential or a manual gearbox.

TECHNICAL SPECIFICATION

ENGINE		CHASSIS	
rear, longitudinal, V8 (90°)		Chassis	steel, integrated with rear
			trellis chassis
Bore and stroke	85x77 mm	Front suspension	independent,
Unitary cubic capacity	436.9		double wishbones,
Total cubic capacity	3495.5		coil springs,
Valve gear	twin overhead camshafts		anti-roll bar, gas-filled dampers
Number of valves	five per cylinder	Rear suspension	independent,
Compression ratio	11:1		double wishbones,
Fuel feed	Bosch Motronic 5.2 injection		coil springs,
Ignition	Bosch Motronic 5.2 static		anti-roll bar, gas-filled dampers
	electronic	Brakes	disc
Coolant	water	Steering	rack
Lubrication	dry sump	Fuel tank	82 litres
Maximum power	380 hp at 8250 rpm	Tyres front/rear	225/40 ZR 18, 265/40 ZR 18
Specific power	108.7 hp/litre		
		DIMENSIONS AND WEIGHT	
TRANSMISSION		Wheelbase	2450
Rear-wheel drive		Track front/rear	1514/1615 mm
Clutch	single dry disc	Length	4250 mm
Gearbox	en bloc with engine	Width	1900 mm
	six gears + reverse	Height	1170 mm
	(six gears + reverse – F 355 F1)	Kerb weight	1350 mm
BODY		PERFORMANCE	
Two-seater roadster		Top speed	295 km/h
		Power to weight ratio	3.5 kg/hp

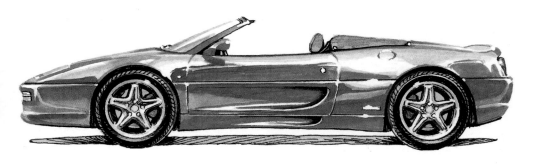

Ferrari F 355 Spider   1995

Maranello's practice of soon following the presentation of a new model with a road-ster version continued with the F 355; in the spring of 1995, Ferrari "uncovered" the car and introduced an open top version of the sports saloon, as always created main-ly with the United States market in mind.

As had already been the case with other models, the absence of a roof group ended up emphasising the assertive and elegant lines of the car even more, although the new Ferrari retained the same shape as its closed sister. The front end was of new concept to the range, although it had been previously seen on the 512 M. There were double air vents along the flanks, an innovative design for the 18-inch, five-spoke alloy rims which boasted 18-inch diameter ultra-low profile tyres, and the tail was slightly in depression in relation to the profile of the engine cover, curved upwards to create the slightest suggestion of a spoiler.

The most important new feature of the roadster was the hood's semi-automatic rais-ing and lowering system. It was a task carried out by an electronic management sys-tem, which had the job of synchronising the hood's movement with that of the seats and side windows, ensuring they took up their positions in perfect unison with each other during the opening and closing procedures. Once down, the hood stored itself behind an elegant material cover, which pushed itself towards the rear mudguards to create an image of considerable aesthetic impact with the car's body, and engine cover, furrowed by a series of straight air vents through which to cool the roadster's V8 engine. From 1997, a six-speed sequential gearbox also became available for the open top F 355, its control behind the steering wheel rim, meaning the disappearance of the gear lever.

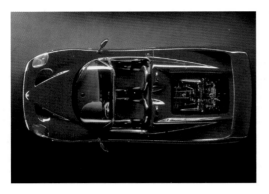

The heir to the Ferrari F40 could be nothing other than another extraordinary car: it was the F 50, which fitted the bill well and was a sort of Grand Prix car in grand tourer garb, to which Maranello transferred much of the technology and experience it had gathered in recent years with its single seaters. That included a monocoque made of composite materials, a fuel tank in rubberised material, which was sourced from the aircraft industry, and hubs in titanium.

TECHNICAL SPECIFICATION

ENGINE		CHASSIS	
central, longitudinal, V12 (65°)		*Chassis*	monocoque in carbon fibre
		Front suspension	F1-type double
Bore and stroke	85x69 mm		wishbones, coil springs
Unitary cubic capacity	391,6		pushrod dampers
Total cubic capacity	4698.5	*Rear suspension*	F1-type double
Valve gear	twin overhead camshafts		wishbones, coil springs,
Number of valves	five per cylinder		pushrod dampers
Compression ratio	11.3:1	*Brakes*	disc
Fuel feed	Bosch Motronic 2.7 injection	*Steering*	rack
Ignition	Bosch Motronic 2.7 static	*Fuel tank*	105 litres
	electronic	*Tyres front/rear*	245/35 ZR 18, 335/30 ZR 18
Coolant	water		
Lubrication	dry sump	DIMENSIONS AND WEIGHT	
Maximum power	520 hp at 8500 rpm	*Wheelbase*	2580 mm
Specific power	111 hp/litre	*Track front/rear*	1620/1602 mm
		Length	4480 mm
TRANSMISSION		*Width*	1986 mm
Rear-wheel drive		*Height*	1120 mm
Clutch	two dry discs	*Kerb weight*	1230 kg
Gearbox	en bloc with engine		
	six gears and reverse	PERFORMANCE	
BODY		*Top speed*	325 km/h
Sports tourer/barchetta		*Power to weight ratio*	3.87 kg/hp

Ferrari F 50   1995

When the Ferrari F 50 was unveiled at the 1995 Geneva Motor Show, it must have created the same kind of impact as Maranello's sports and prototype racing cars of the late Sixties and early Seventies, among them the 512 S and M. The project that gave birth to the F 50, heir to the F 40 of eight years earlier, was grandiose in all respects and represented the most advanced meeting point between cars for road and track use. There were many analogies with the Prancing Horse's Formula One cars, including a monocoque in carbon fibre, the engine group and transmission located at the rear and also playing a load-carrying role, the lower area of the car developed to exploit ground effect to the full, the body made entirely of composite materials and, of course, its performance. Powered by a 65°, 4,698.5 cc V12 engine that put out 520 hp at 8,500 rpm, the F 50 had a top speed of 325 km/h and could accelerate from 0-100 km/h in just 3.87 seconds. There were two version of this covered wheel "Formula One" car - a barchetta with two roll bars - one behind each of the seats – with a hard top and a sports saloon.

The commemorative car's genuine racing pedigree and flair plus its low and aerodynamic line made the F 50 so much like a prototype it encouraged Ferrari to build a competition version of the car in 1996, in which the 12-cylinder engine of the F 93 A was installed for possible use in the Endurance BPR racing series against the McLaren F1 GTr and the Porsche 911 GT1. Unfortunately, after promising tests carried out by Dario Benuzzi at Fiorano, the project went no further. The Ferrari F 50, paragon of design and technology in the unadulterated style of Pininfarina, remained in production until 1997, by which time a total of 349 cars had been built and sold at a price that was way out of mere mortals' reach and strictly the preserve of the elite of the elite.

Winner of two F1 world championships with Benetton in 1994 and 1995, Michael Schumacher joined Scuderia Ferrari at the end of '95. With the F 310 designed by John Barnard, once more head of the team's technical management, the German driver quickly demonstrated his extraordinary talent by winning three Grands Prix and taking third place in the title chase, behind the Williams-Renaults of Damon Hill and Jacques Villeneuve.

TECHNICAL SPECIFICATION

ENGINE		
rear, longitudinal, V10 (75°)		
Bore and stroke	90x47.2 mm	
	(92x45.1 – San Marino GP)	
Unitary cubic capacity	249.8	
Total cubic capacity	2998.1	
Valve gear	twin overhead camshafts	
Number of valves	four per cylinder	
Compression ratio	-	
Fuel feed	Magneti-Marelli electronic	
	injection	
Ignition	single, Magneti-Marelli	
	electronic injection	
Coolant	water	
Lubrication	dry sump	
Maximum power	700 hp at 16,000 rpm	
	(725 hp at 16,500 rpm –	
	San Marino GP)	
Specific power	233.4 hp/litre	
	241.8 – San Marino GP)	
TRANSMISSION		
Rear-wheel drive		
Clutch	multi-disc	
Gearbox	en bloc with engine	
	six gears + reverse	
	(seven + reverse – Belgian GP)	

BODY	
Single-seater	
CHASSIS	
Chassis	monocoque in carbon fibre
Front suspension	independent,
	double wishbones,
	spring-loaded
	pushrods
Rear suspension	independent,
	double wishbones,
	spring-loaded
	pushrods
Brakes	disc
Steering	rack
Fuel tank	140 litres
Tyres front/rear	-
DIMENSIONS AND WEIGHT	
Wheelbase	2900 mm
Track front/rear	1690/1650 mm
Length	4355 mm
Width	1995 mm
Height	970 mm
Weight in running order	600 kg
PERFORMANCE	
Top speed	320 km/h
Power to weight ratio	0,8 kg/hp

Ferrari F 310 1996

A revolutionary car for an extraordinary driver: Michael Schumacher joined Scuderia Ferrari at the express wish of Gianni Agnelli, in whose opinion the German was the best. Those are the words that most suitably describe the story of the Ferrari F 310 and Benetton-Ford's double world champion, who was to drive the 310 when making his debut at the wheel of a Rossa.

The reduction of F1 cars' cubic capacity from 3,500 cc to 3,000 cc and the tough new regulations brought in by FIA for safety purposes at the end of 1995 obliged Ferrari, as well as all other competing teams, to go back to the drawing board and start from scratch again, beginning with designing a new engine. Maranello opted for a normally aspirated 10-cylinder unit built from sophisticated fusions of aluminium alloy, its cylinder banks at a 75° angle: a power unit considered more advantageous than the V12 in both weight saving terms at only 120 kg and in bulk, being 60 cm shorter than the 12-cylinder. John Barnard designed a car of revolutionary shape around the V10, with a low and tapered nose, which was later raised again from the Grand Prix of Canada. The sidepods were also detached from the central part of the chassis and linked to it only by a winged plane, which persevered with the same concept as that used for the unfortunate F 92 A in 1992. Barnard also designed a new gearbox, which he installed in a transverse position. To elongate the car's wheelbase, he went for a spacer positioned between the engine and gearbox, in which the oil reservoir was housed and to which the rear suspension rockers were directly attached. Michael Schumacher's first year at Ferrari, where his team mate was Eddie Irvine, ended up as a positive one: that year, he won the Grands Prix of Spain, Belgium and Italy: his 59 points earned him third place in the drivers' world championship, won by Damon Hill and his Williams-Renault. Ferrari also came second in the world constructors' table with 70 points.

Maranello, the small industrial centre a stone's throw from Modena, earned world fame as the home of Ferrari, so it was only fitting that the town's name became part of the official designation of one of the Prancing Horse's cars. So the 550 Maranello was launched in 1996, a potent grand tourer with which Ferrari went back to the V12 power unit configuration with a 5,473.9 cc, longitudinally mounted front engine. A great classic that quickly became yet another sales success.

TECHNICAL SPECIFICATION

ENGINE
front, longitudinal, V12 (65°)

Bore and stroke	88x75
Unitary cubic capacity	456.2
Total cubic capacity	5473,9
Valve gear	twin overhead camshafts
Number of valves	four per cylinder
Compression ratio	10.8:1
Fuel feed	Bosch Motronic M 5.2 electronic injection
Ignition	Bosch Motronic M 5.2 static electronic
Coolant	water
Lubrication	dry sump
Maximum power	485 hp at 7000 rpm
Specific power	88.6 hp/litre

TRANSMISSION
Rear-wheel drive

Clutch	single dry disc
Gearbox	en bloc with differential six gears + reverse

BODY
Two-seater coupé

CHASSIS

Chassis	tubular, steel
Front suspension	independent, double wishbones, coil springs anti-roll bar, gas-filled dampers
Rear suspension	independent, double wishbones, coil springs, anti-roll bar, gas-filled dampers
Brakes	disc
Steering	rack
Fuel tank	114 litres
Tyres front/rear	255/40 ZR 18, 295/35 ZR 18

DIMENSIONS AND WEIGHT

Wheelbase	2500 mm
Track front/rear	1632/1586 mm
Length	4555 mm
Width	1935 mm
Height	1277 mm
Kerb weight	1690 kg

PERFORMANCE

Top speed	320 km/h
Power to weight ratio	3.48 kg/hp

Ferrari 550 Maranello　　　　1996

It is only fitting that tradition is handed down and refined over time to appear in a new, more modern guise, even many years later. And if that tradition has been the basis of cars that have indelibly marked the history of a company like Ferrari, then such a practice eventually becomes an obligation. Such was the case in the summer of 1996, when Ferrari took the wraps off another of its great classics – the 550 Maranello, powered by a 65° V12 engine up front in a longitudinal position, its traditional location. It was a potent unit of 5,473.9 cc, which generated 485 hp at 7,000 rpm – and that could propel the car to a top speed of 320 km/h and from 0-100 km/h in 4.4 seconds. For a car weighing in at 1,690 kg, figures like those simply underline a scintillating performance capability. Those are the salient facts that concern the prowess of the Ferrari 550 Maranello, a car that honoured its origins by carrying the name of its hometown for all to see. In delineating the new Rossa's shape, Pininfarina was able to steer a course between tradition and innovation. The long bonnet boasted a generous air intake and contrasted with the short rear end, between which was a cockpit set well back, double air vents inclined and slotted into the flanks, which were themselves crossed by an accentuated dihedral line and circular optical groups in the tail. These were all elements that had their roots in classic Ferraris of times gone by, updated by the adoption of the most advanced aerodynamic technology of the day. With a CX of 0.33, which indicates the car's coefficient of aerodynamic penetration or slipperiness as it cuts through the air, the 550 Maranello had an underbody designed to optimise its interaction with the ground; electronic set-up and traction control all helped to make this commemorative car one of the most technologically advanced Ferraris ever built.

With the Maranello, Ferrari set another important standard: the unification of exceptional performance with a leather interior of extremely high prestige and a level of comfort worthy of a saloon of the greatest luxury.

The 1997 F1 season was one in which Ferrari climbed right back to the top of the sport. The F 310 B proved to be a fast and well equilibrated car; better still, it was reliable throughout the season. Michael Schumacher (picture) was the architect of this refound competitiveness and was able to win five Grands Prix to take second place to Williams-Renault's Jacques Villeneuve in the drivers' championship.

TECHNICAL SPECIFICATION

ENGINE
rear, longitudinal, V10 (75°)

Bore and stroke	-
Unitary cubic capacity	299.8
Total cubic capacity	2998.1
Valve gear	twin overhead camshafts
Number of valves	four per cylinder
Compression ratio	12.8:1
Fuel feed	Magneti-Marelli electronic
Ignition	Magneti-Marelli static electronic
Coolant	water
Lubrication	dry sump
Maximum power	750 hp at 17,000 rpm
Specific power	250 hp/litre

TRANSMISSION
Rear-wheel drive

Clutch	three carbon discs
Gearbox	en bloc with engine seven gears + reverse

BODY
Single-seater

CHASSIS

Chassis	monocoque in composite materials
Front suspension	independent, double wishbones, spring-loaded pushrod with coil spring and parallel damper
Rear suspension	independent, double wishbones, spring-loaded pushrod with damper, coil spring and parallel damper
Brakes	disc
Steering	rack
Fuel tank	140 litres
Tyres front/rear	-

DIMENSIONS AND WEIGHT

Wheelbase	2935 mm
Track front/rear	1690/1605 mm
Length	4358 mm
Width	1995 mm
Height	968 mm
Weight in running order	600 kg

PERFORMANCE

Top speed	325 km/h
Power to weight ratio	0.8 kg/hp

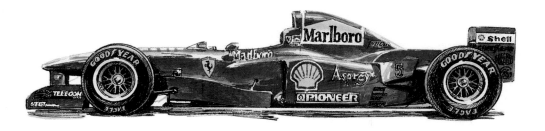

Ferrari F 310 B   1997

Ferrari had never really been in a position to fight for the Formula One World Championship since 1990. But that situation was eventually changed after the slow and laboured reconstruction of the Racing Department, which began in 1993 with the engagement of Jean Todt as its head, and culminated in early 1996 with the acquisition of double world champion Michael Schumacher.

The F 310 B was a logical evolution of the F 310 and retained the 2,998.1 cc, 75° V10 engine, which was further refined in both weight and bulk, but still put out a maximum of 750 hp at 17,000 rpm. At the start of the season, the car boasted a high nose and it continued in an almost straight line right through to the arc; the sidepods were also rather high and wide so that they could convey the maximum amount of air to the radiators. The rear wing with its vertical end plates was the result of much research and crossed two units of horizontal fairing that advanced until they joined the 'pods.

The 310 B showed itself to be as competitive as it was reliable, powering Michael Schumacher to five Grands Prix victories, including a memorable win in Monaco in the pouring rain, and to finally battle it out with Jacques Villeneuve and his Williams-Renault for the world title until the last cliff hanging race of the season. But unfortunately, that fight had an unhappy ending for Ferrari at the Grand Prix of Europe at Jerez, Spain. The German was still in the lead after his second pit stop and, therefore, well on his way to his third world championship: but he was unable to contain Jacques Villeneuve's climb back up the field, during which the Canadian attempted to overtake the Ferrari driver. The two collided as a result of an unethical manoeuvre by Schumacher, but it was Villeneuve who was able to continue and went on to win the world championship, while Schumacher retired. Later, the Ferrari number one was nominally excluded from the championship table, but was allowed to retain the points he had won.

Not even six victories were enough for Michael Schumacher, photographed at Monza, to beat Mika Häkkinen and his McLaren-Mercedes for the world title. The Finn won eight Grands Prix and became champion for the first time in his distinguished career. Ferrari's number two driver, Eddie Irvine, did well and scored eight podium finishes to take fourth place in the championship table, with 47 points.

TECHNICAL SPECIFICATION

ENGINE		CHASSIS	
rear, longitudinal, V10 (80°)		Chassis	monocoque in composite material
Bore and stroke	94x43.1 mm	Front suspension	independent,
Unitary cubic capacity	299.8 mm		double wishbones,
Total cubic capacity	2998.3		torsion spring,
Valve gear	twin overhead camshafts		spring-loaded pushrods
Number of valves	four per cylinder	Rear suspension	independent,
Compression ratio	13.3:1		double wishbones,
Fuel feed	Magneti-Marelli digital electronic injection		torsion spring, spring-loaded pushrods
Ignition	Magneti-Marelli static electronic	Brakes	disc
		Steering	rack
Coolant	water	Fuel tank	200 litres
Lubrication	dry sump	Tyres front/rear	-
Maximum power	760 hp at 17,600 rpm		
Specific power	253.5 hp/litre	**DIMENSIONS AND WEIGHT**	
		Wheelbase	2953 mm
TRANSMISSION		Track front/rear	1490/1405 mm
Rear-wheel drive		Length	4340 mm
Clutch	three carbon discs	Width	1795 mm
Gearbox	en bloc with engine	Height	961 mm
	seven gears + reverse	Kerb weight	500 kg
BODY		**PERFORMANCE**	
Single-seater		Top speed	-
		Power to weight ratio	1.9 kg/hp

Ferrari F 300 1998

After the extraordinary finish to the 1997 world championship, which cost Michael Schumacher his exclusion from the final standings after his unsporting performance at Jerez, Scuderia Ferrari was back for more in the 1998 Formula One World Championship with yet another car derived from its predecessor, without any significant new innovations. John Barnard had left the team, so the F 300 was designed by Rory Byrne and Ross Brawn, both of whom were with Michael Schumacher during his Benetton years. A change in the regulations that meant a return to tyres with grooved treads made it essential to review the aerodynamics of the car. The straight out position of the nose and the fin in the lower area that acted as an air diffuser were both retained, but modifications were made to the sidepods, which narrowed towards the rear. For the third successive year, it was decided to further develop the V10, with the angle of inclination between the cylinder banks taken to 80° and a power output that had risen to 780 hp at 17,600 rpm by the end of the season at Spa.

Mika Häkkinen and his McLaren-Mercedes took over from the Williams-Renault drivers as Michael Schumacher's toughest opponent. The whole season was dominated by the duel between those two drivers, with Häkkinen piling up a reasonable points lead early in the season, having won in Australia, Brazil, Spain and Monaco. But after victory in Argentina, Schumacher won three Grands Prix in a row in Canada, France and Great Britain. Then Häkkinen logged another four victories from the Grand Prix of Austria through to the end of the season, which dashed the German's title hopes for another year: even winning six Grands Prix was not enough to allow him to bring the much coveted title back to Maranello - one that had been anxiously awaited by the Prancing Horse's tifosi for 18 long years.

In 1998, the 456 GT was the object of a profound re-styling. The face-lift affected the nose of the car, in particular, as it was given a radiator grill of different design and directional indicator lights set into the bumper bars. An optional four-speed automatic gearbox could also be fitted to the new grand tourer to turn it into the 456 GTA. The performance of the car is also worthy of note: it had a declared top speed of 298 km/h and a 0-100 km/h acceleration time of 5.5 seconds.

TECHNICAL SPECIFICATION

ENGINE		CHASSIS	
front, longitudinal, V12 (65°)		Chassis	tubular, steel
		Front suspension	independent, double
Bore and stroke	88x75 mm		wishbones, coil springs,
Unitary cubic capacity	456.1		anti-roll bar, gas-filled dampers
Total cubic capacity	5473.9	Rear suspension	independent,
Valve gear	twin overhead camshafts		double wishbones,
Number of valves	four per cylinder		coil springs,
Compression ratio	10.6:1		anti-roll bar, self-levelling
Fuel feed	Bosch Motronic M 5.2		dampers
	electronic injection	Brakes	disc
Ignition	Bosch Motronic M5.2	Steering	rack
	electronic injection	Fuel tank	110 litres
Coolant	water	Tyres front/rear	255/45 ZR 17, 285/40 ZR 17
Lubrication	dry sump		
Maximum power	442 hp at 6250 rpm	DIMENSIONS AND WEIGHT	
Specific power	80.7 hp/litre	Wheelbase	2600 mm
		Track front/rear	1585/1606 mm
TRANSMISSION		Length	4730 mm
Rear-wheel drive		Width	1920 mm
Clutch	single dry disc	Height	1300 mm
Gearbox	en bloc with differential	Kerb weight	1690 kg (1770 – GTA)
	six gears + reverse - automatic		
	(four + reverse – GTA)	PERFORMANCE	
		Top speed	300 km/h
BODY		Power to weight ratio	3.8 kg/hp (4 – GTA)
2+2 coupé			

Ferrari 456 M GT and GTA   1998

At first glance, the 456 GT seemed the same car as its 1992 predecessor when it made its debut at the March 1998 Geneva Motor Show. But in reality, the M that completed the new coupé 2+2's designation stood for the Italian word Modificata or modified. Sure enough, a careful analysis of the car confirmed the 456 M GT offered a series of aesthetic changes with which Ferrari conducted a highly competent re-styling operation with the intention of not disrupting the well-established and much liked line that first saw the light of day six years earlier. The modifications affected the nose in particular: it had become wider and of different profile, inside which were housed circular fog lights, while the indicators located in the fairing had been changed at the same time to a smaller diameter. Two air intakes previously housed in the lower area of the front fairing had also been relocated. Slight styling changes were made to the number plate holder and the lower part of the rear underbody. The nose became more substantial and profiled for aerodynamic reasons. The 5,474 cc, 65° V12 engine remained unchanged, while the most substantial mechanical modifications were made to the car's suspension, which was completely revised. The Ferrari 456 M GT was given independent suspension of transverse parallelograms, managed electronically by a system that checked and modified its attitude in relation to the road conditions it encountered. The new suspension technology worked in unison with the ABS braking system and the distributor of the EBD rear braking network. The 456 M was also offered with a four-speed automatic gearbox and that derivative was christened the GTA. Like the 1992 car, the soft and elegant lines of the 456 M GT and GTA lent themselves effectively to a range of metallic colours – blue, silver and dark burgundy – that were suitable alternatives to the traditional red.

Finnish driver Mika Salo, pictured in the Ferrari F 399, took the place of Michael Schumacher after the German's accident in the Grand Prix of Great Britain at Silverstone. The Finn came second in the German GP and third in the Italian. With Schumacher out of the running for the world championship, Eddie Irvine made his bid for the title and won four races to rival Mike Häkkinen for the crown, right up until the last race of the season in Japan, but he was unable to take the title.

TECHNICAL SPECIFICATION

ENGINE		CHASSIS	
rear, longitudinal, V10 (80°)		*Chassis*	monocoque in composite materials
Bore and stroke	94x41.4	*Front suspension*	independent,
Unitary cubic capacity	299.7		double wishbones,
Total cubic capacity	2997		spring-loaded
Valve gear	twin overhead camshafts		pushrods
Number of valves	four per cylinder	*Rear suspension*	independent,
Compression ratio	13.3:1		double wishbones,
Fuel feed	Magneti-Marelli digital electronic injection		spring-loaded pushrods
Ignition	Magneti-Marelli static electronic	*Brakes*	disc
		Steering	rack
Coolant	water	*Fuel tank*	200 litres
Lubrication	dry sump	*Tyres front/rear*	-
Maximum power	800 hp at 17,500 rpm		
Specific power	267 hp / litre	DIMENSIONS AND WEIGHT	
		Wheelbase	3000 mm
TRANSMISSION		*Track front/rear*	1490/1405 mm
Rear-wheel drive		*Length*	4387 mm
Clutch	three carbon discs	*Width*	1795 mm
Gearbox	en bloc with engine seven gears + reverse	*Height*	961 mm
		Weight in running order	600 kg
BODY		PERFORMANCE	
Single-seater		*Top speed*	-
		Power to weight ratio	0.7 kg / hp

Ferrari F 399 1999

Five victories in 1997, six in 1998 and in both cases Ferrari came second in the Formula One World Championship for constructors. It was with the knowledge that it had been so near and yet so far from the title that Ferrari openly declared its intention to go for it in 1999. The car on which Maranello put its money was the F 399, designed by the dynamic duo of Rory Byrne and Ross Brawn, and was, once more, the logical evolution of its predecessor, which was always able to count on its reliability and performance, right from the first race of the season. Externally, modifications were only made to the profile of the sidepods. They became higher and not so narrow in the cockpit area, which was made more spacious to improve driver safety, plus the exhaust pipe blow at the rear of the car.

Ferrari's plans started to work immediately, with Eddie Irvine winning the season's first race in Melbourne, Australia. Right up until the Grand Prix of Monaco, Ferrari's insistent march towards the title was, to say the least, exciting, Schumacher won at both Imola and in Monte Carlo, but from the Grand Prix of Spain McLaren gave Häkkinen, Schumacher's main rival for world championship honours again, the material with which to win in Barcelona and Canada and to come second in France. Then the German's bid for the title came to a dramatic end on the first lap of the Grand Prix of Great Britain at Silverstone, where he had a frightening accident that fractured his right leg at Stowe. Out of the running, Schumi's bid for the title was passed on to Irvine, who won in Austria and Germany, ahead of his new team mate Salo. Back in the cockpit at Sepang, Schumacher ceded victory to Irvine in an attempt to help the Irishman win the title fight. The matter was decided during the last race of the season in Japan, where Irvine's third place was not enough to earn him the championship. Hä kkinen won the race and became world champion again. But reliability rewarded Scuderia Ferrari: the team brought the world constructors' title back to Maranello after a 16 year absence, with 128 points to McLaren's 124.

In 1999, the genealogy of the eight-cylinder Ferrari engine was once again revitalised with the introduction of the 360 Modena, a car of absolute state-of-the-art technological content, from its aluminium monocoque to the carefully honed aerodynamics of its underbody and optional F1 sequential gearbox. The external shape of the 360 Modena was also a major leap forward from all that had gone before.

TECHNICAL SPECIFICATION

ENGINE
rear, longitudinal, V8 (90°)

Bore and stroke	85x79 mm
Unitary cubic capacity	448.2
Total cubic capacity	3586
Valve gear	twin overhead camshafts
Number of valves	five per cylinder
Compression ratio	11:1
Fuel feed	Bosch Motronic ME 7.3 injection
Ignition	Bosch Motronic ME 7.3 electronic
Coolant	water
Lubrication	dry sump
Maximum power	400 hp at 8500 rpm
Specific power	111.5 hp/litre

TRANSMISSION
Rear-wheel drive	
Clutch	single dry disc
Gearbox	en bloc with engine six gears + reverse manual or F1 sequential

BODY
Two-seater roadster

CHASSIS
Chassis	space frame-type in aluminium
Front suspension	independent, double wishbones, coil springs, anti-roll bar, gas-filled dampers
Rear suspension	independent, double wishbones, pushrod, coil springs, anti-roll bar, gas-filled dampers
Brakes	disc
Steering	rack
Fuel tank	95 litres
Tyres front/rear	215/45 ZR 18, 275/40 ZR 18

DIMENSIONS AND WEIGHT
Wheelbase	2600 mm
Track front/rear	1669/1617 mm
Length	4477 mm
Width	1922 mm
Height	1235 mm
Kerb weight	1350 kg

PERFORMANCE
Top speed	300 km/h
Power to weight ratio	3.2 kg/hp

Ferrari 360 Modena   1999

Renewing a range of cars like the eight cylinders from Maranello was never going to be a simple task, given their immense sales success – greater than the company had ever previously known - enjoyed by earlier such products, like the 308 and then the F 355. But Ferrari and Pininfarina decided together, without hesitation, to create a radically new car from both the appearance and mechanical standpoints – and that is exactly what happened. The fruit of their labours appeared at the 1999 Geneva Motor Show in the form of the 360 Modena. Ferrari wanted to build a car of advanced aerodynamics with its weight pared to the bone, so it sacrificed a number of styling features that were considered indispensable to a Ferrari up until that time, like the classic nose, which was replaced by a single unit of fairing in which were two sizeable air intakes to cool the radiators, positioned in front of the axle. The soft and compact surfaces of the Modena continued along the bonnet and on to the windscreen, which was fairly well inclined, then along the flanks in which there were also pairs of air intakes: two mounted in front of the rear wings, which harked back to the 250 Le Mans design, and two larger ones lower down on the sides. The eight-cylinder engine was positioned longitudinally and was visible through a rear window. The tail of the 360 Modena repeated the double apertures at the front, from each of which emerged double exhaust pipes. Weight containment was possible due to the adoption of a space frame chassis built entirely of aluminium, as was the body.
The power of the 90° V8 engine was upped to 3,586 cc to return 400 hp at 8,500 rpm. On this model, too, the six-speed gearbox was also made available with a sequential control lever behind the steering wheel rim.
At the end of 1999, Ferrari built a corresponding racing version of the Modena, which would enable the Prancing Horse's motor racing customers to take to the track and compete in Ferrari's 2000 Challenge series.

Michael Schumacher brought the Formula One World Championship for drivers back to Maranello at last in 2000 - after a 21-year absence. That was also a record points year, with the German scoring 108 in the drivers' and Ferrari 170 to win the constructors' title, which came from 10 victories – Schumacher's nine and Barrichello's one – plus podium placings. The Brazilian, shown on the left competing at Monza, contributed in a determinate way to bringing the two titles back to Maranello.

TECHNICAL SPECIFICATION

ENGINE		CHASSIS	
rear, longitudinal, V10 (90°)		*Chassis*	monocoque in composite materials
Bore and stroke	96x41.40 mm	*Front suspension*	independent,
Unitary cubic capacity	299.6		wishbones pushrods and
Total cubic capacity	2996.6		torsion springs,
Valve gear	twin overhead camshafts	*Rear suspension*	independent,
Number of valves	four per cylinder		wishbones pushrods and
Compression ratio	13.2;1		torsion springs
Fuel feed	Magneti-Marelli digital electronic	*Brakes*	disc
		Steering	rack
Ignition	Magneti-Marelli static electronic	*Fuel tank*	141 litres
		Tyres front/rear	-
Coolant	water		
Lubrication	dry sump	DIMENSIONS AND WEIGHT	
Maximum power	810 hp at 17,600 rpm	*Wheelbase*	3010 mm
Specific power	270.3 hp/litre	*Track front/rear*	1490/1405 mm
		Length	4397 mm
TRANSMISSION		*Width*	1795 mm
Rear-wheel drive		*Height*	959 mm
Clutch	multi-disc	*Weight in running order*	600 kg
Gearbox	en bloc with engine seven gears + reverse	PERFORMANCE	
		Top speed	over 320 km/h
BODY		*Power to weight ratio*	0.7 kg/hp
Single-seater			

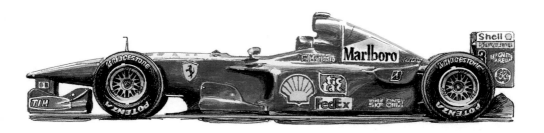

Ferrari F1 2000

2000

After having restored the world constructors championship to Ferrari in 1999, Maranello could do nothing other than renew its challenge to McLaren-Mercedes for the drivers' title in 2000, putting its faith in a team that was, by this time, a consolidated affair with the constant motivation of Michael Schumacher, who was joined by new acquisition Rubens Barrichello, and the new F1 2000. The philosophy of Ross Brawn and Rory Byrne, who were little inclined to disrupt the imposition of previous models, was also reconfirmed with the F1 2000, born from the conceptual basis of the F 399. The car was, naturally, the object of customary aerodynamic refinements, particular attention having been paid to weight distribution and lowering the centre of gravity. The V10 engine, code numbered the 049, was now able to put out 810 hp at 17,600 rpm yet, at the same time; it was made lighter and more compact, having been built from special alloys.

Schumacher was immediately able to exploit the qualities of the F1 2000, winning the season's first three Grands Prix in Australia, Brazil and San Marino, to accumulate a significant advantage over the McLarens of Häkkinen and Coulthard: but he lost the Grands Prix of Great Britain and Spain to the Anglo-German team. Ferrari's number one also lost ground mid-season, in part due to two consecutive accidents, one in Austria and the other in his homeland, which put him out of action on the first lap of each event. But he was soon back on song towards the end of the year, during which he won another four GPs and, at long last, Ferrari's next drivers' world championship, which found its way back to Maranello after a 21-year absence.

The record achievements that season included 10 victories, one of them by Barrichello in Germany, for a total of 170 points, of which 108 were chalked up by Schumacher, to give Ferrari its second world constructors' championship.

Ferrari brought out the roadster version of its closed 360 Modena at the 2000 Geneva Motor Show. The removal of the roof group had required a new body design behind the cab, where a home was also found for the car's ultra-modern hood when down. The soft top's raising and lowering system was completely automatic, able to complete the operation in just a few seconds.

TECHNICAL SPECIFICATION

ENGINE		CHASSIS	
rear, longitudinal, V8 (90°)		Chassis	space frame-type in aluminium
Bore and stroke	85x79 mm	Front suspension	independent, double
Unitary cubic capacity	448.2		wishbones, coil springs,
Total cubic capacity	3586		anti-roll bar, gas-filled dampers
Valve gear	twin overhead camshafts	Rear suspension	independent, double
Number of valves	five per cylinder		wishbones, pushrod, coil
Compression ratio	11:1		springs,anti-roll bar,
Fuel feed	Bosch Motronic ME 7.3 injection		gas-filled dampers
Ignition	Bosch Motronic ME 7.3 electronic	Brakes	disc
		Steering	rack
Coolant	water	Fuel tank	95 litres
Lubrication	dry sump	Tyres front/rear	215/45 ZR 18, 275/40 ZR 18
Maximum power	400 hp at 8500 rpm		
Specific power	111.5 hp/litre	DIMENSIONS AND WEIGHT	
		Wheelbase	2600 mm
		Track front/rear	1669/1617 mm
TRANSMISSION		Length	4477 mm
Rear-wheel drive		Width	1922 mm
Clutch	single dry disc	Height	1235 mm
Gearbox	en bloc with engine	Kerb weight	1350 kg
	six gears + reverse manual		
	or F1 sequential	PERFORMANCE	
		Top speed	300 km/h
		Power to weight ratio	3.3 kg/hp
BODY			
Two-seater roadster			

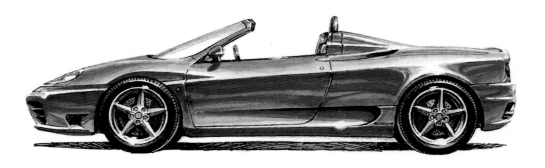

Ferrari 360 Spider   2000

The 2000 Geneva Motor Show was the stage on which the 360 Spider was unveiled, a car that took the place of the F 355 in that configuration, which went out of production in 1999. The front of the new model was unchanged, except for new concept fairing for the nose and double air intakes along the flanks. The most significant amount of re-styling work was carried out by Pininfarina on the rear end immediately behind the cab, where the accommodation of the hood had demanded a re-think of the car's shape.

A completely automatic system of raising and lowering the hood had been installed in the 360 Spider and that enabled the opening and closing operation to be completed in just 20 seconds. Once down, the hood found its place in an small space between the cab and the amidships engine: to cover the soft top, Pininfarina had developed a modern system, which was also in the best traditions of Ferrari barchettas at one and the same time. The two roll bars positioned behind each seat and the colour-keyed body that spilled over into the interior constituted an evident harking back to the open sports racers of the Fifties and Sixties. On each side of the cover that masked the presence of the hood were two spine fins that gave the car an overall equilibrium and symmetry, while also acting as a styling link between the central area of the car and the engine cover. The 360 Spider was powered by the same 3,586 cc, 90° V8 engine as the one installed in the sports saloon.

Using the 360 Spider as a base, Pininfarina built a one-off 360 barchetta in metallic silver in the summer of 2000, a prestigious commission by Gianni Agnelli as a wedding gift for Luca Cordero di Montezemolo, president of Ferrari.

In 2000, Ferrari went back to associating the name Barchetta – used to describe the cars bodied by Carrozzeria Touring in the Forties and Fifties – with its open top cars, this time for a roofless version of the 550 Maranello: it was called the 550 Barchetta Pininfarina. With this car, Maranello offered once more some of the flavour of its great classics of the past, a modern version of a car of unquestioned fascination – a roadster powered by a 65° V12 engine in a front longitudinal position.

TECHNICAL SPECIFICATION

ENGINE		
front, longitudinal, V12 (65°)		
Bore and stroke	88x75 mm	
Unitary cubic capacity	456.1	
Total cubic capacity	5473.9	
Valve gear	twin overhead camshafts	
Number of valves	four per cylinder	
Compression ratio	10.8:1	
Fuel feed	Bosch Motronic M 5.2 digital injection	
Ignition	Bosch Motronic M 5.2 static electronic	
Coolant	water	
Lubrication	dry sump	
Maximum power	485 hp at 7000 rpm	
Specific power	88.6 hp/litre	

TRANSMISSION	
Rear-wheel drive	
Clutch	single dry disc
Gearbox	en bloc with differential six gears + reverse

BODY
Two-seater barchetta

CHASSIS	
Chassis	tubular, steel
Front suspension	independent, double wishbones, coil springs, anti-roll bar, telescopic dampers
Rear suspension	independent, double wishbones, coil springs, anti-roll bar, telescopic dampers
Brakes	disc
Steering	rack
Fuel tank	114 litres
Tyres front/rear	255/40 ZR 18, 295/35 ZR 18

DIMENSIONS AND WEIGHT	
Wheelbase	2500 mm
Track front/rear	1632/1586 mm
Length	4555 mm
Width	1935 mm
Height	1258 mm
Weight in running order	1690 kg

PERFORMANCE	
Top speed	300 km/h
Power to weight ratio	3.48 kg/hp

Ferrari 550 Barchetta 2000

The name Barchetta used to describe a Ferrari immediately conjures up memories of fast and elegant cars like the 166 MM, bodied by Touring at the end of the Forties. A recollection rekindled at the 2000 Frankfurt Motor Show, where the Prancing Horse launched an open version of the 550 Maranello with that same, historic denomination: they called it the 550 Barchetta Pininfarina. The Turin stylist's name became an integral part of the car's official designation, which celebrated a collaboration that began way back in 1952 and became more consolidated and prolific as the years passed. The Barchetta Pininfarina was a thoroughbred roadster, up there with the 275 GTS/4 NART and the 365 GTS/4 Daytona and, like its illustrious predecessors, had a line of extraordinary elegance and cleanliness, combined with a level of absolutely top performance, provided by its 12-cylinder engine located, as tradition required - up front and north-south. The nose on the open version of the 550 Maranello seemed even longer, lower and more profiled, while having maintained unchanged the imposition of both the front end and engine cover. The ample windscreen protruded somewhat from the pillars, which were part colour-keyed with the rest of the body. The sides of the car remained unchanged up to the height of the doors, while the whole of the rear end was rethought. Compared to the closed version, the wings of the Barchetta were made to protrude less and their profile became straighter. As with the 360 Spider, behind each seat were located two roll bars, at the base of which began two slight bulges that gradually emerged from the smooth surface of the body. A small, rectangular air duct was opened up on the driver's side, while on the passenger's there was the kind of fuel filler cap typical of those used on the sports racing cars of the Sixties. The 550 Barchetta's engine was the same as that which powered the 550 Maranello: the 5,473.9 cc V12.

In 2001, Michael Schumacher won the drivers' world championship again and Ferrari topped the constructors' points table for the third consecutive year. At the Grand Prix of Italy at Monza, the Ferraris took to the track without their habitual sponsorship logos, but with a black band painted on their noses as a mark of respect for the people who lost their lives in the World Trade Centre tragedy in New York on 11 September. Rubens Barrichello came second and Schumacher fourth.

TECHNICAL SPECIFICATION

ENGINE		CHASSIS	
rear, longitudinal, V10 (90°)		*Chassis*	monocoque in composite materials
Bore and stroke	96x41.4 mm	*Front suspension*	independent,
Unitary cubic capacity	299.6		wishbones with pushrods
Total cubic capacity	2996.6		and torsion springs
Valve gear	twin overhead camshafts	*Rear suspension*	independent, wishbones
Number of valves	four per cylinder		with pushrods
Compression ratio	13.4:1		and torsion springs
Fuel feed	Magneti-Marelli electronic injection	*Brakes*	disc
		Steering	rack
Ignition	Magneti-Marelli static electronic	*Fuel tank*	141 litres
		Tyres front/rear	-
Coolant	water		
Lubrication	dry sump	DIMENSIONS AND WEIGHT	
Maximum power	840 hp at 18,000 rpm	*Wheelbase*	3010 mm
Specific power	280.3 hp/litre	*Track front/rear*	1470/1405 mm
		Length	4445 mm
TRANSMISSION		*Width*	1796 mm
Rear-wheel drive		*Height*	959 mm
Clutch	multi-disc	*Weight in running order*	600 kg
Gearbox	en bloc with engine seven + reverse		
		PERFORMANCE	
		Top speed	320 km/h
BODY		*Power to weight ratio*	0.7 kg/hp
Single-seater			

Ferrari F 2001 {#title} 2001

From the day of its introduction, the Ferrari F 2001 proudly wore the number 1 on its nose, underlining the fact that Michael Schumacher had brought the world drivers' championship back to Maranello the previous year, after an absence of 21 years.

The most significant difference between the new car and the F 2000, on which the F 2001 was based, was the shape of its nose. Starting from a rather high monocoque in the cockpit area, it inclined itself progressively downwards in correspondence with the front wing, giving it the harmonious appearance of a spoon. The shape of the F 2001 was heavily conditioned by the regulations introduced for 2001 on aerodynamic efficiency and safety, which resulted in a significant strengthening of the chassis and the use of protection elements around the cockpit.

The car was powered once more by Maranello's 90° V10, designated the 050, on which an enormous amount of "miniaturisation" work had been carried out to make it lighter and more compact. In the end, the unit had become 20 mm shorter, 25 mm lower and 8% lighter overall.

A constant yield, the ability to adapt itself to the different characteristics of the various circuits and, most important of all, reliability were the best qualities of the 2001's engine. The car was able to maintain its high level of performance and achievement throughout the season, enabling Michael Schumacher to set yet more records. The German's nine wins and 11 pole positions meant the world champion was able to win the title again, this time by the Grand Prix of Hungary – as did Nigel Mansell in the Williams-Renault in 1992 – with four Grands Prix still to go. That gave the Kerpen driver his fourth world championship and put him within one title of equalling Juan Manuel Fangio's long standing record: Ferrari became the world's top F1 constructor again.

The third successive world drivers' championship for Michael Schumacher, and the fourth constructors' title for Scuderia Ferrari-Marlboro. The Maranello team's domination did not even come to a halt in 2002. Indeed, it became even more absolute and, for some, rather embarrassing as far as the squad's opponents were concerned. This time, Schumacher was able to clinch the world title by the Grand Prix of France at Magny Cours – six races before the end of the season.

TECHNICAL SPECIFICATION

ENGINE
rear, longitudinal, V10 (90°)

Bore and stroke	97x40.5 mm
Unitary cubic capacity	299.7
Total cubic capacity	2997
Valve gear	twin overhead camshafts
Number of valves	four per cylinder
Compression ratio	13.4:1
Fuel feed	Magneti-Marelli electronic injection
Ignition	Magneti-Marelli static electronic
Coolant	water
Lubrication	dry sump
Maximum power	850 hp at 18,000 rpm
Specific power	283.6 hp/litre

TRANSMISSION
Rear-wheel drive

Clutch	multi-disc
Gearbox	en bloc with engine seven + reverse

BODY
Single-seater

CHASSIS

Chassis	monocoque in composite materials
Front suspension	independent, wishbones with pushrods and torsion springs
Rear suspension	independent, wishbones with pushrods and torsion springs
Brakes	disc
Steering	rack and pinion
Fuel tank	-
Tyres front/rear	-

DIMENSIONS AND WEIGHT

Wheelbase	3050 mm
Track front/rear	1470/1405 mm
Length	4495 mm
Width	1796
Height	959 mm
Weight in running order	600 kg

PERFORMANCE

Top speed	330 km/h
Power to weight ratio	0.7 kg/hp

Ferrari F1 2002 2002

As if the five world championships in three years – the drivers' in 2000 and 2001 and three constructors' from 1999 to 2001 inclusive – were not enough, Ferrari made a further effort the following season. They provided Michael Schumacher and Rubens Barrichello with an even more revolutionary car for 2002, designated the F1 2002 and, once more, conceived around the 10-cylinder engine. The key new developments were not, however, to be found in the power unit, which was a logical evolution of the potent and reliable 2001 V10, but in the car's aerodynamics and transmission. The shape and bulk of the F1 2002 were even further reduced and more compact compared to the previous year's car. The higher, narrower nose went straight as far as the centre of the cockpit's arch, which was further forward, partially to allow for a bigger fuel tank. The sidepods were also longer and rounder, all the way back to the gearbox area at the rear. The transmission was the F1 2002's crowning glory, though: it was a miniaturisation in a 'box of cast titanium that took two years to develop and inside which were the car's rear dampers.

Such refined and advanced technology could do nothing other than provide absolute top performance, which was the case from the first race of the season. Schumacher won the Grands Prix of Australia, Brazil, San Marino, Spain, and Austria. Barrichello handed victory to the German driver at the A1 Ring in the last few metres of the race, an incident that provoked both problems and criticism, after which Schumacher went on to also win in Canada and Great Britain. Having returned the favour to Maranello's Brazilian at the Grand Prix of Europe in Germany, the Kerpen driver went to the Grand Prix of France with 86 points, 54 more than his team mate. Ferrari's third consecutive drivers' world championship and Schumacher's fifth were a mere formality. Fangio's record had been equalled.

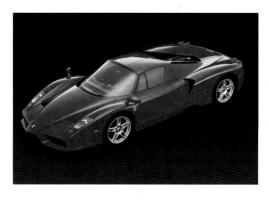

Fourteen years after his death in 1988, Maranello decided to pay tribute to Enzo Ferrari, its founder and creator, by naming a car of absolute top technology and styling after him. The Ferrari Enzo was the most advanced car of its kind, both as far as the materials from which it was built were concerned – composite matter for the monocoque and body, special aluminium alloys for the engine – and its performance capability, which was comparable to that of a Formula One car.

TECHNICAL SPECIFICATION

ENGINE		CHASSIS	
rear, longitudinal, V12 (65°)		*Chassis*	carbon fibre and honeycomb aluminium
Bore and stroke	92x75.2 mm	*Front suspension*	independent,
Unitary cubic capacity	499.8		wishbones, coil springs
Total cubic capacity	5998		anti-roll bar, telescopic
Valve gear	twin overhead camshafts		dampers
Number of valves	four per cylinder	*Rear suspension*	independent, wishbones,
Compression ratio	11.2:1		coil springs,
Fuel feed	Bosch Motronic ME 7		anti-roll bar, telescopic dampers
	integrated digital electronic	*Brakes*	disc
Ignition	Bosch integrated electronic	*Steering*	rack
Coolant	water	*Fuel tank*	110 litres
Lubrication	F1-type coiled sump	*Tyres front/rear*	245/35 ZR 19, 345/35 ZR 19
Maximum power	660 hp at 7800 rpm		
Specific power	110 hp/litre	DIMENSIONS AND WEIGHT	
		Wheelbase	2650 mm
TRANSMISSION		*Track front/rear*	1660/1650 mm
Rear-wheel drive		*Length*	4702 mm
Clutch	double disc	*Width*	2035 mm
Gearbox	en bloc with engine	*Height*	1147 mm
	six gears + reverse	*Weight in running order*	1365 kg
BODY		PERFORMANCE	
Two-seater coupé		*Top speed*	over 350 km/h
		Power to weight ratio	2.07 kg/hp

Ferrari Enzo   2002

Those who thought the collaboration between Ferrari and Pininfarina had reached the highest expression of creation in high class road cars with motor racing performance in the F 50 had to think again when the Ferrari Enzo was launched at the 2002 Paris Motor Show as a supreme tribute by Maranello to its founder, who died in 1988. All of the technical decisions made in relation to this model were taken to perform a precise function from both the styling/aerodynamic and mechanical standpoints. The close relationship of parentage that interplayed between the Ferrari Enzo and a modern Formula One racing car was evident from the start: the front end, with its central area raised and finishing in a narrow, pointed nose from which departed two inclined, vertical supports that framed two ample air intakes together with the lower spoiler, was a clear reminder of the nose of Michael Schumacher's F1 racing car. The Enzo also inherited from the F1 car the composite materials from which its monocoque and body were made, the shape of the lateral air intakes and the painstakingly researched active-type aerodynamics. With the variation of its speed, the car automatically assumed the optimum set-up, all of its components controlled by special electronic management systems. The Enzo's 65°, 5,998 cc V12 engine was also the same as the one used in Formula One in terms of performance, putting out 660 hp at 7,800 rpm for a top speed well in excess of 350 km/h. The car's acceleration times were impressive: 3.65 seconds from 0-100 km/h and 9.5 seconds from 0-200 km/h. The six speed gearbox was also electronically controlled, as was the double disc clutch, with gear changes taking place at an exceptionally fast 150 milliseconds, depending on the way the driver decided to use the transmission, which could be in either the Sport or Race mode. The price of this masterpiece of technology was around 700,000 Euros.

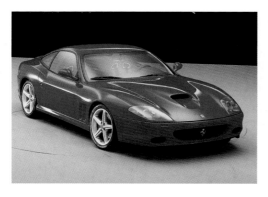

Moving on from the conceptual layout of the Ferrari 550 Maranello, a car that was given a positive press reception, the 575 M came in with a series of modifications imposed by specific technical needs. The front end was given a series of aerodynamic refinements to provide better internal and external fluid dynamics. As well as a more powerful engine, other items worthy of note include the new design of the front optical groups and alloy rims.

TECHNICAL SPECIFICATION

ENGINE
front, longitudinal, V12 (65°)

Bore and stroke	89x77 mm
Unitary cubic capacity	479
Total cubic capacity	5748
Valve gear	twin overhead camshafts
Number of valves	four per cylinder
Compression ratio	11:1
Fuel feed	Bosch Motronic M 7.1 electronic injection
Ignition	Bosch integrated electronic
Coolant	water
Lubrication	dry sump
Maximum power	515 hp at 7250 rpm
Specific power	89.6 hp/litre

TRANSMISSION
Rear-wheel drive

Clutch	single dry disc
Gearbox	en bloc with differential six gears + reverse

BODY
Two-seater coupé

CHASSIS

Chassis	tubular, steel
Front suspension	independent, double wishbones, coil springs, anti-roll bar, telescopic dampers
Rear suspension	independent, wishbones, coil springs, anti-roll bar, telescopic dampers
Brakes	disc
Steering	rack
Fuel tank	114 litres
Tyres front/rear	255/40 ZR 18, 295/35 ZR 18

DIMENSIONS AND WEIGHT

Wheelbase	2500 mm
Track front/rear	1632/1586 mm
Length	4555 mm
Width	1935 mm
Height	1277 mm
Weight in running order	1730 mm

PERFORMANCE

Top speed	325 km/h
Power to weight ratio	3.48 kg/hp

Ferrari 575 M Maranello 2002

The front engined grand tourer still remains an important theme in Ferrari production and that fact was confirmed once more at the 2002 Geneva Motor Show with the presentation of the 575 M Maranello, a substantial revision of the 550 in both styling and mechanics. A further evolution of the car's shape was made necessary due to the innovative technical decisions that had been taken: so the front end of the car assumed a different style, with a smaller grill and air intakes and a modified shape for the lower spoiler. Other fairly extensive aesthetic changes concerned the front optical groups, the area of the body housing the lights colour keyed with the rest of the car. A more refined design of five spoke alloy rims was also adopted. Considerable new developments were incorporated into the car's power unit, which was still the 65° V12, but with its total cubic capacity increased from 5,473.9 cc for a maximum power output of 485 hp at 7,000 rpm to 5,748 cc that produced 515 hp at 7,250 rpm. The new top speed was almost 325 km/h and the 0-100 km/h acceleration time 4.2 seconds. The gearbox en bloc with the differential was at the rear of the car, in line with the transaxle layout, to optimise weight distribution, and was F1 electro-hydraulically controlled: that drastically reduced the time it took to change gear.

The experience gathered with the Ferrari Enzo in terms of adaptive set-up – automatically modified by the car itself in relation to external conditions – was built into the 575 M Maranello, with a suspension that altered itself to perform to the best of its ability in all road conditions. The interior of the car was completely redesigned, with the principal instruments in a single dial in front of the driver. The seats now had six different, electrically regulated positions to provide maximum driving comfort, for which purpose the door panel finish and onboard components were also designed.

The F 2003-GA Formula One car came well up to expectations, confirming it was an heir worthy of the preceding F 2002. The competitiveness of Scuderia Ferrari's opponents had increased considerably over that of the previous season: especially Juan Pablo Montoya and his Williams-BMW, who fought hard for the world drivers' championship until two races from the end of the season. The title went to Michael Schumacher for the fourth consecutive year and Maranello won its fifth constructors' championship.

TECHNICAL SPECIFICATION

ENGINE
rear, longitudinal, V10 (90°)

Bore and stroke	97x40.5 mm
Unitary cubic capacity	299.7
Total cubic capacity	2997
Valve gear	twin overhead camshafts
Number of valves	four per cylinder
Compression ratio	13.3:1
Fuel feed	Magneti-Marelli electronic injection
Ignition	Magneti-Marelli static electronic
Coolant	water
Lubrication	dry sump
Maximum power	830 hp
Specific power	277 hp / litre

TRANSMISSION
Rear-wheel drive

Clutch	multi-disc
Gearbox	en bloc with engine seven gears + reverse

BODY
Single-seater

CHASSIS

Chassis	monocoque in composite materials
Front suspension	independent with double superimposed wishbones, torsion pushrods and spring
Rear suspension	independent, torsion pushrod and spring
Brakes	disc
Steering	rack and pinion
Fuel tank	-
Tyres front/rear	-

DIMENSIONS AND WEIGHT

Wheelbase	-
Track front/rear	1470 / 1405 mm
Length	4545 mm
Width	1796 mm
Height	959 mm
Kerb weight	600 kg

PERFORMANCE

Top speed	over 360 km / h
Power to weight ratio	0.75 kg / hp

Ferrari F 2003-GA   2003

The crushing superiority of Scuderia Ferrari-Marlboro and Michael Schumacher during the 2002 season, a cocktail of technology and talent able to win both the drivers' and constructors' titles well before the end of the season, induced the Federation to bring in important new modifications to Formula One regulations in an effort to create a more even playing field and breathe life back into the championship. The most significant changes were to practice and the means by which points were scored. Drivers were to take to the track for Saturday qualifying on the basis of placings achieved the day before and would have just one opportunity to set their fastest lap. The cars were already obliged to qualify with a quantity of fuel to be used during the Grand Prix, and after doing so were taken to a parc fermé, where they would remain until the Grand Prix, without the mechanics being allowed to carry out more work on them and without taking part in a warm-up. The race winner was assigned 10 points as usual, but the second placed car and driver took eight, the third six, the fourth five, the fifth four, the sixth three, the seventh and eighth two and one respectively.

Those modifications achieved their objective: the world championship saw three drivers battling it out for the title, right up to the last race of the season: Kimi Raikkonen in the McLaren-Mercedes who was constant and scored well throughout the year, Juan Pablo Montoya in the Williams-BMW – winner of two Grands Prix – and, of course, Michael Schumacher in the Ferrari. But as a result of his six victories and a number of podium finishes, the German won the championship once more to make it his fourth consecutive world title, and the Scuderia topped the constructors' table with 158 points, to which Rubens Barrichello's victories in Great Britain and Japan also made a significant contribution.

Taking its cue from the 360 Modena, Ferrari unveiled the Challenge Stradale at the 2003 Geneva Motor Show, the road-going version of the 360 Challenge. The multiplicity of aerodynamic refinements carried out on the car can best be seen in profile, starting with the elongation of the body under the front air intakes, modification of the sills under the doors and the raised rear end in relation to the car's nose, a feature more in tune with cars for track use.

TECHNICAL SPECIFICATION

ENGINE		CHASSIS	
central, longitudinal, V8 (90°)		*Chassis*	aluminium space frame
		Front suspension	independent, double
Bore and stroke	85x79 mm		wishbones, coil springs,
Unitary cubic capacity	448.2		anti-roll bar, gas-filled
Total cubic capacity	3558		dampers
Valve gear	twin overhead camshafts	*Rear suspension*	independent, double
Number of valves	five per cylinder		wishbones pushrod, coil
Compression ratio	11.2:1		springs, anti-roll bar,
Fuel feed	Bosch Motronic 7.3		gas-filled dampers
	electrostatic injection	*Brakes*	disc
Ignition	Bosch Motronic 7.3	*Steering*	rack
	electrostatic	*Fuel tank*	95 litres
Coolant	water	*Tyres front/rear*	225/35 ZR 19, 285/35 ZR 19
Lubrication	dry sump		
Maximum power	425 hp at 8500 rpm	DIMENSIONS AND WEIGHT	
Specific power	118.5 hp/litre	*Wheelbase*	2600 mm
		Track front/rear	1669/1617 mm
TRANSMISSION		*Length*	4477 mm
Rear-wheel drive		*Width*	1922 mm
Clutch	single dry disc	*Height*	1199 mm
Gearbox	en bloc with engine	*Kerb weight*	1180 kg
	six gear + reverse		
	F1 electro-hydraulic	PERFORMANCE	
		Top speed	300 km/h
BODY		*Power to weight ratio*	2.7 kg/hp
Two-seater coupé			

Ferrari Challenge Stradale   2003

Maranello's grand touring cars had been taking to the track since 1993 in a series of Continental racing championships called the Ferrari Challenge, renewing a tradition close to the heart of the Prancing Horse during the Fifties and Sixties. The drivers were Ferrari's sporting customers, who competed on circuits that were often those of the Formula One World Championship. The first car to be used in the single marque series was the 348, followed by the F 355: from the start of the 2000 season, the 360 became the official Challenge car, set up and powered by the eight-cylinder engine the output of which had been increased to over 400 hp. Ferrari applied numerous technical features derived directly from its F1 single-seater to this extreme version of the Modena. The Challenge Stradale displayed for the first time had a white stripe crossed by an Italian tricolour, which ran longitudinally over the whole body, the same livery that had been adopted for the first, legendary 250 GTO in 1962. The exterior already confirmed the car's way-out sporting inclinations, as with door mirrors in carbon fibre, titanium wheels and 19-inch tyres. The overall weight of the car was reduced by no less than 110 kg compared to the standard Modena: that was done through a painstaking lightening exercise, which affected the structural elements with ample use of aluminium and carbon fibre, components like the disc brakes in carbon-ceramics and the interior and exterior finish items.

To the V8 engine, the power output of which had been upped to 425 hp at 8,500 rpm, was fitted an electro-hydraulically controlled transmission of the F1 type, in which the gears and clutch were controlled by levers behind the steering wheel rim: that also provided for functions such as the launch control to eliminate wheel spin at the start of a race.

All of which meant the car's performance capability was at a racing level, with a top speed of 300 km/h and a 0-100 km/h acceleration time of 4.1 seconds.

With the 612 Scaglietti, which was given its debut in January 2004 at the Detroit Motor Show, Ferrari returned to a theme close to its heart – the 2+2. One of Pininfarina's main objectives was to make the car as comfortable as possible for the driver and its passengers. That is confirmed not only by the Scaglietti coupé's overall length of 4,765 mm, but also by its height of 4.4 cm more than the 1992 456 GT, which enabled passengers to reach the rear seats more easily.

TECHNICAL SPECIFICATION

ENGINE		CHASSIS	
front, longitudinal, V12 (65°)		*Chassis*	aluminium space frame
		Front suspension	independent,
Bore and stroke	89x77 mm		double wishbones,
Unitary cubic capacity	479.03		coil springs,
Total cubic capacity	5748.32		hydraulic dampers
Valve gear	twin overhead camshafts	*Rear suspension*	independent,
Number of valves	four per cylinder		double wishbones,
Compression ratio	11.2:1		coil springs,
Fuel feed	Bosch Motronic ME 7		hydraulic dampers
	electronic injection	*Brakes*	disc
Ignition	Bosch Motronic ME 7 electronic	*Steering*	rack
Coolant	water	*Fuel tank*	110 litres
Lubrication	dry sump	*Tyres front/ rear*	245/45-18, 285/40-19
Maximum power	540 hp at 7250 rpm		
Specific power	94 hp/litre	DIMENSIONS AND WEIGHT	
		Wheelbase	2950 mm
TRANSMISSION		*Track front/rear*	1688/1641 mm
Rear-wheel drive		*Length*	4902 mm
Clutch	single dry disc	*Width*	1957 mm
Gearbox	en bloc with differential	*Height*	1344 mm
	six gears + reverse	*Kerb weight*	1840 kg
BODY		PERFORMANCE	
2+2 coupé		*Top speed*	over 315 km/h
		Power to weight ratio	3.4 kg/hp

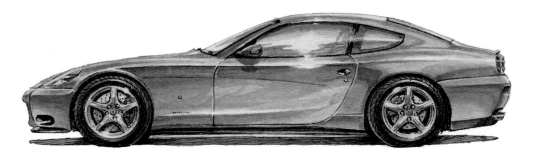

Ferrari 612 Scaglietti

2004

Collaboration between Ferrari and Scaglietti dates back to the early Fifties, when the then small artisan body building shop started to craft Maranello's sports racing cars – the first was the 1953 500 Mondial barchetta, for which the company created a body in beaten aluminium that was sinuous of line and light, the qualities that were to characterise the Ferrari sports racers of the period. To commemorate this long and fruitful relationship, Luca Cordero di Montezemolo, president of Ferrari, decided to name this model after Sergio Scaglietti. It was a car that brought Ferrari back to the 2+2 - the first of the series was the 1960 250 GTE - the creation of which was entrusted to Pininfarina. The line penned by the carrozzeria for the new coupé, which was all in aluminium and assembled in the Scaglietti factory, was an admirable meeting point between tradition and innovation. If the ample front end, with a grill in the centre of which was the Prancing Horse, was itself a clear reference to the grand tourers of the past, the clove like shape of the front optical groups and, more than anything else, the heavily flared flanks close to the wheel housings were elements that had a clear antecedence in the 375 MM Berlinetta Aerodinamica, commissioned in 1954 by film director Roberto Rossellini for actress Ingrid Bergman. The styling of the rear end once again bore the design already much admired in the 456 GT and the 550 Maranello: the Scaglietti was 35 centimetres longer that the Maranello, to provide its driver and passengers with more comfort. The engine of the 612, a designation used previously for a model that was to compete in the CAN-AM series, was a potent 65° V12 of 5,748 cc with a power output of 540 hp, able to carry the muscular coupé to a top speed of 315 km/h. The unit was linked to either a six-speed mechanical gearbox or the alternative electro-hydraulic complex called the FIA, the gears of which were engaged by actioning a lever behind the steering wheel rim or in a completely automatic manner.

The side view of the new F2004 shows the results of careful aerodynamic research, with the car's nose lower and more tapered plus higher sidepods, inside which were radiators of diverse inclination, as with the preceding F2003-GA. The car's superiority on the track was devastating, enabling Michael Schumacher to win the drivers' world championship for the fifth consecutive year and Maranello the constructors' title.

TECHNICAL SPECIFICATION

ENGINE		CHASSIS	
rear, longitudinal, V10 (90°)		*Chassis*	monocoque in composite materials
Bore and stroke	-	*Front suspension*	independent with double
Unitary cubic capacity	299.7		superimposed wishbones,
Total cubic capacity	2997		torsion pushrods and spring
Valve gear	twin overhead camshafts	*Rear suspension*	independent, torsion
Number of valves	four per cylinder		pushrod and spring
Compression ratio	-	*Brakes*	disc
Fuel feed	Magneti-Marelli electronic injection	*Steering*	rack and pinion
		Fuel tank	-
Ignition	Magneti-Marelli static electronic	*Tyres front/rear*	-
Coolant	water	DIMENSIONS AND WEIGHT	
Lubrication	dry sump	*Wheelbase*	3050 mm
Maximum power	900 hp at 18,800 rpm	*Track front/rear*	1470/1405 mm
Specific power	300 hp/litre	*Length*	4545 mm
		Width	1796 mm
TRANSMISSION		*Height*	959 mm
Rear-wheel drive		*Weight in running order*	605 kg
Clutch	multi-disc		
Gearbox	en bloc with engine seven gears + reverse	PERFORMANCE	
		Top speed	over 360 km/h
		Power to weight ratio	0.6 kg/hp
BODY			
Single-seater			

Ferrari F 2004 2004

While Ferrari's main adversaries came up with cars with aerodynamics that were decidedly on the limit, like the Williams-BMW whose FW26 had an original nose connected to the front wing by two fins, which earned it the name of walrus: the feature was dropped mid-season. The Ferrari F2004 looked like a logical evolution of the previous season's F2003-GA, at least as far as its exterior lines were concerned.

But a more careful examination of it confirmed the new car was the result of detailed refinement, partially seen on the 2003 car. Apart from a nose that was more inclined downwards, the most significant work was carried out on the rear end. The sidepods were higher, squarer and positioned further back in relation to the front axle and the Coke bottle plane more pronounced near the tail. The upper part of the engine cover was of new conception and ended with a sort of fin, as required by the regulations. The aerodynamics of the chimneys, which housed the exhausts, was also new as they were further oriented upwards but were closer to the central body.

The F2004 showed its extraordinary potential from the season's first race in Australia, both its drivers dominating qualifying and the race, in which they came first and second. That was the start of a long series of victories, with Schumacher winning again in Malaysia, Bahrain, which was a round in the championship for the first time, San Marino and Spain, where the German celebrated his 200th Grand Prix. After a missing out in Monaco, the Schumacher-Ferrari duo went back to dictating the pace, scoring another impressive series of six consecutive victories, with Maranello taking the constructors' championship again in Hungary. Michael Schumacher secured his seventh world title – two more than Juan Manuel Fangio – at the next Grand Prix of Belgium. Despite winning both championships, Ferrari were still victorious in the Grands Prix of Italy and China – another new F1 location – both of them won by Rubens Barrichello, while the Japanese finale went to the seven times world champion Schumacher.

As well as having an ample rear window through which the potent eight-cylinder, 4308 cc engine could be seen, the rear volume of the F430 embodied styling features inherited from the Enzo. Both the circular double rear light clusters, which were partially set into the body, and the design of the narrow upper air intake in the centre of which was the prancing horse, repeated features introduced for the first time on the Enzo.

TECHNICAL SPECIFICATION

ENGINE

Rear, longitudinal, 90 deg. V8

Bore and stroke	92x81 mm
Unitary cubic capacity	538.5
Total cubic capacity	4308
Valve gear	twin overhead camshaft
Number of valves	four per cylinder
Compression ratio	11.3:1
Fuel feed	Bosch Motronic ME7 electrostatic injection
Ignition	Bosch Motronic ME7 electrostatic
Coolant	water
Lubrication	dry sump
Maximum power	490 hp at 8500 rpm
Specific power	114 hp/litre

TRANSMISSION

Rear-wheel drive

Clutch	single dry disc
Gearbox	en bloc with engine six gears + reverse, electro-hydraulic or manual

BODY

coupé

CHASSIS

Chassis	aluminium space frame
Front suspension	independent, double wishbones, coil springs, anti-roll bar, gas dampers
Rear suspension	independent, double wishbones, coil springs, anti-roll bar, gas dampers
Brakes	disc
Steering	rack and pinion
Fuel tank	95 litres
Tyres front/rear	225/35 ZR 19, 285/35 ZR 19

DIMENSIONS AND WEIGHT

Wheelbase	2600 mm
Track front/rear	1669/1616 mm
Length	4512 mm
Width	1923 mm
Height	1214 mm
Kerb weight	1350 kg

PERFORMANCE

Maximum speed	over 315 km/h
Power to weight ratio	2.8 kg/hp

Ferrari F430 2004

The prestigious family of eight-cylinder engined cars premiered by the Dino 308 GT/4 Bertone in 1973 and inaugurated two years later with the debut of the 308 GTB, was joined by another sports saloon called the F430, the heir to the 360 Modena.

Created in close collaboration with the Maranello racing department, a significant number of the technical features developed in recent years for the F1 cars were incorporated into this car; for the first time in a road car they included an electronically controlled differential, which had five different settings to optimise traction values and worked on suspension components. It was operated by a special paddle switch on the steering wheel, the same as those on the Schumacher and Barrichello cars. The heart of the F430 was a 90 deg. V8 4308 cc engine installed in a rear longitudinal position. In this area, too, experience gathered in Formula One led to the development of a compact and light power unit, controlled by two Bosch Motronic ME7 electronic management systems, with twin overhead camshaft valve gear, which generated a maximum power of 490 hp at 8500 rpm and a top torque of 47.4 kg/m at 5250 rpm. At 315 km/h and a 0-100 km/h time of four seconds, the F430's maximum speed was at the level of the F1 car. This agile and powerful engine worked in unison with a six speed F1 sequential gearbox, although a manual was available: it was connected to an electronic differential with a box entirely in aluminium, which also contained the engine's oil reservoir.

The F430's elegant and assertive lines by Pininfarina were an extraordinary meeting point between suggestions of the past and modern styling. To the first category belong the two large, elliptically shaped front air intakes inspired by the 1961 156 F1 and the early Sixties sports racing cars (see the air intake on the side at the rear, a clear reference to the 250 LM): the second category accounts for the small, horizontal wing down low in the centre of the radiator grill, the task of which was to direct the flow of air toward the car's sophisticated flat underbody; and the front and especially the rear light clusters housed in an overhang, like those of the Enzo.

Despite the sinuous lines of a body that almost faithfully reproduced the shape of the 575 M Maranello, with the prominent front overhang, streamlined and voluminous flanks and especially the rear end with its traditional circular light clusters, the 575 Handling visibly distinguished itself by the adoption of bigger 19-inch diameter rims to which Pirelli P Zero Corsa tyres were fitted.

TECHNICAL SPECIFICATION

ENGINE
Front, longitudinal, V12, 65 deg.

Bore and stroke	89x77 mm
Unitary cubic capacity	479
Total cubic capacity	5748
Valve gear	twin overhead camshaft
Number of valves	four per cylinder
Compression ratio	11:1
Fuel feed	Bosch Motronic electro-static injection
Ignition	Bosch Motronic integrated electronic
Coolant	water
Lubrication	dry sump
Maximum power	515 hp at 5250 rpm
Specific power	89.6 hp/litre

TRANSMISSION
Rear-wheel drive

Clutch	single dry disc
Gearbox	en bloc with differential six gears + reverse, electro-hydraulic F1

BODY
coupé

CHASSIS

Chassis	tubular, steel
Front suspension	independent, double wishbones, coil springs, anti-roll bar, telescopic dampers
Rear suspension	independent, double wishbones, coil springs, anti-roll bar, telescopic dampers
Brakes	disc
Steering	rack and pinion
Fuel tank	105 litres
Tyres front/rear	255/35 ZR 19-305/30 ZR 19

DIMENSIONS AND WEIGHT

Wheelbase	2500 mm
Track front/rear	1632/1586 mm
Length	4550 mm
Width	1935 mm
Height	1277 mm
Kerb weight	1730 kg

PERFORMANCE

Maximum speed	325 km/h
Power to weight ratio	3.3 kg/hp

575 Maranello Handling GTC   2004

Armed with experience and victories gained with the 575 GTC in the FIA Grand Touring Trophy, Ferrari decided to make a road going version of that exceptional car for its more sporting and demanding clients, itself born of the 2002 575 M Maranello. The new front engined, 12-cylinder sports saloon, one of the classical themes of Ferrari production through the years, the exterior of the 575 Maranello Handling GTC was not far off the assertive and elegant lines of the 575 M, the shape of which it perpetuated and was characterised by a prominent front overhang and a second rear volume that was more compact and collected. The 575's GTC elaboration kit offered by Ferrari took the already potent 65 deg. twin overhead cam V12 engine of the Maranello to an impressive 515 hp at 7250 rpm, which increased the car's performance increased sharply to a maximum speed of 325 km/h and a 0-100 km/h acceleration time of 4.2 seconds, figures that are even more meaningful if one considers the 575's weight of 1730 kg. To be able to use so much power, it was necessary to fit the GTC with the new Pirelli P Zero Corsa tyres in sizes 255/35 front and 305/30 rear on 19 inch rims, between the spokes of which the new carbon-ceramic disc brakes – also previously adopted by the Enzo – could be seen. The GTC body also underwent a notable set-up stiffening process with the adoption of harder springs and anti-roll bar on both axles, completely managed by electronics. Drivers had the opportunity of selecting either a touring ride by actioning the Comfort device or a sporting one by switching to Sport. The transmission was also electronically operated and had a six-speed F1 sequential gearbox, as were the suspension components. The new exhaust system with lighter, smaller diameter silencers could be seen by observing the 575 GTC Handling from the outside.

If the dominant features of the front end were imposed in line with those of the 575 M Maranello, with its three element circular light clusters and the large air intake in the centre of the bonnet, the cockpit and the rear end of the Superamerica are completely new. Both were revised to take into account the innovative retractable glass screen, which makes the Superamerica the most exceptional grand touring convertible.

TECHNICAL SPECIFICATION

ENGINE		BODY	
Front, longitudinal, V12 at 65 deg.		*coupé*	
Bore and stroke	89x77 mm	CHASSIS	
Unitary cubic capacity	479	*Chassis*	tubular, steel
Total cubic capacity	5748	*Front suspension*	independent, double
Valve gear	twin overhead		wishbones, coil springs,
	camshaft		anti-roll bar, telescopic dampers
Number of valves	four per cylinder	*Rear suspension*	independent, double
Compression ratio	11:1		wishbones, coil springs,
Fuel feed	Bosch Motronic electrostatic		anti-roll bar, telescopic dampers
	injection	*Brakes*	disc
Ignition	Bosch Motronic integrated	*Steering*	rack and pinion
	electronic	*Fuel tank*	105 litres
Coolant	water	*Tyres front/rear*	255/35 ZR 19, 305/30 ZR 19
Lubrication	dry sump		
Maximum power	540 hp at 7250 rpm	DIMENSIONS AND WEIGHT	
Specific power	94 hp/litre	*Wheelbase*	2500 mm
		Track front/rear	1632/1586 mm
TRANSMISSION		*Length*	4550 mm
Rear-wheel drive		*Width*	1935 mm
Clutch	single dry disc	*Height*	1277 mm
Gearbox	en bloc with differential	*Kerb weight*	1790 kg
	six gears + reverse,		
	electro-hydraulic F1	PERFORMANCE	
	sequential or manual	*Maximum speed*	320 km/h
		Power to weight ratio	3.3 kg/hp

Superamerica   2005

In the long and many faceted production history of Ferrari, the name Superamerica has been linked to cars of extraordinary prestige, always built in limited series, which were the top of the range in the late Fifties and the following decade. The name was first given to an elegant dual-tone coupe called the 410, which was built in 1956 by Pininfarina, and then again in 1960 the 400, another gem built by the Turin stylist. The latest Ferrari to bear the high-sounding name unites the fascination of a front engined V12 with that of a convertible, which was announced at the end of last year and unveiled at the 2005 Los Angeles and Detroit motor shows. One of the remarkable features of the new Superamerica is the modern interpretation of its retractable rigid roof. This original system, created by designer Leonardo Fioravanti, who was also the father of other prestigious sports saloons of the past such as the Daytona, is operated by a sophisticated electronic kinematic mechanism mounted on a carbon fibre structure, which permits a variation of brightness and changes the car's configuration from being a closed to an open roadster in just 10 seconds through the movement of an electro-chromic glass panel. Once open, the glass disappears into a special compartment at the back of the cockpit. The Superamerica inherits the stylistics of its front end from the 575 M Maranello, but the elegant, streamlined profile of its flanks and rear volume are different, centred on two pronounced lateral pillars that act as a roll bar and by retention elements for the glass roof when closed. The interior has ample leather and carbon fibre.

The new Superamerica, which is being built in limited number, has the classic 65 deg. V12 engine of 5748 cc with four overhead camshaft valve gear, four valves per cylinder and with its crank case, cylinder head and oil reservoir made in light alloy; with a maximum power output of 540 hp at 7250 rpm, the Superamerica has a maximum speed of 320 km/h and accelerates from 0-100 km/h in just 4.2 seconds.

The absence of the roof group does not change the elegant and assertive lines of the F430 in any way; at the rear, near the ample rear window through which the potent eight-cylinder engine can be seen, the latest Maranello roadster has two roll bars linked to two light fins, which also act as unifying elements between the body and the raised hood.

TECHNICAL SPECIFICATION

ENGINE
Rear, longitudinal, 90 deg. V8.

Bore and stroke	92x81 mm
Unitary cubic capacity	538.5
Total cubic capacity	4308
Valve gear	twin overhead camshafts
Number of valves	four per cylinder
Compression ratio	11.3:1
Fuel feed	Bosch Motronic ME7 electrostatic injection
Ignition	Bosch Motronic ME7 electrostatic
Coolant	water
Lubrication	dry sump
Maximum power	490 hp at 8500 rpm
Specific power	114 hp/litre

TRANSMISSION
Rear-wheel drive

Clutch	single dry disc
Gearbox	en bloc with engine six gears + reverse, electro-hydraulic F1 or manual

BODY
Roadster

CHASSIS

Chassis	space frame in aluminium
Front suspension	independent, double wishbones, coil springs, anti-roll bar, gas dampers
Rear suspension	independent, double wishbones, coil springs, anti-roll bar, gas dampers
Brakes	disc
Steering	rack and pinion
Tyres front/rear	225/35 ZR 19, 285/35 ZR 19

DIMENSIONS AND WEIGHT

Wheelbase	2600 mm
Track front/rear	1669/1616 mm
Length	4512 mm
Width	1923 mm
Height	mm
Kerb weight	1420 kg

PERFORMANCE

Maximum speed	over 310 km/h
Power to weight ratio	2.3 kg/hp

Ferrari F430 Spider   2005

The debut of an eight-cylinder Ferrari sports saloon is, by tradition, followed some time later by the launch of a corresponding roadster version: a tradition that embraces cars from the 308 GTS, which made its debut at the 1977 Frankfurt Motor Show, to the 360 Spider, which was marketed a year after the coupe at the 2000 Geneva show. The 2005 prestigious Swiss show was the venue at which the F430 Spider made its first public appearance, the latest open top derivative in a long and illustrious line of such cars.

The absence of the roof group takes nothing away from the elegance and aggressiveness of the F430's lines. The front end is unchanged and has the two ample elliptical air intakes and innovative wedge-shaped optical groups, the slightly ascending flanks become even more taut and streamlined. The rear of the car was of new conception, where two paired roll bars and the same number of discreet pillars lead to the engine cover, as always with an ample rear window that gives a glimpse of the imposing 90 deg. V8 engine. There are no major new engine developments in relation to that of the sports saloon, which puts out 490 hp at 8500 rpm and develops a maximum speed of over 310 km/h. With the exception of the controls that operate the kinematic mechanism of the hood, which disappears into its own compartment between the engine and the cockpit once it is closed, that area is of no substantial difference to the sports saloon. The F430 Spider also has all the electronic devices of the corresponding closed version, including the sophisticated system by which to calibrate the suspension, speed of gear change, electronic differential, traction and stability control. All of those parameters can be varied just as on the Formula One car by selecting the appropriate set-up, which can be actioned with a small lever on the steering wheel, where the start button is also located.

The absence of the roof group obliged Maranello's technicians to stiffen the chassis, which is made of aluminium and composites. The Spider weighs 70 kg more than the 430 Coupe, an increment that has no repercussions on the car's performance. The Ferrari F430 Spider costs about 177,000 euro.

The latest Formula One racing car from Maranello. Due to the radical modifications carried out to meet the Federation's regulations for the 2005 world championship, the car has not been able to repeat the extraordinary results achieved by the preceding F2004. Problems of reliability and performance often held back Schumacher and Barrichello, who found it hard to constitute a real danger for their adversaries, especially Renault and McLaren.

TECHNICAL SPECIFICATION

ENGINE
rear, longitudinal, V10 (90°)

Bore and stroke	-
Unitary cubic capacity	299.7
Total cubic capacity	2997
Valve gear	twin overhead camshafts
Number of valves	four per cylinder
Compression ratio	-
Fuel feed	Magneti-Marelli electronic injection
Ignition	Magneti-Marelli static electronic
Coolant	water
Lubrication	dry sump
Maximum power	900 hp at 18,800 rpm
Specific power	300 hp / litre

TRANSMISSION
Rear-wheel drive

Clutch	multi-disc
Gearbox	en bloc with engine seven gears + reverse

BODY
Single-seater

CHASSIS

Chassis	monocoque in composite materials
Front suspension	independent with double superimposed wishbones, torsion pushrods and spring
Rear suspension	independent, torsion pushrod and spring
Brakes	disc
Steering	rack and pinion
Fuel tank	-
Tyres front/rear	-

DIMENSIONS AND WEIGHT

Wheelbase	3050 mm
Track front/rear	1470 / 1405 mm
Length	4545 mm
Width	1796 mm
Height	959 mm
Weight in running order	605 kg

PERFORMANCE

Top speed	over 360 km/h
Power to weight ratio	0.6 kg/hp

Ferrari F 2005   2005

The new Ferrari Formula one car for the 2005 season was unveiled at the end of February, as is Maranello's tradition. The number one had pride of place on a Rossa's nose for the fifth consecutive year, the 2004 championship having been won for the seventh time by Michael Schumacher. But for the first time in many years, Rory Byrne was not responsible for the car's design, as he only played a supervisory role in the project: the car was the work of a group of young engineers comprising, among others, Aldo Costa, who was responsible for the project and the development of the car, and Tiziano Battistini, who had assumed control of the technical office. This revolution within Maranello's racing department spawned an equally innovative, design in relation to the new regulations for the 2005 season. In an attempt to reduce the cost and performance of cars, the international federation, had introduced rules that would radically change the Formula One scenario. As well as a series of significant aerodynamic restrictions that affected the cars in all sectors, engines were required to cover the distance of testing, qualifying and races of two Grands Prix, which meant double the kilometres of the previous season - and it was no longer permitted to change tyres during a race.

As had happened in 2003, the new Ferrari did not make its debut in Australia, the first round in the championship: two F2004 Ms, the latter standing for modified, took to the grid for the first three races. The car was a sort of halfway house between the previous season's Ferrari and the F2005. From that first race, it seemed that Maranello's crushing supremacy of the preceding year's F2004 was a distant memory. Barrichello's second place in Australia and Schumacher's modest seventh in Malaysia were the only positive results achieved with the F2004 M. And unfortunately, the situation did not improve at the Grand Prix of Imola, where the new F2005 did eventually make its debut. Up until the Grand Prix of Canada, Ferrari's drivers only made it to the podium another four times – two second places for Schumacher and two thirds for Barrichello – and were never able to fight on equal terms with the Renaults of Alonso and Fisichella or the McLarens of Raikkonen and Montoya.

Over 50 years of victory

From the moment it was established in 1947, Ferrari has always identified itself with the world of motor racing, which has been the central theme of Maranello's activities over the years. Perhaps no other car manufacturer can boast such a wealth of first class results, yet even today nobody really knows the limits of the Prancing Horse. The respected list of Ferrari's most important victories compiled by Gianni Cancellieri in 1997 was published as an appendix to the book commemorating 50 years of Ferrari called Ferrari 1947-1997 by Karl Ludvigsen and Gianni Cancellieri. It covered about 15,000 races, which led to 1,500 overall victories, a figure that would have risen to almost 5,000 if class and category wins had also been taken into account.

It would not have been difficult but, perhaps, too ambitious a task to have tried to improve on the contents of that book; it was, therefore, considered opportune to publish here the full list of Ferrari victories that appeared in the Ludvigsen-Cancellieri publication. We have updated them to the end of 2004 with the long series of successes attained during the Michael Schumacher era and the equally glorious and fascinating achievements of the F 333 SP barchettas, with which Ferrari returned to sports car racing.

The following data is listed chronologically here on each of Ferrari's victories:
- the date of the race
- the name of the location or circuit at which the event took place
- the official name of the race
- the name of the winning driver or crew
- the car model

Where a victory has contributed to an international championship such as the Formula One, Sports Car or Prototype world titles and European Hillclimbing Championship - and only in such cases - the official name of the series has been included in full.

Palmarès

1947

May 25 / Terme di Caracalla
Rome Grand Prix
Franco Cortese
125 S

June 1
Vercelli Circuit
Franco Cortese
125 S

June 15
Vigevano Circuit
Franco Cortese
125 S

June 29
Varese Circuit
Franco Cortese
125 SC

July 6
Forlì Circuit
Tazio Nuvolari
125 SC

July 13
Parma Circuit
Tazio Nuvolari
125 SC

October 12
City of Turin Grand Prix
Raymond Sommer
159 SC

1948

April 4
Sicily Tour/Targa Florio
C. Biondetti/I. Troubetzkoy
166 S

May 2
Mille Miglia
C. Biondetti/G. Navone
166 S

May 30
Bari Grand Prix
Francisco Landi
166 SC

May 30 / Skarpnäck
Summer Grand Prix
Clemente Biondetti
166 SC

July 18 / Rheims
Coupe des Petites Cylindrées
Raymond Sommer
166 SC

September 12 / Montlhéry
Paris 12 Hours
L. Chinetti/Lord Selsdon
166 SC

September 26
Florence Circuit
Raymond Sommer
166 F2

October 24 / Salò
Garda Circuit
Giuseppe Farina
125 F1

November 3 / Montlhéry
1 Hour International Record
Luigi Chinetti
166 SC

November 3 / Montlhéry
200 Kms International Record
Luigi Chinetti
166 SC

November 3 / Montlhéry
100 Miles International Record
Luigi Chinetti
166 SC

November 14
Vermicino-Rocca di Papa
Giovanni Bracco
166 SC

1949

February 13
Rosario Grand Prix
Giuseppe Farina
166 C

March 20
Sicily Tour / Targa Florio
C. Biondettti/A. Benedetti
166 Inter

April 18 / Goodwood
Lavant Cup
Dudley Folland
166 SC

April 24
Mille Miglia
C. Biondetti / E. Salami
166 MM

May 21
Brussels Grand Prix
Luigi Villoresi
166 F2

May 26
Luxembourg Grand Prix
Luigi Villoresi
166 MM

May 29 / Monza
Inter-Europa Cup
Bruno Sterzi
166 S

June 2
Rome Grand Prix
Luigi Villoresi
166 F2

June 12
Bari Grand Prix
Alberto Ascari
166 F2

June 19
Naples Grand Prix
Roberto Vallone
166 Inter

June 25-26
Le Mans 24 Hours
L. Chinetti / Lord Selsdon
166 MM

June 26 / Monza
Autodrome Grand Prix
Juan Manuel Fangio
166 F2

June 29
Umbria Tour
Roberto Vallone
166 Inter

July 3 / Bern
Switzerland Grand Prix
Alberto Ascari
125 F1

July 9-10
Spa-Francorchamps 24 Hours
L. Chinetti / J. Lucas
166 MM

July 10 / Salò
Garda Circuit
Luigi Villoresi
166 F2

July 17 / Rheims
Coupe des Petites Cylindrées
Alberto Ascari
166 F2

July 17
Dolomite Cup
Roberto Vallone
166 Inter

July 31
Zandvoort Grand Prix
Luigi Villoresi
125 F1

August 20 / Silverstone
Daily Express Trophy
Alberto Ascari
125 F1

August 21
Senigallia Circuit
Franco Cornacchia
166 MM

September 4
Trieste Circuit
Franco Cornacchia
166 MM

September 11 / Monza
Italian and European Grand Prix
Alberto Ascari
125 F1

September 17 / Watkins Glen
Seneca Cup
Briggs Cunningham
166 SC

September 25 / Brno
Masaryk Circuit
Peter Whitehead
125 F1

December 18 / Buenos Aires
Premio Juan Domingo Perón
Alberto Ascari
166 C

1950

January 8 / Buenos Aires
Premio Eva Perón
Luigi Villoresi
166 C

January 15
Mar del Plata Grand Prix
Carlos Menditeguy
166 MM

January 15 / Mar del Plata
General San Martín Grand Prix
Alberto Ascari
166 C

January 22 / Rosario
Acción de San Lorenzo Cup
Luigi Villoresi
166 C

March 19
Marseille Grand Prix
Luigi Villoresi
166 F2

March 26 / Monza
Inter-Europa Cup
Antonio Stagnoli
166 MM

April 23
Mille Miglia
G. Marzotto / M. Crosara
195 S

May 7 / Modena
Autodrome Grand Prix
Alberto Ascari
166 F2

May 7 / Erlen
Eastern Switzerland Grand Prix
Luigi Villoresi
166 F2

May 7 / Roubaix
A.C. du Nord Grand Prix
Raymond Sommer
166 F2

May 14
Mons Circuit
Alberto Ascari
166 F2

May 18
Luxembourg Grand Prix
Alberto Ascari
166 MM

May 28 / Monza
Autodrome Grand Prix
Luigi Villoresi
166 F2

May 28
Aix-les-Bains Circuit
Raymond Sommer
166 F2

June 4 / Bern
Swiss F2 Grand Prix
Raymond Sommer
166 F2

June 4
Tuscany Cup
D. Serafini/E. Salami
166 MM

June 10
Rome 3 Nocturnal Hours
Giannino Marzotto
195 S

June 11
Rome Grand Prix
Alberto Ascari
166 F2

July 2 / Rheims
Jean-Pierre Wimille Cup
Alberto Ascari
166 F2

July 13
Jersey Road Race
Peter Whitehead
125 F1

July 16
Dolomite Cup
Giannino Marzotto
195 S

July 23
Naples Grand Prix
Franco Cortese
166 F2

July 23 / Montlhéry
Paris 12 Hours
L. Chinetti/J. Lucas
166 MM

August 6
Calabria Tour
D. Serafini/E. Salami
195 S

August 12 / Dundrod
Ulster Trophy
Peter Whitehead
125 F1

August 20 / Nürburgring
German Grand Prix
Alberto Ascari
166 F2

August 20
Senigallia Circuit
Antonio Stagnoli
166 MM

August 26 / Silverstone Production Car Race
Alberto Ascari
166 MM

October 1 / Interlagos
Interstate Race
Francisco Landi
125 F1

October 15 / Salò
Garda Circuit
Alberto Ascari
166 F2

October 29 / Barcelona-Pedralbes
Peña Rhin Grand Prix
Alberto Ascari
375 F1

November 12
City of Paraná Grand Prix
Juan Manuel Fangio
166 C

December 18
Santiago Grand Prix
Juan Manuel Fangio
166 C

1951

January 25
City of São Paulo Grand Prix
Francisco Landi
125 F1

February 18 / Buenos Aires
General Perón Grand Prix
José Froilán González
166 C

February 24 / Buenos Aires
Eva Perón Grand Prix
José Froilán González
166 C

March 11
Syracuse Grand Prix
Luigi Villoresi
375 F1

March 26
Pau Grand Prix
Luigi Villoresi
375 F1

April 1
Sicily Tour
V. Marzotto/L. Fontana
212 Export

April 8
Marseille Grand Prix
Luigi Villoresi
166 F2

April 15 / Monza
Inter-Europa Cup
Luigi Villoresi
212 Export

April 22
San Remo Grand Prix
Alberto Ascari
375 F1

April 28-29
Mille Miglia
L. Villoresi/P. Cassani
340 America

May 5 / Silverstone
Daily Express Trophy
Reg Parnell
375 F1 Thinwall Special

May 13 / Monza
Autodrome Grand Prix
Alberto Ascari
166 F2

May 14 / Goodwood
Festival of Britain Trophy
Reg Parnell
375 F1 Thinwall Special

May 20 / Genoa
Columbus 5th Century Grand Prix
Luigi Villoresi
166 F2

May 20 / Interlagos
Governador Noguera Garcez Race
Francisco Landi
125 F1

June 3
Tuscany Cup
G. Marzotto/M. Crosara
212 Export

June 3
Aix-les-Bains Circuit
Rudi Fischer
166 F2

June 10 / Angoulême
Remparts Circuit
Rudi Fischer
166 F2

June 10
Rome Grand Prix
Mario Raffaeli
166 F2

June 17 / Oporto
Portuguese Grand Prix
Casimiro De Oliveira
340 America

June 24
Naples Grand Prix
Alberto Ascari
166 F2

June 28 / Rio de Janeiro
Bôa Vista Grand Prix
Francisco Landi
125 F1

July 8
Rouen Grand Prix
Giannino Marzotto
166 F2

July 14 / Silverstone
British Grand Prix
F1WC
José Froilán González
375 F1   [2]

July 15
Vila Real Circuit
Giovanni Bracco
340 America

July 29 / Nürburgring
German Grand Prix
F1WC
Alberto Ascari
375 F1   [2]

August 12 / Erlen
Eastern Switzerland Grand Prix
Peter Whitehead
166 F2

August 12
Senigallia Circuit
Luigi Villoresi
340 America

August 15
Pescara Circuit
José Froilán González
375 F1

August 30 - September 10
Tour de France Automobile
'Pagnibon'/A. Barraquet
212 Export

September 16 / Monza
Italian Grand Prix
F1WC
Alberto Ascari
375 F1   [5]

September 23
Modena Grand Prix
Alberto Ascari
500 F2

November 20-25
Carrera Panamericana México
P. Taruffi/L. Chinetti
212 Inter

1952

January 13 / Interlagos
City of São Paulo Grand Prix
Juan Manuel Fangio
166 C

January 19 / Gavea
Rio de Janeiro Grand Prix
José Froilán González
166 C

February 3 / Rio de Janeiro
Quinta da Bôa Vista Grand Prix
Juan Manuel Fangio
166 C

March 9 / Buenos Aires
Presidente Perón Grand Prix
Juan Manuel Fangio
166 C

March 9
Sicily Tour
P. Marzotto/M. Marini
166 MM

March 16 / Buenos Aires
Eva Perón Grand Prix
Juan Manuel Fangio
166 C

March 16
Syracuse Grand Prix
Alberto Ascari
500 F2

March 19 / Syracuse
Sicily Gold Cup
Eugenio Castellotti
195 S

March 23 / Montevideo
1st Piriapolis Circuit
Juan Manuel Fangio
166 C

March 30
Montlhéry Circuit
'Pagnibon'
225 S

March 30 / Montevideo
2nd Piriapolis Circuit
Juan Manuel Fangio
166 C

April 6 / Turin
Valentino Grand Prix
Luigi Villoresi
375 Indianapolis

April 6
Nîmes Grand Prix
'Pagnibon'
225 S

April 14
Pau Grand Prix
Alberto Ascari
500 F2

April 14 / Goodwood
Richmond Trophy
José Froilán González
375 F1 Thinwall Special

April 27
Marseille Grand Prix
Alberto Ascari
500 F2

May 3-4
Mille Miglia
Giovanni Bracco
250 S

May 4
Bordeaux Circuit
'Pagnibon'
225 S

May 11
Naples Grand Prix
Giuseppe Farina
500 F2

May 18 / Bern
Bremgarten Grand Prix
Hans Karl von Tscharner
212 Export

May 18 / Bern
Swiss Grand Prix
F1WC
Piero Taruffi
500 F2   [3]

May 25 / Nürburgring
Eifelrennen
Rudi Fischer
500 F2

May 25 / Montlhéry
Paris Grand Prix
Piero Taruffi
500 F2

May 25
Santa Monica Circuit
Phil Hill
212 Export

June 1
Tuscany Cup
B. Sterzi / N. Rovelli
212 Export

June 1
Albi Grand Prix
Louis Rosier
375 F1

June 2 / Monte Carlo
Monaco Grand Prix
Vittorio Marzotto
225 S

June 7 / Dundrod
Ulster Trophy
Piero Taruffi
375 F1 Thinwall Special

June 8 / Monza
Autodrome Grand Prix
Giuseppe Farina
500 F2

June 8
Orléans Circuit
Jean Lucas
225 S

June 21 / Oporto
Portuguese Grand Prix
Eugenio Castellotti
225 S

June 21 / Spa-Francorchamps
Belgian and European Grand Prix
F1WC
Alberto Ascari
500 F2   [5]

July 6 / Rouen-les-Essarts
A.C. de France Grand Prix
F1WC
Alberto Ascari
500 F2   [5]

July 6
Vila Real Circuit
Casimiro De Oliveira
225 S

July 13
Les Sables d'Olonne Grand Prix
Luigi Villoresi
500 F2

July 13
Dolomite Gold Cup
P. Marzotto / M. Marini
225 S

July 19 / Silverstone
British Grand Prix
F1WC
Alberto Ascari
500 F2   [5]

July 19
Silverstone 100 Miles
Piero Taruffi
375 F1 Thinwall Special

August 2 / Boreham
Daily Mail Trophy
Luigi Villoresi
375 F1

August 3
Calabria Tour
Paolo Marzotto
225 S

August 3 / Nürburgring
German Grand Prix
F1WC
Alberto Ascari
500 F2   [5]

August 3
Race at the Nürburgring
Piero Carini
225 S

August 10 / St.-Gaudens
Comminges Grand Prix
A. Simon / A. Ascari
500 F2

August 10
Senigallia Circuit
Paolo Marzotto
225 S

August 15
Pescara 12 Hours
P. Marzotto / G. Bracco
250 S

August 17 / Zandvoort
Dutch Grand Prix
F1WC
Alberto Ascari
500 F2   [5]

August 24
Messina 10 Nocturnal Hours
C. Biondetti / F. Cornacchia
212 Export

August 24
La Baule Grand Prix
Alberto Ascari
500 F2

August 31
Pergusa Circuit
Luigi Bordonaro di Chiaramonte
212 Export

September 7 / Monza
Inter-Europa Cup
Bruno Sterzi
212 Export

September 7 / Monza
Italian Grand Prix
F1WC
Alberto Ascari
500 F2   [5]

September 14
Modena Grand Prix
Luigi Villoresi
500 F2

September 14
Cadours Circuit
Louis Rosier
500 F2

September 19 / Buenos Aires
Premio Eva Perón
Roberto Bonomi
212 Export

September 28
Bari Grand Prix
Francisco Landi
195 S

September 28 / Berlin
Avusrennen
Rudi Fischer
500 F2

October 4 / Castle Coombe
F2 Race
Roy Salvadori
500 F2

1953

January 18 / Buenos Aires
Argentine Grand Prix
F1WC
Alberto Ascari
500 F2   [5]

February 1
Buenos Aires Grand Prix
Giuseppe Farina
625 F1

April 6
Pau Grand Prix
Alberto Ascari
500 F2

April 12
Sicily Tour
L. Villoresi / P. Cassani
340 MM

April 25-26
Mille Miglia
SCWC
G. Marzotto / M. Crosara
340 MM   [0280 AM]

May 3
Bordeaux Grand Prix
Alberto Ascari
500 F2

May 9 / Silverstone
Daily Express Trophy
Mike Hawthorn
500 F2

May 9 / Silverstone
Sports Car Race
Mike Hawthorn
340 MM

May 10
Naples Grand Prix
Giuseppe Farina
500 F2

May 16 / Dundrod
Ulster Trophy
Mike Hawthorn
500 F2

May 17
Coupes de Spa
Olivier Gendebien
166 MM

May 24
Algiers 3 Hours
'Pagnibon'
340 MM

May 24
Cagliari-Sassari-Cagliari
Eugenio Castellotti
225 S

May 31
Albi Grand Prix
Louis Rosier
375 F1

May 31 / Montlhéry
Paris Cup
'Pagnibon'
340 MM

June 7 / Zandvoort
Dutch Grand Prix
F1WC
Alberto Ascari
500 F2   [5]

June 20 / Oporto
Portuguese Grand Prix
José Antonio Nogueira Pinto
225 S

June 21 / Spa-Francorchamps
Belgian Grand Prix
F1WC
Alberto Ascari
500 F2   [5]

June 28
Rouen Grand Prix
Giuseppe Farina
625 F1

June 29 / Monza
Autodrome Grand Prix
Luigi Villoresi
250 MM

July 5 / Rheims
A.C. de France Grand Prix
F1WC
Mike Hawthorn
500 F2   [1]

July 12
Dolomite Gold Cup
Paolo Marzotto
250 MM

July 12 / Berlin
Avusrennen
Jacques Swaters
500 F2

July 18 / Silverstone
British Grand Prix
F1WC
Alberto Ascari
500 F2   [5]

July 18 / Silverstone
Formule Libre Trophy
Giuseppe Farina
375 F1 Thinwall Special

July 25-26
Spa-Francorchamps 24 Hours
SCWC
G. Farina / M. Hawthorn
375 MM   [0320 AM]

July 26
Messina 10 Nocturnal Hours
E. Castellotti / G. Musitelli
250 MM

August 2 / Nürburgring
German Grand Prix
F1WC
Giuseppe Farina
500 F2   [4]

August 9
Senigallia Circuit
Paolo Marzotto
340 MM

August 9
Les Sables d'Olonne Grand Prix
Louis Rosier
500 F2

August 15
Pescara 12 Hours
U. Maglioli/M. Hawthorn
375 MM

August 15 / Charterhall
Daily Record Trophy
Giuseppe Farina
375 F1 Thinwall Special

August 23 / Bern
Swiss Grand Prix
F1WC
Alberto Ascari
500 F2   [5]

August 30
Nürburgring 1000 Kilometres
SCWC
A. Ascari/G. Farina
340 MM   [0286 AM]

September 13 / Monza
Inter-Europa Cup
Franco Cornacchia
212 Inter

September 26
Goodwood Trophy
Mike Hawthorn
375 F1 Thinwall Special

September 26 / Goodwood
Woodcote Cup
Mike Hawthorn
375 F1 Thinwall Special

December 20
Casablanca 12 Hours
G. Farina/P. Scotti
375 MM

1954

January 24
Buenos Aires 1000 Kilometres
SCWC
G. Farina/U. Maglioli
375 MM   [0370 AM]

January 31
City of Buenos Aires Grand Prix
Maurice Trintignant
625 F1

February 27
Agadir Circuit
Giuseppe Farina
375 Plus

March 7 / Dakar
Senegal Criterium
Piero Scotti
375 Plus

April 11
Tuscany Cup
Piero Scotti
375 MM

April 11
Syracuse Grand Prix
Giuseppe Farina
625 F1

April 19 / Goodwood
Lavant Cup
Reg Parnell
500 F2/625 F1

April 19
Marrakech Circuit
François Picard
500 Mondial

May 9
Bordeaux Grand Prix
José Froilán González
625 F1

May 15 / Silverstone
Sports Car Race
José Froilán González
375 Plus

May 15 / Silverstone
Daily Express Trophy
Trintignant/González
625 F1

May 22
Bari 3 Nocturnal Hours
Clemente Biondetti
735 Mondial

May 23
Bari Grand Prix
José Froilán González
625 F1

June 6
Hyères 12 Hours
M. Trintignant/L. Piotti
250 Monza

June 7 / Goodwood
Whitsun Trophy
Peter Collins
375 F1 Thinwall Special

June 12-13
Le Mans 24 Hours
SCWC
J.F. González/M. Trintignant
375 Plus   [0396 AM]

June 20
Imola Gold Shell
Umberto Maglioli
500 Mondial

June 27 / Monza
Supercortemaggiore Grand Prix
U. Maglioli/M. Hawthorn
735 S

July 11
Rouen Grand Prix
Maurice Trintignant
625 F1

July 17 / Silverstone
British Grand Prix
F1WC
José Froilán González
625 F1   [4]

July 25 / Monsanto
Portuguese Grand Prix
José Froilán González
750 Monza

July 25 / La Prairie
Caen Circuit
Maurice Trintignant
625 F1

August 2 / Crystal Palace
August Trophy
Reg Parnell
500 F2/625 F1

August 8
Senigallia Circuit
Umberto Maglioli
750 Monza

September 25 / Goodwood
Woodcote Cup
Peter Collins
375 F1 Thinwall Special

October 23 / Barcelona-Pedralbes
Peña Rhin Grand Prix
François Picard
500 Mondial

October 24 / Barcelona-Pedralbes
Spanish Grand Prix
F1WC
Mike Hawthorn
553 F1   [2]

November 19-23
Carrera Panamericana México
SCWC
Umberto Maglioli
375 Plus   [0392 AM]

1955

January 23
Buenos Aires 1000 Kilometres
SCWC
E. Díaz Saenz Valiente/J.M.
Ibáñez
375 Plus   [0398 AM]

February 27
Agadir Circuit
'Mike Sparken'
750 Monza

March 13
Dakar Grand Prix
Piero Carini
750 Monza

April 3
Sicily Tour
Piero Taruffi
118 LM

May 22 / Monte Carlo
Monaco and European Grand Prix
F1WC
Maurice Trintignant
625 F1   [2]

May 29
Hyères 12 Hours
A. Canonica/G. Munaron
750 Monza

May 29
Rafaela 500 Miles
Alberto Rodríguez Larreta
625 TF

June 5
Targa Mugello
Umberto Maglioli
750 Monza

June 18 / Toronto
Edenvale Grand Prix
Jim Pauley
340 MM

July 23-24
Messina 10 Nocturnal Hours
E. Castellotti/M. Trintignant
750 Monza

July 24 / Monsanto
Lisbon Grand Prix
Masten Gregory
750 Monza

August 7 / Kristianstad
Swedish Grand Prix
Gunnar Carlsson
750 Monza

September 10 / Elkhart Lake
Road America Race
Phil Hill
750 Monza

October 10 / Havana
Cuban Grand Prix
Santiago Gonzáles
225 S

December 3
Palm Springs Race
Ernie McAfee
750 Monza

December 6 / Nassau
Governor's Trophy
Alfonso De Portago
750 Monza

December 11
Nassau Trophy
Phil Hill
750 Monza

December 11
Nassau Race
Alfonso De Portago
250 GT

1956

January 22 / Buenos Aires
Argentine Grand Prix
F1WC
L. Musso/J.M. Fangio
D 50   [0003]

February 5 / Mendoza
Buenos Aires Grand Prix
Juan Manuel Fangio
D 50

February 10
Palm Springs Race
Carroll Shelby
500 TR

February 26
Agadir Circuit
Maurice Trintignant
860 Monza

March 11
Dakar Grand Prix
Maurice Trintignant
860 Monza

March 24
Sebring 12 Hours
SCWC
J.M. Fangio/E. Castellotti
860 Monza   [0604]

April 8
Sicily Tour
P. Collins/L. Klemantaski
857 S

April 15
Syracuse Grand Prix
Juan Manuel Fangio
D 50

April 18
Pebble Beach Race
Carroll Shelby
500 TR

April 28-29
Mille Miglia
SCWC
Eugenio Castellotti
290 MM   [0616]

June 3 / Spa-Francorchamps
Belgian Grand Prix
F1WC
Peter Collins
D 50   [0008]

June 13
Elkhart Lake Race
Carroll Shelby
500 TR

June 17
Oporto Grand Prix
Alfonso De Portago
250 GT

June 24 / Monza
Supercortemaggiore Grand Prix
P. Collins/M. Hawthorn
500 TR

July 1 / Rheims
A.C. de France Grand Prix
F1WC
Peter Collins
D 50   [0008]

July 8
Rouen Grand Prix
Eugenio Castellotti
860 Monza

July 14 / Silverstone
British Grand Prix
F1WC
Juan Manuel Fangio
D 50   [0010]

August 5 / Nürburgring
German Grand Prix
F1WC
Juan Manuel Fangio
D 50   [0010]

August 12 / Kristianstad
Swedish Grand Prix
SCWC
M. Trintignant/P. Hill
290 MM   [0606]

August 25-26
Messina 5 Nocturnal Hours
Phil Hill
500 TR

September 17-23
Tour de France Automobile
A. De Portago/E. Nelson
250 GT

October 7 / Montlhéry
Paris Coupe du Salon
Alfonso De Portago
250 GT

November 4
Palm Springs Race
Carroll Shelby
500 TR

1957

January 20
Buenos Aires 1000 Kilometres
SCWC
L.Musso/M.Gregory/E.Castellotti
290 MM   [0626]

April 7
Syracuse Grand Prix
Peter Collins
D 50

April 14
Sicily Tour
O. Gendebien/J. Washer
250 GT

April 24-28
Acropolis Rally
ERCD
J. Estager/Mme Estager
250 GT   [0443 GT]

April 28
Naples Grand Prix
Peter Collins
D 50

May 11-12
Mille Miglia
SCWC
Piero Taruffi
315 S   [0684]

July 13-14
Rheims 12 Hours
O. Gendebien/P. Frère
250 GT

July 14 / Rheims
Coupe de vitesse F2
Maurice Trintignant
156 F2

July 14 / Rheims
Coupe de vitesse F1
Luigi Musso
D 50

August 4 / Nürburgring
Rhineland Cup
Wolfgang Seidel
250 GT

September 8 / Monza
Inter-Europa Cup
Camillo Luglio
250 GT

September 8
Elkhart Lake 500 Miles
P. Hill/G. Greenspun
250 GT

September 16-22
Tour de France Automobile
O. Gendebien/L. Bianchi
250 GT

October 6 / Montlhéry
Paris Coupe du Salon
Olivier Gendebien
250 GT

October 13 / Monza
Leopoldo Carri Cup
Edoardo Lualdi Gabardi
250 GT

November 3 / Caracas
Venezuelan Grand Prix
SCWC
P. Hill/P. Collins
335 S   [0700]

December 7 / Nassau
Governor's Trophy
Phil Hill
335 S

December 8
Nassau Trophy
Stirling Moss
290 MM

1958

January 26
Buenos Aires 1000 Kilometres
SCWC
P. Collins/P. Hill
250 TR 58   [0704]

February 24 / Havana
Cuban Grand Prix
Stirling Moss
335 S

March 22
Sebring 12 Hours
SCWC
P. Collins/P. Hill
250 TR 58   [0704]

April 7
Pau 3 Hours
O. Gendebien/C. Bourillot
250 GT

April 7 / Goodwood
Glover Trophy
Mike Hawthorn
246 F1

April 13
Syracuse Grand Prix
Luigi Musso
246 F1

May 3 / Silverstone
Daily Express Trophy
Peter Collins
246 F1

May 11
Targa Florio
SCWC
L. Musso/O. Gendebien
250 TR 58   [0726]

May 18
Spa Grand Prix
Nano Da Silva Ramos
250 GT

June 21-22
Le Mans 24 Hours
SCWC
O. Gendebien/P. Hill
250 TR 58   [0728]

July 6 / Rheims
A.C. de France Grand Prix
F1WC
Mike Hawthorn
246 F1   [0003]

July 6
Rheims 12 Hours
O. Gendebien/P. Frère
250 GT

July 19 / Silverstone
British Grand Prix
F1WC
Peter Collins
246 F1   [0002]

September 7 / Monza
Inter-Europa Cup
Luigi Taramazzo
250 GT

September 7
Elkhart Lake 500 Miles
L. Reventlow/G. Andrey
335 S

September 14-21
Tour de France Automobile
O. Gendebien/L. Bianchi
250 GT

October 5 / Nürburgring
Eifelrennen
Wolfgang Seidel
250 GT

October 5 / Montlhéry
Paris Coupe du Salon
Luciano Bianchi
250 GT

October 6 / Bathurst
Australian Grand Prix
Lex Davison
500 F2

November 4 / Monza
Sant'Ambroeus Cup
Edoardo Lualdi Gabardi
250 GT

1959

March 21
Sebring 12 Hours
SCWC
P. Hill/O. Gendebien/
D. Gurney/C. Daigh
250 TR 59   [0766]

April 18
Aintree 200 Miles
Jean Behra
246 F1

May 3 / Monza
Sant'Ambroeus Cup
Giulio Cabianca
196 S

May 3 / Montlhéry
Prix de Paris
Olivier Gendebien
250 GT

June 28 / Monza
Lottery Grand Prix
Alfonso Thiele
250 GT

July 5 / Rheims
A.C. de France and European
Grand Prix
F1WC
Tony Brooks
256 F1   [0002]

August 2 / Avus
German Grand Prix
F1WC
Tony Brooks
246 F1   [0002]

September 13 / Monza
Inter-Europa Cup
Alfonso Thiele
250 GT

September 18-25
Tour de France Automobile
O. Gendebien/L. Bianchi
250 GT

September 27 / Montlhéry
Coupe du Salon de Paris
Jean-Pierre Schild
250 GT

October 11 / Riverside
Los Angeles Times Grand Prix
Phil Hill
250 TR

1960

January 31
Buenos Aires 1000 Kilometres
SCWC
P. Hill/C. Allison
250 TR 59/60 [0774]

March 19
Syracuse Grand Prix
Wolfgang von Trips
256 F1

May 15 / Montlhéry
Prix de Paris
André Simon
250 GT

384

June 25-26
Le Mans 24 Hours
SCWC
O. Gendebien/P. Frère
250 TR 59/60 [0772]

July 3 / Nuremberg
Norisring Race
Wolfgang Seidel
250 GT

July 24 / Stuttgart
Solitude Grand Prix
Wolfgang von Trips
156 F2

July 31 / Nürburgring
Rhineland Cup
Jo Schlesser
250 GT

August 20 / Goodwood
RAC Tourist Trophy
Stirling Moss
250 GT

August 27 / Brands Hatch
Redex Trophy
Stirling Moss
250 GT

September 4 / Monza
Inter-Europa Cup
Carlo Mario Abate
250 GT

September 4 / Monza
Italian and European Grand Prix
F1WC
Phil Hill
246 F1 [0007]

September 15-23
Tour de France Automobile
W. Mairesse/G. Berger
250 GT

October 16 / Modena
ACI Gold Cup
Carlo Mario Abate
250 GT

October 23 / Montlhéry
Paris 1000 Kilometres
O. Gendebien/L. Bianchi
250 GT

November 27
Nassau Tourist Trophy
Stirling Moss
250 GT

December 3 / Nassau
Governor's Trophy
Ricardo Rodríguez
196 S

1961

March 25
Sebring 12 Hours
SCWC
P. Hill/O. Gendebien
250 TR 61 [0792]

March 25 / Snetterton
Lombank Trophy
Mike Parkes
250 GT

April 3 / Goodwood
Fordwater Trophy
Mike Parkes
250 GT

April 25
Syracuse Grand Prix
Giancarlo Baghetti
156 F1

April 30
Targa Florio
SCWC
W. von Trips/O. Gendebien/
R. Ginther
246 SP [0790]

May 14
Naples Grand Prix
Giancarlo Baghetti
156 F1

May 14
Spa Grand Prix
Willy Mairesse
250 GT

May 14 / Montlhéry
Prix de Paris
André Simon
250 GT

May 22 / Zandvoort
Dutch Grand Prix
F1WC
Wolfgang von Trips
156 F1 [0004]

May 27-28
Mille Miglia Rally
ERCD
G. Andersson/C. Lohmander
250 GT [2439 GT]

June 3 / Brands Hatch
Peco Trophy (no. 1)
Mike Parkes
250 GT

June 10-11
Le Mans 24 Hours
SCWC
P. Hill/O. Gendebien
250 TR 61 [0794]

June 18 / Spa-Francorchamps
Belgian Grand Prix
F1WC
Phil Hill
156 F1 [0003]

July 2 / Rheims
A.C. de France Grand Prix
F1WC
Giancarlo Baghetti
156 F1 [0008]

July 8 / Silverstone
British Empire Trophy
Stirling Moss
250 GT

July 9 / Clermont-Ferrand
Auvergne 6 Hours
W. Mairesse/P. Dumay
250 GT

July 15 / Aintree
British Grand Prix
F1WC
Wolfgang von Trips
156 F1 [0004]

July 23 / Meadowdale
Wisconsin Grand Prix
Denise McCluggage
250 GT

July 30
Rhodes Circuit
Gino Munaron
250 TR

August 6 / Nürburgring
Rhineland Cup
Carlo Mario Abate
250 GT

August 7 / Brands Hatch
Peco Trophy (no. 2)
Stirling Moss
250 GT

August 15
Pescara 4 Hours
SCWC
L. Bandini/G. Scarlatti
250 TR P 61 [0780]

August 19 / Goodwood
RAC Tourist Trophy
Stirling Moss
250 GT

September 10 / Monza
Inter-Europa Cup
Pierre Noblet
250 GT

September 10 / Monza
Italian Grand Prix
F1WC
Phil Hill
156 F1 [0002]

September 14-23
Tour de France Automobile
W. Mairesse/G. Berger
250 GT

September 23
Watkins Glen Grand Prix
George Constantine
196 S

September 24 / Montlhéry
Paris Cup
Henri Oreiller
250 GT

October 3 / Snetterton
Molyslip Trophy
Mike Parkes
250 GT

October 8 / Montlhéry
Paris Coupe du Salon
Henri Oreiller
250 GT

October 22 / Montlhéry
Paris 1000 Kilometres
P. Rodríguez/R. Rodríguez
250 GT

December 4
Nassau Tourist Trophy
Stirling Moss
250 GT

December 9 / Nassau
Governor's Trophy
Pedro Rodríguez
250 TRi 61

December 26 / Brands Hatch
Christmas Trophy
Graham Hill
250 TRi 61

1962

March 24
Sebring 12 Hours
J. Bonnier/L. Bianchi
250 TR 61 [0792]

April 1 / Heysel
Brussels Grand Prix
Willy Mairesse
156 F1

April 15 / Monza
Grand Touring Trophy
Edoardo Lualdi Gabardi
250 GT

April 15
Coupes de Bruxelles
Pierre Noblet
250 GT

May 6
Targa Florio
W. Mairesse/R. Rodríguez/
O. Gendebien
246 SP 62 [0796]

May 8 / Silverstone
Scalextric Trophy
Mike Parkes
250 GTO

May 13 / Berlin
Avus Grand Prix
Edgar Berney
250 GT

May 20
Naples Grand Prix
Willy Mairesse
156 F1

May 20
Spa Grand Prix
Edgar Berney
250 GT

May 26 / Brands Hatch
Peco Trophy (no. 1)
Innes Ireland
250 GTO

May 27
Nürburgring 1000 Kilometres
P. Hill/O. Gendebien
246 SP 62 [0790]

June 10
Parma-Poggio di Berceto
EHC
Lodovico Scarfiotti
196 SP [0804]

June 11
Mallory Park Race
Mike Parkes
250 GTO

June 17
Marlboro 6 Hours
C. Hayes/G. Hobbs
250 GT

June 17
Mont-Ventoux Hillclimb
EHC
Lodovico Scarfiotti
196 SP [0804]

June 23
Riverside 6 Hours
K. Miles/B. Drake
250 GTB

June 23-24
Le Mans 24 Hours
SEWC
P. Hill/O. Gendebien
330 TRi LM [0808]

July 8
Trento-Bondone
EHC
Lodovico Scarfiotti
196 SP [0804]

July 15 / Clermont-Ferrand
Auvergne Trophy
CIGTC/III
Carlo Mario Abate
250 GTO [3445 GT]

July 22
Freiburg-Schauinsland
EHC
Lodovico Scarfiotti
196 SP [0804]

Palmarès

August 6 / Brands Hatch
Guards Trophy
Mike Parkes
246 SP

August 6 / Brands Hatch
Peco Trophy (no. 2)
Mike Parkes
250 GTO

August 18 / Goodwood
RAC Tourist Trophy
CIGTC/III
Innes Ireland
250 GTO   [3505 GT]

August 19 / Pergusa
Mediterranean Grand Prix
Lorenzo Bandini
156 F1

September 9
Albi Grand Prix
Henri Oreiller
250 GT

September 15-23
Tour de France Automobile
A. Simon/M. Dupeyron
250 GTO

September 16
Bridgehampton 400
Pedro Rodríguez
330 TRi LM

September 23
Mosport Park Race
Pedro Rodríguez
330 TRi LM

September 29
Snetterton 3 Hours
Mike Parkes
250 GTO

October 7 / Montlhéry
Coupe du Salon de Paris
Edgar Berney
250 GTO

October 14 / Monza
Autumn Cup
Edoardo Lualdi Gabardi
250 GTO

October 21 / Montlhéry
Paris 1000 Kilometres
CIGTC/III
P. Rodríguez/R. Rodríguez
250 GTO   [3987 GT]

November 3 / Kyalami
Rand 9 Hours
D. Piper/B. Johnstone
250 GTO

December 2 / Luanda
Angola Grand Prix
Luciano Bianchi
250 GTO

December 3
Nassau Tourist Trophy
Roger Penske
250 GTO

1963

February 17
Daytona 3 Hours
CIGTC/III
Pedro Rodríguez
250 GTO   [4219 GT]

March 23
Sebring 12 Hours
IGTPT - SEWC
J. Surtees/L. Scarfiotti
250 P   [0810]

April 7
Dakar 6 Hours
P. Noblet/J. Guichet
250 GTO

May 4
Japanese Grand Prix
Pierre Dumay
250 GTO

May 12
Spa 500 Kilometres
CIGTC/III
Willy Mairesse
250 GTO   [3757 GT]

May 19
Nürburgring 1000 Kilometres
J. Surtees/W. Mairesse
IGTPT - SEWC
250 P   [0812]

June 3 / Goodwood
Whitsun Trophy
Mike Parkes
250 GTO

June 15-16
Le Mans 24 Ore Hours
IGTPT - SEWC
L. Scarfiotti/L. Bandini
250 P   [0814]

June 30
Rheims International Trophy
Carlo Mario Abate
250 TR

July 6 / Silverstone
Martini Trophy
Mike Parkes
250 GTO

July 7 / Clermont-Ferrand
Auvergne 3 Hours
Lorenzo Bandini
250 TR

August 4 / Nürburgring
German Grand Prix
F1WC
John Surtees
156 F1   [0002]

August 18 / Pergusa
Mediterranean Grand Prix
John Surtees
156 F1

August 24 / Goodwood
RAC Tourist Trophy
CIGTC/III
Graham Hill
250 GTO   [4399 GT]

September 14-22
Tour de France Automobile
CIGTC/III
J. Guichet/José Behra
250 GTO   [5111 GT]

September 28 / Mosport Park
Canadian Grand Prix
Pedro Rodríguez
250 P

November 2 / Kyalami
Rand 9 Hours
D. Piper/T. Maggs
250 GTO

December 14 / Kyalami
Rand Grand Prix
John Surtees
156 F1

1964

February 16
Daytona 2000 Kilometres
CIGTC/III - FAT
P. Hill/P. Rodríguez
250 GTO   [5571 GT]

March 21
Sebring 12 Hours
IGTPT - SEWC
M. Parkes/U. Maglioli
275 P   [0816]

March 30 / Goodwood
Sussex Trophy
Graham Hill
250 GTO

April 12
Syracuse Grand Prix
John Surtees
158 F1

May 2 / Silverstone
BRDC Trophy
Graham Hill
250 GTO

May 17
Spa 500 Kilometres
CIGTC/III
Mike Parkes
250 GTO   [4399 GT]

May 31
Nürburgring 1000 Kilometres
IGTPT - SEWC
L. Scarfiotti/N. Vaccarella
275 P   [0820]

June 20-21
Le Mans 24 Hours
IGTPT - SEWC
J. Guichet/N. Vaccarella
275 P   [0816]

July 5
Rheims 12 Hours
G. Hill/J. Bonnier
250 LM

July 19 / Zolder
Limburg Grand Prix
Luciano Bianchi
250 LM

August 2 / Nürburgring
German Grand Prix
F1WC
John Surtees
158 F1   [0005]

August 23 / Zeltweg Airport
Austrian Grand Prix
F1WC
Lorenzo Bandini
156 F1   [0004]

August 29 / Goodwood
RAC Tourist Trophy
Graham Hill
330 P

September 6 / Monza
Inter-Europa Cup
Nino Vaccarella
250 LM

September 6 / Monza
Italian Grand Prix
F1WC
John Surtees
158 F1   [0006]

September 12-20
Tour de France Automobile
CIGTC/III
L. Bianchi/G. Berger
250 GTO   [4153 GT]

September 12-20
Tour de France Automobile
Coupe des Dames
A. Soisbault/N. Roure
250 GTO

September 13 / St.-Jovite
Québec Race
Pedro Rodríguez
275 P

September 13
Elkhart Lake 500 Miles
W. Hansgen/A. Pabst
250 LM

September 27 / Mosport Park
Canadian Grand Prix
Pedro Rodríguez
250 LM

October 11 / Montlhéry
Paris 1000 Kilometres
G. Hill/J. Bonnier
330 P

October 25 / Monza
Bettoja Trophy
Lodovico Scarfiotti
330 P

October 31 / Kyalami
Rand 9 Hours
D. Piper/T. Maggs
250 LM

November 29 / Luanda
Angola Grand Prix
Willy Mairesse
250 LM

1965

March 21 / Spa-Francorchamps
Coupes de Belgique
Willy Mairesse
250 LM

April 25
Monza 1000 Kilometres
IGTPT
M. Parkes/J. Guichet
275 P2   [0836]

May 9
Targa Florio
IGTPT - SEWC
L. Bandini/N. Vaccarella
275 P2   [0828]

May 16
Spa 500 Kilometres
Willy Mairesse
250 LM

May 23
Nürburgring 1000 Kilometres
IGTPT - SEWC
J. Surtees/L. Scarfiotti
330 P2   [0828]

June 6
Mugello Circuit
M. Casoni/T. Nicodemi
250 LM

June 7
Perth 6 Hours
Spencer Martin
250 LM

June 19-20
Le Mans 24 Hours
IGTPT - SEWC
J. Rindt/M. Gregory
250 LM   [5893]

July 4
Rheims 12 Hours
P. Rodríguez / J. Guichet
365 P

July 11
Trento-Bondone
EHC
Lodovico Scarfiotti
Dino 206 P   [0834]

July 25
Cesana-Sestrière
EHC
Lodovico Scarfiotti
Dino 206 S   [0834]

August 8
Freiburg-Schauinsland
EHC
Lodovico Scarfiotti
Dino 206 S   [0834]

August 15 / Pergusa
City of Enna Cup
Mario Casoni
250 LM

August 22 / Zeltweg Airport
Austrian Grand Prix
Jochen Rindt
250 LM

August 29
Ollon-Villars
EHC
Lodovico Scarfiotti
Dino 206 S   [0834]

November 7 / Kyalami
Rand 9 Hours
D. Piper / R. Attwood
365 P

November 28 / Luanda
Angola Grand Prix
David Piper
365 P

November 29
Nassau Tourist Trophy
Charlie Kolb
275 GTB

1966

March 13 / Monza
FISA Cup
Edoardo Lualdi Gabardi
250 LM

March 27 / Zolder
Grand National de Belgique
'Beurlys'
250 LM

April 25
Monza 1000 Kilometres
ISPCC
J. Surtees / M. Parkes
330 P3   [0848]

May 1
Syracuse Grand Prix
John Surtees
312 F1

May 22
Spa 1000 Kilometres
ISPCC
M. Parkes / L. Scarfiotti
330 P3   [0848]

June 12 / Spa-Francorchamps
Belgian Grand Prix
F1WC
John Surtees
312 F1   [0010]

June 26 / Clermont Ferrand
Auvergne Trophy
David Piper
365 P

July 24
Cesana-Sestrière
EHC
Lodovico Scarfiotti
Dino 206 S   [0842]

August 6
Race at Crystal Palace
David Piper
250 LM

August 7 / Pergusa
City of Enna Cup
'Pam'
Dino 206 S

August 21
Surfer's Paradise 12 Hours
J. Stewart / A. Buchanan
250 LM

August 28
Sierre-Montana-Crans
EHC
Lodovico Scarfiotti
Dino 206 S   [0842]

September 4 / Monza
Italian Grand Prix
F1WC
Lodovico Scarfiotti
312 F1   [0011]

September 4 / Vallelunga
Ettore Bettoja Trophy
Edoardo Lualdi Gabardi
Dino 206 S

September 17 / Snetterton
Autosport Trophy
David Piper
250 LM

October 16 / Montlhéry
Paris 1000 Kilometres
M. Parkes / D. Piper
250 LM

November 6 / Kyalami
Rand 9 Hours
D. Piper / R. Attwood
365 P

November 21
Capetown 3 Hours
David Piper
365 P

1967

February 4-5
Daytona 24 Hours
ISPCC
L. Bandini / C. Amon
330 P4   [0846]

April 10 / Zolder
Grand National de Belgique
'Beurlys'
250 LM

April 25
Monza 1000 Kilometres
ISPCC
L. Bandini / C. Amon
330 P4   [0856]

April 29 / Silverstone
Daily Express Trophy
Mike Parkes
312 F1

May 21
Syracuse Grand Prix
Mike Parkes (dead heat)
312 F1

May 21
Syracuse Grand Prix
Lodovico Scarfiotti (dead heat)
312 F1

July 15
Race at Silverstone
Richard Attwood
250 LM

August 28
Race at Brands Hatch
David Piper
250 LM

1968

January 6 / Pukekohe
New Zealander Grand Prix
TC
Chris Amon
Dino 246/T   [0004]

January 13
Levin Grand Prix
TC
Chris Amon
Dino 246/T   [0004]

June 30 / Norisring
Nuremberg 200 Miles
David Piper
330 P3

July 7 / Rouen-les-Essarts
French Grand Prix
F1WC
Jacky Ickx
312 F1   [0009]

July 21 / Stuttgart
Solitude Grand Prix
David Piper
330

August 11 / Karlskoga
Swedish Grand Prix
David Piper
330 P3

September 29
Surfer's Paradise 3 Hours
L. Geoghegan/Geoghegan
250 LM

October 13 / Hockenheim
Baden-Württemberg Trophy
F2ET
Tino Brambilla
Dino 166 F2   [0004]

October 27 / Vallelunga
Rome Grand Prix
F2ET
Tino Brambilla
Dino 166 F2   [0004]

November 23
Capetown 3 Hours
Paul Hawkins
330 P4

December 1
Buenos Aires Grand Prix
Tino Brambilla
Dino 166 F2

December 1 / Bulawayo
Rhodesian Grand Prix
Paul Hawkins
330 P4

December 8
Córdoba Grand Prix
Andrea De Adamich
Dino 166 F2

December 15 / San Juan
Zonda Grand Prix
Andrea De Adamich
Dino 166 F2

December 28
Pietermaritzburg 3 Hours
Paul Hawkins
330 P4

1969

January 4 / Pukekohe
New Zealander Grand Prix
TC
Chris Amon
Dino 246/T 69 [0008]

January 4
East London 500 Miles
Paul Hawkins
330 P4

January 11
Levin Grand Prix
TC
Chris Amon
Dino 246/T 69 [0008]

February 2 / Lakeside
Australian Grand Prix
TC
Chris Amon
Dino 246/T 69 [0008]

February 16
Sandown Park 100 Miles
TC
Chris Amon
Dino 246/T 69 [0008]

May 1
Race at Magny-Cours
Mike Hailwood
350 Can-Am

May 25
Montseny Hillclimb
EHC
Peter Schetty
212 E   [0862]

June 8
Rossfeld Hillclimb
EHC
Peter Schetty
212 E   [0862]

June 22
Mont-Ventoux Hillclimb
EHC
Peter Schetty
212 E   [0862]

July 13
Trento-Bondone
EHC
Peter Schetty
212 E   [0862]

July 27
Freiburg-Schauinsland
EHC
Peter Schetty
212 E   [0862]

August 3
Cesana-Sestrière
EHC
Peter Schetty
212 E   [0862]

August 31
Ollon-Villars
EHC
Peter Schetty
212 E   [0862]

1970

January 2
Levin Grand Prix
TC
Graeme Lawrence
Dino 246/T 69   [0008]

March 21
Sebring 12 Hours
ICCS
I. Giunti/N. Vaccarella/M.
Andretti
512 S   [1026]

March 30
Singapore Grand Prix
Graeme Lawrence
Dino 246/T 69

April 5
Selangor Grand Prix
Graeme Lawrence
Dino 246/T 69

April 19 / Spa-Francorchamps
Belgium 500 Kilometres
Georg Loos
512 S

August 16 / Zeltweg
Austrian Grand Prix
F1WC
Jacky Ickx
312 B/F1   [001]

September 6 / Monza
Italian Grand Prix
F1WC
Clay Regazzoni
312 B/F1   [004]

September 6
Fuji Grand Prix
C. Manfredini/G.P. Moretti
512 S

September 20 / St.-Jovite
Canadian Grand Prix
F1WC
Jacky Ickx
312 B/F1   [001]

October 25
Mexican Grand Prix
F1WC
Jacky Ickx
312 B/F1   [001]

November 8 / Kyalami
Rand 9 Hours
J. Ickx/I. Giunti
512 M

1971

March 6 / Kyalami
South African Grand Prix
F1WC
Mario Andretti
312 B/F1   [002]

March 21 / Brands Hatch
Race of Champions
Clay Regazzoni
312 B2/F1

March 28 / Ontario
Questor Grand Prix
Mario Andretti
312 B/F1

May 2
Imola 300 Kilometres
Arturo Merzario
512 M

June 13 / Hockenheim
Jochen Rindt Memorial
Jacky Ickx
312 B/F1

June 20 / Zandvoort
Dutch Grand Prix
F1WC
Jacky Ickx
312 B2/F1   [006]

July 4 / Zandvoort
Benelux Cups
Hughes de Fierlant
512 M

September 12
Imola 500 Kilometres
Clay Regazzoni
312 P

November 6 / Kyalami
Rand 9 Hours
C. Regazzoni/B. Redman
312 P

1972

January 9
Buenos Aires 1000 Kilometres
WCCS
R. Peterson/T. Schenken
312 P   [0886]

February 6
Daytona 6 Hours
WCCS
J. Ickx/M. Andretti
312 P   [0888]

March 25
Sebring 12 Hours
WCCS
J. Ickx/M. Andretti
312 P   [0882]

April 16
Brands Hatch 1000 Kilometres
WCCS
J. Ickx/M. Andretti
312 P   [0888]

April 25
Monza 1000 Kilometres
WCCS
C. Regazzoni/J. Ickx
312 P   [0882]

May 7
Spa-Francorchamps 1000 Kilome-
tres
WCCS
B. Redman/A. Merzario
312 P   [0890]

May 21
Targa Florio
WCCS
A. Merzario/S. Munari
312 P   [0884]

May 28
Nürburgring 1000 Kilometres
WCCS
R. Peterson/T. Schenken
312 P   [0886]

June 25 / Zeltweg
Austria 1000 Kilometres
WCCS
J. Ickx/B. Redman
312 P   [0888]

July 22
Watkins Glen 6 Hours
WCCS
J. Ickx/M. Andretti
312 P   [0896]

July 30 / Nürburgring
German Grand Prix
F1WC
Jacky Ickx
312 B2/F1   [005]

September 14-24
Tour de France Automobile
EGTT - ERCD
J.C. Andruet/'Biche'
365 GTB/4-C [15667]

September 17
Imola 500 Kilometres
Arturo Merzario
312 P

November 4 / Kyalami
Rand 9 Hours
C. Regazzoni/A. Merzario
312 P

1973

April 25
Monza 1000 Kilometres
WCCS
J. Ickx/B. Redman
312 P   [0888]

May 27
Nürburgring 1000 Kilometres
WCCS
J. Ickx/B. Redman
312 P   [0888]

1974

April 28 / Jarama
Spanish Grand Prix
F1WC
Niki Lauda
312 B3/F1   [015]

June 23 / Zandvoort
Dutch Grand Prix
F1WC
Niki Lauda
312 B3/F1   [015]

August 4 / Nürburgring
German and European Grand
Prix
F1WC
Clay Regazzoni
312 B3   [016]

1975

April 13 / Silverstone
Daily Express Trophy
Niki Lauda
312 T/F1

May 11 / Monte Carlo
Monaco Grand Prix
F1WC
Niki Lauda
312 T/F1   [023]

May 25 / Zolder
Belgian Grand Prix
F1WC
Niki Lauda
312 T/F1   [023]

June 8 / Anderstorp
Swedish Grand Prix
F1WC
Niki Lauda
312 T/F1   [023]

July 6 / Le Castellet
French Grand Prix
F1WC
Niki Lauda
312 T/F1   [022]

August 24 / Dijon-Prenois
Swiss Grand Prix
Clay Regazzoni
312 T/F1

September 7 / Monza
Italian Grand Prix
F1WC
Clay Regazzoni
312 T/F1   [024]

October 5 / Watkins Glen
United States Grand Prix
F1WC
Niki Lauda
312 T/F1   [023]

1976

January 25 / Interlagos
Brazilian Grand Prix
F1WC
Niki Lauda
312 T/F1   [023]

March 6 / Kyalami
South African Grand Prix
F1WC
Niki Lauda
312 T/F1   [023]

March 28 / Long Beach
United States Grand Prix West
F1WC
Clay Regazzoni
312 T/F1   [024]

May 16 / Zolder
Belgian Grand Prix
F1WC
Niki Lauda
312 T2/F1   [026]

May 30 / Monte Carlo
Monaco Grand Prix
F1WC
Niki Lauda
312 T2/F1   [026]

July 18 / Brands Hatch
British Grand Prix
F1WC
Niki Lauda
312 T2/F1   [028]

1977

January 23 / Interlagos
Brazilian Grand Prix
F1WC
Carlos Reutemann
312 T2/F1   [029]

March 5 / Kyalami
F1WC
South African Grand Prix
Niki Lauda
312 T2/F1   [030]

July 31 / Hockenheim
German Grand Prix
F1WC
Niki Lauda
312 T2/F1   [031]

August 28 / Zandvoort
Dutch Grand Prix
F1WC
Niki Lauda
312 T2/F1   [030]

1978

January 15 / Rio de Janeiro
Brazilian Grand Prix
F1WC
Carlos Reutemann
312 T2/F1   [031]

April 2 / Long Beach
United States Grand Prix West
F1WC
Carlos Reutemann
312 T3/F1   [032]

July 16 / Brands Hatch
British Grand Prix
F1WC
Carlos Reutemann
312 T3/F1   [033]

October 1 / Watkins Glen
United States Grand Prix East
F1WC
Carlos Reutemann
312 T3/F1   [035]

October 8 / Montréal
Canadian Grand Prix
F1WC
Gilles Villeneuve
312 T3/F1   [034]

1979

March 3 / Kyalami
South African Grand Prix
F1WC
Gilles Villeneuve
312 T4/F1   [037]

April 8 / Long Beach
United States Grand Prix West
F1WC
Gilles Villeneuve
312 T4/F1   [037]

April 15 / Brands Hatch
Race of Champions
Gilles Villeneuve
312 T3/F1

May 13 / Zolder
Belgian Grand Prix
F1WC
Jody Scheckter
312 T4/F1[040]

May 27 / Monte Carlo
Monaco Grand Prix
F1WC
Jody Scheckter
312 T4/F1   [040]

September 9 / Monza
Italian Grand Prix
F1WC
Jody Scheckter
312 T4/F1   [040]

October 7 / Watkins Glen
United States Grand Prix East
F1WC
Gilles Villeneuve
312 T4/F1   [041]

1981

May 31 / Monte Carlo
Monaco Grand Prix
F1WC
Gilles Villeneuve
126 C/F1   [052]

June 21 / Jarama
Spanish Grand Prix
F1WC
Gilles Villeneuve
126 C/F1   [052]

September 15-20
Tour de France Automobile
ERCD
J.C. Andruet/C. Bouchetal
308 GTB   [26713]

1982

April 25 / Imola
San Marino Grand Prix
F1WC
Didier Pironi
126 C2/F1   [059]

July 3 / Zandvoort
Dutch Grand Prix
F1WC
Didier Pironi
126 C2/F1   [060]

August 8 / Hockenheim
German Grand Prix
F1WC
Patrick Tambay
126 C2/F1   [061]

September 19-25
Tour de France Automobile
ERCD
J.C. Andruet/'Biche'
308 GTB   [21071]

1983

May 1 / Imola
San Marino Grand Prix
F1WC
Patrick Tambay
126 C2B/F1 [065]

June 12 / Montréal
Canadian Grand Prix
F1WC
René Arnoux
126 C2B/F1 [064]

August 7 / Hockenheim
German Grand Prix
F1WC
René Arnoux
126 C3/F1   [066]

August 28 / Zandvoort
Dutch Grand Prix
F1WC
René Arnoux
126 C3/F1   [066]

1984

April 29 / Zolder
Belgian Grand Prix
F1WC
Michele Alboreto
126 C4/F1   [074]

1985

June 16 / Montréal
Canadian Grand Prix
F1WC
Michele Alboreto
156-85/F1   [081]

August 4 / Nürburgring
German Grand Prix
F1WC
Michele Alboreto
156-85/F1   [080]

1987

November 1 / Suzuka
Japanese Grand Prix
F1WC
Gerhard Berger
F1-87   [098]

November 15 / Adelaide
Australian Grand Prix
F1WC
Gerhard Berger
F1-87   [097]

1988

September 11 / Monza
Italian Grand Prix
F1WC
Gerhard Berger
F1-87/88C   [102]

1989

March 26 / Rio de Janeiro
Brazilian Grand Prix
F1WC
Nigel Mansell
F1-89   [109]

August 13 / Hungaroring
Hungary Grand Prix
F1WC
Nigel Mansell
F1-89   [109]

September 24 / Estoril
Portuguese Grand Prix
F1WC
Gerhard Berger
F1-89   [112 bis]

1990

March 25 / Interlagos
Brazilian Grand Prix
F1WC
Alain Prost
641   [116 bis]

June 24 / México City
Mexican Grand Prix
F1WC
Alain Prost
641/2   [116 bis]

July 8 / Le Castellet
French Grand Prix
F1WC
Alain Prost
641/2   [119]

July 15 / Silverstone
British Grand Prix
F1WC
Alain Prost
641/2   [119]

September 23 / Estoril
Portuguese Grand Prix
F1WC
Nigel Mansell
641/2   [120]

September 30 / Jerez
Spanish Grand Prix
F1WC
Alain Prost
641/2   [121]

1994

April 17 / Braselton
Road Atlanta 2 Hours
IMSA
Jay Cochran
F 333 SP

May 30 / Lakeville
Lime Rock 2 Hours
IMSA
G.P. Moretti / E. Salazar
F 333 SP

June 26
Watkins Glen 3 Hours
IMSA
G.P. Moretti / E. Salazar
F 333 SP

July 3
Suzuka 500 Kilometres
A. Oloffson / L. Della Noce
F 40

July 10
Vallelunga 4 Hours
A. Oloffson / L. Della Noce
F 40

July 10
Indianapolis 2 Hours
IMSA
G.P. Moretti / E. Salazar
F 333 SP

July 24 / Laguna Seca
Monterey Grand Prix
IMSA
T. Evans / F. Vélez
F 333 SP

July 31 / Hockenheim
German Grand Prix
F1WC
Gerhard Berger
412 T1   [153]

October 31
Vallelunga 6 Hours
GGTE
A. Oloffson / L. Della Noce
F 40

1995

March 18
Sebring 12 Hours
IMSA
T. Evans / F. Vélez / E. van de Poele
F 333 SP

May 21 / Shearwater
Halifax 3 Hours
IMSA
M. Baldi / F. Vélez
F 333 SP

May 29 / Lakeville
Lime Rock Grand Prix
IMSA
Wayne Taylor
F 333 SP

June 11 / Montréal
Canadian Grand Prix
F1WC
Jean Alesi
412 T2   [161]

July 2
Anderstorp 4 Hours
GGTE
M. Ferté / O. Thévenin
F 40   [74045]

September 10 / College Station
Texas 3 Hours
IMSA
Wayne Taylor
F 333 SP

September 24 / Le Mans
Autumn Cup
L. Drudi / C. Rosenblad
F 40

October 1
Phoenix 200 Miles
IMSA
Fermín Vélez
F 333 SP

1996

April 21 / Braselton
Road Atlanta 3 Hours
IMSA
M. Papis / G.P. Moretti
F 333 SP

May 27 / Lakeville
Lime Rock Grand Prix
IMSA
G.P. Moretti / M. Papis
F 333 SP

June 2 / Barcelona-Montmeló
Spanish Grand Prix
F1WC
Michael Schumacher
F 310   [171]

June 9
Watkins Glen 6 Hours
IMSA
G.P. Moretti / M. Papis
F 333 SP

July 14
Anderstorp 4 Hours
GGTE
A. Olofsson / L. Della Noce
F 40 GTE   [90001]

August 25 / Spa-Francorchamps
Belgian Grand Prix
F1WC
Michael Schumacher
F 310   [167]

September 8
Italian Grand Prix
F1WC
Michael Schumacher
F 310   [171]

1997

March 15
Sebring 12 Hours
IMSA
T. Evans / F. Vélez / Y. Dalmas /
S. Johansson
F 333 SP

May 11 / Monte Carlo
Monaco Grand Prix
F1WC
Michael Schumacher
F 310/B   [177]

May 26 / Lakeville
Lime Rock Grand Prix
IMSA
A. Montermini / A. Hermann
F 333 SP

June 15 / Montréal
Canadian Grand Prix
F1WC
Michael Schumacher
F 310/B   [177]

June 29 / Magny-Cours
French Grand Prix
F1WC
Michael Schumacher
F 310/B   [177]

August 2
Race at Zolder
F. Lienhard / D. Theys
F 333 SP

August 24 / Spa-Francorchamps
Belgian Grand Prix
F1WC
Michael Schumacher
F 310/B   [179]

August 31
Mosport 3 Hours
IMSA
R. Morgan / D. Fellow
F 333 SP

September 12 / Suzuka
Japanese Grand Prix
F1WC
Michael Schumacher
F 310/B   [178]

September 28
Pikes Peak 2 Hours
IMSA
A. Montermini / A. Hermann
F 333 SP

October 18 / Sebring
Octoberfest 2 Hour Race
IMSA
A. Montermini / A. Hermann
F 333 SP

Update palmarés:

1998

January 31 / February 1
Daytona 24 Hours
IMSA
G. Moretti / D.Theys /
A. Luyendyk / M. Baldi
F 333 SP

March 22
Sebring 12 Hours
IMSA
D. Theys / G. Moretti /
M. Baldi
F 333 SP

April 12 / Buenos Aires
Argentina Grand Prix
F1WC
M. Schumacher
F300

April 13
Paul Ricard
Sport International Series
Lienhard / D. Theys
F 333 SP

April 26
Las Vegas
SportsCar
W. Taylor / E. Van de Poele
F 333 SP

May 10
Brno
Sport International Series
V. Sospiri / E. Collard
F 333 SP

June 7 / Montréal
Canadian Grand Prix
F1WC
M. Schumacher
F300

June 28 / Magny Cours
France Grand Prix
F1WC
M. Schumacher
F300

July 12 / Silverstone
British Grand Prix
F1WC
M. Schumacher
F300

July 12 / Donington
Tourist Trophy
Sport International Series
V. Sospiri / E. Collard
F 333 SP

August 16 / Hugaroring
Hungary Grand Prix
F1WC
M. Schumacher
F300

August 16
Anderstorp
Sport International Series
V. Sospiri / E. Collard
F 333 SP

August 23
Watkins Glen 6 Hours
IMSA
G. Moretti / M. Baldi
D. Theys
F 333 SP

September 6
Nürburgring
Sport International Series
V. Sospiri / E. Collard
F 333 SP

September 13 / Monza
Italian Grand Prix
F1WC
M. Schumacher
F300

September 20 / Le Mans
Autumn Cup
Sport International Series
V. Sospiri / E. Collard
F 333 SP

October 10 / Road Atlanta
Petit Le Mans
SportsCar
W. Taylor / E. Van de Poele
E. Collard
F 333 SP

1999

March 7 / Melbourne
Australian Grand Prix
F1WC
E. Irvine
F399

March 28
Barcelona
Sport International Series
E. Collard / V. Sospiri
F 333 SP

April 11
Monza 500 Kilometres
Sport International Series
E. Collard / V. Sospiri
F 333 SP

May 2 / Imola
San Marino Grand Prix
F1WC
M. Schumacher
F399

May 16 / Monte Carlo
Monaco Grand Prix
F1WC
M. Schumacher
F399

May 16
Spa-Francorchamps
Sport International Series
M. Baldi / L. Redon
F 333 SP

June 27
Pergusa
Sport Racing World Cup
C. Pescatori / E. Moncini
F 333 SP

July 25 / A1 Ring
Austrian Grand Prix
F1WC
E. Irvine
F399

August 1 / Hockenheim
German Grand Prix
F1WC
E. Irvine
F399

September 19
Magny-Cours
Sport Racing World Cup
G. Sospiri / G. Mazzacane
F 333 SP

October 17 / Sepang
Malaysia Grand Prix
F1WC
E. Irvine
F399

2000

March 12 / Melbourne
Australian Grand Prix
F1WC
M. Schumacher
F1-2000

March 26 / Interlagos
Brasil Grand Prix
F1WC
M. Schumacher
F1-2000

March 26
Barcelona
Sport Racing World Cup
C. Pescatori / D. Terrien
F 333 SP

April 9 / Imola
San Marino Grand Prix
F1WC
M. Schumacher
F1-2000

May 21 / Nürburgring
Europe Grand Prix
F1WC
M. Schumacher
F1-2000

June 18 / Montréal
Canadian Grand Prix F1WC
M. Schumacher
F1-2000

July 30 / Hockenheim
German Grand Prix
F1WC
R. Barrichello
F1-2000

August 6
Brno
Sport Racing World Cup
C. Pescatori / D. Terrien
F 333 SP

August 27
Donington
SRWC
Pescatori / Terrien
F 333 SP

September 10 / Monza
Italian Grand Prix
F1WC
M. Schumacher
F1-2000

September 17
Nürburgring
Sport Racing World Cup
C. Pescatori / D. Terrien
F 333 SP

September 24 / Indianapolis
United States Grand Prix
F1WC
M. Schumacher
F1-2000

October 1
Magny Cours
Sport Racing World Cup
C. Pescatori/D. Terrien
F 333 SP

October 8 / Suzuka
Japan Grand Prix
F1WC
M. Schumacher
F1-2000

October 22 / Sepang
Malaysia Grand Prix
F1WC
M. Schumacher
F1-2000

2001

March 4 / Melbourne
Australian Grand Prix
F1WC
M. Schumacher
F1-2001

March 18 / Sepang
Malaysia Grand Prix
F1WC
M. Schumacher
F1-2001

April 8
Barcelona
Sport FIA
C. Pescatori/M. Zadra
F 333 SP

April 29 / Barcelona
Spanish Grand Prix
F1WC
M. Schumacher
F1-2001

May 13
Spa-Francorchamps
Sport FISA
J.M. Gounon/M. Zadra
F 333 SP

May 27/Monte Carlo
Monaco Grand Prix
F1WC
M. Schumacher
F1-2001

June 24 / Nürburgring
Europe Grand Prix
F1WC
M. Schumacher
F1-2001

July 1 / Magny Cours
France Grand Prix
F1WC
M. Schumacher
F1-2001

August 19 / Hungaroring
Hungary Grand Prix
F1WC
M. Schumacher
F1-2001

August 26 / A1 Ring
500 Kilometres
GT FIA
R. Rydell-P. Kox
550 Maranello

September 2 / Spa-Francor-
champs
Belgian Grand Prix
F1WC
M. Schumacher
F1-2001

September 28-30 / Jarama
500 Kilometres
GT FIA
R. Rydell-A.Menu
550 Maranello

October 14 / Suzuka
Japan Grand Prix
F1WC
M. Schumacher
F1-2001

2002

March 3 / Melbourne
Australian Grand Prix
F1WC
M. Schumacher
F1-2001

March 31 / Interlagos
Brasil Grand Prix
F1WC
M. Schumacher
F2002

April 14 / Imola
San Marino Grand Prix
F1WC
M. Schumacher
F2002

April 28 / Barcelona
Spanish Grand Prix
F1WC
M. Schumacher
F2002

May 12 /A1 Ring
Austrian Grand Prix
F1WC
M. Schumacher
F2002

June 2 / Jarama
500 Kilometres
GT FIA
A. Piccini-J. D. Deletraz
550 Maranello

June 9 / Montréal
Canadian Grand Prix
F1WC
M. Schumacher
F2002

June 23 / Nürburgring
European Grand Prix
F1WC
R. Barrichello
F2002

June 30 / Anderstorp
500 Kilometres
GT FIA
A. Piccini-J. D. Deletraz
550 Maranello

July 7 / Silverstone
British Grand Prix
F1WC
M. Schumacher
F2002

July 14 / Oschersleben
500 Kilometres
GT FIA
A. Piccini-J. D. Deletraz
550 Maranello

July 21 / Magny Cours
France Grand Prix
F1WC
M. Schumacher
F2002

July 28 / Hockenheim
German Grand Prix
F1WC
M. Schumacher
F2002

August 18 / Hungaroring
Hungary Grand Prix
F1WC
R. Barrichello
F2002

September 1 / Spa-Fancorchamps
Belgian Grand Prix
F1WC
M. Schumacher
F2002

September 15 / Monza
Italy Grand Prix
F1WC
R. Barrichello
F2002

September 29 / Indianapolis

United States Grand Prix
F1WC
R. Barrichello
F2002

October 13
Japan Grand Prix / Suzuka
F1WC
M. Schumacher
F2002

October 20 / Estoril
500 Kilometres
GT FIA
A. Piccini-J. D. Deletraz
550 Maranello

2003

April 4 / Barcelona
500 Kilometres
GT FIA
T. Biaggi-M. Bobbi
550 Maranello

April 20 / Imola
San Marino Grand Prix
F1WC
M. Schumacher
F2003-GA

April 27 / Magny-Cours
500 Kilometres
GT FIA
T. Biaggi-M. Bobbi
550 Maranello

May 4 / Barcelona
Spanish Grand Prix
F1WC
M. Schumacher
F2003-GA

May 11 / Pergusa
500 Kilometres
GT FIA
T. Biaggi-M. Bobbi
550 Maranello

May 18 / A1 Ring
Austrian Grand Prix
F1WC
M. Schumacher
F2003-GA

May 25 / Brno
500 Kilometres
GT FIA
T. Biaggi / M. Bobbi
550 Maranello

June 9 / Donington
500 Kilometres
GT FIA
T. Biaggi / M. Bobbi
550 Maranello

June 14-15
Le Mans 24 Hours
Davies / Enge / Kox
550 Maranello
[1° GTS]

June 15 / Montréal
Canadian Grand Prix
F1WC
M. Schumacher
F2003-GA

July 20 / Silverstone
British Grand Prix
F1WC
R. Barrichello
F2003-GA

September 14 / Monza
Italy Grand Prix
F1WC
M. Schumacher
F2003-GA

September 21 / Oscersleben
500 Kilometres
GT FIA
T. Biaggi-M. Bobbi
550 Maranello

September 28 / Indianapolis
United States Grand Prix
F1WC
M. Schumacher
F2003-GA

October 5 / Estoril
500 Kilometres
GT FIA
F. Babini-P. Peter
575 GTC

October 12 / Suzuka
Japan Grand Prix
F1WC
R. Barrichello
F2003-GA

October 19 / Monza
500 Kilometres
GT FIA
L. Cappellari / F. Golin
550 Maranello

2004

March 7 / Melbourne
Australian Grand Prix
F1WC
M. Schumacher
F2004

March 21 / Sepang
Malaysia Grand Prix
F1WC
M. Schumacher
F2004

March 28 / Monza
500 Kilometres
GT FIA
L. Cappellari / F. Golin
550 Maranello

April 4 / Bahrain
Bahrain Grand Prix
F1WC
M. Schumacher
F2004

April 18 / Valencia
500 Kilometres
GT FIA
L. Cappellari / F. Golin
550 Maranello

April 25 / Imola
San Marino Grand Prix
F1WC
M. Schumacher
F2004

May 9 / Barcelona
Spanish Grand Prix
F1WC
M. Schumacher
F2004

May 9 / Barcelona
Monza 1000 Kilometres
Le Mans Endurance Series
Davies / Herbert
550 Maranello (1° GTS)

May 19 / Hockenheim
500 Kilometres
GT FIA
M. Bobbi / Gardel
550 GT

May 30 / Nürburgring
European Grand Prix
F1WC
M. Schumacher
F2004

June 13 / Montréal
Canadian Grand Prix
F1WC
M. Schumacher
F2004

June 20 / Indianapolis
United States Grand Prix
F1WC
M. Schumacher
F2004

July 3 / Nürburgring
1000 Kilometres
Le Mans Endurance Series
Lamy-Bouchut-Zacchia
550 Maranello (1° GTS)

July 4 / Magny-Cours
France Grand Prix
F1WC
M. Schumacher
F2004

July 11 / Silverstone
British Grand Prix
F1WC
M. Schumacher
F2004

July 25 / Hockenheim
German Grand Prix
F1WC
M. Schumacher
F2004

July 31
Spa-Francorchamps 24 Hours
GT FIA
Cappellari / Gollin / Byner / Calder-
ari
550 GT

August 14
Silverstone 1000 Kilometres
ALMS
Daoudi-Rusinov
360 Modena (1° N-GT)

August 15 / Hungaroring
Hungary Grand Prix
F1WC
M. Schumacher
F2004

September 12 / Monza
Italian Grand Prix
F1WC
R. Barrichello
F2004

September 26 / Shanghai
China Grand Prix
F1WC
R. Barrichello
F2004

October 8 / Dubai
500 Kilometres
GT FIA
M. Bobbi / Gardel
550 GT

October 10 / Suzuka
Japan Grand Prix
F1WC
M. Schumacher
F2004

Bibliography

Ferrari 1946-1990. Opera Omnia. Catalogue raisonné, Automobilia, Milan 1990

Serge Bellu, *Guida all'identificazione Ferrari*, Giorgio Nada Editore, Milan 1990

Keith Bluemel, Jess G. Pourret, *Ferrari 250 GTO*, Giorgio Nada Editore, Milan 1998

Gianni Cancellieri, Cesare De Agostini, *F 1. Trentatré anni di Gran Premi iridati*, Autosprint/Conti Editore, Bologna 1982

Piero Casucci, *Ferrari F1 1948-1963*, Profili Quattroruote, Editoriale Domus, Milan 1985

Piero Casucci, *Ferrari F1 1964-1976*, Profili Quattroruote, Editoriale Domus, Milan 1986

Piero Casucci, *Ferrari F1 1977-1985*, Profili Quattroruote, Editoriale Domus, Milan 1986

Etienne Cornil, *Ferrari Pininfarina*, Giorgio Nada Editore, Milan 1997

Andrea Curami, Daniele Galbiati, Luca Ronchi, *1000 km di Monza. Trofeo Filippo Caracciolo*, Edizione del Soncino, Soncino 1998

Enzo Ferrari, *Le briglie del successo*, Poligrafici il Borgo, Bologna 1970

Jean-Pierre Gabriel, *Dino. Le altre Ferrari*, Giorgio Nada Editore, Milan 1989

Alan Henry, *Ferrari. Les monoplaces de Grand Prix*, Editions ACLA, Paris 1984

Karl Ludvigsen, Gianni Cancellieri, *Ferrari 1947-1997*, Giorgio Nada Editore, Milan 1997

Michele Marchianò, *Ferrari by Zagato*, Giorgio Nada Editore, Milan 1988

Giannino Marzotto, *Frecce Rosse. Le Ferrari alla Mille Miglia*, Giorgio Nada Editore, Milan 2001

Marcel Massini, *Ferrari by Vignale*, Giorgio Nada Editore, Milan, 1993

Corrado Millanta, Luigi Orsini, Franco Zagari, *Ferrari Automobili 1947-1953*, Editoriale Olimpia, Florence 1985

Antoine Prunet, *Ferrari. Le Granturismo*, L.D.A., Milan 1980

Antoine Prunet, *Ferrari Sport e Prototipi*, Automobilia - L.D.A., Milan 1983

Franco Varisco, *L'Anteprima Ferrari*, Ferrari World, 1990

Index of names and places

Index of names and places

Finito di stampare presso
D'Auria Industrie Grafiche S.p.A
nel mese di ottobre 2005